Android for Absolute Beginners

Getting Started with Mobile Apps Development Using the Android Java SDK

Grant Allen

Apress®

Android for Absolute Beginners: Getting Started with Mobile Apps Development Using the Android Java SDK

Grant Allen
LONDON, UK

ISBN-13 (pbk): 978-1-4842-6645-8 ISBN-13 (electronic): 978-1-4842-6646-5
https://doi.org/10.1007/978-1-4842-6646-5

Managing Director, Apress Media LLC: Welmoed Spahr
Acquisitions Editor: Steve Anglin
Development Editor: Matthew Moodie
Coordinating Editor: Mark Powers

Cover designed by eStudioCalamar

Cover image by Dollar Gill on Unsplash (www.unsplash.com)

Distributed to the book trade worldwide by Apress Media, LLC, 1 New York Plaza, New York, NY 10004, U.S.A. Phone 1-800-SPRINGER, fax (201) 348-4505, e-mail orders-ny@springer-sbm.com, or visit www.springeronline.com. Apress Media, LLC is a California LLC and the sole member (owner) is Springer Science + Business Media Finance Inc (SSBM Finance Inc). SSBM Finance Inc is a **Delaware** corporation.

For information on translations, please e-mail booktranslations@springernature.com; for reprint, paperback, or audio rights, please e-mail bookpermissions@springernature.com.

Apress titles may be purchased in bulk for academic, corporate, or promotional use. eBook versions and licenses are also available for most titles. For more information, reference our Print and eBook Bulk Sales web page at http://www.apress.com/bulk-sales.

Any source code or other supplementary material referenced by the author in this book is available to readers on GitHub via the book's product page, located at www.apress.com/978-1-4842-6645-8. For more detailed information, please visit http://www.apress.com/source-code.

Printed on acid-free paper

To all the aspiring new Android developers in the world,
may you have fun while you learn to build new and wonderful applications!

Table of Contents

About the Author

Grant Allen, **PhD**, has worked in the technology field for over 20 years, as a CTO, entrepreneur, and emerging technology expert. After successful startup exits and a decade at Google, Grant's focus is now mentoring and coaching startups and hi-tech companies on building great teams and great technology. He is a frequent speaker on topics such as big data, mobile ecosystems, Android, wearables, IoT, disruptive innovation, and more. Grant has a PhD in computer science based on research he performed while at Google and an MBA specializing in technology management, and he is the author of seven books on various mobile platform and data technology topics.

About the Technical Reviewer

Val Okafor is a software architect with expertise in Android development and resides in sunny San Diego of California, USA. He has over 14 years of industry experience and has worked for corporations such as Sony Electronics, The Home Depot, San Diego County, and American Council on Exercise. Val earned his BSc in IT from National University, San Diego, and master's in software engineering from Regis University, Colorado. He is the creator and principal engineer of the Pronto line of mobile apps including Pronto Journal, Pronto Invoice, and Okason Contractor App. His passion for software development goes beyond his skill and training; he also enjoys sharing his knowledge with other developers. He has taught Android development to over 5,000 students through Udemy.

Acknowledgments

Writing a book during a global pandemic is a strange experience and only made possible with the help of all the folks at Apress and the technical reviewer. I'd like to thank Steve Anglin, Val Okafor, Mark Powers, Matthew Moodie, and all the other people at Apress who made this book a reality.

I would also like to thank Google for continuing to make Android a fun and dynamic platform on which to learn to develop applications.

Introduction

A book for beginners with Android development should provide enough subject matter to spur the imagination and lay a foundation for future learning and experimentation. The trick is to make sure the content doesn't overload you, the reader, or leave you at your wit's end as to how to get started.

In this book, I have tried to balance giving you a firm foundation in the core concepts and techniques you will need to get started, without packing in every possible topic that might be of use to you eventually. That would have resulted in thousands and thousands more pages of content, which gets to the point of being counterproductive.

You will see and create a wide range of applications based on the topics covered in the 20 chapters presented here, and I've also provided a range of pointers to more online content at Apress, Google, and other websites that take some of the topics beyond the beginner's realm. This book is a beginning, and where you go from here is entirely up to you!

Part I

Get Android, Get Started

Chapter 1

Introducing Android

Welcome to the start of your developer journey with Android. Perhaps you already own and use an Android phone, tablet, or other devices. You would be in great company, with over a billion devices around the world used every day based on the Android operating system. Even if you think you don't already use Android, you may be surprised to learn that it has made its way into an astonishing range of devices and products, many of which you might have used without even realizing the power of Android was helping you out.

Android now powers an amazing range of devices beyond phones and tablets, including smart watches, fitness devices, car entertainment and navigation systems, game consoles, toys, kitchen appliances, garden watering systems, plumbing and heating controls, and even barbecues! Yes, barbecues! This expansion in devices that use Android shows no signs of slowing down, but the most popular and likely place in which to find Android is still on phones and tablets. As a budding developer for Android, this means that you'll learn many aspects that apply to all – or at least many – of the types of devices mentioned here, but your initial focus is likely to be best applied learning to build applications for Android phones and tablets.

Working with Android: The Best Parts

Mobile and smartphone development has been one of the most exciting technology stories of the last decade or more. You might not personally have experienced every twist and turn, but you are likely to have been exposed to devices across one or more of the recent eras of smartphones, and you have likely heard names like Nokia, Apple, Microsoft, Google, and Android mentioned in many combinations.

Today, Android presents you with the benefits learned from all of the great technology battles between these companies and platforms over the last 10 years and lets you ride that wave, serving up fantastic tools, capabilities, and help to get you on the path to Android application development. That is perhaps Android's most compelling appeal right now,

G. Allen, *Android for Absolute Beginners*, https://doi.org/10.1007/978-1-4842-6646-5_1

as this book is written. It is neck and neck at the forefront of all smartphone and mobile technology (along with iOS from Apple), and by choosing Android, you immediately gain access to the benefits it provides, which include

- Developer tools and platforms: We'll cover many of these items in this very book, from Android Studio, the Android SDK, Google Play services, and the Google Play online store, to name just a few.
- A massive existing market: I'm not joking when I say a billion-plus users are waiting for your application, with many more potential future users on the horizon. As Figure 1-1 shows, the global market penetration for Android is breathtaking.
- A global community of like-minded developers: You are not alone in pursuing your Android application development dreams. There are tens of thousands, hundreds of thousands, or possibly even millions of other developers who have experiences to share.
- A rock-solid technology foundation: Android started life using the Java programming language as the predominant technology with which to build applications. Today it also supports Kotlin and C++. We will stick to Java for the examples and techniques explored in this book, as it is one of the most widely used, widely respected, and mature development technologies in existence – the vast majority of Android applications are built with Java.

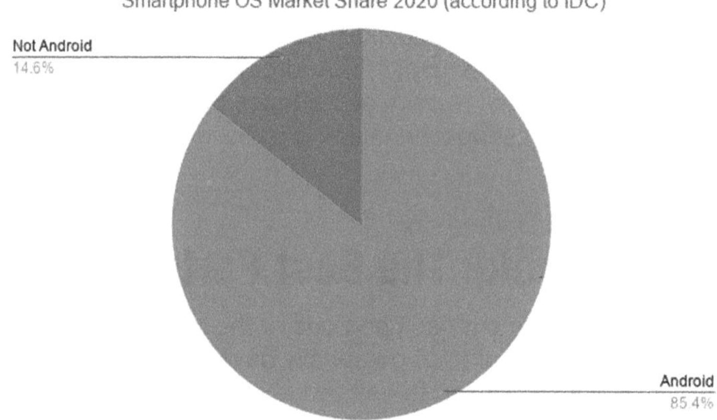

***Figure 1-1.** Android's global market share among smartphone users*

I could go on with more examples of the breadth and depth of the Android development world and its advantages, but instead I'll let the rest of this book help demonstrate many more of them.

Working with Android: The Challenges

I wouldn't be honest if I didn't flag that Android is blessed in many ways, but also has challenges. The good news is that many of these challenges are both well known and easily accommodated. Here are some of the areas that a new developer is likely to encounter before too long:

- You are developing for small devices. Whether we are talking Android phones, Android tablets, in-car dashboards, or a range of other form factors, one common constraint you will need to deal with is the size of the screen. We will explore this topic in depth when we discuss emulating Android devices with virtual devices, but always remember that your experience sitting at a desktop or laptop computer, building for Android, is different from the experience your users will have on the phones and tablets.
- Think beyond the screen. Don't let small screens be your only avenue for providing great features and cool capabilities in your applications! As you will see, later chapters will explore things like sound and audio, on-board sensors, vibration, and more. Don't become a captive to the screen – you have many more tools at your disposal.
- Alternatives are a single swipe away. Everyone with an Android device – or indeed any smartphone – has first-hand experience of many applications. Users have choice, and users will also be running a range of other applications on their phones. This means your application might be sharing resources and user attention, and users can do all kinds of things you never expected!
- Android isn't always Android. We will be covering the latest versions of Android in this book, including Android version 11, which at the time of writing is nearly one year old, and previewing Android version 12, which will be released later this year as part of Google's typical annual release cycle for Android updates. However, out in the marketplace, the billion or more users I mentioned earlier in this chapter are using earlier Android versions. And not just Android 10 or Android 9, but versions all the way back to Android 4 and even earlier! Android has a complicated history when it comes to encouraging (or even allowing) users to upgrade, and this is something to keep in mind when deciding how much of that billion-user market to target.

Whatever you do, do not get disheartened by these points. Think of them more as the first set of lessons to learn as you embark on developing Android applications.

Understanding Android's Heritage and How It Affects You

Android dates back to 2003, when in October of that year a group of developers in Palo Alto got together and used the Linux kernel as the basis for their dream of a new age of devices with much more capable interfaces. After struggling in its formative years, Google bought the Android business in 2005, and its pre-Google cofounder Andy Rubin joined Google to continue the effort developing an operating system for smartphones and other gadgets.

In 2008, after a few false starts, Google and its partners HTC and T-Mobile released the first handset, known as the "Dream" or "G1," depending on which country you were in. My very own G1 still runs to this day, but is no longer my daily go-to phone. Figure 1-2 shows my G1 at the original lock screen.

***Figure 1-2.** The author's original G1 Android phone, from 2008*

After this first release, momentum slowly ramped up for Android, and updates to the operating system started appearing with the names of sweet treats as code names – Cupcake, Donut, Eclair, and so on, representing versions 1.5, 2.0, and 2.1.

Around the time of first public release, Google also partnered with telcos, chip companies, and handset manufacturers to create the Open Handset Alliance, which was aimed at building a broad coalition to support Android into the future. Google also moved to establish the "Android Open Source Project" as the custodian for the base open source code for Android.

There is much more to the story of Android, with many new versions of software and many new manufacturers joining in the fun. But the preceding points were the unheralded start of several of the issues that Android developers must contend with as they build applications.

With many companies moving to build Android-powered phones, Google did not directly control how Android was maintained on each manufacturer's devices nor how telcos in major markets managed the consumer lifecycle of phones as part of contracts, sales, and so forth. What emerged over the coming years after the initial releases of Android was a market with many different devices, running many different versions of Android, with very patchy upgrade guarantees. This is known in the Android world as the fragmentation problem.

For developers, this means that building applications for Android requires some extra effort in thinking about the population of devices in the wild and what versions of Android they run. At the time of writing this book, Google has made a range of efforts to make this less of a concern and encourage manufacturers to upgrade devices. This is having some impact. Google has also added a range of developer features to ease the effort required of you, the developer, to handle this varied market, and we will discuss several of these features in later chapters.

In closing this topic, Figure 1-3 shows a view of the current distribution of Android versions in use throughout the world in mid-2020.

ANDROID PLATFORM VERSION	API LEVEL	CUMULATIVE DISTRIBUTION
4.0 Ice Cream Sandwich	15	
4.1 Jelly Bean	16	99.8%
4.2 Jelly Bean	17	99.2%
4.3 Jelly Bean	18	98.4%
4.4 KitKat	19	98.1%
5.0 Lollipop	21	94.1%
5.1 Lollipop	22	92.3%
6.0 Marshmallow	23	84.9%
7.0 Nougat	24	73.7%
7.1 Nougat	25	66.2%
8.0 Oreo	26	60.8%
8.1 Oreo	27	53.5%
9.0 Pie	28	39.5%
10. Android 10	29	8.2%

***Figure 1-3.** Android versions and API levels in use in 2020*

Note the somewhat self-flattering presentation of these numbers. Instead of reporting the absolute fraction of devices in use for each version of Android, you are instead shown the "cumulative distribution" for devices running a particular version or later. It is easy enough to perform the arithmetic to work out the real absolute percentages. For example, 11.2% of devices run Android 6.0 "Marshmallow," being the difference between its 84.9% cumulative distribution and Android 7.0's 73.7% cumulative distribution. At the time of writing, Android 11 had been released for several months, but was not yet showing in the statistics. Android 12 is slated for release later in this current year, with only minor tweaks to Android 11. Rest assured both Android 11 and then Android 12 will rocket up the charts and be a good basis for learning Android development.

The takeaway from this discussion is that to target a meaningful percentage of Android devices, you will want to embrace Android capabilities from several versions in the past, rather than only cater to the bleeding edge.

Understanding Android's Future

A system like Android, with billions of users already, can already be considered a roaring success. But there's plenty of growth and opportunity left for Android, in a wealth of new areas. For instance, a great deal of attention is now centered on how Android will be part of "hybrid" computing in the future. This hybrid model is where some devices use Android for part of the operation, serving up applications just as your smartphone does today, but switch to using a second operating system like Chrome OS for other tasks.

Android will also follow a regular path of updates itself, as will many of the great online services like Google Play and other cloud offerings, which will further push the boundaries of what's possible with Android devices and Android applications.

What to Expect for the Rest of This Book

Android for Absolute Beginners is written to take you, the reader, on your first journey writing software, learning the practices, techniques, and approaches that will arm you for your future application development goals, as well as many of the fundamentals upon which computer programs are built. We will of course be using Android as both the target environment for your learning, as well as the inspiration for what's possible, and the basis for covering many topics that you'll encounter in other areas of software development as well.

I have laid out the book in four broad parts, each targeting your growing understanding of how to write apps for Android, and Android itself, as you progress through the content and examples. The chapters in each part cover the following topics.

Detailing More of the Remaining Chapters

Chapter 1, Introducing Android: You're reading it! You have already covered much of the introduction to Android and in just a few pages will embark on your first Android application.

Chapter 2, Introducing Android Studio: We will look at the most popular toolset with which to build Android applications – Android Studio – and how to go about getting this free software. We will also briefly examine some alternatives to Android Studio and how to stay informed about new releases, new features, and other changes in how Android applications can be built. Lastly, we'll introduce the idea of an "emulated" Android phone – an Android Virtual Device (AVD) – which is a way of having your computer simulate an Android handset and provides a playground on which to test your applications without needing to tinker with your actual phone.

Chapter 3, Your First Android Application, Already!: Yes, that's right. You'll get straight into creating your very first Android application. No need to wait until you've finished the book! Our first example will be very simple, but it will lay the foundation from which we will expand in all of the remaining chapters.

Chapter 4, Exploring Your First Project: In this chapter, we will take a virtual magnifying glass to the example you created in Chapter 3 and walk through each of the pieces of your first application to begin understanding where they came from, what they do, and why they are where they are.

Chapter 5, Android Studio In-Depth: If you are going to use an integrated set of tools for your future development, then diving deep into their capabilities will be a must. In this chapter, we will explore all of the key aspects of Android Studio, including code editing features, debuggers, profiling tools, and more.

Chapter 6, Mastering Your Entire Developer Ecosystem: This rounds out your understanding of all of the tools you can, and will, use in your development journey. This chapter will explore the tools that sit outside Android Studio's integrated environment, but nevertheless are vital to it, including the Java Developer Kit (JDK), Gradle, source control systems for your code and applications, management of Android Virtual Devices, and other key parts of your environment. We'll also look at aspects of your developer hardware that can influence your path to Android development.

Chapter 7, Introducing Java for Android Development: Ready to "level up" with Java? Regardless of your current knowledge level, this chapter will highlight the key areas of Java coding that you need for Android development, along with further resources to expand your Java expertise.

Chapter 8, Introducing XML for Android Development: Many aspects of Android application behavior are controlled by XML (Extensible Markup Language) data. This chapter walks you through the fundamentals of XML and how to apply XML for various aspects of your Android applications, including an application's manifest, its user interface, and more.

Chapter 9, Exploring Android Concepts: Core UI Widgets: Building on Chapter 8, we explore how to lay out Android user interfaces with stock components such as menus, on-screen widgets like fields, lists, images, and other visual items. This chapter will also introduce the key concept of an activity – the fundamental building block of Android user interfaces. Lastly, we will give an overview of Android Jetpack, which is a modern library offering contemporary layout approaches while offering backward compatibility.

Chapter 10, Exploring Android Concepts: Layouts and More: This chapter expands your repertoire and breadth of understanding for all of Android's user interface components and builds further on the work from Chapters 8 and 9.

Chapter 11, Understanding Activities: Armed with the UI concepts from earlier chapters, you will explore the full power of activities as the basic building block of all Android applications.

Chapter 12, Introducing Fragments: You will learn the wider concept of fragments that power development for many different screen sizes and layout options.

Chapter 13, Working with Sound, Audio, and Music for Android: In this chapter, we will explore all aspects of audio for your applications, including playback of audio and use of sounds in applications, recording audio, and even creating audio on Android devices.

Chapter 14, Working with Video and Movies for Android: If you are a budding Steven Spielberg, Sophia Coppola, or even just YouTube star, this chapter is for you. We will cover Android's video capabilities for both capture and playback and how to work these capabilities into your applications.

Chapter 15, Introducing Notifications: Branch out beyond the boundaries of your application by using the event frameworks and notification systems that Android provides.

Chapter 16, Exploring Device Capabilities with Calls: There is more to your Android world of possibilities than just what can be shown on-screen. We will look at call capabilities, accessing sensors, and other information.

Chapter 17, Understanding Intents, Events, and Receivers: Behind the scenes of every Android application, a wealth of background features keep things moving. This chapter covers the core concepts central to the Android platform and shows how they shape and influence your applications.

Chapter 18, Introducing Android Services: In this chapter, we'll explore working with other code and other applications to enrich your own application and what it can do for your users.

Chapter 19, Working with Files in Android: Android enables you to work with many kinds of data, configuration, and other files. This chapter will start your journey understanding where and how Android applications can leverage traditional files for powering your user experiences.

Chapter 20, Working with Databases in Android: Data drives every application, and knowing how to store, manage, and use data for applications is key to making them great. This chapter will cover the many ways Android provides for working with data.

With that foretaste of what's to come complete, there's no time like the present to get started. Chapter 2 awaits on the next page!

Chapter 2

Introducing Android Studio

In this chapter, we will introduce Android Studio, the primary tool you will use to write the software for your Android applications. While there are a range of other pieces of software you will rely on, the Android Studio Integrated Development Environment (IDE) will be central to bringing your ideas to life. You can think of it as the software you use to write further software.

If you have done any kind of software development in the past, you might find some of the concepts familiar. If that is the case, feel free to skip ahead to the sections later in this chapter that dive straight into the mechanics of installing Android Studio for your chosen platform. You can of course keep reading, to see if there's anything new or interesting on the topic.

Let's now delve into the most important toolset you will use as an Android apps developer – Android Studio!

Understanding What Is Meant by Integrated Development Environment, or IDE

Before we dive in, let's define what is meant by IDE for those who haven't encountered the term or are completely new to programming. The term Integrated Development Environment is almost self-explanatory, but not quite. If we pull it apart, the "Development Environment" bit is simply referring to the fact that it is the environment (in the software sense) where developers develop. That's akin to saying Microsoft Word, or Google Docs, is an author's "Writing Environment" – the place where they do their writing.

The term "Integrated" is also straightforward, but knowing what is being integrated is key to an overall understanding of an IDE. To extend our writing analogy a little further, as a software developer you will also be writing, but in your case, it will be human-readable programming code in Java and potentially several other languages. To that end, every IDE includes (integrates) a code editor, where you write the actual raw code. So far, so good.

G. Allen, *Android for Absolute Beginners*, https://doi.org/10.1007/978-1-4842-6646-5_2

Just as Microsoft Word provides some extra bundled tools for an author, like spelling check and online dictionary definition lookup, so too an IDE pulls in other tools and makes them available in an integrated way to a software developer. Alongside the code editor, there are usually language reference tools so you can look up how a software library works, build tools that take your written code and compile it into a working piece of software, debugging tools to help you identify and understand problems and errors, and a host of other tools like performance profilers, code formatters, syntax highlighters, live inspection tools, network monitors, and more.

The crux of the IDE is that all of these tools are integrated, and more or less work well together, without needing the developer to manually pass things around between the tools. Prior to the emergence of IDEs, this was the less glamorous life of a developer. With an IDE like Android Studio in place to handle mundane, convoluted, and repetitive actions, you are left free to focus on the creative problem-solving aspects of writing applications, worrying less about the low-level plumbing.

The History and Provenance of Android Studio

When Google first released developer tools for Android, it targeted one of the most popular open source development environments of the day, Eclipse. It released a set of tools that plugged into Eclipse, known as the Android Developer Tools, or ADT. This combination – Eclipse and ADT – satisfied many Android developers for many years. Fast-forward over a decade, and while Eclipse is still a hugely popular IDE, a range of other IDEs have risen and fallen in prominence, and Google is nothing if not keen to be at the leading edge of these sorts of changes.

In 2013, Google announced that it was cooperating with JetBrains, a company that had developed a modern IDE known as IntelliJ IDEA that focused primarily on first-class developer experiences for those building Java-based applications, and the new collaborative product would be based on IntelliJ IDEA and known as Android Studio and released as a completely free IDE for Android development. Android Studio version 1.0 was released later in 2014. In subsequent years, Google announced that Android Studio would be the premier IDE for developing Android applications and it would cease focusing on and investing in other tools. This hasn't stopped Eclipse fans from continuing to use Eclipse, the ADT, and a range of other tools – we'll touch on such alternatives at the end of this chapter.

Downloading the Android Studio Installer for Your Platform

You now have enough context to understand why Android Studio is important and the role it will play for you in your future Android application development. It's time to get Android Studio and get coding!

The number one location for downloading the installation packages for Android Studio is the official Android web page itself. You can start at the home page, at `www.android.com/`, or dive straight into the developer download page at `https://developer.android.com/studio`.

I should note that the normal caveats apply when calling out website URLs in printed (or electronic) books. URLs can and do change over time. If you are reading this sometime after publication, the direct link at `https://developer.android.com/studio` may have changed – but the home page at `www.android.com/` will always exist and help you navigate to wherever Google may have moved the download page in the future.

For Linux operating system users, there is at least one other option, using the Snap packaging approach, which we will discuss in a moment.

Working with Android Studio Versions

Upon arriving at the download website, you see an immediate "Download Android Studio" option, as shown in Figure 2-1. Look carefully at the text under the button. In my example, it reads "4.0 for Linux 64-bit (865 MB)."

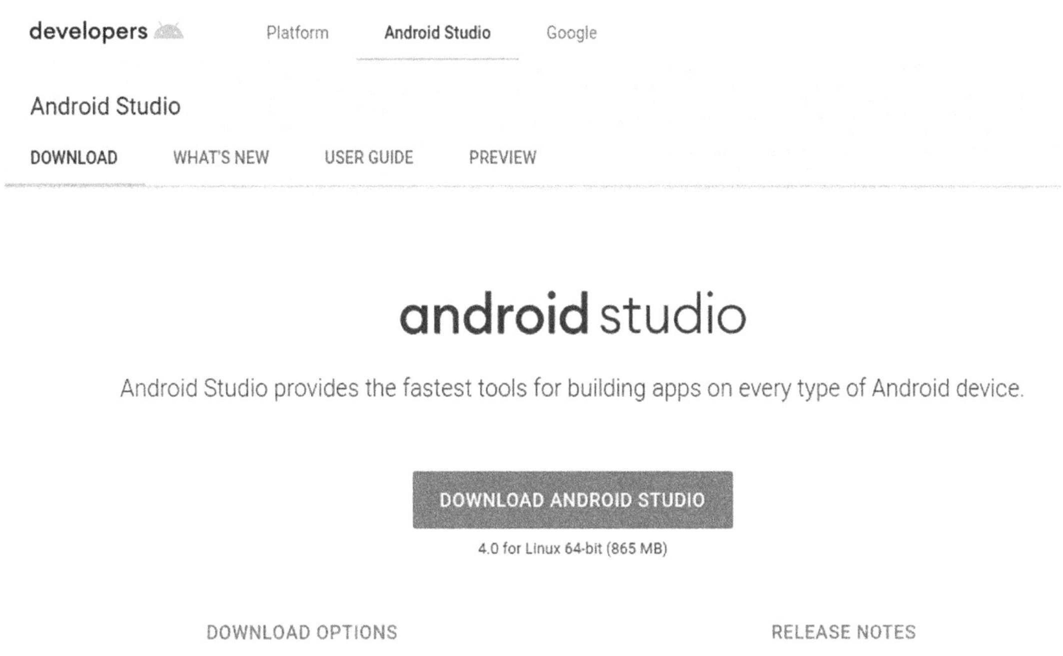

***Figure 2-1.** The developer.android.com/studio download page, showing Android Studio 4.0*

The "4.0" refers to the version of Android Studio, and this opens up the topic of versions, Android, Android Studio, and Android Software Development Kits (SDKs). The overarching aspect you as a developer need to know is that versions of Android – the software running on people's devices – are not tied directly to versions of Android Studio, meaning that when you use Android Studio to develop applications, you are given a variety of means to control what versions of Android (and therefore what devices) your application will support.

Understanding How Android Studio and the Android SDK Work Together

Android operating system releases provide a range of features, and developers are given access to these features via incorporating the Android SDK in their code. Google releases Android SDK versions regularly, several times a year in some cases. Your installation of Android Studio can install and use many different releases of the Android SDK – and in fact you almost certainly will. You will then be able to specify how to pick an SDK version and the Android versions supporting the SDK's features, as you create your applications. We'll walk through this process in detail in Chapter 3, so don't feel overwhelmed by the version "dance" at this point.

Preparing for Android Studio

Android Studio is the leading IDE for Android development, for many of the reasons outlined earlier in this chapter. It has almost everything needed for both new and experienced Android developers making applications of all sorts. Almost! There are a few other considerations that you, as a new Android apps developer, will need to take into account to round out your developer working environment.

Broadly, these considerations are thankfully few in number and easily grasped. In essence, they are the following:

- What desktop or laptop hardware will I use for my Android development?
- What operating system will I run on my desktop/laptop?
- What prerequisites will my system need prior to using Android Studio?
- What Android handsets, if any, will I make use of during development?

Let's look at each of these in turn, from the perspective of the recommended minimums to get started, so you can get moving quickly on the installation of Android Studio itself later in this chapter.

Choosing Desktop or Laptop Hardware for Android Development

First, the good news. Almost any existing computer you have will be a great starting point for your Android development journey. Pretty much any computer from the last decade has the basic computational "grunt" to support Android Studio and allow you to learn the core concepts while building your first applications. In fact, some developers never bother moving past their "daily driver" machine that they've used for everything else, because their demands are just not that taxing.

There might come a time, however, when you want to think about how seriously you are pursuing Android apps development and what benefit you could get from better equipment. Or you might be in the market for a new computer now and want to plan ahead for the computation resources that make apps development faster, more efficient, and so on.

We will explore all aspects of more powerful development hardware, accessories, and the complete developer environment in Chapter 6. You can feel free to jump ahead and read Chapter 6 if you are contemplating how to supercharge your computer or purchase new equipment for Android development. But for those who would just like to ensure they are covered by their existing equipment, here are some key considerations should you confirm based on Google's recommended minimum configuration for Android Studio:

- CPU: The good news here is that pretty much any CPU from the last few years will be more than enough to get started with Android development.
- Memory: Google recommends a minimum of 4 GB of RAM and suggests 8 GB is the preferred base level. Much of this memory will be used for virtual device emulation, with the balance for Android Studio itself. You can squeeze by with less than the minimum, but performance when it comes to trying out your applications will suffer.
- Storage: While the minimum recommended is 2 GB and the preference Google states is for 4 GB, the reality is that more storage is always better. 2 GB will get you a base Android Studio installation, one virtual device, and a lot of regular housecleaning trying to delete unneeded items to free up space. 4 GB is a little better. If you can, clean up to ensure you have 5–10 GB to make life easier for yourself.
- Screen: Google recommends a screen resolution of at least 1280 × 800. However, what isn't stated is that this is the recommendation for Android Studio itself, where you will be writing code and testing your application. There are a rabbit hole of considerations for screen resolution when you consider how your development environment is very different from the screens on users' phones. For now, pay attention to Google's guidelines, but we will revisit the topic of screens in Chapter 6 and other chapters.

Choosing the Operating System for Your Computer

Google makes Android Studio available for all popular operating systems, including Linux, macOS, Windows, and its very own Chrome OS (which is essentially a reskinned version of Linux). Unless you are in the market for a new computer, whatever operating system your current computer has is a fine choice. We'll delve further into the details of an ideal developer setup, including operating system choice, in Chapter 6.

Continuing with Downloading the Installer

Now that you have acquainted yourself with the nuances of Android Studio versions and your hardware and operating system choices, you can now continue to download and install Android Studio. As mentioned earlier in the chapter, from the page `https://developer.android.com/studio`, your operating system should be automatically detected, and a download button for that platform should be prominent. You saw this in the previous example when visiting the site from a Linux machine. From my MacBook, I see an option presented front and center to "Download Android Studio" with the text "4.0 for Mac" beneath it.

If you are downloading from a different machine instead of the one you plan to use for Android development, ensure you choose the right flavor of Android Studio for the machine you intend to use. If that target machine has a different operating system, scroll down the page to the heading "Android Studio downloads," where you will see options for each operating system that Android Studio supports.

WINDOWS ALTERNATIVES

The list of installation options on the Android developer website includes two flavors for Windows. The first is an executable installer, with a filename of the form "android-studio-ide-193.6514223-windows.exe" (the string of digits after "android-studio-ide" is the build and release number, which will vary over time). The second is a zip file, with a filename of the form "android-studio-ide-193.6514223-windows.zip." I recommend you use the first option of the regular executable installer. This will deal with a variety of concerns for you, including directory placement and Windows permissions for the account you normally use under Windows, as well as any other accounts on a shared machine.

Click the relevant option to download the appropriate version of Android Studio for your operating system, and make a note of where the download is being placed by your browser. This is typically the "Downloads" directory for your user on macOS, Linux, and Windows, but can differ if you choose to place it elsewhere.

With the release of Android Studio 4.0, the total download size is nearly 1 GB in size, so it may take a few minutes to complete the download.

Installing Android Studio on Windows

Assuming you are following the recommended path of using the executable installer for Windows, you can launch the installer from your download location by double-clicking the executable file. As of this writing, that means the file android-studio-ide-193.6514223-windows.exe. All recent versions of Windows will prompt you to allow the installation to continue via the User Access Control (UAC) mechanism, to ensure you explicitly consent to the elevated privileges required to complete installation.

Once installation is complete, you should see a new Start menu item for Android Studio.

Installing Android Studio on macOS

As with most application installations on macOS, installing Android Studio is very straightforward. Open Finder on your Mac, and browse to the directory into which you downloaded the Android Studio installer. You should see a DMG file with a name similar to "android-studio-ide-193.6514223-mac.dmg" – this was the DMG file for the Android Studio 4.0 installer. Double-click this disk image file, and your Mac will first verify the download, which really means it will check the code signing certificate and/or notarization used by Google to prepare the disk image. Once verification is complete, you should see the typical DMG installation window as shown in Figure 2-2.

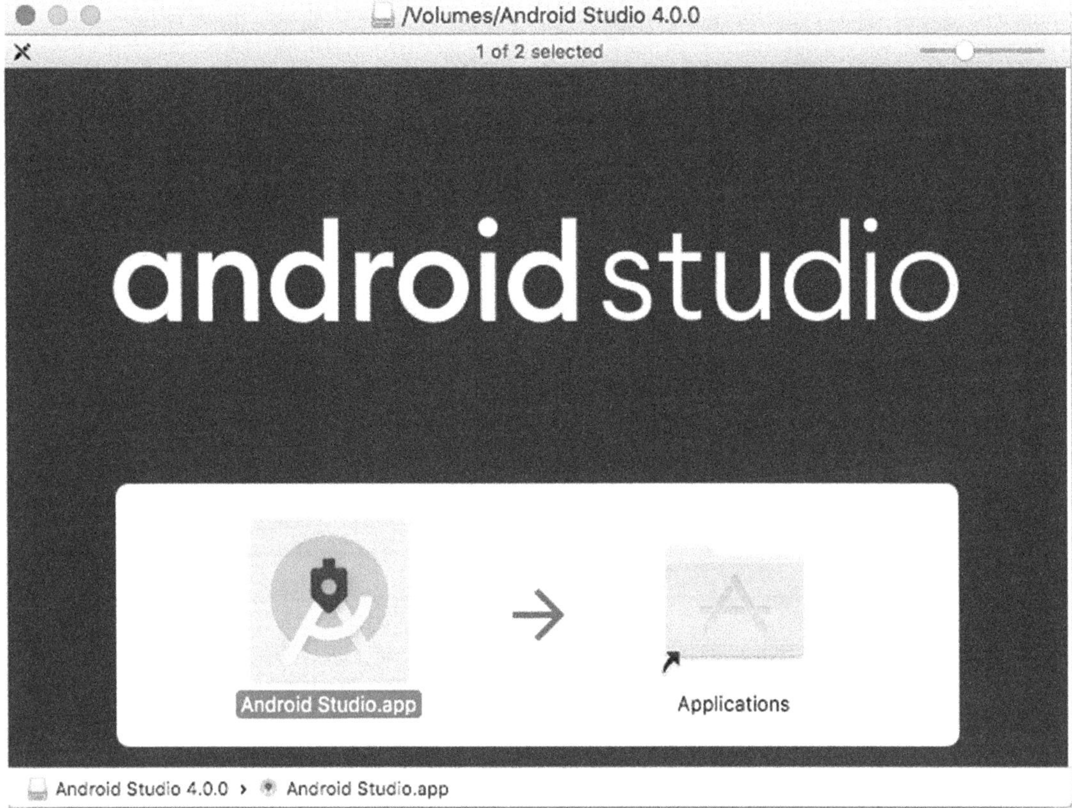

Figure 2-2. The Android Studio DMG installation window for macOS

Drag the Android Studio app icon to the Applications folder, and this will trigger your Mac to copy the installation package as normal for any Mac application. Once complete, Android Studio will be ready to use from the Applications menu and folder.

Installing Android Studio on Linux

The Android Studio installer you downloaded for Linux is a gzip compressed tarball, with a file name such as `android-studio-ide-193.6514223.tar.gz`. Unpacking this file to a directory of your choice is what constitutes installation, as far as Android Studio is concerned. Decide where you would like to install Android Studio: for instance, you might want this under your user account's home directory or some other directory such as `/opt`. When you do unpack the compressed tarball, you see it create a directory called "android-studio" in the location you specify, and all the files and subdirectories will live under that. This means it is not necessary for you to create a similarly named parent directory. For example, there is no need for me to create a `/home/grant/android-studio` directory, as unpacking the tarball will also create the leaf level – and I don't really want a `/home/`

grant/android-studio/android-studio path, as that is needlessly redundant. The directory you chose for Android Studio will be referred to as the "installation home" by much of the internal Android Studio documentation.

Open your favorite shell, such as bash or zsh, and change the directory into the parent directory under which you want Android Studio placed. Make sure you have write permissions to your intended location. Note where you downloaded the compressed tarball file – in my case, that is the /home/grant/Downloads directory, which I can also refer to as ~/Downloads. Run the tar command as follows, which instructs it to unzip, uncompress, and verify the final expanded set of files:

```
tar -xvzf ~/Downloads/android-studio-ide-193.6514223.tar.gz
```

A few screenfuls of status should scroll by, and eventually you should be returned to your shell prompt. Run ls or open your favorite file manager, and you should see the android-studio directory now created. In that directory, you'll find a file named Install-Linux-tar.txt, which you read for some basic instructions on further tweaking the installation and how to actually run the Android Studio binary. I'll ruin the suspense for you! You will see a bin directory under the android-studio directory, and within is a shell script named studio.sh. Execute this shell script to start Android Studio. We will return to some of the other configuration options mentioned in the Install-Linux-tar.txt file later in the book.

SNAP TO IT!

There are alternatives to the typical installation option for Linux, and one of these follows the trend in recent years for packaged versions of applications on Linux that are entirely self-contained, bundling all dependencies and libraries into one package. This approach is typified by the Snap bundling promoted by Canonical (of Ubuntu fame) and Flatpak, which grew out of the freedesktop.org work by XDG.

For Linux distributions that support the Snap package (which in theory is all of them), you can instead have your package manager install the Snap for Android Studio. For instance, under Ubuntu 20.04, you can simply run

```
sudo snap install android-studio
```

A word of caution over the Snap approach: Where downloading from the official site at https://developer.android.com will provide the latest patched version of Android Studio, relying on the Snap approach implicitly means relying on the maintainers and packagers of the Snap package keeping it up to date. In theory this maintenance is entirely possible, and some people claim it as easy, or easier than relying on maintenance and fixes for normally installed software. However, the Snap package you retrieve from your online package repository may not be up to date.

Continuing with Android Studio Setup After Installation

With Android Studio installed on your computer, there are a handful of one-time setup actions that need to be performed to get you started. Fortunately, Android Studio itself will guide you through these setup steps. If you haven't already started Android Studio subsequent to installation, you should do that now. You should see the splash screen shown in Figure 2-3.

Figure 2-3. *The splash screen shown when starting Android Studio*

Once Android Studio loads for the first time, the splash screen will disappear and you should see the start of the setup wizard, which might flash by, and then you will be prompted to import settings from any prior version of Android Studio on your machine, as shown in Figure 2-4.

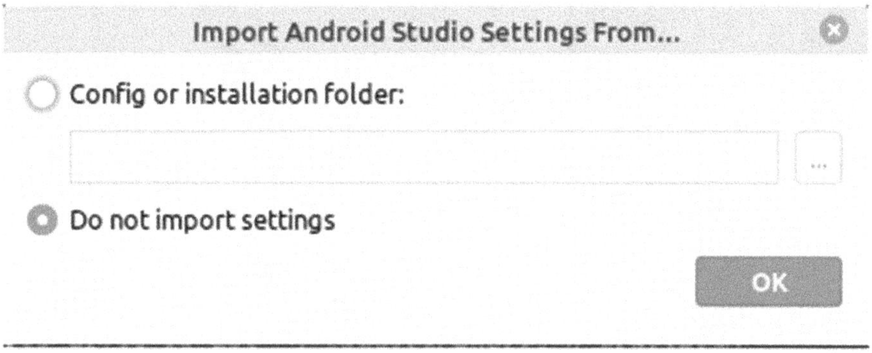

Import Android Studio Settings From...

Config or installation folder:

Do not import settings

OK

Figure 2-4. *Import settings option displayed when you run Android Studio for the first time*

For the purposes of this chapter, we will assume there are no older settings to import. You can choose the "Do not import settings" option and click the OK button. The setup process will then prompt you with a question about sharing usage data, such as features used and libraries accessed, in a prompt as shown in Figure 2-5.

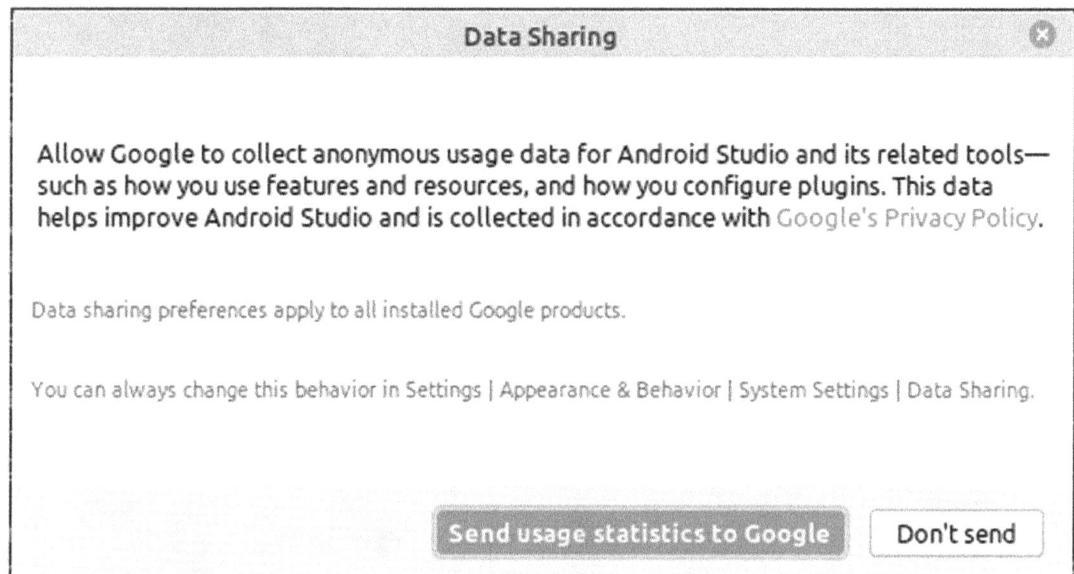

Figure 2-5. Data sharing prompt during Android Studio setup

It is entirely up to you if you want to share your usage statistics with Google or not. It will not affect the features or behavior of Android Studio as you are using it – though it can help with bug fixes and improvements in future versions.

After you make your usage statistics choice, you will see the landing page for the setup wizard for Android Studio, as shown in Figure 2-6.

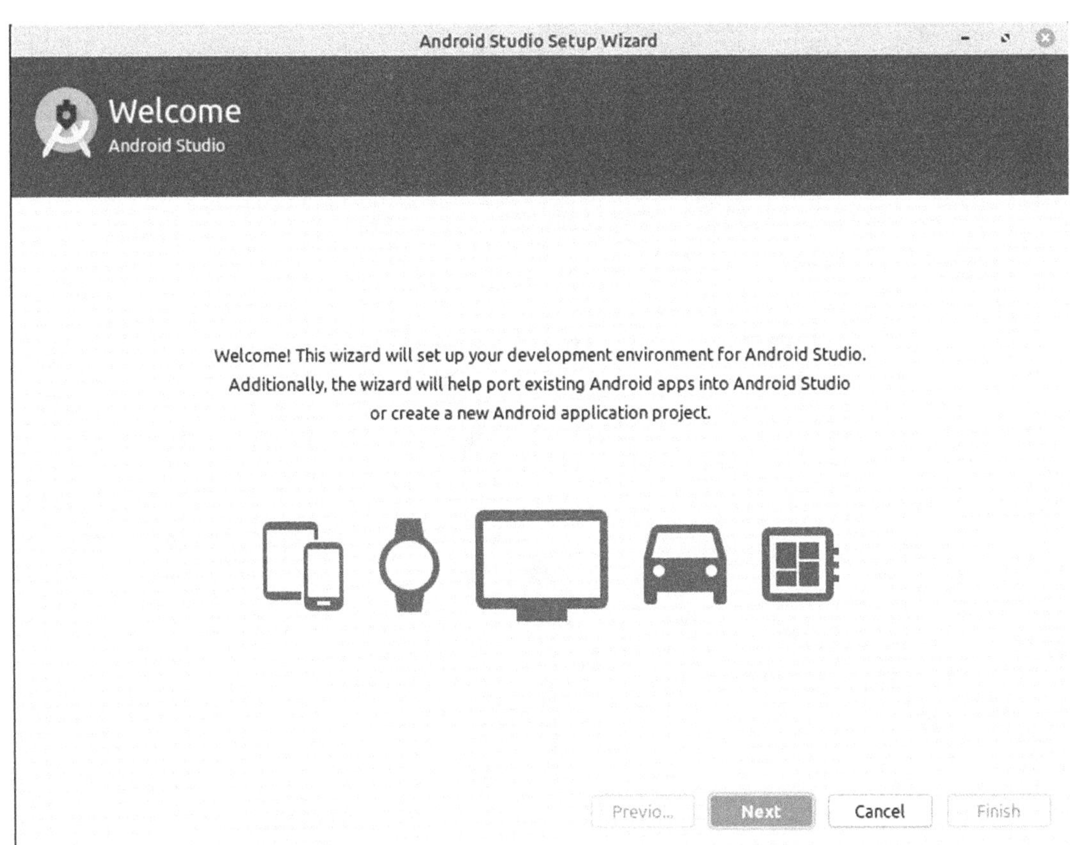

Figure 2-6. The Android Studio setup wizard home page

There are not really many options you have at this point. You can either click the Next button to progress through the setup wizard or click the Cancel button to return to this at a future time.

Assuming you are feeling adventurous – and I feel that's a safe bet as you have already bought this book – click Next to get started with the final pieces of the setup wizard. You will be presented with the choice to select a standard or custom Install Type, as shown in Figure 2-7.

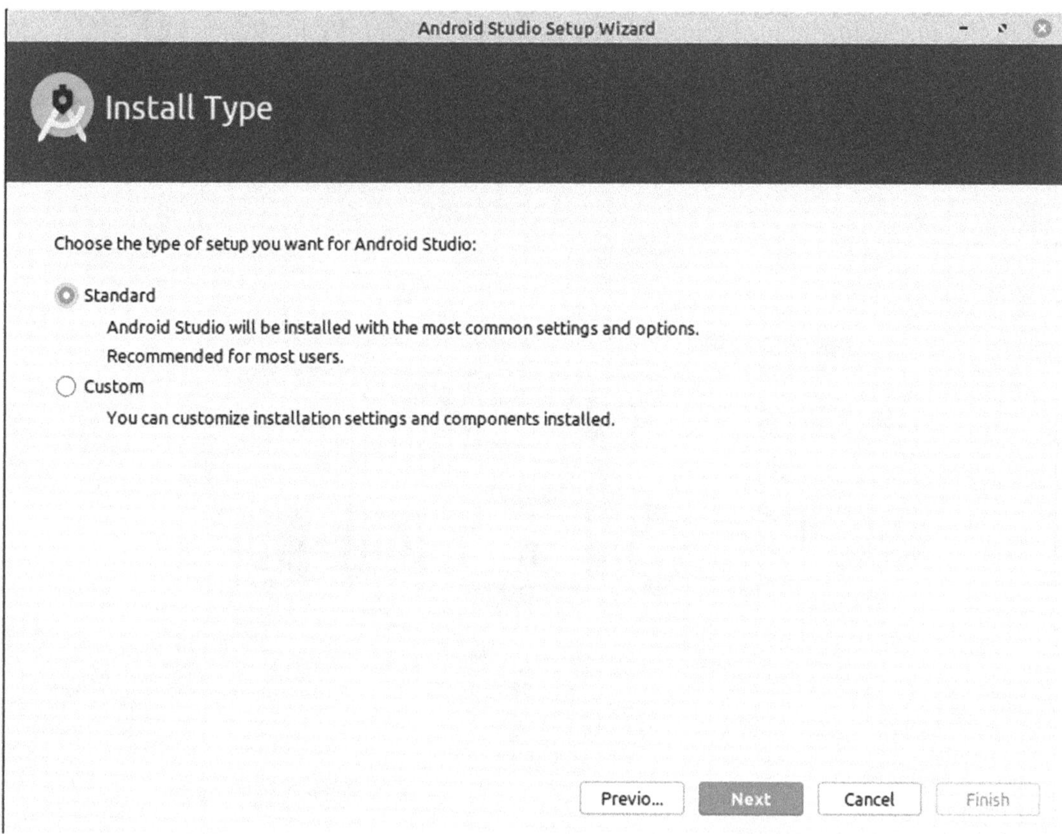

Figure 2-7. The Install Type selection page in the Android Studio setup wizard

The Custom setup option will allow you to do things like change the installation location, choose which versions of the Android SDK to download, and similar selections. We will return to these items in more detail in Chapter 5. For now, you can select the Standard Install Type and click the Next button.

You next choice will be largely cosmetic in nature, where you will be offered the option to have the user interface use a "light" or "dark" theme, as you can see in Figure 2-8.

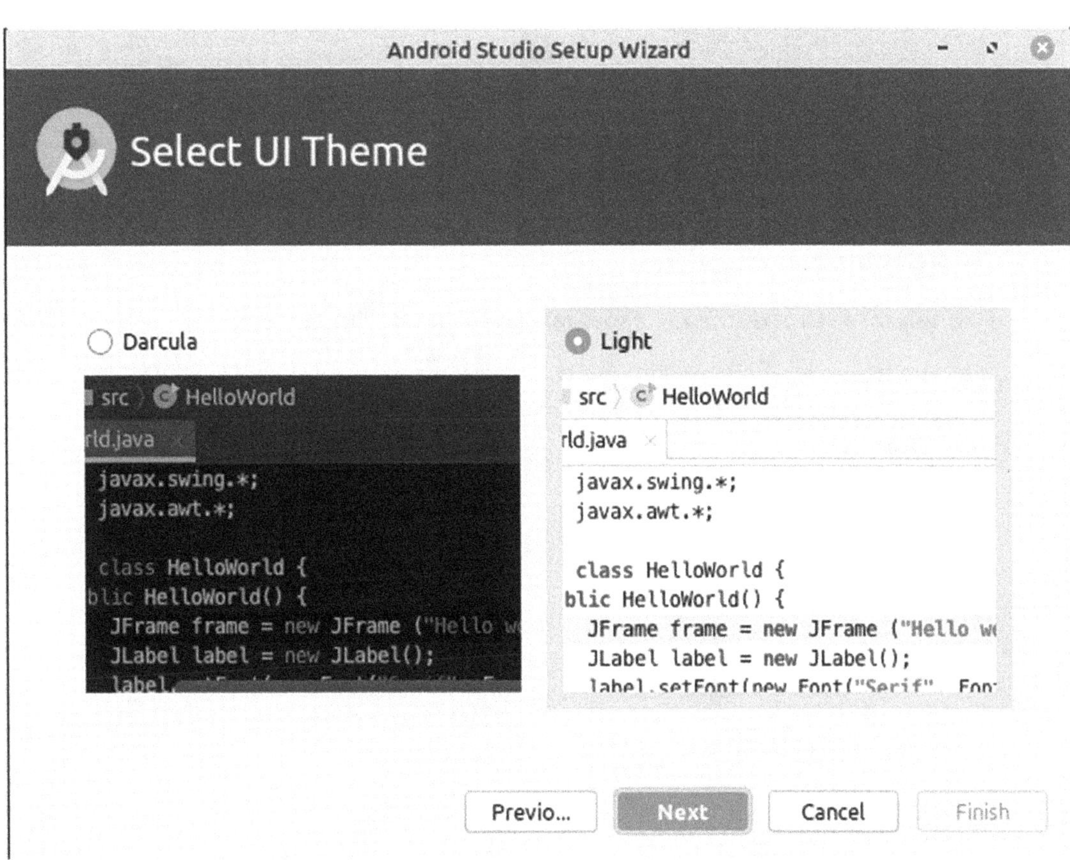

Figure 2-8. The option to Select UI Theme in Android Studio

For those of you with OLED-based displays, there is a miniscule difference in power usage between light and dark themes. For everyone else, this is just a cosmetic preference. For the purposes of this book, I will be using the Light theme, as this will save ink for any printed version of the book. Once you have decided on your own preference, click the Next button to continue.

Your penultimate setup wizard screen will appear, which is the Verify Settings view shown in Figure 2-9.

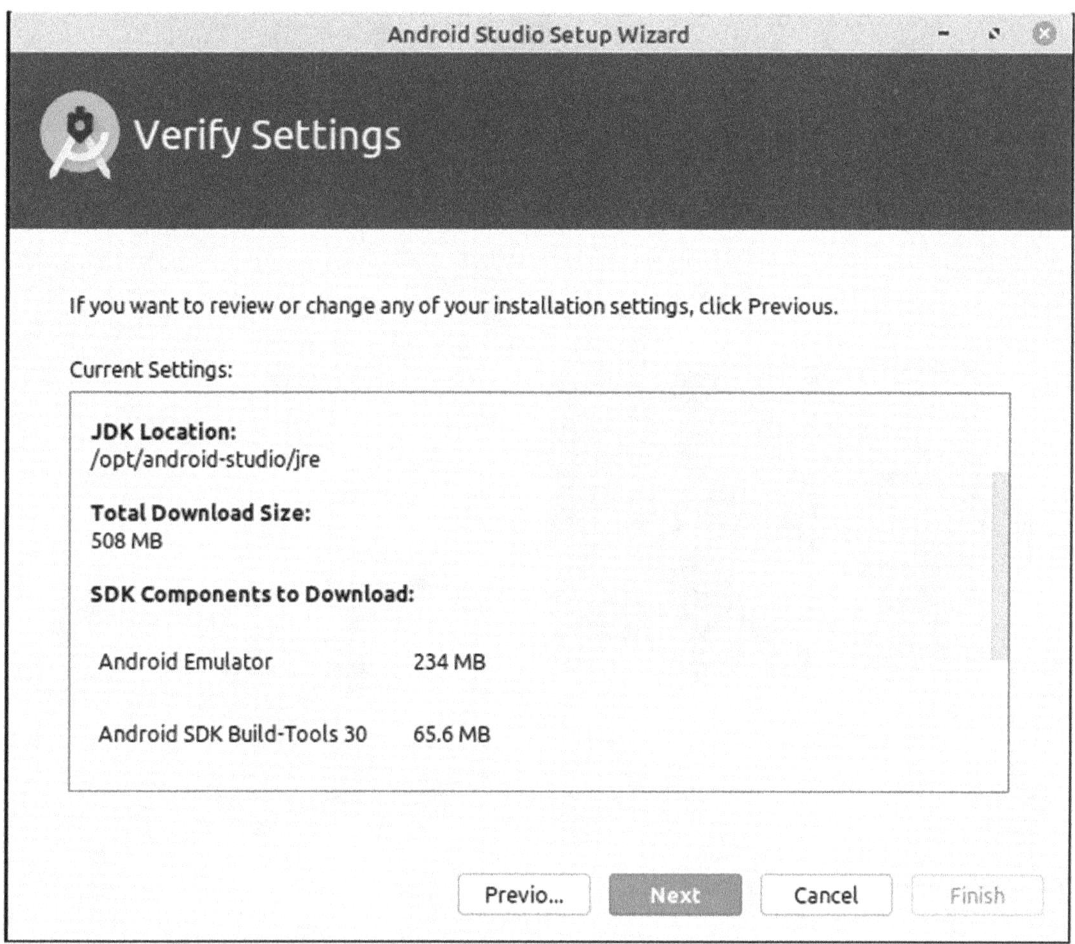

Figure 2-9. The Verify Settings screen in the Android Studio setup wizard

You might be accustomed to simply skipping past these sorts of confirmation screens, but I'd encourage you to scroll through the summary shown. Not because there are any hidden "gotchas" in there, but primarily to ensure you realize how much more will be downloaded as part of the setup process. If you choose the Standard Install Type as described earlier, Android Studio will continue to download the latest Android SDK version and the latest virtual device emulator for your platform. These can easily total another 500 MB–1 GB of downloads, which you should at least know about. If you've already experimented with the Custom Install Type option, at this stage you might be downloading quite a few SDK versions and emulator engines, which can quickly grow to many gigabytes of additional downloads. Once you are happy with the choices you have made, click the Next button, and Android Studio will commence all the remaining automation and download steps automatically. In some circumstances, if your hardware has direct emulation support, you will see an additional screen as shown in Figure 2-10.

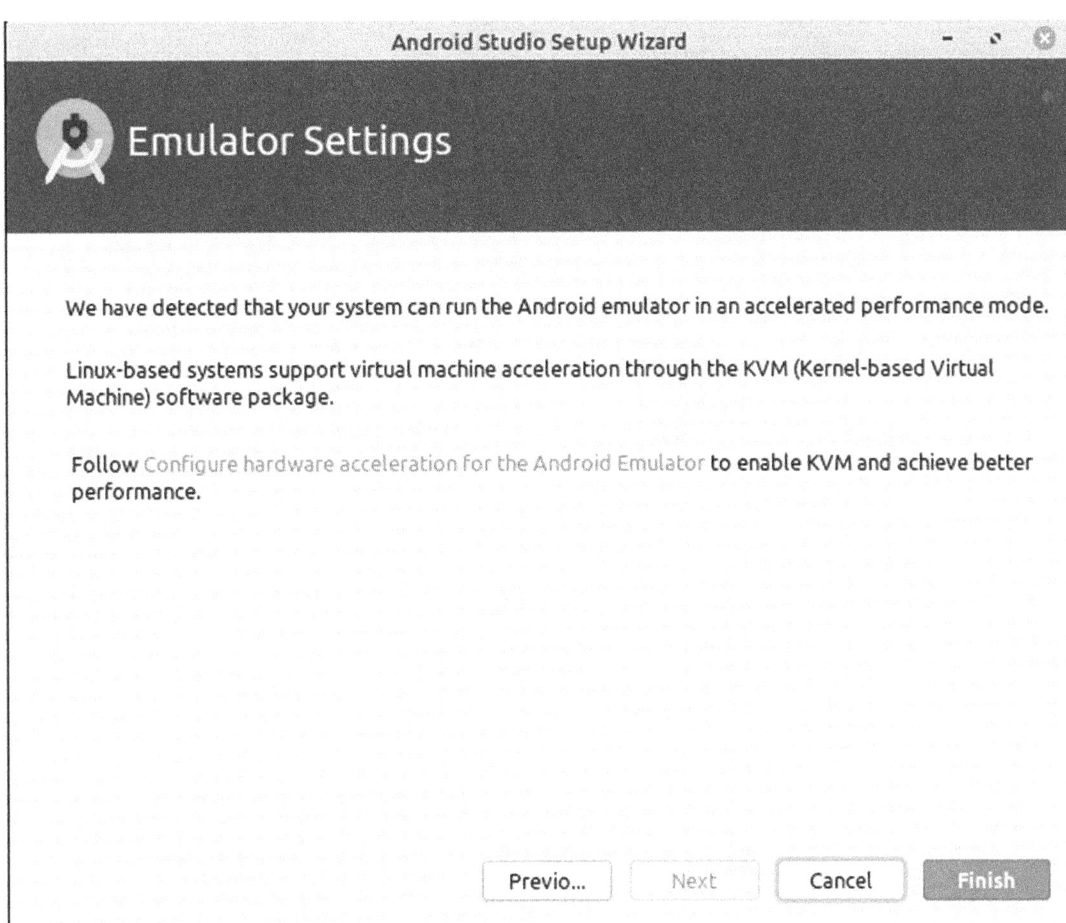

Figure 2-10. Android Studio's advisory screen informing you of accelerated emulation performance

There is no downside to using your hardware emulation acceleration features, so accept this option, and you will eventually be presented with the Downloading Components progress screen, as shown in Figure 2-11.

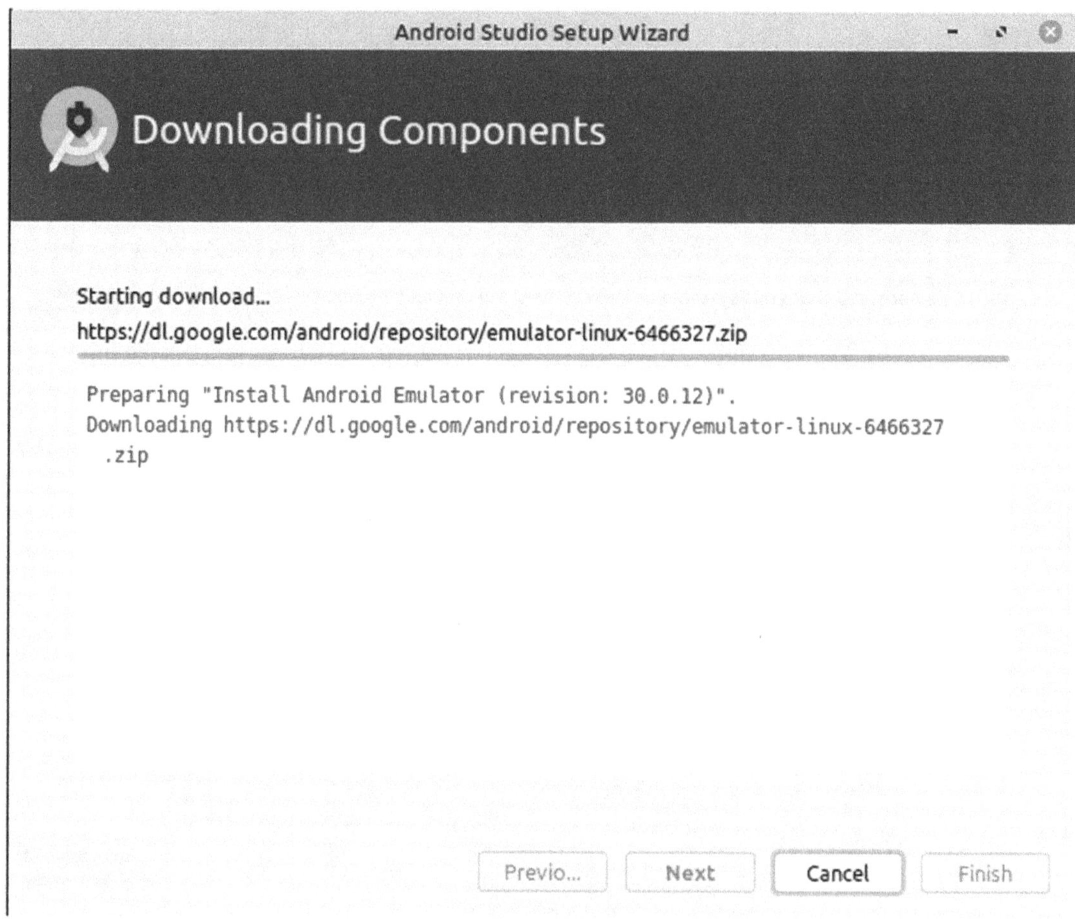

Figure 2-11. *The initial view of the Downloading Components progress screen*

Depending on the speed of your computer and your Internet connection, the component download and configuration process will take at least a few minutes. Do not panic if you see the details stall at points, as this usually represents where the Android Studio setup wizard is downloading large components, such as Android SDK packages. Eventually, you should see the details stop scrolling past, with one magic line showing at the bottom of the window, as shown in Figure 2-12.

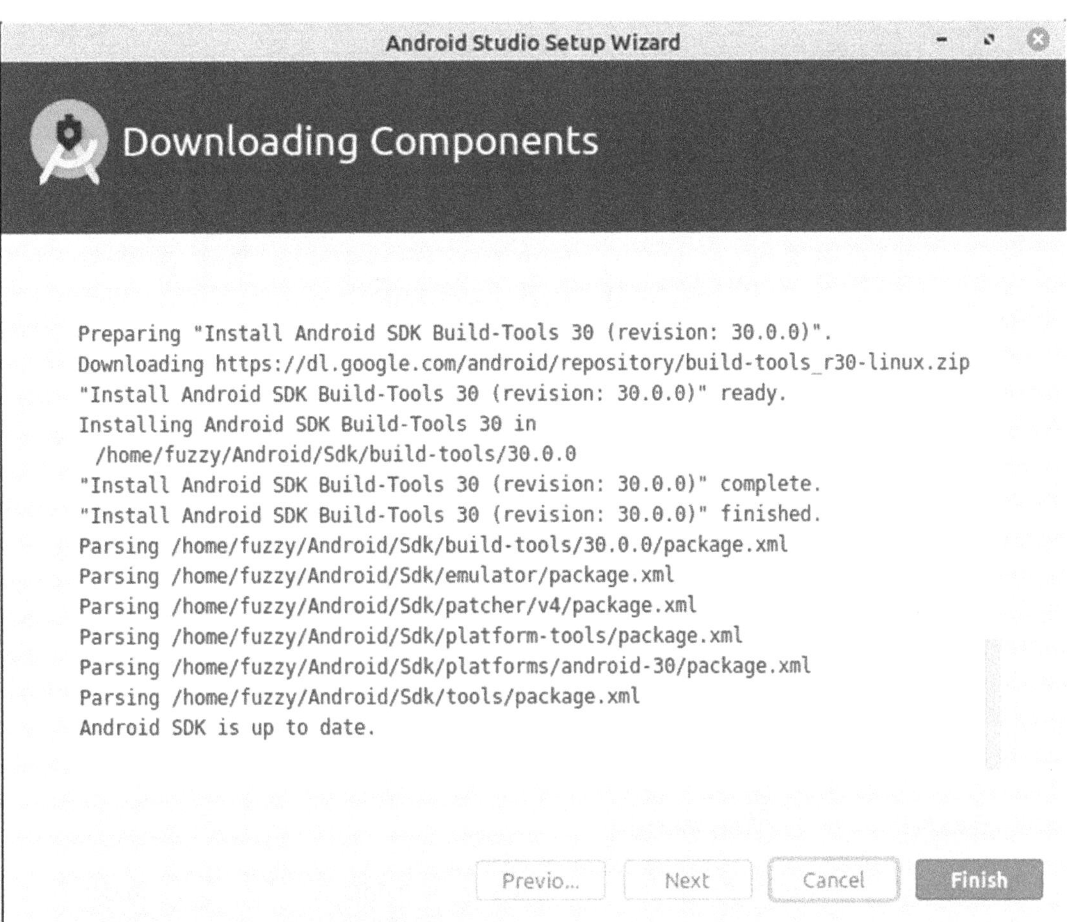

Figure 2-12. *The completed component download view in the Android Studio setup wizard*

The magic line of text you want to see at the end of the process is "Android SDK is up to date." This means that the download and configuration steps are complete and Android Studio is ready to roll. You can click the Finish button, and you will be presented with the startup screen for Android Studio itself, shown in Figure 2-13.

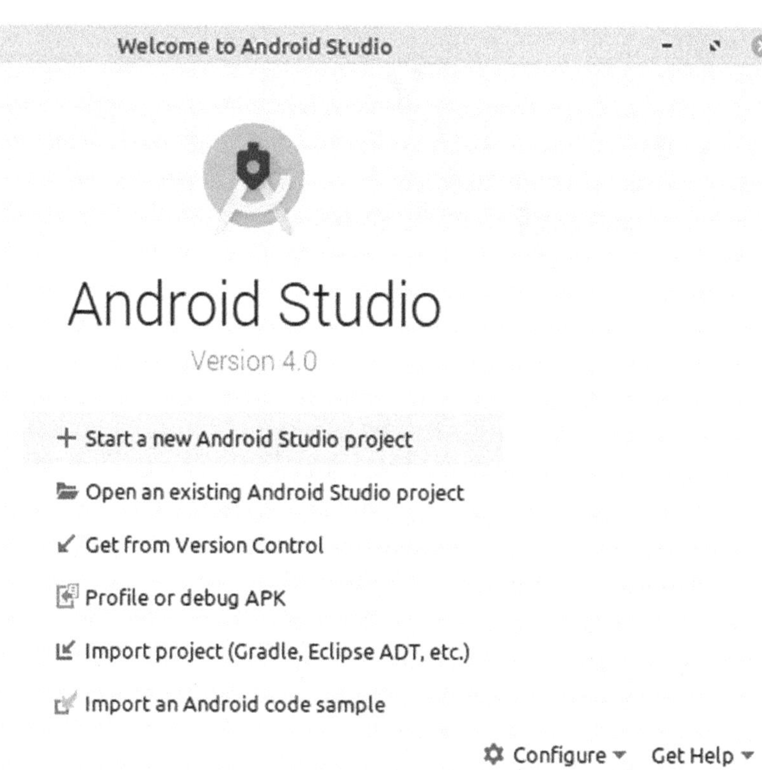

Figure 2-13. The Welcome to Android Studio screen

We will return to the options presented here in the coming chapters. For now, you can relax in the knowledge that you have successfully installed Android Studio and the SDK and emulator components we will be using in the next chapters.

Working with Alternatives to Android Studio

If there is one thing that the software world – and software development in particular – offers, it is choice! Whether it's web browsers, email packages, or your preference in games, choice abounds. Developing applications for Android is no different, though there is a strong default in Android Studio. Nevertheless, other options are out there, and even if you don't plan to use any of them, it can be useful to be aware alternative IDEs and other tools exist, because you will see them mentioned online, at conferences, and in other forums where Android development is discussed.

Here is a short, though not exhaustive, list of alternatives you might encounter in your budding Android application development career.

Eclipse

As mentioned earlier in the chapter, Eclipse was the first IDE Google supported for Android development. At the dawn of Android around 2007, Google needed to provide a compelling developer offering so that its newly acquired smartphone operating system had the appeal to draw developers to it. At the time, it chose the open source Eclipse IDE as the officially endorsed development environment. That choice was universally accepted and acknowledged as a great multiplier and enabler, letting literally millions of Android developers access tools for free that enabled them to make wave after wave of Android applications.

Eclipse had a decade in the limelight, right though until the launch of Android Studio 1.0 in 2014. Even after that launch, Eclipse still enjoyed full support from Google, until the release of Android Studio 2.2 in 2016. Google announced at that point that it would no longer support Eclipse as a first-class development environment nor would it certify that the Android Developer Tools would work bug-free in the future.

This might sound like Eclipse is no longer a viable environment in which to build Android applications. Nothing could be further from the truth. The reality is that Google no longer provides the polish, the convenience, or the direct support for developers wanting to use Eclipse. However, two major themes ensure that Eclipse remains an option for developers who seek to use it.

First, Eclipse has over a decade of accumulated fine-tuning, integrations, and know-how on the basics of dealing with Android applications. At the end of the day, the work of building Android apps boils down to working with textual Java code, XML data, and related artifacts. As we will see in Part 2 of this book, those facets do not change just because you choose a different IDE to help you in the process.

Second, Eclipse is one of the most popular IDEs over time, and it has strengths beyond Android that mean it is very often the IDE of choice in development environments that are dealing with building applications beyond a single target platform.

This isn't to suggest that choosing Eclipse as your IDE will be as smooth or as efficient as Android Studio. Once you move beyond the scope of this book, you'll find many contemporary online sources of information will assume you are using Android Studio and not Eclipse. But some of you – particularly the experienced developers – will look beyond this to where Eclipse already appeals. If you are embarking on your developer journey and have not already a healthy dose of experience with Eclipse, then I strongly suggest you go with Android Studio as your IDE.

IntelliJ IDEA

At the beginning of this chapter, I explained the genesis of Android Studio and outlined its foundation being based upon IntelliJ IDEA. So you may be thinking, if that is what Android Studio is based upon, why would I choose IntelliJ IDEA instead, what is the difference, and why would I care?

Great questions! In essence, as a new developer, there are no overwhelming reasons to think about choosing IntelliJ IDEA as your IDE of choice. However, seasoned developers, or those who develop Java-based applications for more platforms than just Android, often find standardizing on one IDE to be a significant driver for efficiency. There are also features that JetBrains, the company behind IntelliJ, only makes available in the full commercial package, such as the ability to work seamlessly with the Spring Framework for Java. If you fall into those categories, you are more than welcome to adopt IntelliJ IDEA as your preferred IDE.

To find out more about how to use IntelliJ IDEA specifically for Android development, check out the web pages dedicated to this topic from JetBrains, the company that owns and builds IntelliJ IDEA, at `www.jetbrains.com/help/idea/android.html` and `www.jetbrains.com/help/idea/getting-started-with-android-development.html`.

Tools That Target Multiple Operating Systems and Mobile Platforms

In Chapter 1, you saw the breakdown of smartphone market share, where Android held a massive majority. Don't let that blind you to the reality that alternatives exist, such as Apple's iPhone, and tools exist to help developers target both platforms and even a few others you may not have heard of. Some of the key multiplatform IDEs and development environments include products such as Xamarin, PhoneGap, Flutter, and Apache Cordova.

Cross-platform tools deserve a book in their own right, and in fact these aforementioned tools have more than one book dedicated to them, as well as countless pages of content available online. If you are interested in what they have to offer, I strongly recommend starting with their respective product home pages on the Internet and then expanding your search from there.

Traditional Platform-Agnostic Development Tools

To wrap up this chapter and the topic of developer tools, I should take you back to the very beginning of the chapter. IDEs came into existence to help developers wrangle all of the tools that are used to create modern applications. This includes code editors, debuggers, compilers, and more. But IDEs are not for everyone.

Some readers are likely to be seasoned developers, who are quite comfortable assembling their own set of tools to aid in creating Android applications. There are plenty of developers who prefer to choose their own editor, such as Vim, Emacs, or Sublime Text; compilation and build pipeline tools such as Ant, Jenkins, and Hudson; and other tools for performance management, debugging, and more.

If you want to pursue this path, Google makes a set of Android command-line development tools available from the Android Studio download page mentioned at the beginning of the chapter. These tools include sdkmanager, which takes care of downloading and managing multiple Android SDK packages; adb, which is the Android Developer Bridge utility for moving your applications from your developer machine to your virtual and real devices; and more.

While this book isn't targeted at developers who want to take this path, at least you know that it is a viable alternative. For now, we'll assume you are content working with Android Studio, and we'll delve straight into developing your first Android application in the very next chapter, starting on the next page!

Chapter 3

Your First Android Application, Already!

With Android Studio in place on your computer, you are ready to begin creating your very first Android application. Yes, right now! For those readers who are not familiar with Java code development, do not panic. We will start our examples in this chapter with no assumed Java knowledge or know-how. For those readers who do know Java, read on in any case as we will cover the important first step of creating an Android Virtual Device, or AVD, on which to run the example in this chapter, as well as the examples in future chapters.

Creating Your First Android Virtual Device

One of the most useful features provided in the wider Android Studio integrated environment is the ability to create Android Virtual Devices, or AVDs. With an AVD, you get the ability to emulate a real Android device, controlling a range of its capabilities and features, without having to have an actual physical device.

The AVD approach isn't meant to prohibit you from using a real device on which to test and use your applications, but if you think about the plethora of Android devices, versions, and form factors that we've touched on in the first two chapters, you can see how it would be impractical for you as a developer to own even a fraction of the number of devices found in the wild running Android. AVDs help you bridge the gap between what you have (and can afford) and what your user base will actually be using.

To start creating your first AVD, start Android Studio if it is not already running, and you will see the splash screen and then the Welcome to Android Studio screen as you might remember from Chapter 2. In the lower right of the welcome screen, you should see a cog icon and the menu option `Configure`, which you should click to reveal a range of configuration options as shown in Figure 3-1.

G. Allen, *Android for Absolute Beginners*, https://doi.org/10.1007/978-1-4842-6646-5_3

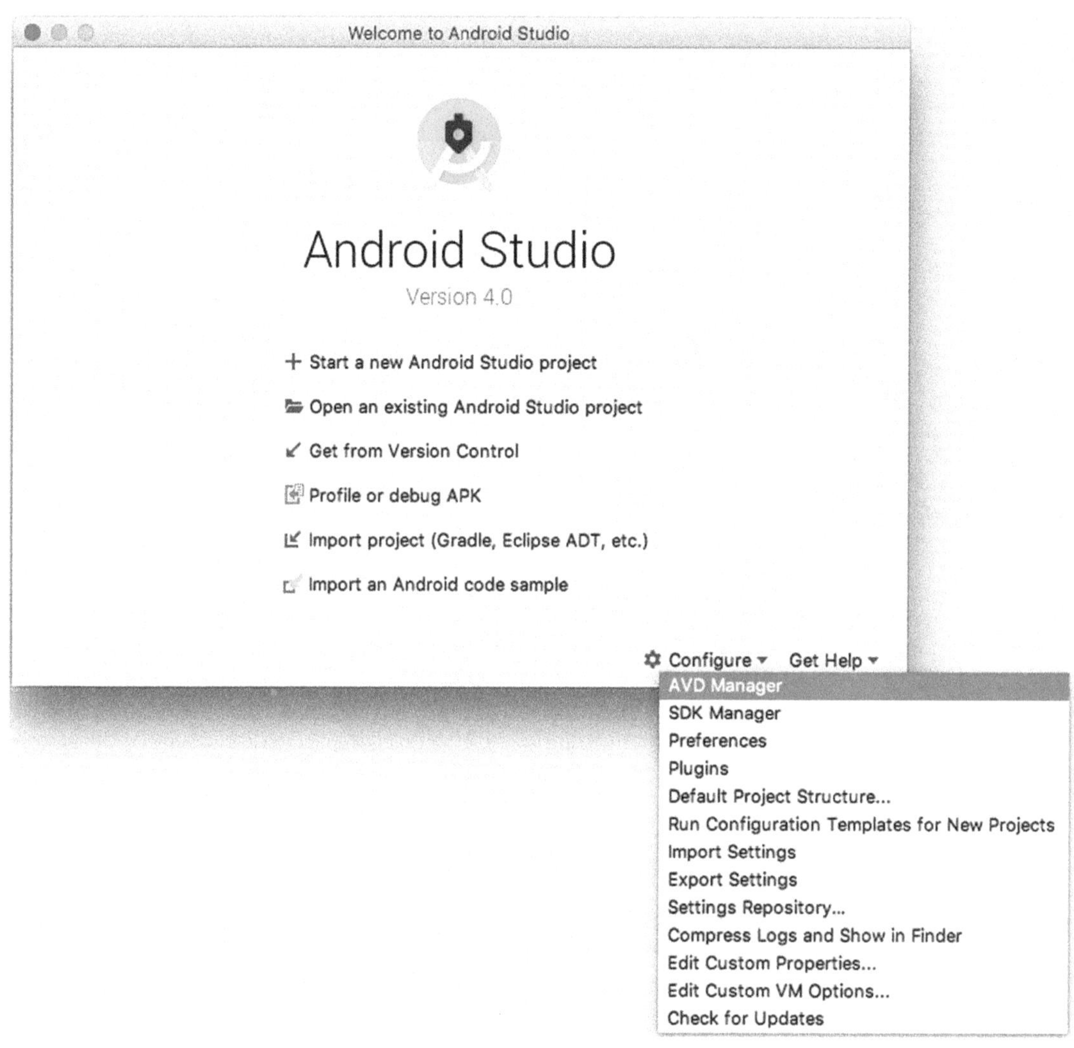

Figure 3-1. *The Configuration menu from the Welcome to Android Studio screen*

You will see that the very first option on the list of configuration items presented is the AVD Manager option. Click this option, and the AVD Manager will start after a few seconds, and you should be presented with the introductory Android Virtual Device Manager screen shown in Figure 3-2.

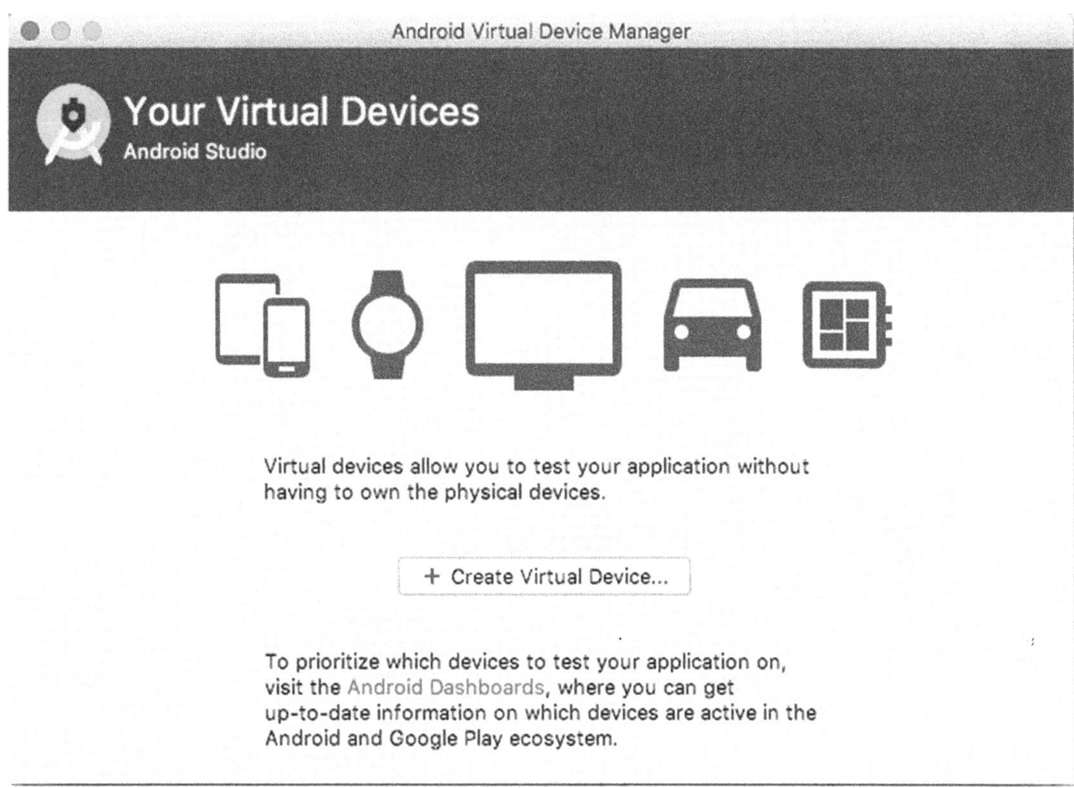

Figure 3-2. The Android Virtual Device Manager welcome screen

In the middle of the screen, you should see the button as shown in Figure 3-2 that reads `+ Create Virtual Device...`. Go ahead and click that button to start the AVD creation process. You will then see the Virtual Device Configuration hardware selection screen, as shown in Figure 3-3.

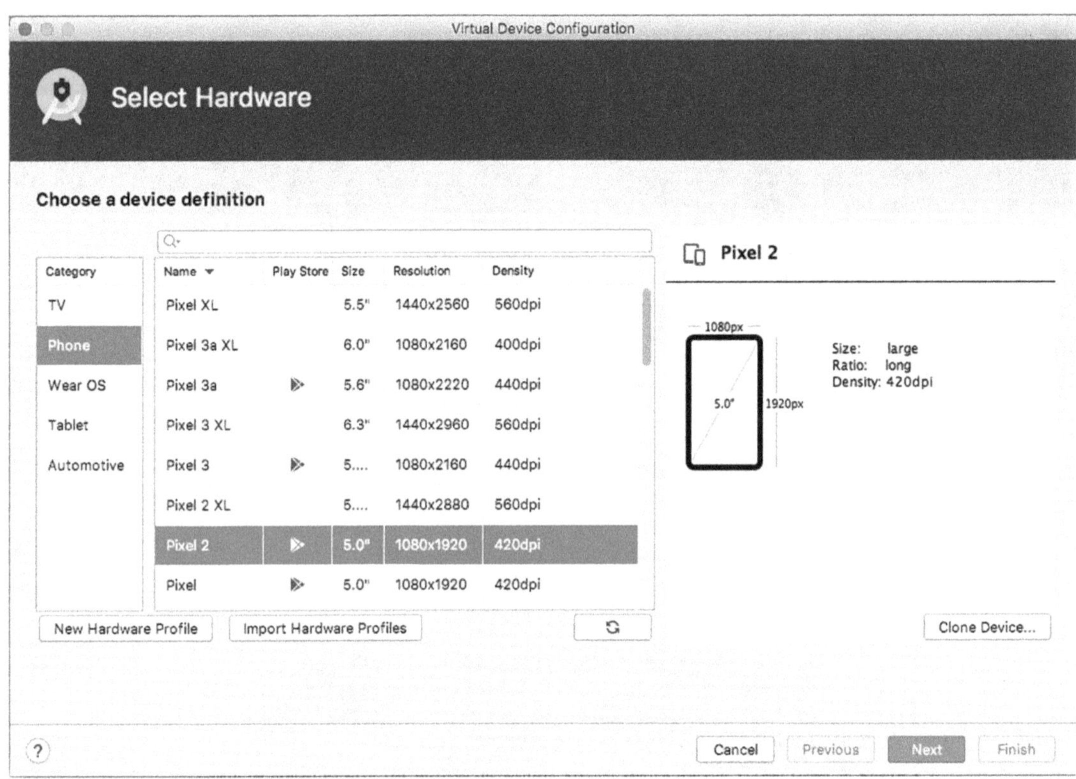

Figure 3-3. The Select Hardware option for new AVD creation

There is a lot going on in the hardware selection screen, but don't feel overwhelmed. The multitude of options here convey the variables you will find in devices in the real world, so it really isn't surprising. Let's step through the areas one by one so you begin to feel at home with the AVD Manager and creating and using AVDs.

Starting on the left-hand side of the hardware selection screen, the Category list provides a grouping of device emulators based on form factor and usage pattern. You should see at least the five normal options shown in Figure 3-3, TV, Phone, Wear OS (formerly Android Wear), Tablet, and Automotive. Feel free to click through each of these to see how the device list (middle of the screen) and dimension detail window change, but when you're done, choose Phone as the Category. With Phone selected, you should then see the original list of prepackaged emulated devices originally shown in Figure 3-3.

At this point, we won't just race ahead to choose one of the first devices shown as the basis for our AVD. Instead, spend a moment to scroll through the list, and take note of a few data points that will resurface later in the book and will gradually make more sense and have more impact on your application design.

From the upper end of the list of device definitions, you will see makes and models of smartphones and brands, some of which might be very familiar. The various Pixel options, like Pixel 3, Pixel 2, and so on, and AVD images emulate as near as possible the real, physical devices that bear those names. Similarly, Nexus 6, Nexus 5, and so on are virtual devices that mimic the physical characteristics of their namesakes, whether it is on-board storage, working memory, screen resolution, or other capabilities. Before you scroll to see the rest of the list, take a look at the values shown in the `Resolution` and `Density` columns. You'll see measurements for both, expressed in pixel layout for Resolution (e.g., 1080 × 1920 for the Pixel 2 AVD) and dots per inch, or dpi, for Density (again, 420 dpi for Pixel 2). You might be familiar with resolution and density measures for laptop or desktop screens and not give a second thought to the values you see here. But it is worth comparing these to the other AVDs in the list.

If you scroll further toward the bottom of the list, you will start to see a range of more cryptic device names, as shown in Figure 3-4.

Name ▾	Play Store	Size	Resolution	Density
3.7" WVG...		3.4"	480x800	hdpi
3.7" FWVG...		3.7"	480x854	hdpi
3.4" WQVGA		3.4"	240x432	ldpi
3.3" WQVGA		3.3"	240x400	ldpi
3.2" QVGA...		3.2"	320x480	mdpi
3.2" HVGA...		3.2"	320x480	mdpi
2.7" QVGA...		2.7"	240x320	ldpi
2.7" QVGA		2.7"	240x320	ldpi

***Figure 3-4.** Further AVD templates available to you*

These devices don't have any brand names associated with them, but they do possess some indicators of what they offer, through using the abbreviations commonly associated with various screen sizes and resolutions. We will encounter these terms throughout this book, so for now you can bookmark names like QVGA, WQVGA, mdpi, hdpi, and so on and not labor over their meaning.

As if all of those current and historic options weren't enough, you'll see two buttons below the device definition list that allow for specifying your own custom virtual device profile and for importing a profile from another source. For our purposes, these options won't be needed, but you can appreciate the value they offer – in particular for those of you who might eventually want to design applications targeting very specific, atypical devices.

We will revisit the concepts and principles of Android device resolution and density in Chapters 9, 10, and 11 when we delve into the depths of user interface design. For now, you can scroll back to the top of the device definition list and choose the Pixel 2 pre-configured device definition. Click the Next button, and you should see the System Image selection screen shown in Figure 3-5.

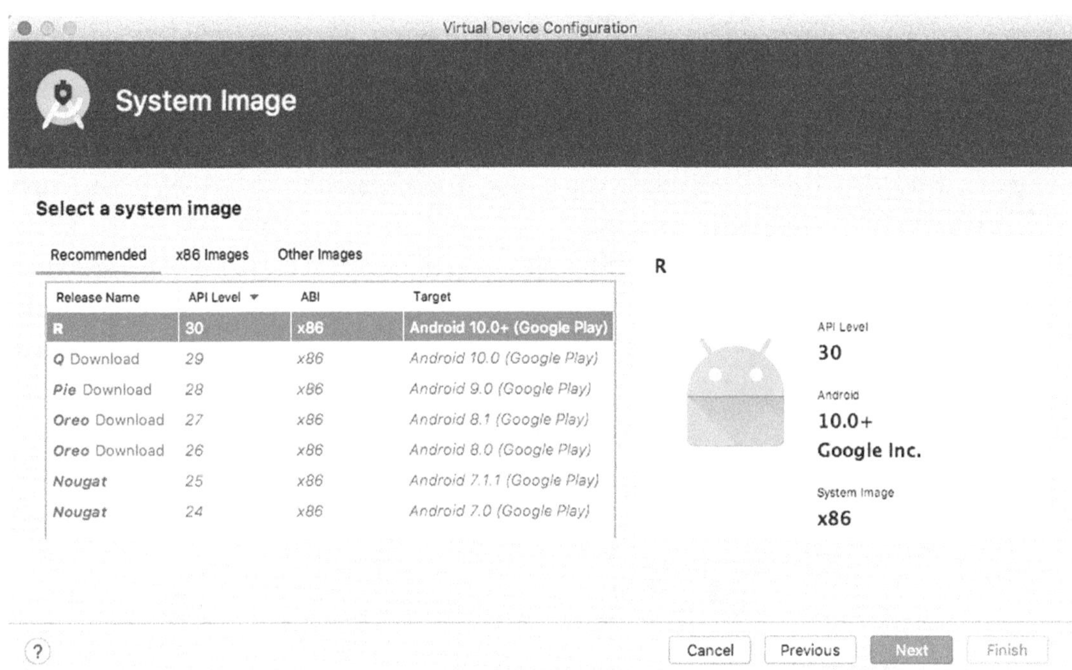

Figure 3-5. *The AVD System Image selection screen in AVD Manager*

Choosing a system image can be considered the complementary step to your earlier choice of device definition. Whereas your device choice selected the hardware aspects of your AVD, the system image determines the key software aspects: Android API/SDK level and ABI, which is basically a decision of which chip architecture to emulate in software, Intel's x86 or one of the Arm-based architectures, and which release of Android these pieces most closely match.

ANDROID SOFTWARE DEVELOPMENT KIT: A SECOND LOOK

In Chapter 2 I introduced the term SDK, or Software Development Kit. While it's easy to parse that phrase and think "Great, a kit to help me develop software," it's worth reviewing what the Android SDK really offers. First and foremost, the Android SDK is a set of software libraries, which are the fundamental tools needed to access the capabilities and power of any Android smartphone and its operating system. You can think of the SDK as the lever that lets you bring all of the power and capabilities Google has built into Android to bear in your own application, without needing to build everything from the ground up.

The Android SDKs – and there are successive versions released for every version of Android – provide the connection to Android Studio that lets you easily invoke Android behavior; build tools that let you turn your code into a working Android program; platform tools that let you manage applications that are still in development and running in "draft" form, including "adb," the Android Debug Bridge, for controlling behavior on an emulator or real device from still-in-development code; and more. Oh, and the SDK provides the emulator framework and device emulation itself!

Depending on whether you have ever previously used a version of Android Studio on the computer you've chosen to use or have stepped through this wizard before, you will see the listed release names like "R" or "Oreo" with or without a download link next to the name. In short, if the system image is already available on your machine, it won't show a download link. If it is yet to be used on your machine, the download link will show, and you can click it straight from the system image stage to fetch the relevant system image.

You will need to have at least one system image for your AVDs to use, so if all you see are system image names accompanied by download links, you should choose to download the latest one. In the example shown in Figure 3-5, this would be the Android "R" system image. Selecting the download will trigger a license acceptance screen, shown in Figure 3-6.

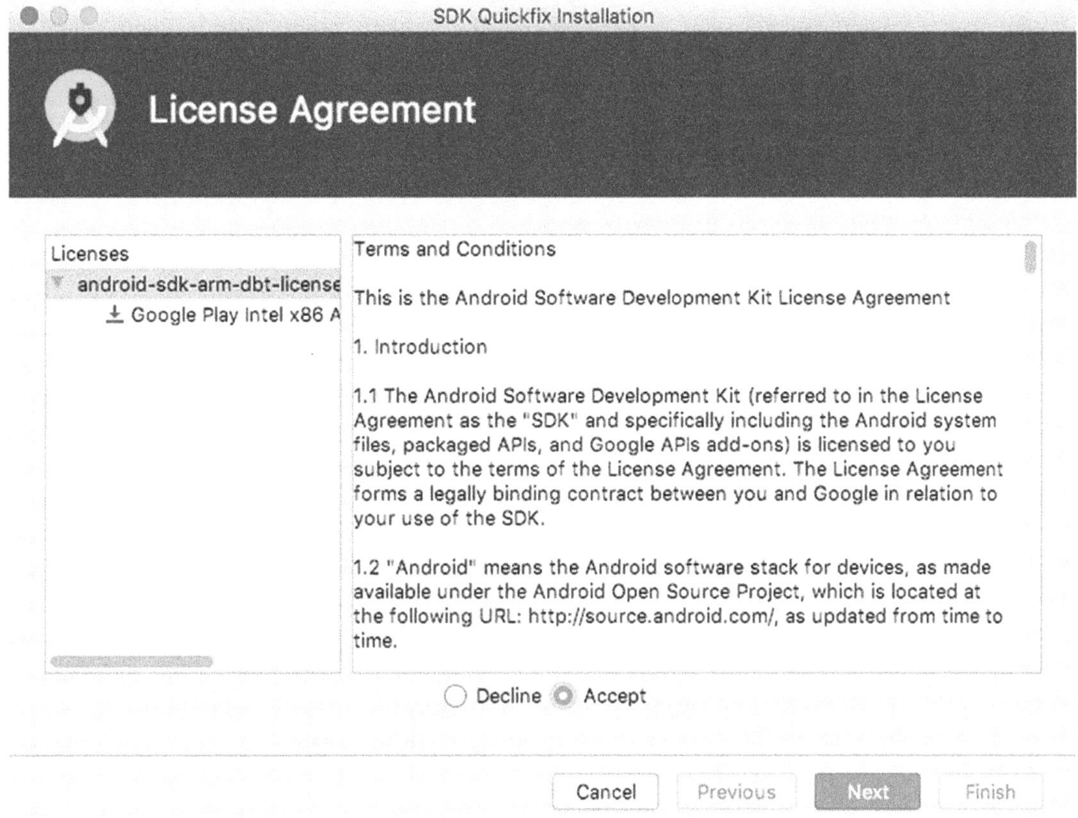

Figure 3-6. *An example license acceptance screen for AVD system images*

I am not a lawyer, and I certainly don't play one on TV! More seriously, that means I can't advise you what the text of the license means or implies. If you are at all worried, seek legal counsel. But from a layperson's perspective, the open source licenses used for Android system images are generally nothing to lose sleep over. I will assume you accept the text shown and, having clicked the Next button, are now staring at the Android Virtual Device (AVD) configuration verification screen shown in Figure 3-7.

Figure 3-7. The Android Virtual Device (AVD) configuration verification screen

Use this screen to check you are happy with the configuration of your new AVD and, most importantly, to give it a memorable name. You can call your AVDs anything you like – there's no need to keep model or make names that might have been inherited from one of the pre-configured system images, though it can help to keep it as part of the name as a quick reminder of the features of your emulated device. Choose a name, and then click the Finish button, to head to the AVD Manager home screen, as shown in Figure 3-8.

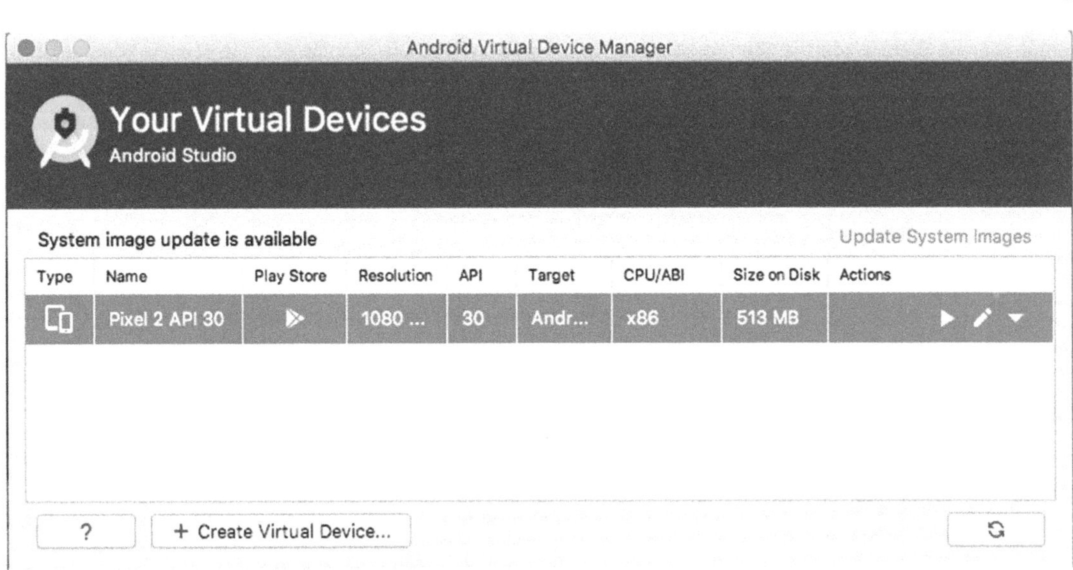

Figure 3-8. The populated AVD Manager home screen

You should now see your newly created AVD in the list of available emulated devices. That's it for creating your first Android Virtual Device – you are now ready to get your own application written and running on it!

Creating Your First Android Application, Already!

You have all the prerequisites in place to get started with your first Android application. There is still a great deal to learn, but you already have the key pieces at hand, including Android Studio and a newly created Android Virtual Device ready to try out whatever you write. Hopefully this ready-to-go status isn't surprising to you. I outlined some of the benefits of IDEs in Chapter 2, and you're about to experience this directly in the area of setting up the scaffolding and framework of a new application.

Without any further suspense, let's get started. If you have followed along with the earlier steps in this chapter, completing the creation of an AVD, you will likely be back at the Android Studio home screen you saw earlier in the chapter, in Figure 3-1. From that home screen, choose the `Start a new Android Studio project` option at the top of the screen, and you will shortly see the first screen of the Create New Project wizard.

If, for whatever reason, you don't have that home screen visible or have restarted Android Studio and it doesn't show the home screen wizard, you might instead be looking at an empty Android Studio screen or one that has loaded a pre-existing project, as shown in Figure 3-9.

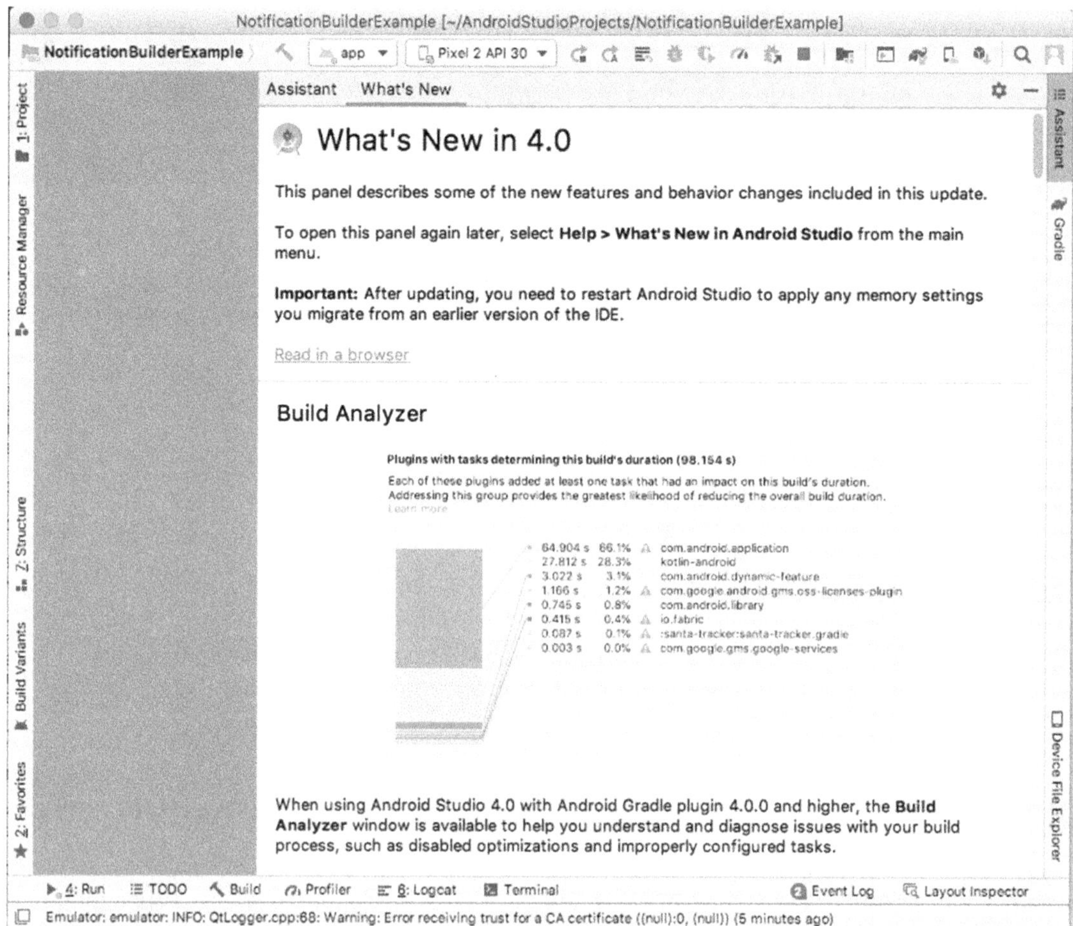

***Figure 3-9.** Android Studio as it appears when the home screen disappears*

Don't panic! You can also initiate a new project from here, but opening the File menu and choosing `New` ➤ `New Project`. This will also launch the Create New Project wizard. Regardless of the path you've taken, you should shortly see the wizard as shown in Figure 3-10

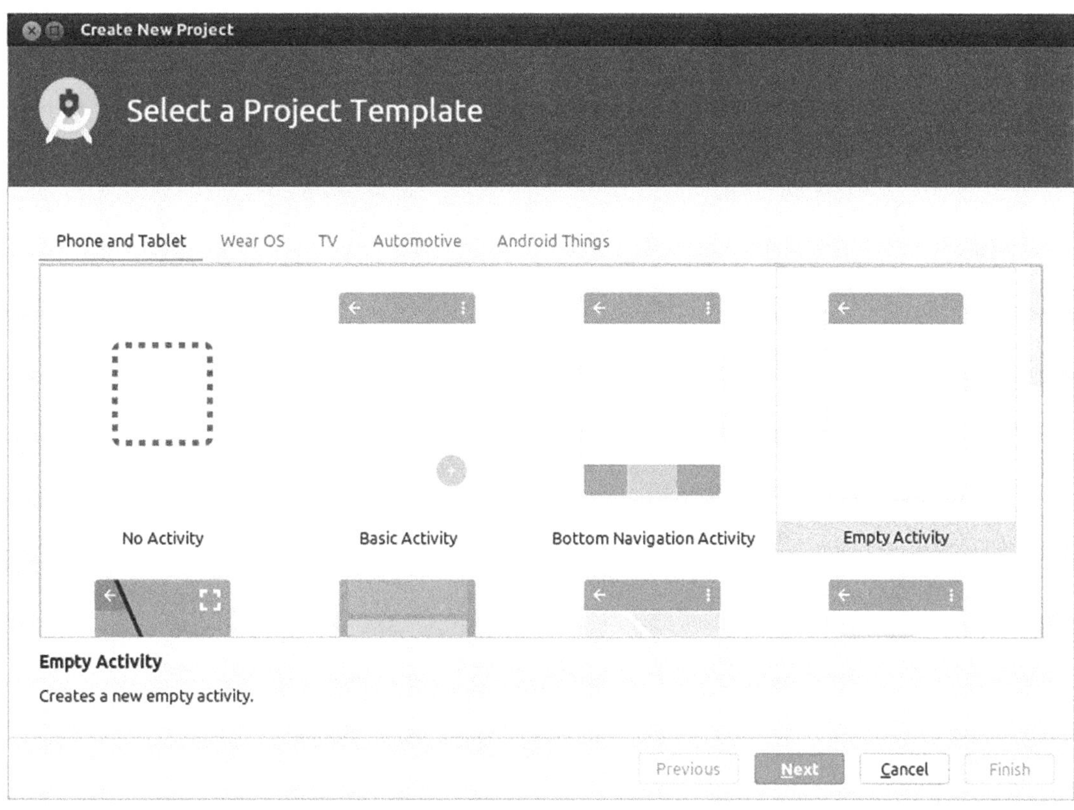

Figure 3-10. The Create New Project wizard in Android Studio

The first page of the wizard is already prompting you to make some choices about what kind of application you would like to build. Across the top of the screen, you will see device categories, such as Phone and Tablet, Wear OS, TV, and so on. At this moment, we will stick with the Phone and Tablet wizard option. Looking at the icons displayed beneath Phone and Tablet, you are likely scratching your head, perplexed as to what terms like `activity`, `fragment`, and so forth mean. Fear not. You'll soon master these. At this stage, you can treat this screen as Android Studio asking you exactly how much bootstrapping you want for your new application and what ready-made pieces you would like it to put in place on your behalf. For instance, if you anticipate making an application reliant on maps and navigation capabilities, the Google Maps Activity template adds in a bunch of mapping, GPS, and location support options ready-made for developers. Other options on this screen similarly pull in other goodies, such as Ad library support for the Google AdMob Ads Activity.

We are going to start with a very plain, vanilla Android application, creating variants of this simple application showing each feature discussed as we work through the coming chapters. So for now, you can choose the Empty Activity option. Don't let the word Empty fool you, as the Empty Activity option still deploys much of the boilerplate and basic project structure you need for your application. With Empty Activity selected, click the Next button, and you should see the Configure Your Project screen, as shown in Figure 3-11.

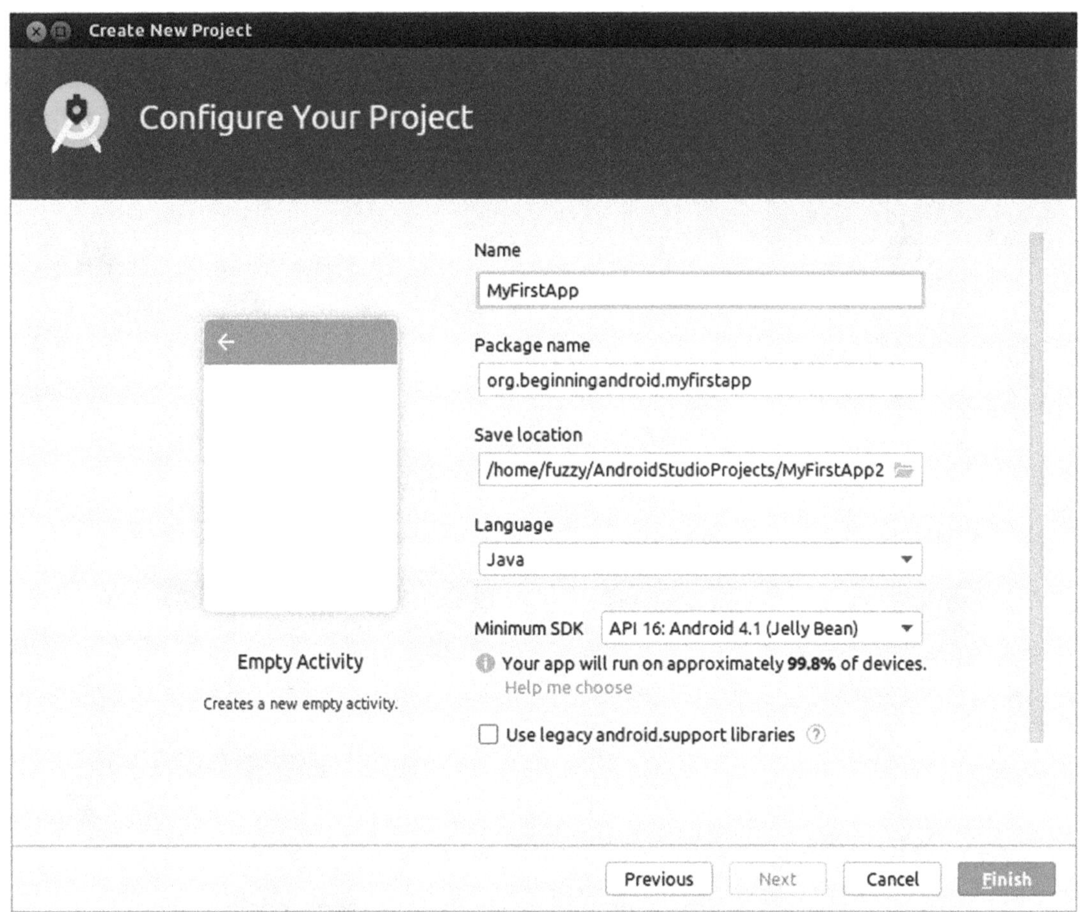

***Figure 3-11.** The Configure Your Project screen in Android Studio*

The options shown on this screen are all that stand between you and adding your own code and touches to your application. For your current MyFirstApp project, you will want to specify the following settings:

Name: This should be a meaningful name for your application. It's the title that will appear on-screen when running the app, it's the caption that will appear under the app's icon from Android launcher screens, and should you even publish this app in the Google Play store or elsewhere, it's the name that will appear there. For our purposes, enter `MyFirstApp` as the name.

Package name: In a world with tens of thousands of developers creating hundreds of thousands of applications for Android, how do you ensure no two apps conflict when it comes to naming? Rather than enforce unique names (though places like Google Play do have some restrictions in this regard), Android leverages the fundamental mechanism of package names derived from the Java standard. We will talk more about Java package naming in Chapter 7, so for now you can use a package name derived from one of my own domain names – `org.beginningandroid.myfirstapp`.

Save location: The save location is the folder on disk where the entire hierarchy of code for this application will be stored. This will include menu subfolders, holding contents like source code, configuration files, images, video, and more, depending on how sophisticated we make this application. To begin with, the space used by a new project will be under 1 MB. But this can grow quickly, so it's best to choose a location on disk that you know has ample spare space. If you're happy with the default, you can accept it – a directory named `AndroidStudioProject/MyFirstApp` under your user's home directory on your operating system.

Language: Open the pick list you see, and you are presented with two options: Kotlin or Java. Kotlin is a newer addition to the family of languages that Android supports for authoring applications. Java is the first and still by a massive margin the largest used and most popular language for Android development. Choose Java as the language for MyFirstApp.

Minimum SDK: Here is where our discussion of Android versions, Android Studio versions, and Android SDK versions from Chapter 2 and this chapter starts to pay off. Your selection here will dictate what version of the SDK is used for this application and therefore to a large degree what devices it will be compatible with from the history of Android devices. Newer releases of the Android SDK provide support for newer features, whereas older releases are more likely to be supported on older – and therefore more – devices. You will see the additional text next to your selection that indicates what percentage of activated Google devices in use throughout the world would support the SDK version of your choice. There is no perfect answer to the best trade-off between new features and broad support. For now, our initial application is not going to use any cutting-edge features from the latest release of the Android SDK, so you can go with the default, choosing API 16, which was first released to coincide with the Android 4.1 Jelly Bean release from several years ago. You can scroll through the list to choose another SDK release if you wish. If your chosen SDK version is not currently installed on your computer, it will be downloaded along with the steps taken to complete setting up this initial application – be sure to account for the 100+ MB of disk space used for each SDK version.

Use legacy android.support libraries: Over the years, Google has tried a number of approaches to deal with the version fragmentation seen in use by active Android devices. One approach was (and still is) to use an additional support library not tied to any one particular SDK version and have applications utilize this support library. The subtlety was that Google was much more able to push updates for the support library, as compared to the Android installation of any particular device. We will talk more about this in coming chapters when we discuss androidx and Jetpack. For now, you can leave this setting at the default of unchecked, meaning we won't pull in support for these libraries.

You are now one step away from a runnable Android application. Click the Finish button, and Android Studio will spring to life, generating the structure and scaffolding for your new Android application and its project folders. After a short time, you should eventually see the full project and the full developer interface for Android Studio appear, as shown in Figure 3-12.

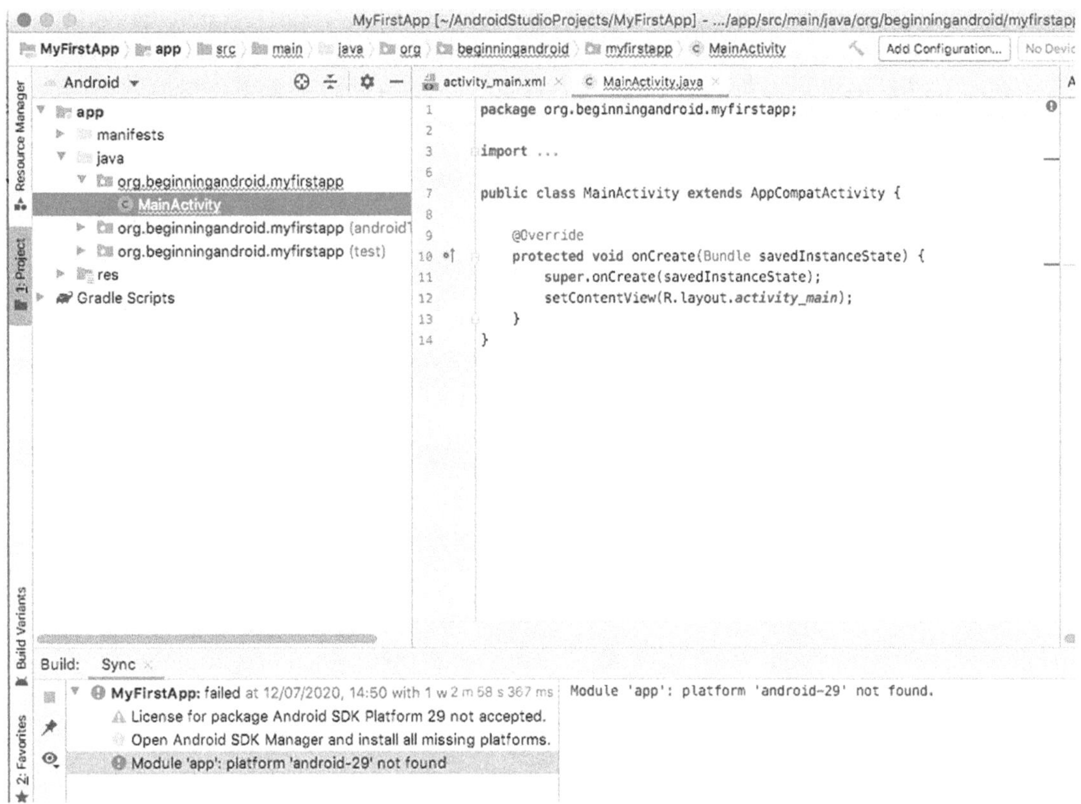

Figure 3-12. Android Studio showing the MyFirstApp project open for editing

Getting Your First Code Written

If you review the layout of your new project as shown in Figure 3-12, you will see a folder/directory hierarchy with all manner of names, such as `manifests`, `java`, `res`, and more. We are going to explore the full project layout, the directories you see, the starter files that populate them, and the pieces you build in the very next chapter.

Right now, in the interests of getting you a working application with your own personal touch, we are going to skip the explanations of those items and dive straight into editing your first application component. Use the Project hierarchy view you see on the left of the Android Studio layout, and click down through the `res` folder and then the `layout` subfolder. You should see a file-like entry named `activity_main.xml` (because these are, actually, files!). Double-click the `activity_main.xml` file, and it will open in the editor view of Android Studio, as you can see in Figure 3-13.

***Figure 3-13.** Opening your first source file in Android Studio*

Looking at screenshots of code is tedious, so let's look at the content of the `activity_main.xml` file. Your file should look like Listing 3-1.

***Listing 3-1.** The contents of the activity_main.xml file in a new Android Studio project*

```
<?xml version="1.0" encoding="utf-8"?>
<androidx.constraintlayout.widget.ConstraintLayout
xmlns:android="http://schemas.android.com/apk/res/android"
    xmlns:app="http://schemas.android.com/apk/res-auto"
    xmlns:tools="http://schemas.android.com/tools"
    android:layout_width="match_parent"
    android:layout_height="match_parent"
    tools:context=".MainActivity">

    <TextView
        android:layout_width="wrap_content"
        android:layout_height="wrap_content"
       android:text="Hello World!"
        app:layout_constraintBottom_toBottomOf="parent"
        app:layout_constraintLeft_toLeftOf="parent"
        app:layout_constraintRight_toRightOf="parent"
        app:layout_constraintTop_toTopOf="parent" />

</androidx.constraintlayout.widget.ConstraintLayout>
```

There are a few different parts of this file that will interest us in the future, but for now we are only interested in one part of the code here, which you see in bold. You will note that about halfway through the file is the line

```
android:text="Hello World!"
```

Go ahead and edit the string within the double quotes, so instead of reading "Hello World!", it reads something like "Hello Android!" or whatever takes your fancy. Once you are done editing this file, save your changes. You've just made your first custom edit to an Android application!

Getting Ready to Run Your Application

You are now ready to have Android Studio run your new application inside the AVD emulator you created earlier in the chapter. In order for Android Studio to do this, it needs to know what your particular preferences are when you ask it to run the application. For example, do you just want it to run normally, so you can interact with it, or do you want it to run in a debugging mode or some other way that lets you carefully examine what is happening in the code or to the interactions between your application and the Android host device, other APIs you may be calling, or external services such as cloud-based APIs?

Android Studio controls these alternative approaches to running your applications through what are known as run configurations. These are preset instructions on exactly what you mean by "run" when running an application.

You can trigger Android Studio to walk you through setting up your first run configuration by simply trying to run your application right now. Open the `Run` menu, and choose the `Run...` option. Without any pre-existing run configurations in place, Android Studio will now prompt you to edit a configuration, as shown in Figure 3-14.

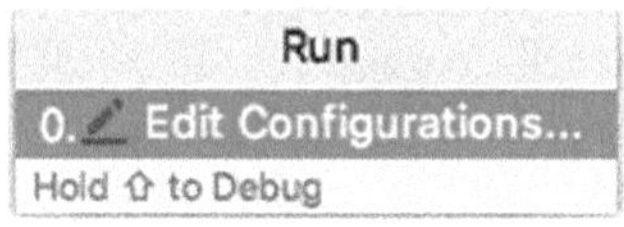

***Figure 3-14.** The prompt to edit your first run configuration*

> **Note** You can always directly edit run configurations without forcibly running an application, by choosing the Edit Configurations... option from the Run menu.

Whichever way you've triggered the creation of your first run configuration, you will see the Run/Debug Configurations screen displayed. The text on that screen will indicate to click the "+" button to add a new configuration, and you should do that. You will see the list of options shown in Figure 3-15.

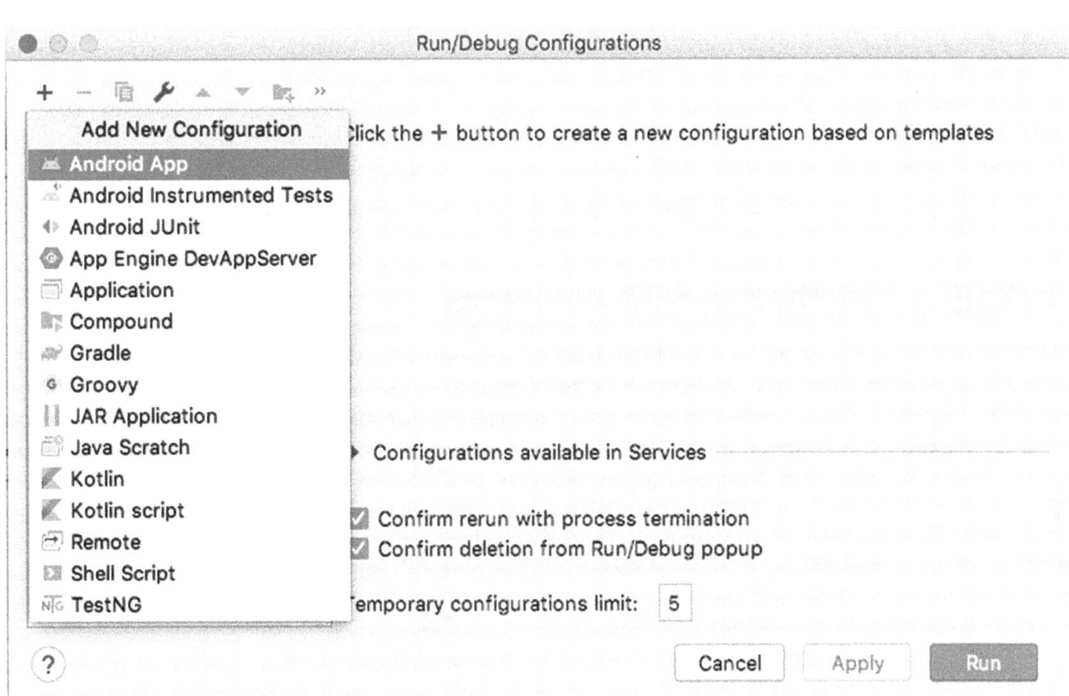

Figure 3-15. Selecting a new base run configuration

Choose the Android App option at the top of the list presented, and you will then see the detailed configuration screen as shown in Figure 3-16.

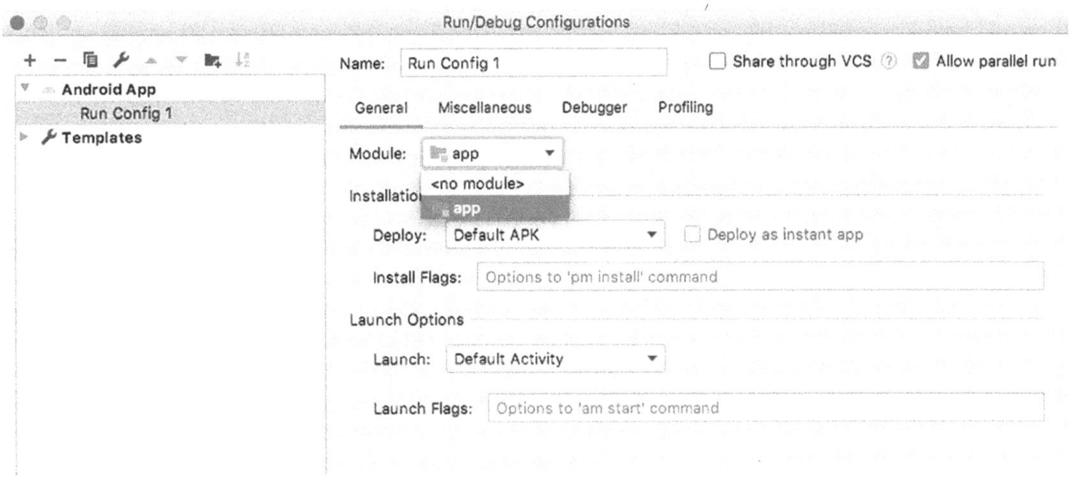

Figure 3-16. Detailed configuration for a new run configuration

There are two settings you will need to make. The first setting is to provide your run configuration with a memorable name. I am going to suggest you use the name Run Config 1. Next, you need to nominate which module of code the run configuration should initiate when running your application. The only option in the list is app, which is fortunate, as that's the option you want. You can see both of these settings in Figure 3-16.

Click the Apply and OK buttons to save away your configuration.

Installing (Additional) SDK Packages

Depending on how you choose your application's minimum SDK setting earlier in this chapter and the options you selected when first installing Android Studio, you might not have the relevant SDK bundle installed on your machine for Android Studio to use in building your application. You can spot this easily, as you're default view in Android Studio includes the current build status in the lower left of the screen.

If you look at the "Build: Sync" area and see an error or warning worded as follows, you likely need to download an SDK package to match the one selected for your project:

```
License for package Android SDK Platform 29 not accepted
```

or

```
Module 'app': platform 'android-29' not found
```

The version number mentioned in the warnings or errors might differ in your installation. Whatever the version, this is easily fixed by invoking the SDK Manager feature (yet another piece of integration offered by the IDE). From the Tools menu of Android Studio, choose the SDK Manager option, and you should see the SDK Manager appear as shown in Figure 3-17.

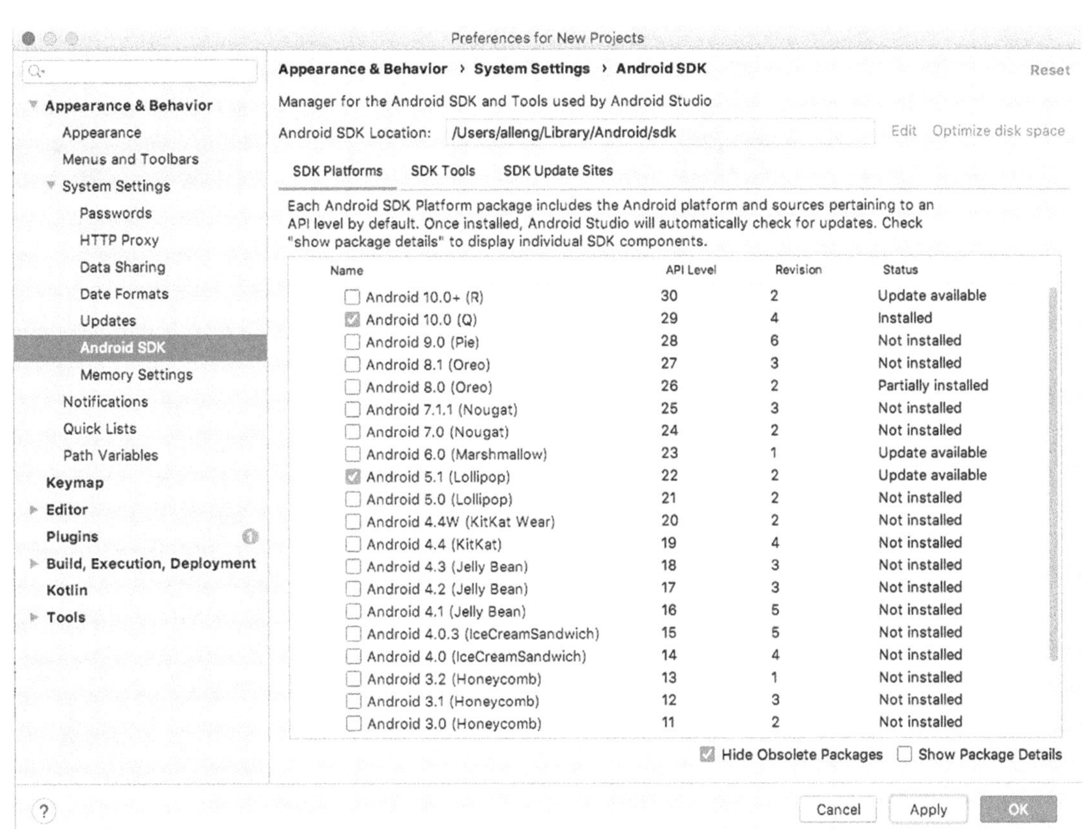

***Figure 3-17.** The Android SDK Manager*

To add the SDK needed for your project, simply check the box next to the relevant version – in my case, that is "Android 10.0 (Q)," which equates to API level 29 or, in other words, version 29 of the Android SDK. Click the Apply button, and the SDK Manager will then trigger the download of this version of the SDK. If you sit back and think about it for a moment, you will realize that as you build more and more applications and potentially choose different target SDK versions for them, you will likely end up with quite a few different versions of the Android SDK installed on your machine, and together, these will take a considerable amount of disk space. We'll revisit this topic in Chapter 6, when we look in depth at your overall developer system setup.

Once the download of any needed Android SDK version is complete, you should see the status as shown in Figure 3-18.

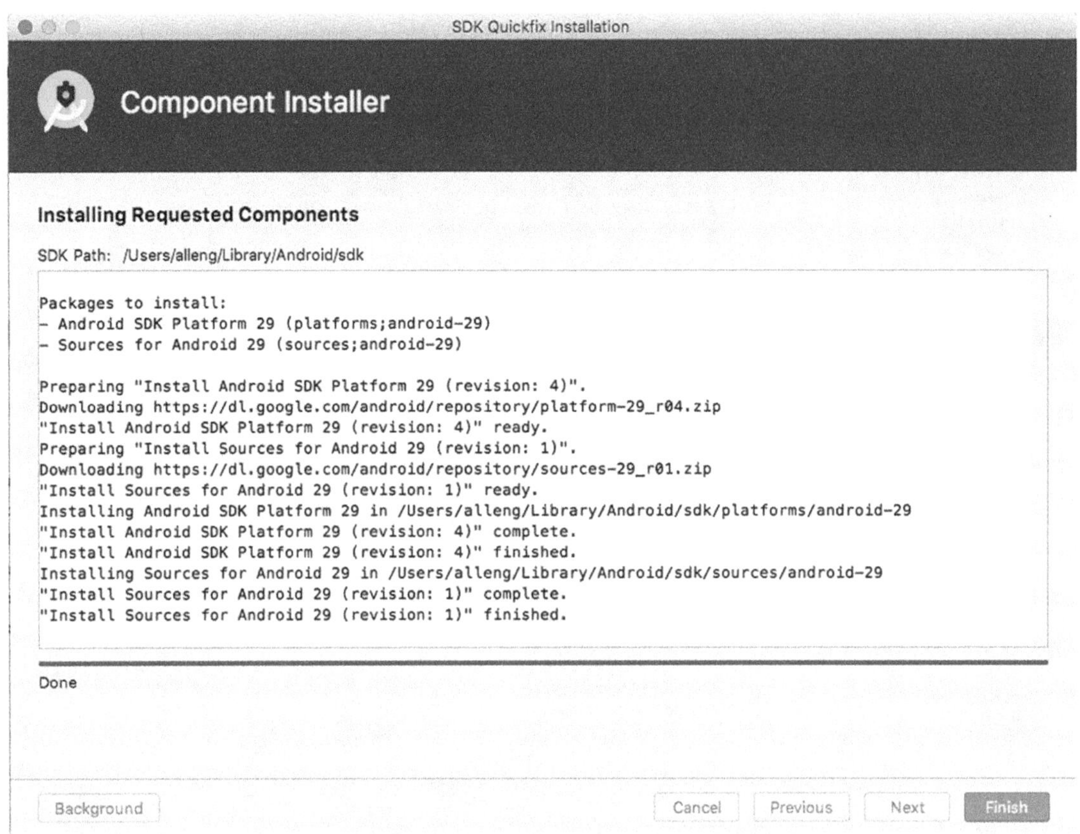

Figure 3-18. *The Android SDK Manager indicating successful download and install of a new SDK version*

At this point, you will need to have Android Studio refresh the configuration for the integrated Gradle build tool so it realizes the new SDK is in place. Android Studio can take all the necessary steps to do this – so don't panic at this point if you know nothing about Gradle as a build tool. Simply open the `File` menu, and select the option that reads `Sync Project with Gradle Files`.

When this sync activity completes, in the Build window in the lower left of the screen, you should see the previous warnings and errors are now gone, and the only message present should read `MyFirstApp successful at` *some-date-and-time*.

Running Your Application

With a completed setup in Android Studio matching the needs of your application and Gradle in sync and ready to build your application, your run configuration should now be able to actually run your new application. Go ahead and choose Run from the Run menu, or directly choose `Run 'Run Config 1'` to skip the run configuration selection step.

A bunch of actions will now happen automatically, but they can take a little time – up to a few minutes depending on the capabilities of your computer. First, Gradle will be invoked to build your application. We will cover this process in more detail in later chapters, but for now what you need to know is that Gradle is pulling together all of the code you wrote, the libraries referenced by your application, the relevant Android SDK, and other plumbing and generating a bundle ready to deploy as your application. This is known as an Android Package, or APK.

Next, Android Studio invokes your AVD, and after the time it takes for that emulator to start, it copies over the APK built by Gradle. Based on your run configuration, Android Studio knows that you want to run the app module, in effect triggering your new MyFirstApp application to run in the AVD, just as if you'd pressed its icon in the Android launcher window.

Your app will run, and your immortal words "Hello Android!" (or whatever you chose) should appear within an app screen titled MyFirstApp, just as you see in Figure 3-19.

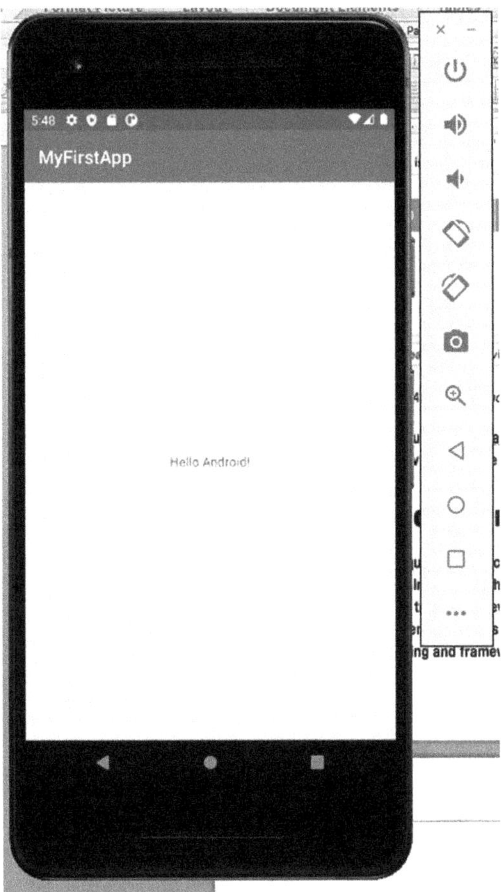

***Figure 3-19.** Your running MyFirstApp Android application within your AVD*

That's it! You have written and run your first Android application. Well done. Take a deep breath, because in Chapter 4 we are going to dive under the hood and examine everything that Android Studio has just built for you in great detail.

Chapter 4

Exploring Your First Project

In Chapter 3, I introduced you to setting up everything you needed to get your first Android application written and running on an AVD, with the goal of very quickly getting you immersed in Android Studio, emulators, and your first part of coding. We got results fast! But you almost certainly have a whole bunch of unanswered questions that cropped up as we zoomed through. In this chapter, we'll start a deeper dive into many of the topics, starting with the structure and features of your new Android project. This should start to answer those questions and build your knowledge.

Viewing the Whole Android Project Structure

To get familiar with the structure and purpose of the various parts of an Android project, it can help to start with the view from 30000 feet up (or 10000 meters, for the metric-minded). Looking at the entire layout of your project from the previous chapter, it turns out to be surprisingly large. While you only edited one file, many others were created for you by the new project wizard, and other files like Java libraries, the Android SDK, and so on were copied or had references added as your project was created.

To see this full view, use the left-hand pane of the Android Studio window, known as the Project Explorer view, to expand the app folder; then the folders under it such as manifests, java, and so on; and all the other folders from the top level down. You will end up with a view of the entire project that looks similar to Figure 4-1 (note that I am showing successive views of the long Project Explorer side by side, to save space).

G. Allen, *Android for Absolute Beginners*, https://doi.org/10.1007/978-1-4842-6646-5_4

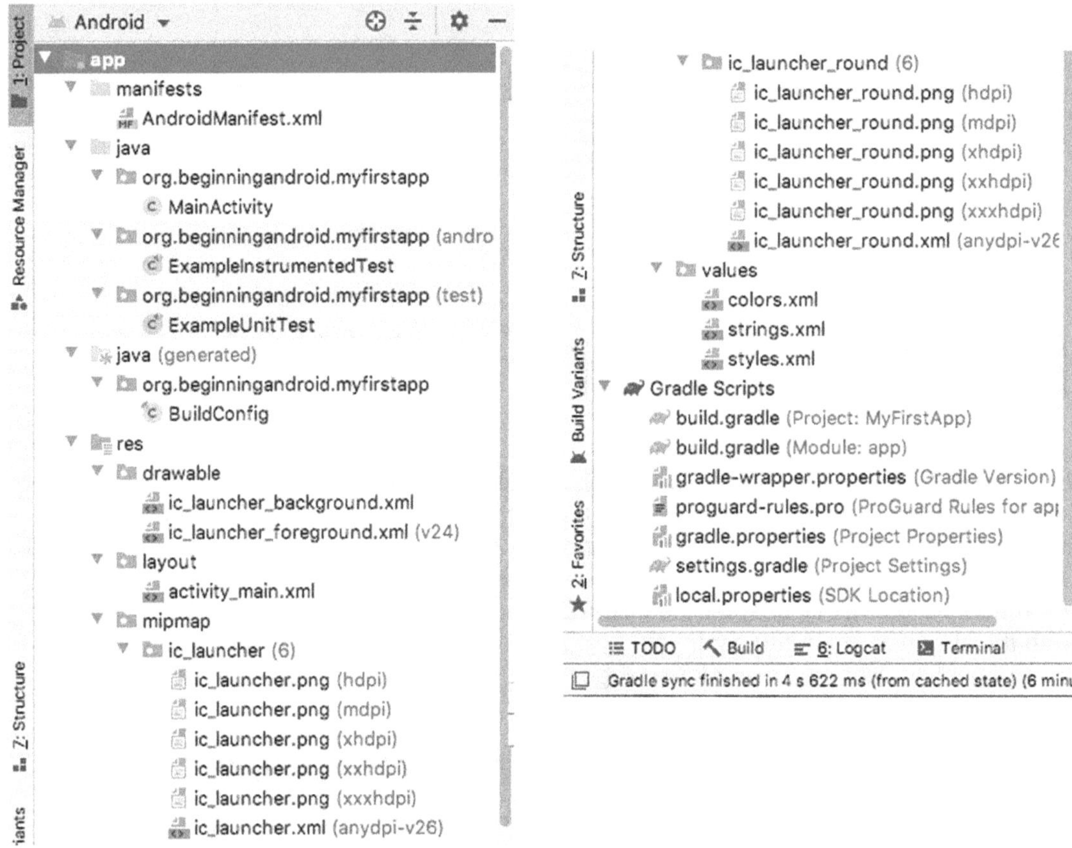

Figure 4-1. The logical Android view of your project in the Project Explorer

The default view you see is known as the Android view and is designed to simplify the way all of your project's constituent parts are displayed to you. The goal with this simplification is to let you focus on the parts you, the developer, write or edit and to keep much of the rest of the supporting files out of the way.

From this whole-of-project Android view, you can see that the project is broken down into five major groups of files that represent different parts of your project.

Working with Manifests

The first group of files shown in the Android view in Project Explorer are your manifest files. With a new project such as MyFirstApp, there is only one manifest file that will concern you, which is the one named `AndroidManifest.xml`.

This is your Android Manifest file and acts almost like a master control file for your Android application. Within the Android Manifest file, you are able to control many major parameters and behaviors of your application, including declaring what permissions your application will require to operate, what services it may interact with, the activities that comprise the application, and the Android SDK levels that the application both needs and supports.

We'll cover more depth on some of these core concepts later in the chapter, including defining what activities and services mean in the Android sense. For now, let's look at the content of your AndroidManifest.xml file, which you see in Listing 4-1.

***Listing 4-1.** The contents of your new AndroidManifest.xml file*

```
<?xml version="1.0" encoding="utf-8"?>
<manifest xmlns:android="http://schemas.android.com/apk/res/android"
    package="org.beginningandroid.myfirstapp">

    <application
        android:allowBackup="true"
        android:icon="@mipmap/ic_launcher"
        android:label="@string/app_name"
        android:roundIcon="@mipmap/ic_launcher_round"
        android:supportsRtl="true"
        android:theme="@style/AppTheme">
        <activity android:name=".MainActivity">
            <intent-filter>
                <action android:name="android.intent.action.MAIN" />

                <category android:name="android.intent.category.LAUNCHER" />
            </intent-filter>
        </activity>
    </application>

</manifest>
```

As you might have guessed from the filename, the contents are in XML format. For those of you encountering XML for the first time, Chapter 8 provides a full introduction to XML for Android development. It's fine to jump ahead and cover that topic and return to this point once you are comfortable with the basics of XML.

Android uses the root element `<manifest>` for the XML document and then introduces two key attributes: a namespace declaration and a package declaration. Where namespaces are concerned, the Android convention is to use them only at the attribute level, rather than also using them for elements. The package name `org.beginningandroid.myfirstapp` should look familiar to you, as this was the package name we provided in the project setup wizard in Chapter 3. As well as providing this essential mapping to ensure uniqueness for your application's fully qualified package name, this technique allows us to then use shorthand in the future when wanting to refer to aspects of the application with itself.

You can see this in action a little further down the manifest, where the first `<activity>` element is introduced, in the form `<activity android:name=".MainActivity">`. Here, the leading dot is shorthand for the full package name referenced in the `<manifest>` package attribute. In practice, it means much shorter names for internal references, so in this example, `.MainActivity` instead of `org.beginningandroid.myfirstapp.MainActivity`. I know which one I'd prefer to type.

The manifest file also includes other key features. For instance, the android:icon and android:roundIcon attributes reference two resource files that provide the square and round icon versions for your application in an Android device's launcher screen and widget screen. The android:label attribute holds the name of your application.

One further important entry is the <activity android:name=".MainActivity"> mentioned earlier. This entry, including the child element <intent-filter>, indicates to Android which activity it should respond with when the application launches and the key intent android.intent.action.MAIN is triggered. We'll cover exactly what these concepts are shortly in this chapter, but for now you can think of this as an Android way of flagging what your application first shows a user when it starts.

Jiving with Java

The second and third main areas of your Android Project Explorer view are for your Java source files. These are the text files in which Java code is written to bring your application to life and have it perform the actions, features, and behaviors you intend for your app to have.

You will see two high-level folders, one for Java and one for Java (generated). In fact at this stage, all of the files in both areas have been generated for you, but in general as you develop your application, you will change the files in the Java tree, add new ones, and so on and leave Android Studio and its integrated tools to automatically handle the Java (generated) files.

There is one file in particular to spot right now, and that is the MainActivity file under the Java ➤ org.beginningandroid.myfirstapp folder. The file on disk is actually called MainActivity.java, and the Android view in Project Explorer is hiding the file extension. This MainActivity file is the code that will run when your application starts, based on the configuration mentioned earlier in the Android Manifest file.

We will look at what is meant by activity both later in this chapter and in depth in many future sections of the book.

Getting Resourceful with Resources

The fourth main area of files within your new project are the resource files, found in the res folder and its subfolders. There are quite a number of items generated for you to begin with, in different categories of resources.

Drawables

Drawables are those things that Android will draw, or render, on-screen as part of your application. This means both normal images, such as artwork, diagrams, and other static images, and images it will have to generate at runtime based on instructions given to it.

The first kind of drawables are represented in typical image files that you might be familiar with, such as GIF, JPEG, and PNG files. Android has mechanisms to scale images up and down to suit various density screens/displays and also lets you store different resolution versions of the same image so as to avoid scaling. We will delve into the world of image, photo, and artwork creation and techniques for Android applications in Chapter 14.

The second kind of drawables Android supports are vector images that it creates at runtime, based on specifications provided in XML files. You can see two examples of XML files providing vector graphics instructions in your new project – `ic_launcher_background.xml` and `ic_launcher_foreground.xml`.

Layouts

In Chapters 9 and 10, we will explore layouts and designing the UI of your application in detail, covering a range of options and styles. When you created your new project in Chapter 3, you will remember choosing the "Empty Activity" option for your project. This choice was used by Android Studio to put in place a default layout, which appears in the file `activity_main.xml` under the layout subfolder.

Once again, this is an XML file, and Android makes extensive use of XML in defining the initial layout and behavioral characteristics of activities. If you think of an activity as a screen or window in your Android application, which is then used by users, it is the XML layout that provides the description of how to create and render the interface. This `activity_main.xml` layout is used by your `MainActivity` Java code when it wants to draw the activity on-screen. This process is known as "inflation" in the Android world and applies to the process for laying out an entire activities interface, as well as any subset of it such as creating a menu or dynamically adding one layout inside another. As your application grows, so too will the number of activity layout XML files in this folder.

Mipmaps

You can think of the `mipmap` folder as a special case of the `drawable` folder. Where drawables are images or artwork for any purpose, the mipmap entries are specifically for the icon files used for your application and an Android device's launcher screen(s). The `ic_launcher` folder holds square versions of the icons, and the `ic_launcher_round` holds rounded versions of the same icons. Multiple instances of each file are stored at different resolutions (display densities), and Android will automatically determine which density version to use based on display characteristics of a device and any explicit configuration overrides an application or device might use.

We will talk more about display densities and their implications in later chapters.

Finding Value in Values

Within the `values` folder, you will find files dedicated to holding data about strings, dimensions, styles, and other reference information. This approach embodies the simple abstraction technique you will find in almost all programming languages and environments. Rather than peppering your application code and configuration files with hard-coded values that might often be repeated in many places, using an abstraction to reference a single definition of a value away from the code makes for cleaner, less error-prone code. This helps in many ways, such as providing a well-managed mechanism for creating and using value resources for many different screen sizes and resolutions.

In your current project, you can see the application name is present in the `strings.xml` file. Rather than embed our "`MyFirstApp`" as a literal string everywhere it is needed through the project, a reference to this entry in the `strings.xml` file can be used. If we ever need to change this value, we can do it in one place, and know that all references will be updated automatically and correctly. While we won't be doing this ourselves, this has concrete benefits in areas such as internationalization and localization of your application into other languages.

Building Everything with Gradle Files

By now, your tally of the number of separate files of various types that make up even your first Android application is growing, well into double digits. Bringing all these files together to create a final, working Android application is the job of the build system, and Android Studio by default relies on a build toolset known as Gradle.

The `Gradle Scripts` folder shows you the various scripts that exist to do the work of building a complete application from its constituent components. The two most notable files right now are the identically named `build.gradle` files. You'll notice the first one flagged as being for the project – in this case, `Project: MyFirstApp`. The second is labeled as `Module: app`.

"Why two `build.gradle` files?" you might ask. The long answer is that you could in fact have more than two. What you are seeing is the project-level `build.gradle` file that all Android projects have one of. Then you are seeing one additional `build.gradle` file for each module your project defines, allowing each module to handle any module-specific build activities and parameters. As your project only defines a single "`app`" module, you only see one more `build.gradle` file, giving you a total of two. As we progress through the book, we'll work with examples that have multiple modules incorporated into a given project, and thus you'll see additional `build.gradle` files in the relevant projects.

Right now, the project-level build.gradle file is of most interest, and you can review its contents in Listing 4-2.

***Listing 4-2.** The project-level build.gradle file*

```
apply plugin: 'com.android.application'

android {
    compileSdkVersion 29
    buildToolsVersion "30.0.0"

    defaultConfig {
        applicationId "org.beginningandroid.myfirstapp"
        minSdkVersion 16
        targetSdkVersion 29
        versionCode 1
        versionName "1.0"

        testInstrumentationRunner "androidx.test.runner.AndroidJUnitRunner"
    }
```

```
    buildTypes {
        release {
            minifyEnabled false
            proguardFiles getDefaultProguardFile('proguard-android-optimize.txt'),
            'proguard-rules.pro'
        }
    }
}

dependencies {
    implementation fileTree(dir: "libs", include: ["*.jar"])
    implementation 'androidx.appcompat:appcompat:1.1.0'
    implementation 'androidx.constraintlayout:constraintlayout:1.1.3'
    testImplementation 'junit:junit:4.12'
    androidTestImplementation 'androidx.test.ext:junit:1.1.1'
    androidTestImplementation 'androidx.test.espresso:espresso-core:3.2.0'
}
```

You have a variety of configuration settings that control how your application is built, which fall into a few key areas. These are SDK versioning and application versioning, the type of application build being targeted, and the inclusion of dependencies, plugins, and libraries that are required as the foundation for your project.

Understanding SDK Version Parameters

There are several parameters you'll observe that mention SDK versions, including `compileSdkVersion`, `minSdkVersion`, and `targetSdkVersion`. These serve different but complementary purposes:

- compileSdkVersion: Instructs Android Studio what version of the SDK – from the potentially many versions you have installed – to use when actually compiling and building your application. Normally you will choose the latest version of the Android SDK you have available.
- minSdkVersion: Sets the threshold for native API feature use in your application and, by implication, determines the oldest versions of Android and Android SDK that would support your application. This in turn sets the oldest devices that could use your application. Features introduced in newer API levels will be handled by Support Libraries or Android Jetpack (discussed in a moment), where possible.
- targetSdkVersion: Controls the newest API features your application will attempt to use, even if the `compileSdkVersion` is a later release than this. This means that you can benefit from efficiencies at compile time offered by newer SDKs, but not be forced to adopt sometimes significant changes to your application's behavior until you explicitly advance the `targetSdkVersion`.

Understanding Application Versioning

When releasing Android applications, just as with almost all other software, the concept of versioning is used to indicate later releases that fix bugs, add new features, improve existing behavior, and so on.

Android uses two parameters that you'll find in the build.gradle file. The most important is the `versionCode` parameter, which traditionally has been the parameter that tracks the version number for a given build/release of your application. The `versionCode` parameter is an integer that should only ever increase as you release new values.

> **Note** Internally, since SDK version 28, Android has also offered the newer `versionCodeMajor` parameter. This is a `long` value, rather than an `integer`, so can hold much higher values. This can currently only be successfully set by incorporating `versionCodeMajor="n"` notation in your Android Manifest XML file. Gradle build files don't currently support this parameter.

Android provides a mechanism to show some kind of meaningful human-readable version to your users as well, sourced from the `versionName` string value. This helps you as a developer if you want to try to signal things like major and minor releases to your users, which is a traditional (though not essential) habit for software development.

Including Libraries for Forward and Backward Version Support

The last aspect of your Gradle build files to note for now is the dependencies section. I won't go into each dependency that is being declared at this stage, as we'll return to each one when we discuss their particulars in later sections on testing, handset/version compatibility, and more. The one common aspect I will highlight is the namespace for many of the dependencies. You will note the leading component name is `androidx`. The name `androidx` refers to Android Jetpack, which was a recent update and refresh of the way Android allows you as a developer to target many different versions of SDK without needing to know of them in advance – in effect, future-proofing your application against some of the changes that get incorporated into later SDK releases while also allowing you to build applications with the capabilities of contemporary SDK releases and letting Android and Jetpack worry about how to mimic such newer behavior when running on devices with older versions of Android that don't support your SDK version explicitly. Jetpack also helps reduce some of the verbosity of writing software in Java, by reducing boilerplate code and helping you follow good practices that have been learned by the Android developer community over time.

Jetpack is replacing an older approach, known as the Android Support Libraries, but you will still see Support Libraries in many references and discussions, and the two will live side by side for some time to come.

Explaining the Key Android Application Logical Building Blocks

You now have some view of the project structure and layout within Android Studio. But at several points in this chapter, I have mentioned some of the fundamental logical building blocks of an Android application, such as activities and services. Now's the time to get a little more understanding of what these building blocks are and how they fit together to bring your application to life.

Activities

If you have used any existing Android application, you would have experienced that it has some themes in common with most software that comes with a user interface. Like other software with UIs, Android uses the concept of a "screen" or "view" where users actually interact with your program. Android calls these activities, and whether you want your users to read text, watch a video, enter data, make a phone call, play a game, or what have you, your users will do this by interacting with one or many activity screens or layouts that you design.

Activities are one of the easiest, and computationally cheapest, parts of Android to develop, and you should be generous with your creation and use of them in your application. Not only will this help your users get a great experience from your application but the Android operating system is designed with the proliferation of activities in mind and provides lots of help in managing them.

Intents

Intents are the internal messaging system of Android, allowing pieces of information to be passed between applications and to and from the Android environment. In this way, your application can trigger actions and share data with Android and other applications, and it can also listen out for events that are happening and take action when appropriate.

The Android operating system already has a very wide range of intents that your application can interact with, and as a developer you can also define and develop your own intents for your own uses.

Services

Services are a common concept in much of the computing world, and while there are slight differences when dealing with them in Android, many of the common concepts still apply. Services are applications that typically have no user interface and instead run in the background. Services offer up a range of features, capabilities, or behaviors that are typically in demand by multiple applications. Services typically are long-lived, humming along in the background helping out your application and others as demanded.

Content Providers

There are many types and derivations of data that your application might want to use that you yourself don't control. Lots of other applications have similar data demands, and so Android ships with the concept of Content Providers, which are a way of abstracting datasets and data sources. This abstraction tries to simplify interacting with lots of varied data sources, including files, databases, streaming protocols, and other ways of accessing data, bringing some logical consistency to you as the developer. Rather than having to learn a different custom way of working with data for every set or type of data you want to use, you learn the Content Provider approach once and can use it repeatedly across many different Content Provider data sources.

You can also build and share your own Content Providers, facilitating data sharing and interaction with other applications.

Summary

You now have a feel for how a typical Android development project is structured and how some of the major building blocks of an Android application are brought together both logically and during building the application, to create a single finished application. We will continue building on the pieces described in this chapter, expanding our exploration of many of them so that you appreciate how more and more sophisticated applications are built.

Chapter 5

Android Studio In-Depth

Long-time users of IDEs like Android Studio usually develop a very strong, very parochial view of how important their chosen IDE is – not only to their productivity but also to their enjoyment of writing applications. In this chapter, my goal is to expose and explore some of the key features of Android Studio that will make you more productive and happier as you build your Android applications.

Android Studio by itself is a huge topic. There are entire books written just on Android Studio itself and how to squeeze the most out of it as an IDE. Some great examples from Apress – the publisher of this book – are *Android Studio IDE Quick Reference* (authored by Ted Hagos, ISBN 978-1-4842-4953-6) and the *Learn Android Studio* series (also authored by Ted Hagos). We don't have the luxury in this book to devote all the remaining chapters to Android Studio itself, but if this chapter gets you excited for the possibilities a great IDE provides, you know where to go next. For now, let's delve into some of the key parts of Android Studio you should get to know right now.

Starting with the Project Explorer

Back in Chapter 4, we briefly introduced the Project Explorer and a few of its capabilities, showing off the Android perspective and the Project Files perspective. We briefly explored those two views of your project, but didn't dwell on the other Project Explorer view options. That leaves us wondering, what are all those other views for?

I'm glad you asked. Broadly, the other view options for Project Explorer are meant to satisfy two compatible desires. First, these views provide you with different ways to look into your project, often emphasizing or focusing on one particular area so that your time can be spent getting things done, rather than fighting the layout of Android Studio. Second, these views also support your personal preferences and desires as a developer and how you prefer to work.

G. Allen, *Android for Absolute Beginners*, https://doi.org/10.1007/978-1-4842-6646-5_5

Getting Comfortable Switching Project Explorer Views

Let's look at some of these views in action, and you can explore all the others to get a feel for what you like. Figure 5-1 shows our MyFirstApp project switched to use the Project Source Files view (again, instead of a very long image, I've pasted two screens side by side).

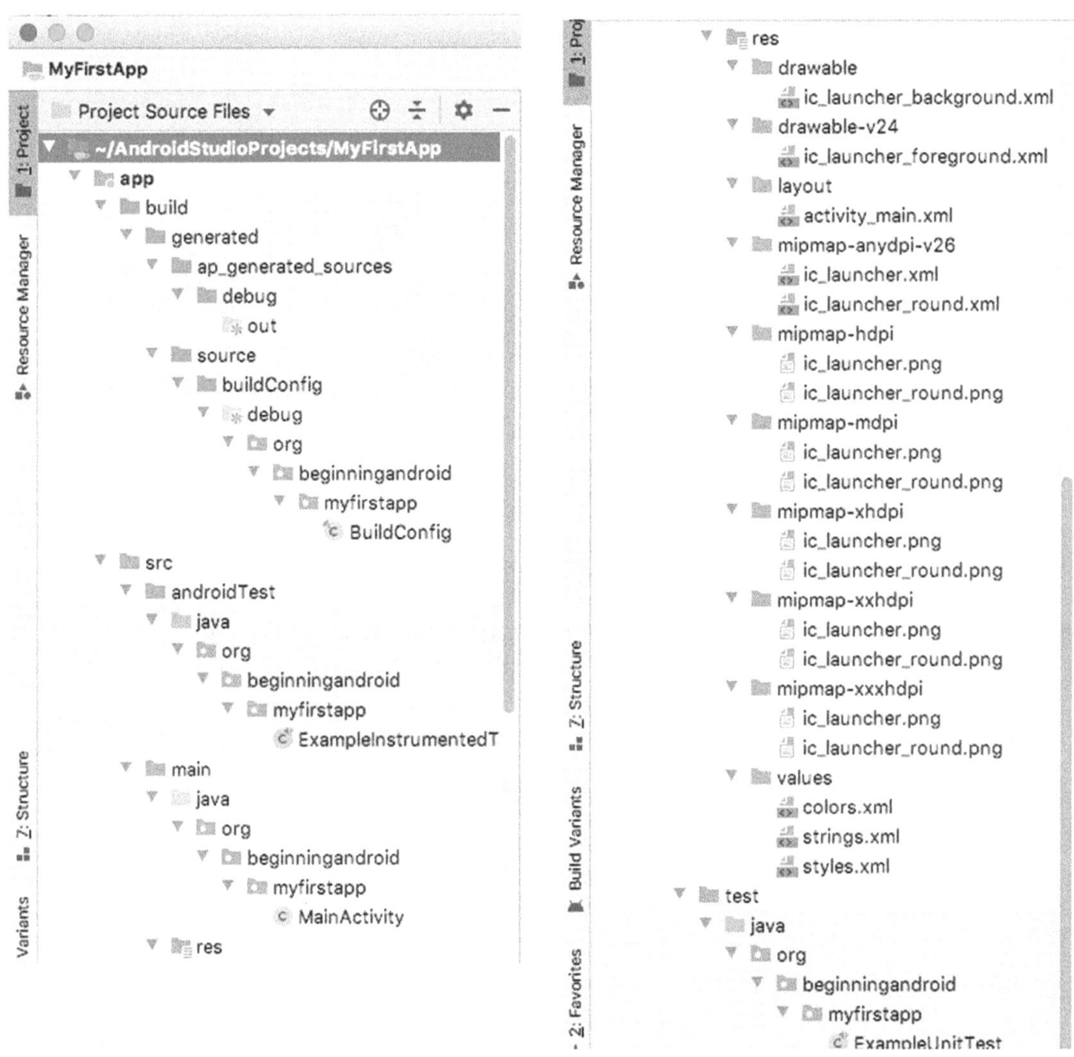

Figure 5-1. The Project Source Files view in Android Studio Project Explorer

You can see some familiar entries there under the src folder hierarchy, for instance, your myfirstapp Java source file and its MainActivity code. If you browse around a little in this view, you will see other source files, such as the template files for testing your code, and some of the editable XML files that control things like visual layout, reusable string values, and more.

But what is most notable is what is not shown. You are no longer seeing things like Gradle build files nor IntelliJ IDEA preference and configuration files, build artifacts, and other non-code items. All of those are hidden, so you can focus on the code! "Why do this?" I hear you ask. As well as the personal preference and specialization points I made in the preceding, the Project Files view in particular is a favorite of some developers who find they work best when they are in "the flow": a state of mind where you are deeply enmeshed with your code, without distractions.

Another popular view is the Project view, which arranges itself to look like many traditional Java IDEs in how they lay out the elements and constituent parts of a project. Figure 5-2 shows this view, and you will note some immediate differences particularly with how external libraries and references are surfaced.

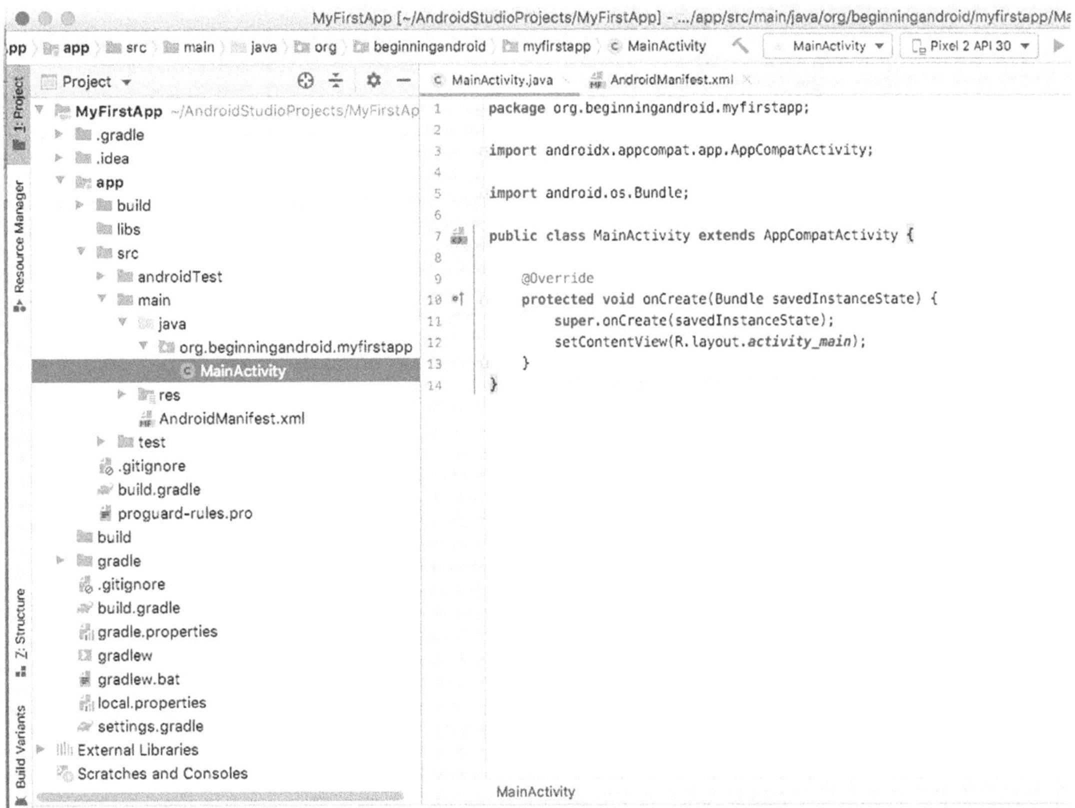

Figure 5-2. The Project view in Android Studio Project Explorer

I strongly encourage you to explore all of the view options in the Project Explorer and find the variants that best suit your way of working.

One really useful point to remember is that, regardless of what view you use or how many times you switch views, Android Studio isn't physically changing your project or moving files. It is just giving you a different virtual view.

Using the Project Explorer Context Menu

As with many other applications you might have used, Android Studio provides context menus that you can access with a right-click of a mouse (or command-click on a Mac). As you explore views in Project Explorer, you should invoke the context menu on everything you see, to get a feel for what is offered. Whether it's file management actions like comparison, find, and so on, quick editing choices, or starting a more serious code management action, the context menu is one of the pro tools you should get familiar with using.

All of the options in the context menus can be found in the main menus in Android Studio, but these can often be buried three or four menu levels deep.

Running and Debugging with Android Studio

As you saw in Chapter 3, one of the principal ways to have Android Studio run your program, in either an emulated or on-device way, is to configure a run configuration. We will revisit run configurations in just a moment, but it is good to know that there are other ways to run your applications as well.

Running with Run Configs: A Recap

Our goal in Chapter 3 was to get your first application running as quickly as possible, so we skipped many of the details of run configurations. There are some key aspects that are worth revisiting, as you will soon want to start creating further run configurations with different characteristics to help you in different phases of application development.

Bring up the details of "Run Config 1" (or whatever name you used to save your run configuration earlier) via the Run ➤ Edit Configurations... menu of Android Studio. You should see the familiar screen showing your run configurations, as per Figure 3-16 from Chapter 3. There are various options spread over four subwindows for any run configuration. Some of these you can explore in your own time, but the major configuration items to familiarize yourself with are as follows.

Run Configuration: General Options

Module: Specifies which specific module to target for the make process, or, if not specified, implies that the whole project should be the target. In practical terms, this helps with larger multimodule projects, where in certain circumstance you might only want to rebuild/remake one specific module – typically because that's the only one that's changed.

Install Options – Deploy: Indicates what should happen once the Android application is built. Should it be run on a device or emulator, and therefore it needs to be deployed, or are you only interested in confirming the application will build cleanly and without errors, without needing to actually run it?

Launch Options – Launch: This setting controls what happens when a successful build is deployed and launched. Should the application run as per the Android Manifest XML file and launch the default activity, or is there a different starting point that should be used in this particular run configuration (such as a substitute activity in the application or no activity at all)?

Install Flags and Launch Flags are beyond the scope of our coverage of run configurations for now.

Run Configuration: Miscellaneous

The miscellaneous options control how "clean" your target environment is when a build is deployed and launched. By clean, I mean what artifacts like logs, prior versions of the application, and so forth are left behind or cleaned up as part of a run configuration.

Logcat: We'll talk more about Logcat later in this chapter, but these settings determine if Logcat output should always be shown to you via the Logcat tool by default and whether output from prior runs should be cleaned up. These logs can get very large if left to grow, so remember the clear log setting if these get unwieldy for you.

Installation Options: You might like to skip deploying your application again if nothing has changed, which can save time in your wider workflow. Knowing that you are not impacting a running instance of your application can be important, for example, when it comes to saving state or running from a known good starting condition.

Run Configuration: Debugger

Those readers who are seasoned in writing any kind of software will appreciate that it is not a task that is ever perfect. Things go wrong, unexpected behaviors happen, applications fail for unpredictable reasons, and more!

The options presented on the Debugger screen make more sense over time, once you have spent some time writing, debugging, and reviewing code. The key options to pay attention to regardless of your experience level are as follows:

Debug Type: Essentially, this provides the guidance to Android Studio about what kind of code to expect in your project. This can set explicitly to Java, Native (which typically means C++ via the Native Development Kit extensions for Android), Dual (both Java and Native), or autodetect. The one advantage of specifying exactly what language to expect, rather than relying on autodetect, is you will save a small amount of time in having Android Studio review your project for language types and not have it load debugging tools for a language that isn't present.

Show static/global variables: One of the first tools many developers reach for when things go wrong is an inspection tool – that is, something that shows the current state of parts of the code when there are problems, such as the value assigned to particular variables. This option adds static/global variables to your view along with the variables you define in methods throughout your code.

Warn when debugging optimized code: One very useful feature of language compilers is their ability to optimize code written by humans to run more efficiently. When this happens, the code being run is not strictly the code you wrote, even though the outcomes should be identical. This setting allows you to be warned when you have moved to debugging code that has been optimized on your behalf.

Other settings such as symbol directories and LLDB options are beyond the scope of the book.

Run Configuration: Profiling

It has taken a long time for Android profiling tools in any form to reach the kind of maturity and insight developers need to help them understand the environmental demands their applications are making. Even a few years back, in both Android Studio and Eclipse, the tooling was still short of what most people would expect. Today, the tools are getting better all the time, and we'll touch on some of them as we look at areas in depth in later chapters. Some of these improved options can be configured directly in your run configuration, as follows:

Enable Advanced Profiling: For anyone working with target SDKs at API level 26 or below, it can be frustrating trying to determine what is happening in your application's immediate environment, for instance, with network behavior and traffic, events handled or dropped, and so forth. The Enable Advanced Profiling option turns on the ability to capture more metrics for older target API levels. For anyone targeting contemporary API levels, for example, 30+, this is now a default part of the standard profiling behavior in Android Studio and associated tools.

Start recording CPU activity on startup: This setting is targeted at profiling where CPU cycles are being spent as your application is used. This has at least two benefits: The first is understanding how various parts of your application will perform, which is important when considering user happiness – a slow application can lead to users getting frustrated with your app. The second benefit is one level of abstraction removed. Because CPU use is the most taxing thing for a smartphone's battery, the CPU activity record can help you understand if your application will be a significant contributor to battery drain when in use. The CPU activity setting is probably not one to start using in your very early Android learning experience, but it will become a mainstay of your developer workflow once you start exploring CPU-heavy Android features, like video use, on-device computation, and so on.

Running Farther with AVDs and Connected Devices

In Chapter 3, we went through the steps of creating an initial run configuration that then used the first AVD we created – named `Pixel 2 API 30` – in order to actually run your application and show you the resulting activity screens. Using AVDs is one of the most powerful capabilities that Android Studio provides for you, enabling you to test and experiment across a huge range of virtual devices.

Technically, the AVD Manager is a separate tool that Android Studio integrates and makes available to streamline your life – the "integration" mantra that I introduced in Chapter 2. As well as being able to launch the AVD Manager from the Tools menu in Android Studio or the toolbar button that appears as the tiny mobile phone icon, you can also run a command-line version of the AVD Manager directly from the command line or shell, as a stand-alone tool from the SDK Tools directory.

To find the SDK Tools directory, from the root directory of your Android installation path (e.g., `~/Library/Android` on macOS or the Android directory you choose for your install under Linux or Windows in Chapter 2), you will find an `sdk` subdirectory. Within the `sdk` subdirectory, follow the further subdirectories `tools` ➤ `bin`. Contained within, you'll find a binary executable file named `avdmanager`. You can guess from its name that this is the stand-alone AVD Manager executable file. If you have any problems finding the SDK Tools directory, use the search feature of your operating system.

When you run from the command line, you get command-line output, as you can see in Listing 5-1, depending on what options you pass to the avdmanager command.

***Listing 5-1.** Command-line output for the avdmanager tool*

```
$ avdmanager list avd

Available Android Virtual Devices:
    Name: Pixel_C_Tablet_API_30
  Device: pixel_c (Google)
    Path: /Users/alleng/.android/avd/Pixel_C_Tablet_API_30.avd
  Target: Google APIs (Google Inc.)
          Based on: Android API 30 Tag/ABI: google_apis/x86
    Skin: pixel_c
  Sdcard: 128 MB
```

Revisiting the AVD Manager

Now that you have many ways of launching the AVD Manager, go ahead and launch it from the Android Studio Tools menu, as we will create a second AVD for future exercises. You can revisit the screen-by-screen how-to instructions from Chapter 2 if you need help, but here are our goals for this second AVD:

Category – Tablet: We want to create a tablet-sized AVD, which will help with testing larger devices with the examples in the book.

Name and type – Pixel C Tablet API 30: This is one of the best all-purpose tablets and one of the most recently launched with a no-frills Android installation directly from Google and is an excellent baseline for testing tablet devices.

System image – R (API level 30): This is the latest SDK and brings with it the latest capabilities Android offers for tablet form factor devices.

> **Note** You might see that the R system image is listed with a download link next to it, in blue. This indicates the necessary Intel x86 system image is not yet installed on your machine. You will need to click the download link and proceed to install the system image in order for this AVD to successfully launch and work.

AVD name – Pixel C Tablet API 30: You can use any name you like, but this example name adds some helpful clues when we see the AVD in AVD Manager or as one of the running emulator processes when actively running, testing, and debugging your code.

When you're done, you should see (at least) two AVDs in the Your Virtual Devices window, as shown in Figure 5-3.

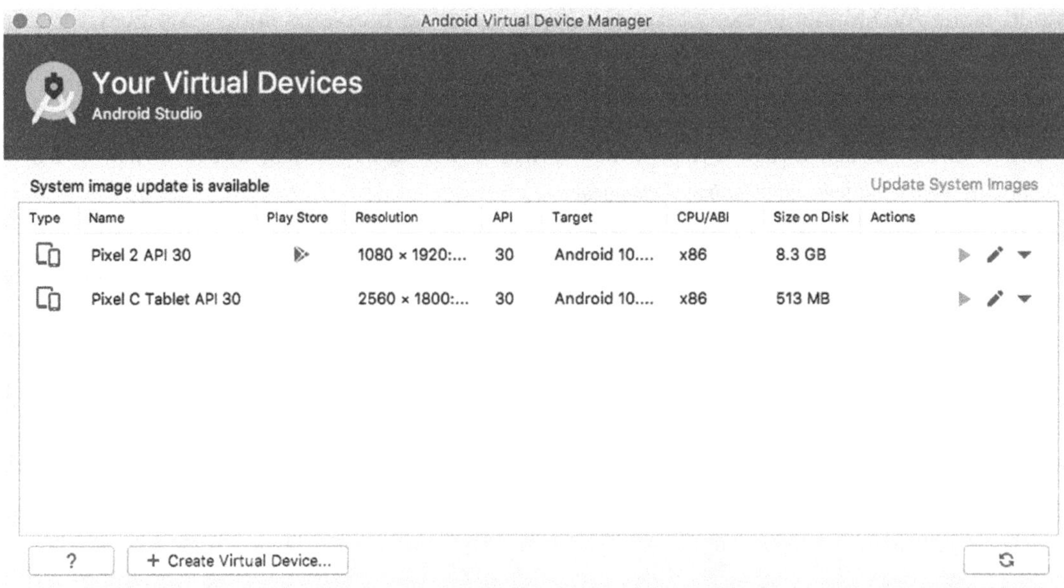

***Figure 5-3.** Multiple AVDs configured in AVD Manager*

The purpose of creating a second (or third or fourth) AVD is not just to show another screenshot of the AVD Manager. Having two or more AVDs is required in order to use Android Studio's ability to run the same code on multiple devices or AVDs simultaneously.

There are many reasons you will want to exercise this ability to test simultaneously on different AVDs and devices in your Android development work. In earlier chapters, we mentioned the diversity of devices sold and in use across the world, the fragmented nature of which Android releases and SDK versions were supported, and other factors that meant your application could be running in a multitude of subtly different settings. First, running your application side by side across several devices helps you spot some of the quirks and differences your users might see in the real world. A second major benefit of this capability is to see how your application might look on a small screen that shows one activity at a time vs. larger screens – such as tablets – where your activity might scale to a different size or appear as part of a multi-activity display using fragments (which we will introduce in Chapter 11). A third reason to use multidevice or AVD testing is to view how Android scales or interpolates images of a particular resolution on screens of different display densities and resolutions.

You should go ahead and test running your MyFirstApp application on multiple AVDs right now. You can trigger this from the Tools ➤ Select Device menu option or the equivalent toolbar dropdown for device selection shown in Figure 5-4.

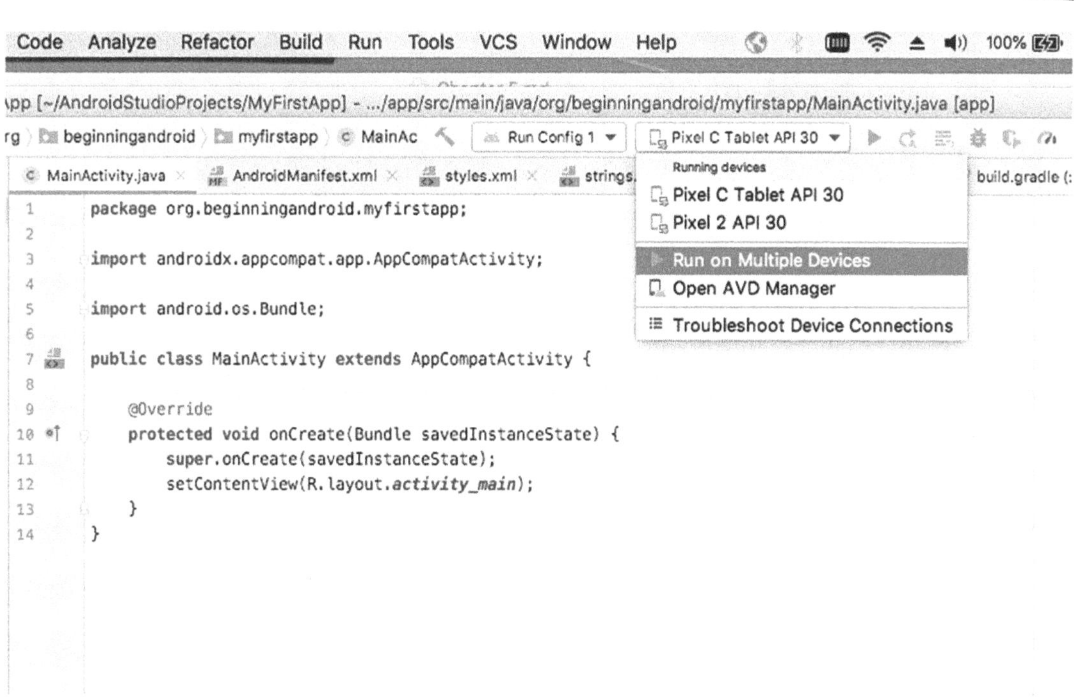

Figure 5-4. *The device selection toolbar dropdown*

Choose the Run on Multiple Devices option, and you will be prompted with the dialog box titled Select Deployment Targets. Choose two or more devices or AVDs, for instance, the Pixel C Tablet and Pixel 2 AVDs we've created so far in the book, as shown in Figure 5-5.

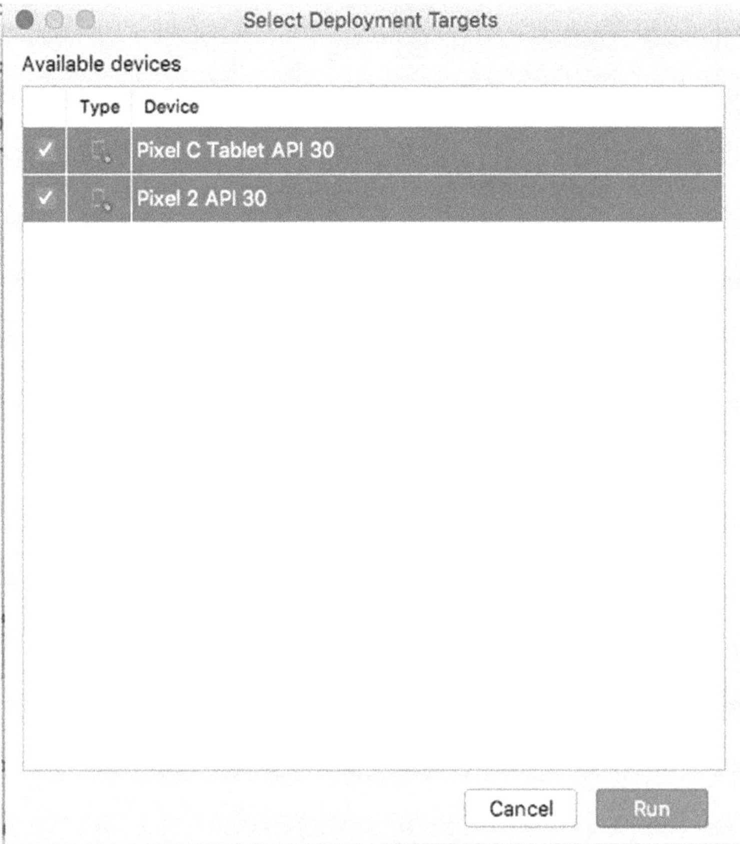

Figure 5-5. Selecting multiple targets to launch your application in Android Studio

Launching multiple AVDs simultaneously will take some time, but after a little patience, you should see your AVDs start and the MyFirstApp application deployed and running on all of them, as shown in Figure 5-6.

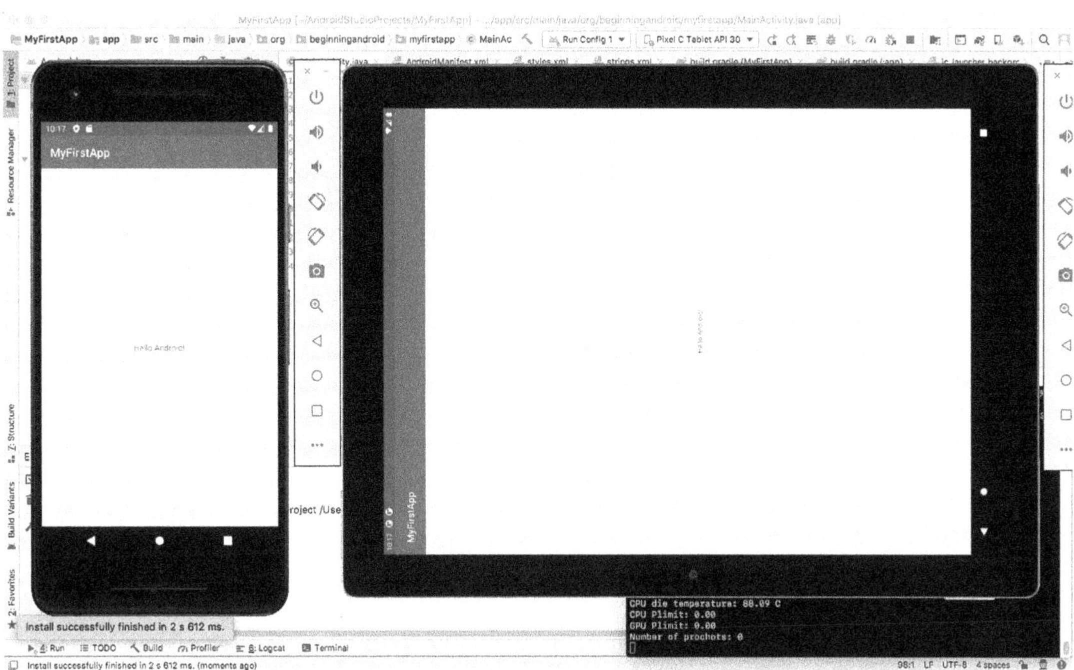

Figure 5-6. App deployed on multiple AVDs simultaneously

Running Your Code on a Real Device

Virtual devices are a boon for any developer, but there will be times when seeing your code in action on a real device is the order of the day. Google has made enormous strides in testing and running your applications on real devices in recent releases of Android Studio. Historically, there was a long chain of command-line steps needed to deploy an application to a real handset, and while you can still take that path today, Android Studio makes it easy to detect and use an Android device connected via a USB cable to your developer machine.

In order to use an Android phone to test your applications as you develop them, you will need to enable developer options on your handset. Google has always had a trick to enable this, which is to open Settings on your phone and scroll to the About Phone option. The last option on the About Phone screen is the build number. Tap the number shown seven times (yes, seven times), and you'll see a countdown appear letting you know you have only a few taps left before developer mode is enabled.

Once you've tapped the build number enough, you'll see an on-screen notice that developer options are now enabled, and a new menu option will appear under Settings that reads Developer options. By default, this will have a suboption named USB debugging enabled. Double-check this is the case on your handset, and turn it on if it is not already enabled.

With developer mode enabled on your phone, connect it via USB cable to your developer computer. Your phone should automatically be detected, and Android Studio will then recognize it as a potential target for running your Android applications.

To test this out, choose `Run` ➤ `Select Device` from the menus, or open the dropdown on the toolbar for AVDs/devices, as shown in Figure 5-7.

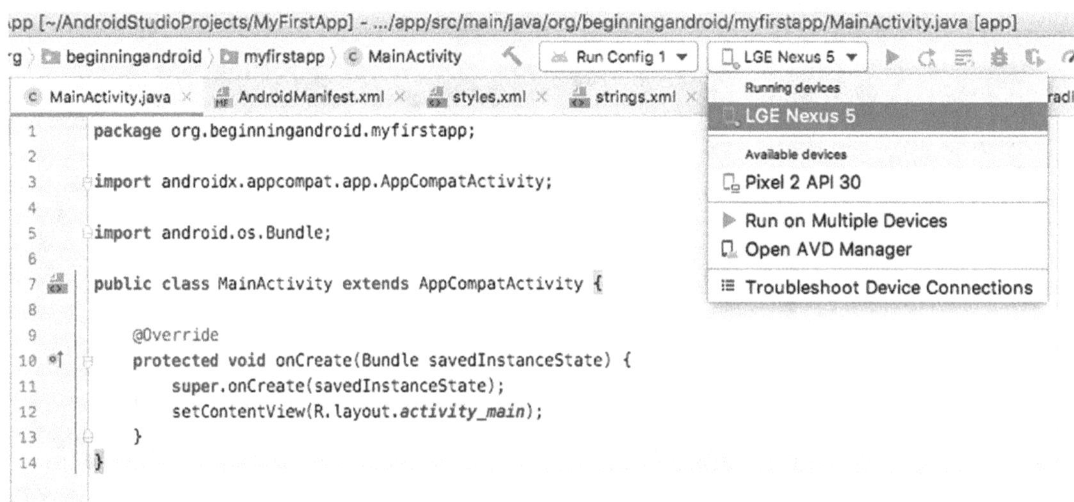

Figure 5-7. Choosing a connected developer-mode Android device from Android Studio

Choose your connected device, which in my case is the Nexus 5 handset. Wait for the few seconds it will take for Android Studio to build, package, and deploy the application to the connected device, and then you should see your application load and run on your phone, as shown in Figure 5-8.

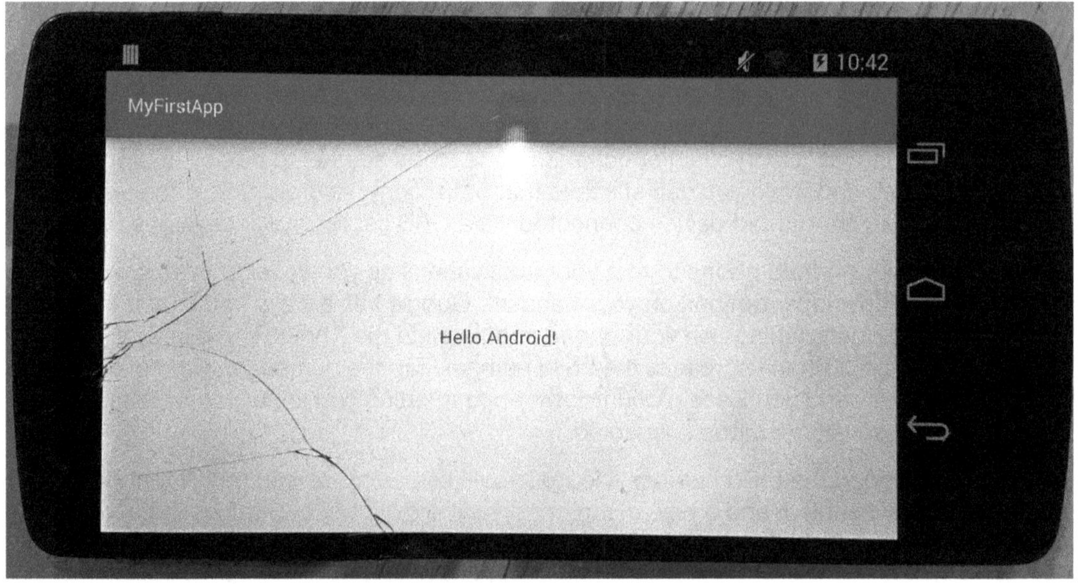

Figure 5-8. Running MyFirstApp on a connected Android handset

Debugging Instead of Running Your Code

Anyone new to application development eventually needs to grapple with what happens when your code "goes wrong." Whether it is unexpected results, strange behavior, application crash, or other problems, debugging is the principal approach to working out what is happening with your application.

Debugging is a huge topic, so rather than attempt to master it here in a chapter dedicated to Android Studio tools, we'll focus first on the principal debugging tools at hand in Android Studio, and then throughout the book we'll expand on debugging and related topics as we introduce more complex Android applications. You can also read more on the topic of debugging on the book website, at `www.beginningandroid.org`.

The four key concepts you should be aware of in Android Studio that help with debugging are as follows.

Setting and Clearing Breakpoints

A breakpoint is a marker in your source code that indicates where you want to break, or stop, execution of your code, in order to then examine behavior or problems in more detail. To set a breakpoint in your code, open the code you want to work with by double-clicking the file or object in the Project Explorer – in my case, it will be the MainActivity.java file. With the file open, click in the darker gray margin just to the right-hand side of the line numbers shown next to your file, as you see in Figure 5-9.

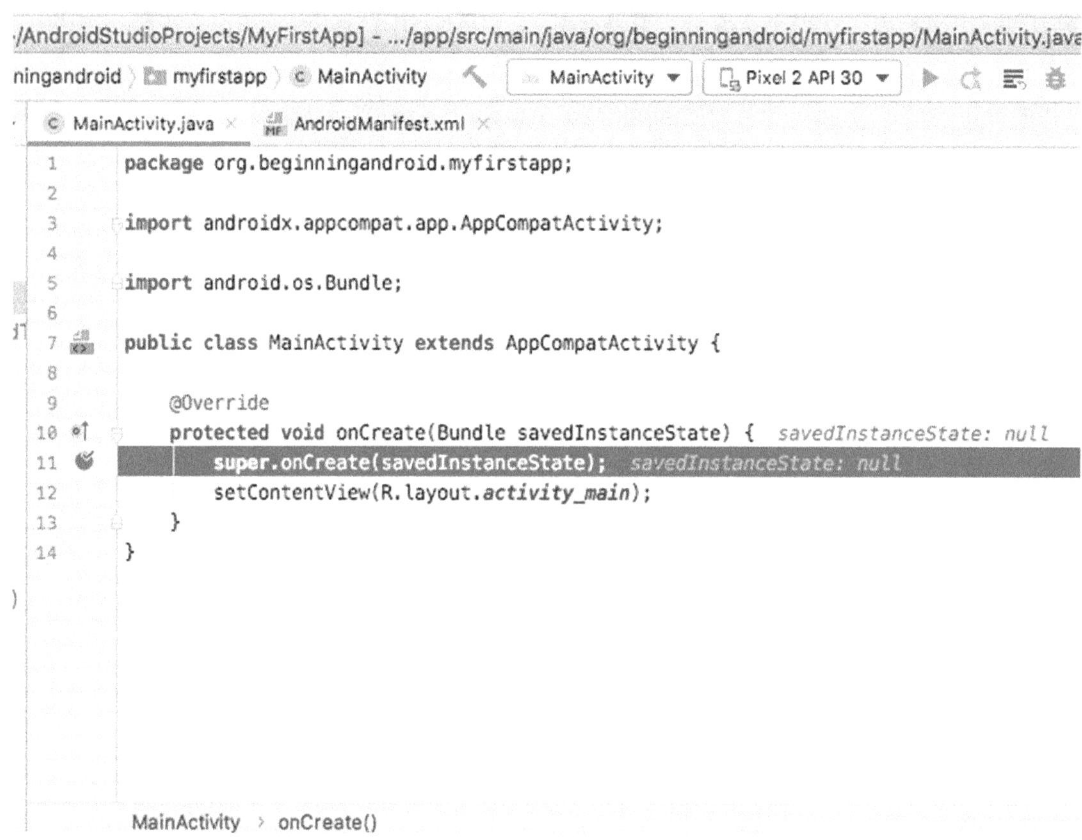

***Figure 5-9.** Setting a breakpoint for debugging in Android Studio*

You should see a red circle appear where you clicked, indicating a breakpoint is set. If for any reason this doesn't seem to make the red circle representing a breakpoint appear, open the Tools menu and choose Toggle Line Breakpoint. Clicking again, or choosing the toggle option again, will remove the breakpoint.

Starting Applications for Debugging

Just as you can run your application with one click of the Run option or choosing a run configuration you have set up, so you can also start your application for debugging. This essentially does the same thing, invoking Gradle to build your application, deploying the application to the nominated device or AVD, and so forth. The one difference is that Android Studio will prime itself to help you with debugging.

To launch your application in debug mode, simply choose the Debug 'Run Config 1' (or similar option) from the Run menu. As well as the build and deployment steps, you will see the lower view in Android Studio automatically open and display the Debug window, with access to Debugger, Console, and other debugging tools, as shown in Figure 5-10.

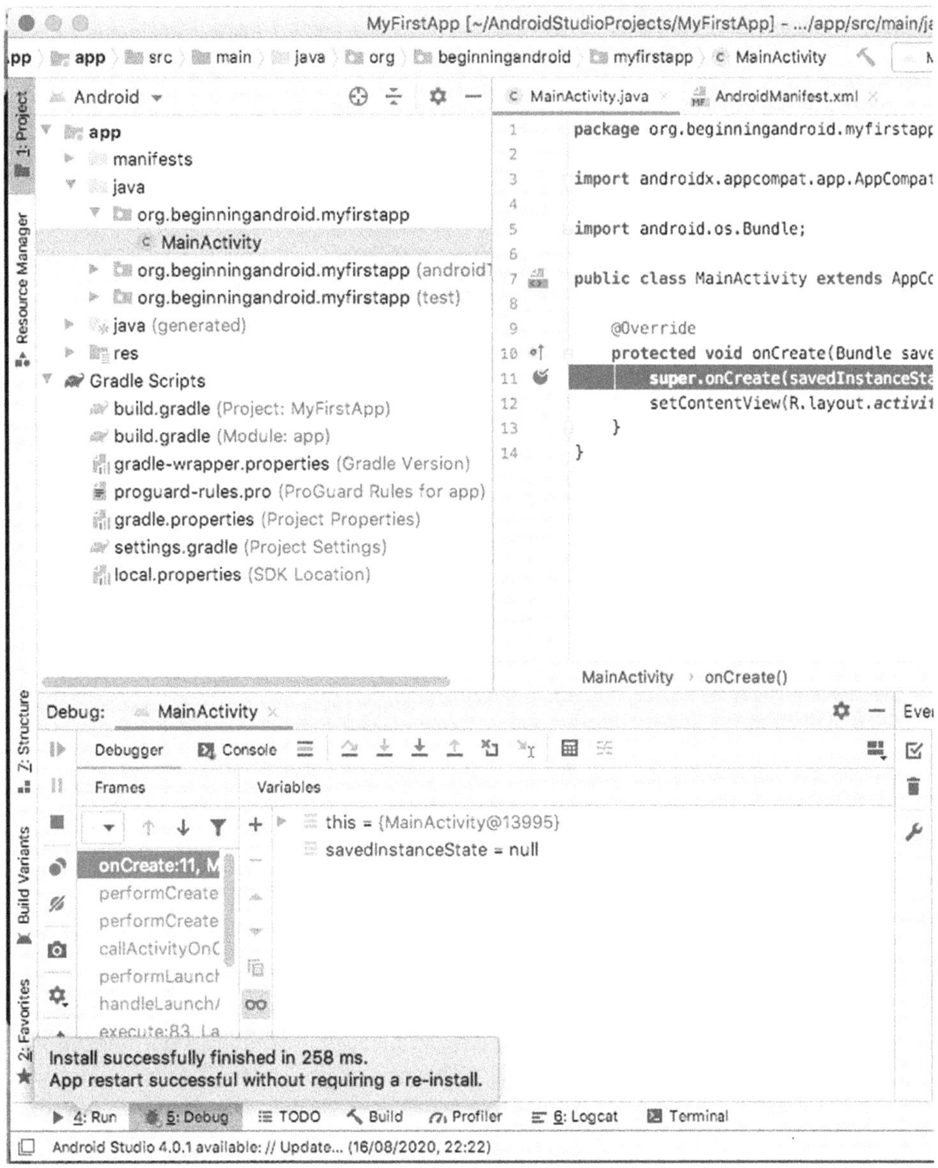

Figure 5-10. The Debug view automatically triggered in Android Studio

Depending on what you're debugging and if you've set breakpoints, you will also see additional menu items in the Run menu activated, as shown in Figure 5-11.

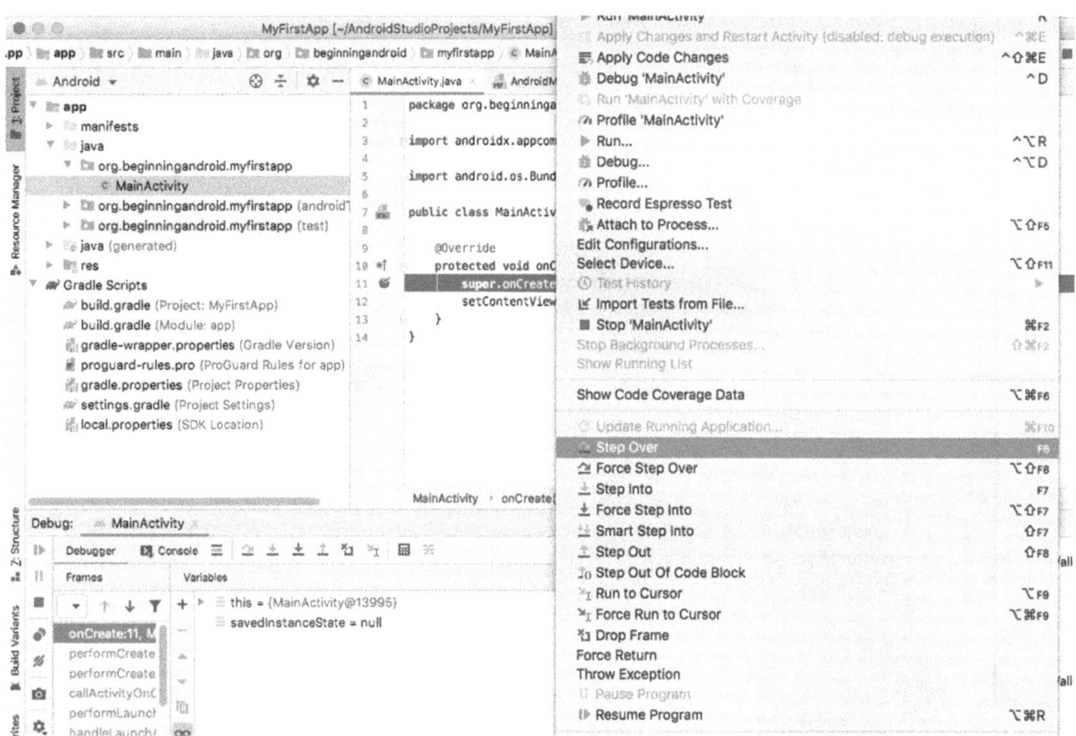

Figure 5-11. Debug options to step into, over, and out of parts of your code in Android Studio

I will explain these "stepping" options under the next heading.

Stepping Through Code While Debugging

The options to "Step Over," "Step Into," "Step Out," and so forth you see in Figure 5-11 are integral to carefully examining what your code is doing. Instead of running your entire code base, by stepping into, over, or out of your code one line at a time, you can step through your application logic one action at a time, and in conjunction with other tools like variable inspection and looking at visual or behavioral changes in activity UIs, you can see the results of each line of logic.

Attaching the Debugger

You may not always have a clear idea of where to set breakpoints or step into or through code. At times, you might want to simply get a deeper look at what is happening in your application to understand some inexplicable behavior or problem. This is where the Debugger tool comes in. We can't do justice to the Debugger in just a few pages, or even an entire chapter, so we won't stress over that. You can find out more about the great capabilities of the Debugger on the book's website, at `www.beginningandroid.org`.

To invoke the Debugger and have it attach itself to a running application to help you in learning what's going on, you can use the very last option in the Run menu – Attach Debugger to Android Process. Your application must be running already for this to work.

Viewing What You've Run

You have now seen enough examples of your first application running on an AVD or on a real device that you might be wondering what I mean by "viewing what you've run." To clear up the mystery, there is more to "seeing" your application running than just looking at the activities being rendered in the finished application.

Android Studio offers several very useful, and some would say critical, tools that let you view what has happened as your application was built by your Gradle scripts (or other tools) and diagnostic and logging information for what is happening as the application runs.

Across the bottom of your Android Studio window, just above the status bar, you will see a set of buttons that give you quick access to these tools, with names like `TODO`, `Build`, `Logcat`, and so on, which you can see in Figure 5-12.

***Figure 5-12.** Easily accessing Event Log, Build Output, Logcat, and more in Android Studio*

Let's look at some of the key tools here so you feel comfortable incorporating their use into your expanding developer toolset.

Understanding Your Build

The Build tool shows you the summary of the build process in the Build Output window, which will either be a "Build: finished" message, with a green tick and some timing information as you can see in Figure 5-13, or a set of errors or issues that prevented the build from working.

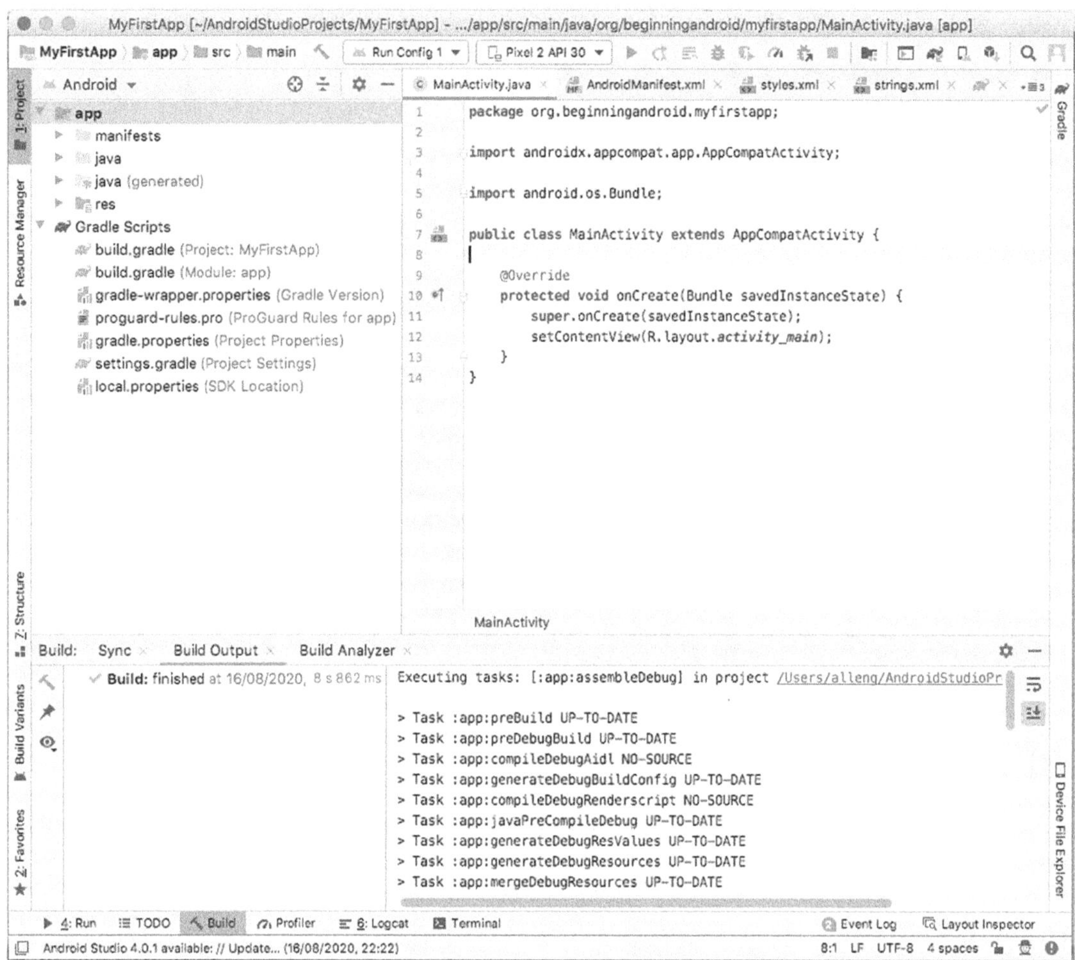

Figure 5-13. The Build Output view of your project build in Android Studio

You will also see a list of the tasks that were performed to actually do the application building (in my case, 20 separate build steps) and a link to the Build Analyzer, which offers a deeper dive into what time each task took and how that might be improved.

Understanding Events in the Event Log

Another of the tools that complements the Build tool is the Event Log. The Event Log shows a higher-level view of action that took place, such as steps taken to load your newly built application onto a device or AVD and any issues identified from those steps. Listing 5-2 shows the Event Log output from building the MyFirstApp application and launching it on multiple AVD instances.

***Listing 5-2.** The Event Log from building and launching MyFirstApp on two AVDs*

```
22:17 Executing tasks: [:app:assembleDebug] in project /Users/alleng/AndroidStudioProjects/
MyFirstApp
22:17 Gradle build finished in 9 s 5 ms
22:17 Install successfully finished in 11 s 455 ms.
22:17 Install successfully finished in 2 s 612 ms.
22:18 Emulator: emulator: INFO: QtLogger.cpp:68: Warning: Error receiving trust for a CA
certificate ((null):0, (null))
22:18 Emulator: Process finished with exit code 0
```

Typical errors you might see in the Event Log are things that may have stopped the build or post-build activity, like specifying an SDK or base image for an emulated device that is not present on the machine. An example of the latter issue would look like this in the Event Log:

```
Emulator: emulator: ERROR: This AVD's configuration is missing a kernel file! Please ensure
the file "kernel-ranchu" is in the same location as your system image.
```

Understanding Logcat

Logcat is one of the most useful tools in your testing and debugging arsenal. Its job is to help collect diagnostic and runtime information from a device or AVD as your application is running and also when your application stops running unexpectedly, crashes, has problems, freezes, and so on.

Logcat will provide a console-like interface to examine and review key system messages from the device or emulator, including things like all-important stack traces of what happened and what went wrong, when an application encountered an error or exception when running. This ability is tremendously useful in situations where code might run perfectly well in one environment, such as an AVD on your developer workstation, but when run on a particular brand or model of phone encounters an unexpected problem.

To use Logcat, just click the button on the bar while you have your application running or while your device or AVD is performing other tasks like starting up. You will see by default a long list of Logcat entries gathered from what's happening with your application and device, as shown in Figure 5-14.

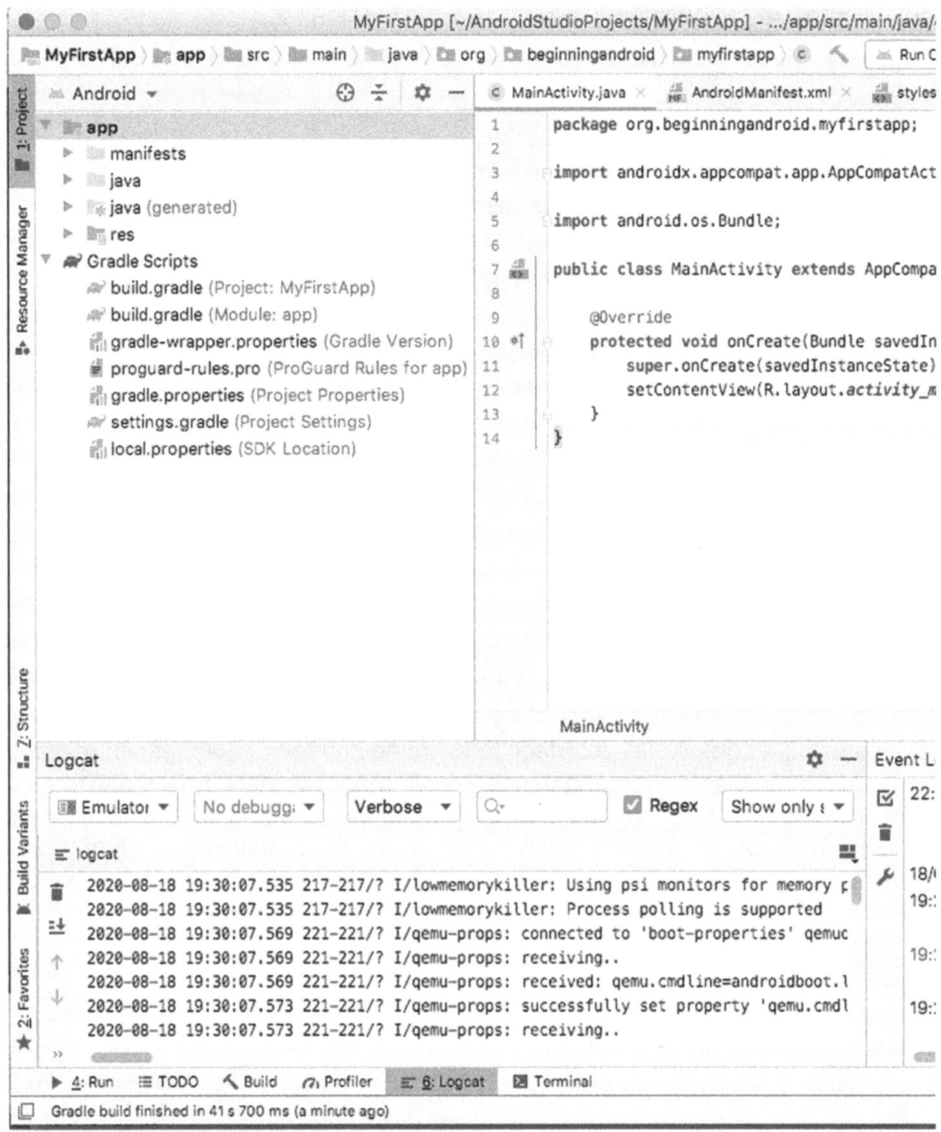

Figure 5-14. Logcat output in Android Studio

This example Logcat output is fairly innocuous, but when things go wrong, the stack traces and other diagnostic information in Logcat are invaluable.

Revisiting the SDK Manager

One last aspect of the major tools available via Android Studio is to revisit the SDK Manager you first saw in Chapter 3. You can invoke and use the SDK Manager at any time, by opening the Tools menu and choosing the SDK Manager entry. You can do this to see the SDK versions you have already installed and any that are not installed or that have updates available, as shown in Figure 5-15.

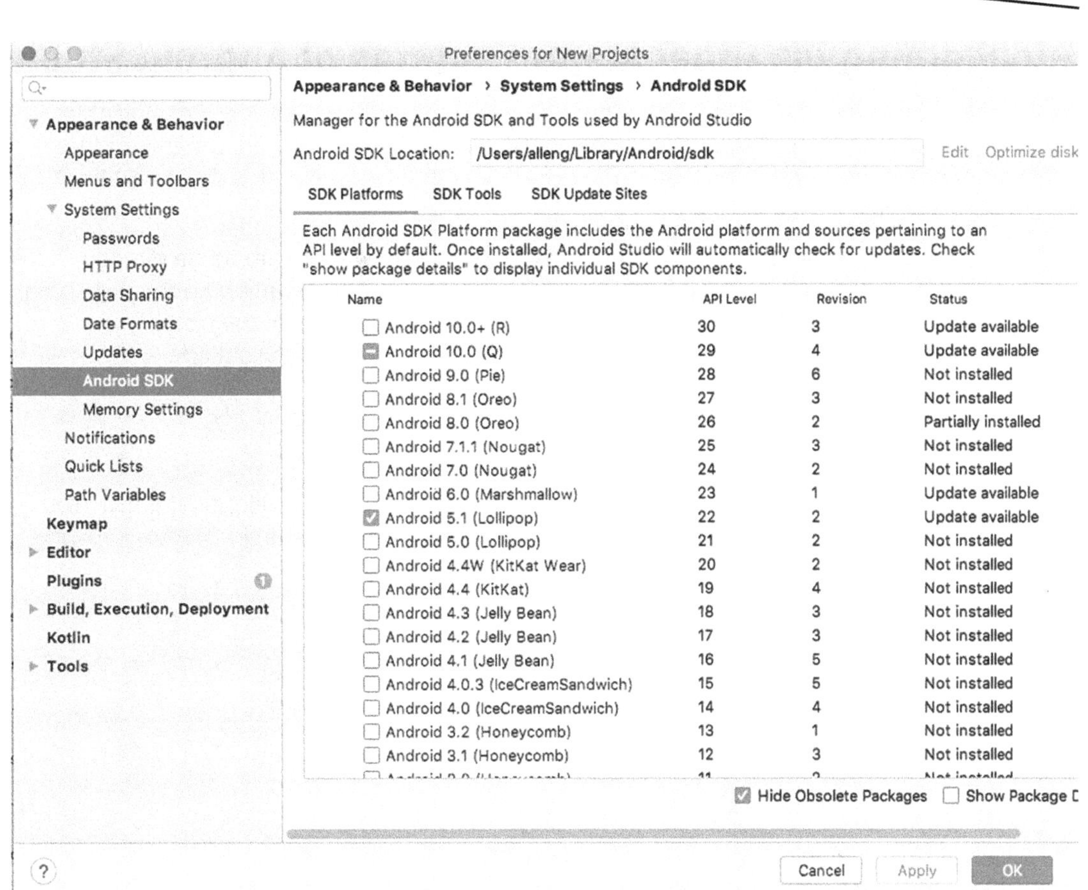

***Figure 5-15.** Revisiting the Android SDK Manager*

As you would expect, you can check any SDK versions you don't have and click Apply, and the SDK Manager will commence downloading and installing those versions in the background. You are most likely going to need to do this as you work in two scenarios: first, when ensuring you have SDKs that represent common or popular Android releases, such as 4.4 "KitKat" and, second, when you are testing out new capabilities as Google releases new SDKs in conjunction with new versions of Android.

But there is another reason to reach for the SDK Manager, and that is its ability to help you add extra goodies to your Android Studio experience. Switch to the second tab in SDK Manager, titled SDK Tools, and you will see a treasure trove of extras that will soon become some of your best-loved tools. We will revisit some of these tools in relevant chapters throughout the rest of the book, but I'll flag two types of tools that are frequently used by developers. These are the Android SDK Command-Line Tools, which offer extra features for managing and controlling SDK packages from the command line, and the various additional Google Play libraries and SDKs, which help you build applications that use dependencies and libraries from Google's proprietary Google Play services.

You can check these for download now or wait until later in the book to do so.

Highlighting the Other Major Features of Android Studio

This chapter has looked at some of the key features of Android Studio that are available to manage, execute, examine, and diagnose your applications as you build them and to manage and use the associated SDKs and other tools that form part of your application development work.

But by far the biggest set of tools in Android Studio that you will use are those directly related to writing code, reviewing code, examining code in detail, rewriting code, and so on. We will introduce many of those aspects of Android Studio in Part 2 of the book, in conjunction with introducing the many parts of coding for Android applications.

Summary

This chapter has introduced you to the main tools of any software developer, the IDE. You should now feel comfortable exploring more of the options within Android Studio, knowing that you can always find the core tools you need for your project.

Chapter 6

Mastering Your Entire Developer Ecosystem

There is more to getting set up for Android development than just installing Android Studio. While you can do just that – and only that – you will eventually find there are other aspects of your computer, and the software it runs, that will make a big difference to your productivity, ambition, and competence as an Android developer. This chapter is not exhaustive, but does give you a lot of important foundational considerations, as well as links to where to go next to learn more. Read on!

Choosing Dedicated Developer Hardware

In Chapter 2, I introduced a short checklist for the aspects of your computer that might be of interest to the serious Android developer. Here is the summary again:

- What desktop or laptop hardware will I use for my Android development?
- What operating system will I run on my desktop/laptop?
- What prerequisites will my system need prior to using Android Studio?
- What Android handsets, if any, will I make use of during development?

The maxim I set out then still applies. Pretty much any computer made in recent years that you have at hand will serve as a decent developer workstation. Whether that is a desktop computer or a notebook, it will get the job done.

But this book isn't just about getting the job done. If you really thirst to be a professional Android developer, then just as other professionals rely on tools and equipment for efficiency and leverage, you too should think about what tools will boost your development work and your ability to make great applications.

G. Allen, *Android for Absolute Beginners*, https://doi.org/10.1007/978-1-4842-6646-5_6

Let's start by looking at the factors you might want to consider if you are looking for developer hardware that will give you an unfair advantage when building Android applications.

Determining Which CPU Is Right for You

The year 2020 sees a lot of choices for x86_64 CPUs: AMD with Ryzen and Threadripper and Intel with their Core series of CPUS. You can find many opinions as to which is the best, and typically these judgments look at raw CPU speed (clock frequency), number of cores in the package, on-board cache at various levels, and several other features.

For the purposes of a dedicated Android developer machine, any contemporary Intel or AMD CPU is ample. If you were looking for specific recommendations for a 2020-era CPU, you should look at Intel Core i5 and Core i7 CPUs and AMD Ryzen 7 and Ryzen 9 CPUs. These have ample speed, a decent core count (typically four or more), and good L1/L2/L3 cache.

There are beefier CPUs from both AMD and Intel, but typically you will see these differentiating themselves with even more cores and occasionally support for other things. In the world of Android development, more cores is not always better. The key activities that are running in parallel for you are any simultaneous activity where you are working in Android Studio and looking at results in one or more AVDs and, for sufficiently large multiproject applications, parallel build activities if Gradle is configured to support them. My advice would be spare your wallet the cost of the most expensive Core i9 and similar AMD processors and use those funds on other parts of your developer setup, such as more memory or a better screen.

Another CPU architecture growing in popularity is Arm. Arm is at the heart of almost every mobile device on the planet today, based on the immense popularity of designs for "systems-on-a-chip," or SoCs, that license the Arm architecture. Arm-based desktop machines are available, and even a nascent market for Arm servers, but there is an interesting conundrum here.

While the vast majority of Android devices sold and used globally today are built with Arm processors, using an Arm-based computer for computationally heavy workloads – such as building/compiling Android applications – is still a challenge. It can be done; there's no doubt. But the speed and performance trade-offs are still significant. And the biggest impediment is whether the tools you expect to use are available for an Arm-based computer. Most notably, Android Studio is not available for Arm – it only runs on x86 architecture computers. Likewise, Google only packages the Android SDK in its many versions for x86, not Arm. This means if you choose an Arm-based development machine, you will need to bootstrap all of your work with your own build tools, work around the absence of easily bundled Android SDKs, and more. That's not a challenge I would recommend.

Too Much Memory Is Never Enough!

I sometimes wish it was as easy to add memory to myself as it is to add it to a desktop computer. For now, you and I will just have to be satisfied with the buying RAM for the sake of better developer firepower.

If you think back to Chapter 2, you'll recall that Google recommends a minimum of 4 GB of RAM for Android Studio and a preferred base level of 8 GB. It's actually quite difficult to buy new computers with only 4 GB of RAM. So, to quote a famous movie, 8 is enough, right?

Not so fast! You can certainly be productive and make Android applications on a computer with 8 GB of RAM. In fact, I'm writing a good portion of this book, and building some of the examples you see, on a 2015-era MacBook Air with 8 GB of memory, so it is more than just theoretically possible. However, I can tell you that it has its clear limitations and frustrations. Some notable examples are where I am trying to run Android Studio and an AVD, plus one of the open source tools I discuss later in this chapter and throughout the book for image and video manipulation. That 8 GB gets exhausted quickly, and the MacBook dutifully starts increasing – and increasingly using – swap space on disk to juggle real memory and the greater demands I'm placing on it.

Contrast this with my trusty desktop machine. It is even older, being a "vintage" Dell Precision workstation from nearly a decade ago – I'm not sure Dell even makes these any more. But it has 32 GB of memory and does not skip a beat using Android Studio, multiple AVDs simultaneously, and several other tools thrown in for good measure.

> **Note** You can tell from my setup that I'm not exactly taking affiliate fees or kickbacks on recommending hardware for you to buy. If you have a time machine, please do jump back to 2010 or 2015 to buy your version of my hardware!

My succinct advice to you if you are specifying your own Android developer system is this: no one ever complained they had too much RAM! If you can, get at least 32 GB; and for luxury, 64 GB will be ample for years of Android development to come.

For those of you looking to buy or acquire a notebook as your primary development machine, pay particular attention to what is the maximum memory your preferred model can take and whether memory can be changed after purchase. That is, is the memory soldered or fixed in place, such that it can't be changed or swapped without expensive, and possibly warranty-voiding, actions? You might find yourself limited to 16 GB – if you can pick a model that supports 32 GB, you will thank yourself in the future (and maybe me as well!).

Storing It All!

As you start building more and more Android applications, your need for disk space will increase to accommodate a wide range of projects, resources, and more. There are obvious areas where you would expect disk space to be consumed, such as the space on disk for your source code files (which are quite small) and image and video files (which can be very, very large).

There are Android development–specific aspects that are obvious when you think about them, such as different versions of the Android SDKs, which can need up to 1 GB per version.

AVDs are the hidden factor when thinking about your storage needs. Because it is so easy to whip up a new AVD image to test out a screen size or device format, it is very easy to end up with 20, 30, or more AVDs before you know it. If you are serious about testing across a lot of screen sizes and resolutions, having dozens of AVDs is the minimum to expect.

With tens or scores of AVDs in place, you can easily chew up 50 GB or more. One of the biggest storage hogs for AVDs is your choice of how much on-board storage, or emulated SD card storage, to allow. These options are mimicked by allocating your on-disk storage, which means if you want to emulate the latest OnePlus 7 device with 128 GB of storage, then your AVD will consume 128 GB or more of your actual disk space! Of course you don't have to use such large allocations for emulated SD cards and on-device storage, but typically you will have at least a workable amount, and this all adds up.

A pragmatic allowance for storage when starting out on your Android application development journey would be on the order of 50 GB. This will let you make several generations of the Android SDK and a useful number of AVDs of various sizes and configurations available, along with Android Studio and other tools. To be comfortable into the future, particularly with a wide range of AVDs for testing purposes, you should aim for 100 GB or more.

Just as important as the size of your storage is the type of storage and its associated speed. Traditional spinning hard disk drives are certainly cheap, but the trade-off is data transfer speed, or IOPS (input/output operations per second). Modern storage options such as solid-state drives, or SSDs, give a considerable boost in terms of data transfer performance and therefore speed of operation for everything from building and running AVDs, deploying large applications and those that rely on significant image and video aspects, and any data-intensive computations or actions.

If you have the choice, always opt for a solid-state storage option, particularly if you plan to do any data-heavy or computation-heavy development. For those of you looking at dedicated notebook computers for your development needs, you will find yourself spoiled for choice given the very large shift toward SSDs in this market in recent years.

Viewing It All!

If you are going to become a dedicated developer of Android applications, you are going to be staring at screens a lot. Given that, you might want to consider how to make the most of the screen you will be viewing and whether you want more than one.

When it comes to monitors or displays, a lot of developer happiness will be based on deeply personal factors. Do you like large screens? Do you prefer multiple screens? Will screens in different orientations help you – landscape or portrait? And will you be mixing screens from a laptop or notebook, with fixed screens? There are more considerations than just this, but I will flag two key characteristics that will make a long-term beneficial impact for you: size and density.

When it comes to screen size, there are some practicalities that will convince you that at least one large screen is worth the expenditure. Look back at Figure 5.6 in Chapter 5, and you will see two AVDs running side by side, one representing a normal phone screen and the other a tablet screen. You will not be surprised to learn that the view in that figure consumed pretty much all of the 13-inch screen on my MacBook Air. If you look really closely, you can see hidden behind the AVD screens tiny fragments of my Android Studio session. But that's all you can see. There's no chance with this size screen to do significant side-by-side development in Android Studio and observation in an AVD, without a set of hugely awkward compromises. You can resize screens and windows in Android Studio, and you can tile windows to try to squeeze everything in with a single AVD running, as shown in Figure 6-1

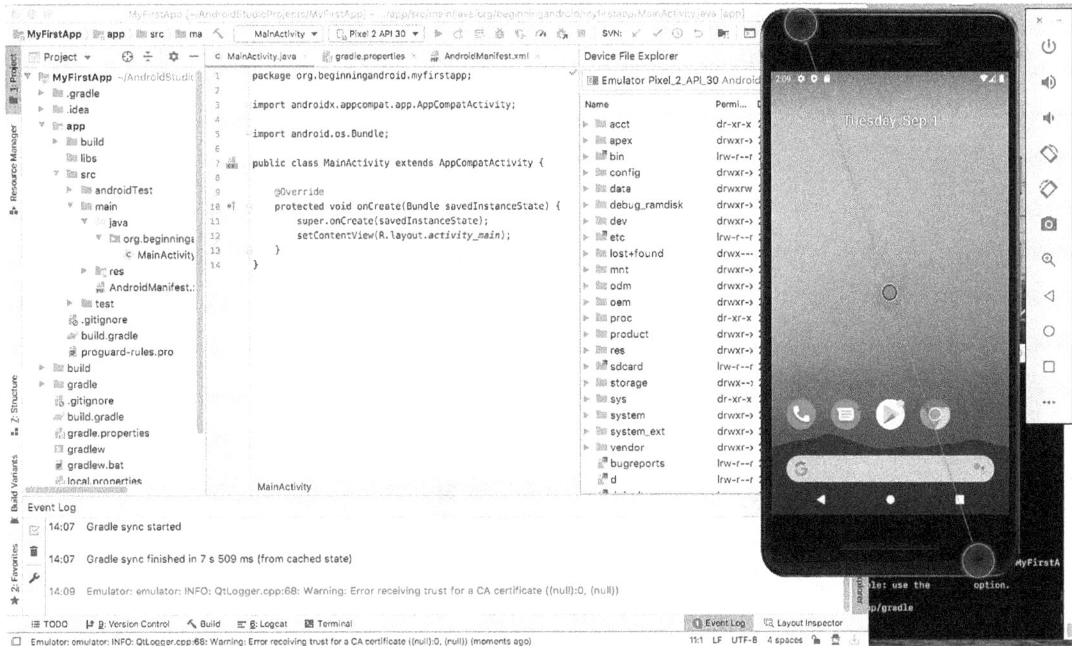

Figure 6-1. Running Android Studio and an AVD side by side on a 13-inch laptop screen

If you think that helps with live debugging or comparing different layouts simultaneously, let me state that it's nothing of the sort. It's just a big pain! Contrast that with the view on a 24-inch screen, with Android Studio and multiple AVDs happily living on a screen blessed with ample real estate, as shown in Figure 6-2.

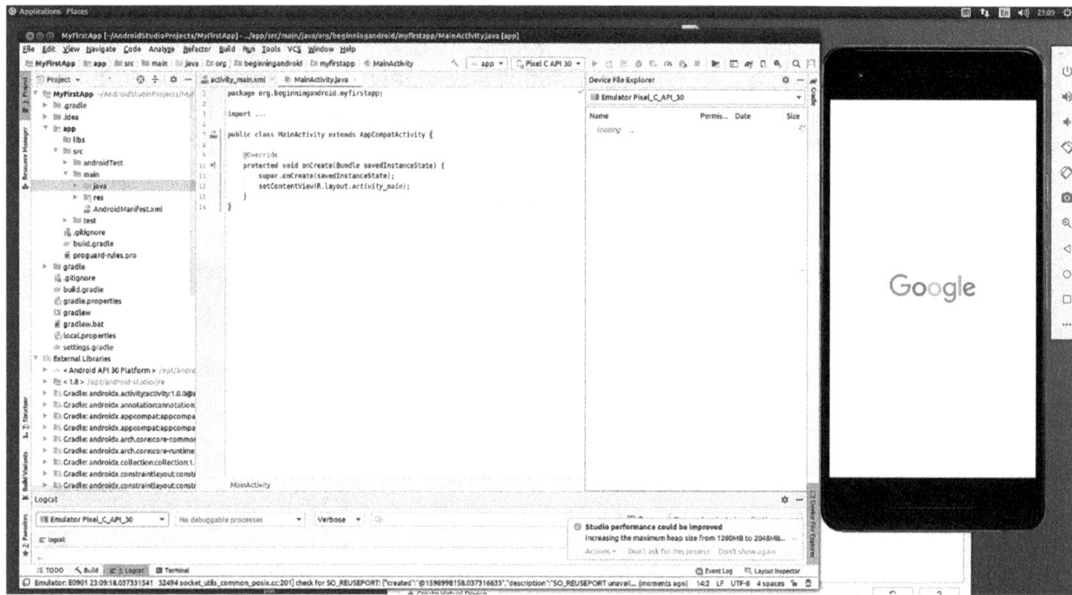

***Figure 6-2.** Running Android Studio and multiple AVDs on a 24-inch screen*

I will let those figures speak a thousand words. When you are done soaking them in, my closing statement on screen size will need no further support. If you can, buy a big screen!

When it comes to screen quality, and specifically pixel density, we again enter some very subjective territory. In the market of 2020, when this book is being written, you can choose from multiple generations of "high density," as well as 4k, 5k, and even 8k! Your personal taste and preferences will be the most important thing to consider, but I will recommend you keep in mind the following two points:

- **See the screen in action**. If you can, visit a retailer that can show you the screen actually hooked up to any kind of computer. This lets you get a feel for how the display actually behaves and lets you play with things like brightness, white balance, contrast, and refresh rate, to satisfy yourself that the screen performs in ways that please you.

- **Aim for a screen with as high, or higher, resolution density as the apps you plan to build**. We will talk more about Android screen resolution options and mechanisms throughout the rest of the book. To ensure that your development and testing show you as best as possible how your artwork, images, video, and other application resources will look on real devices, ensure you choose a screen for your development system that is at least as good as, if not better than, the devices you are targeting. Otherwise, you will get a distorted idea of how things look when running in the real world.

Connecting It All!

Other aspects of your developer setup to consider include the following:

- Keyboard and mouse: It seems mundane, but you will be using these peripherals a lot. Don't settle for ones you don't like!
- USB ports and cables: If you plan on extensive testing of your applications with tethered Android devices, then it pays to have ample available USB ports and cables with appropriate adapters. Most older Android devices use micro-USB connectors, with recent models switching to USB-C-style connectors.
- Charging cables, cradles, and devices: Again, if you plan on using a lot of real Android devices, keeping them powered up becomes somewhat of a chore. While they can be charged via the USB connection to your developer machine, the power drawn over historic USB protocol versions was limited. It was not until USB-C that "standard" USB could draw more than 500 mA current. Where possible, make space and account for power charges that plug into a wall socket.

It's easy to overlook these points, but they can contribute to making your developer experience smoother and more enjoyable, and if you ignore them, you can find them adding friction and frustration that undermine your best endeavors.

Test Handsets and Tablets

Let me start the topic of test handsets by stating that there is no cast-iron rule that says you must have physical Android phones on which to test your applications. Many apps are built and launched based on testing in entirely simulated environments, such as AVDs and the like.

Many applications, however, are built based on real-world testing and feedback on a range of Android devices, where the quirks and differences are detected and addressed in real-world situations. And there are differences! While the Android SDK and the core platform features of Android are (almost) universal, there are countless ways in which both handset vendors and phone companies tweak and change Android's default behavior. Often these "telcos" are doing this to attempt to differentiate themselves from other phone companies, or from a more cynical perspective, they are trying to inject themselves into a position that hopes their users think they are more important than they really are.

Whatever the reason, you will find yourself at some point in your Android developer journey asking if you need to spend money to acquire different Android handsets on which to test your application. I can't give you a definitive answer, but I can make some recommendations to help you decide how much of your precious time and money to devote to acquiring test handsets.

Option 1: All-Virtual Testing

Sticking with Android Virtual Devices is a perfectly good strategy when you are beginning your development journey. And to be honest, it serves many successful developers throughout their entire career. With each release of Android Studio, Android SDKs, and supporting tools from other vendors like Intel, it is more and more feasible to take this path and not spend any additional time or money on dedicated testing hardware.

The drawbacks are that you will sometimes struggle to replicate real-world experiences, such as appreciating the true performance of your application, and you might also fall victim to the "special features" introduced by telcos that I alluded to in the preceding.

Option 2: Start Virtual and Augment with Top Devices

The blended approach of using AVDs extensively and selectively augmenting with some key hardware choices happens to be my preference. This is for several reasons:

- Using AVDs is increasingly effective, as outlined in option 1 in the preceding.
- A huge part of the market is represented by just one vendor: Samsung. Purchasing one Samsung device (or a few devices) will give you exposure to the majority of real Android devices used around the world.
- Google themselves have pushed several generations of stock Android devices under successive brands, first with the Nexus line and more recently with the Pixel line. Having one of these devices allows you to see your application as it looks and behaves on a device free of telco "enhancements."

If you take this approach, buying a small number of handsets gives you the ability to test the real-world experience of a significant number of your potential users.

Option 3: Buy, Buy, and Buy Some More

The option of trying to test all edge cases, quirks, strange behaviors, and bugs appeals to some developers. To do this in the Android space requires a lot of patience and more importantly deep pockets! You could easily amass dozens, scores, or even hundreds of devices and still not cover all of the strange devices – and their strange issues – that your users might encounter in the real world. Your bank balance might be showing a few strange issues by this point as well!

I don't recommend this approach, but I will admit I do not push Android development and applications into the kinds of demanding spaces that uncover lots of these issues. My attempt at amassing a testing library of devices is shown in Figure 6-3.

Figure 6-3. My collection of Android devices, spanning over a decade of Android history

I stopped at 20-odd devices, and my bank balance thanked me!

Option 4: Other People's Hardware

One of my favorite jokes about cloud computing is that it is just running your code on other people's hardware. It's funnier still if you understand what I do as my day job! Behind the humor is a useful insight, however, that testing your Android application on real devices is best done when someone else is taking care of owning and provisioning those devices.

There are a range of commercial options available as of the time of writing this book that let you test your application on a bank of real devices that you don't have to buy yourself. You rent or pay for access as a service and get all the benefits of testing across a wide variety of handsets, with none of the up-front cost of buying them nor the trailing cost of maintaining them.

It's beyond the scope of this book to present an exhaustive list of such services, but here are the dominant options you can access from commercial vendors today, and from there you can certainly search for competing options:

- AWS Device Farm: From the vendor of all things cloud – Amazon – comes AWS Device Farm. Amazon offers access to around 400 different devices from a huge range of manufacturers, with useful tools to manage your testing workloads from within your browser. More details at `https://aws.amazon.com/device-farm/`.
- Google Firebase Test Lab: Google's version of lots of Android devices available remotely (they also include access to various Apple iPhones and iPads). Google also provides some great add-on tools for UI testing and automating your test runs across their fleet of devices. More details at `https://firebase.google.com/docs/test-lab/`.
- Samsung Remote Test Lab: As the 800-pound gorilla of Android devices, Samsung is the obvious choice against which to test your applications. With almost every device they've ever made available in their test lab, plus handy tools, Samsung's Remote Test Lab should be on your shortlist for testing-as-a-service. More details at `https://developer.samsung.com/remote-test-lab`.

There are other commercial services available, as well as options to share or borrow devices from Android developer communities around the world. Consider the preceding a starting point, rather than a definitive guide.

Building with Build Tools

As mentioned in earlier chapters, Gradle is the build tool used by Android Studio to bring together all of the pieces of your Android application and create the finished product. Gradle also has a wealth of options that could (and in fact do) span entire books. I encourage you to start exploring Gradle options to expand your powers when it comes to building your Android applications. Here are three quick tips to get you started and help you find more.

Update Your gradle.properties File

Don't be afraid to open the gradle.properties file for your project and look at the settings it presents you. There are a lot of explanatory comments in the default file, and you should feel comfortable experimenting. For example, you will see an entry that sets the memory for the Java VM that looks like this:

```
org.gradle.jvmargs=-Xmx2048m
```

Try changing that value to `Xmx1024m` and see how that affects build time – you are effectively halving your JVM's available memory. If you have ample memory, try `Xmx4096m` to give the JVM double the default memory, and see if that speeds things up. As you learn more about Gradle config, revisit your properties file to apply what you have learned.

Use the Gradle Command Line

Many of Gradle's features are neatly integrated into Android Studio and triggered when you perform a wide array of actions. But your project will also have a command-line tool for Gradle, named gradlew. It is in the root directory of your project. If you open a shell or command prompt there and run the command-line executable as follows

```
./gradlew
```

you'll see a useful listing of the immediately useful command-line options and tools Gradle makes available. You can also run

```
./gradlew --help
```

for an exhaustive list of all command-line options and tools. One very useful to explore to begin with is the profiling option, which looks at what takes the time when building your application. Invoke it and see the results as follows in Listing 6-1.

***Listing 6-1.** Invoking Gradle profiling from the command line*

```
Welcome to Gradle 6.1.1.
To run a build, run gradlew <task> ...
To see a list of available tasks, run gradlew tasks
To see a list of command-line options, run gradlew --help
To see more detail about a task, run gradlew help --task <task>
For troubleshooting, visit https://help.gradle.org

BUILD SUCCESSFUL in 24s
1 actionable task: 1 executed

See the profiling report at: file:///Users/alleng/AndroidStudioProjects/MyFirstApp/build/
reports/profile/profile-2020-09-01-10-08-13.html
A fine-grained performance profile is available: use the --scan option.
```

Gradle has generated an HTML-formatted report and placed it in the file shown in the output. Opening that file in your browser of choice will show you Gradle's insights on build time for your project, as shown in Figure 6-4.

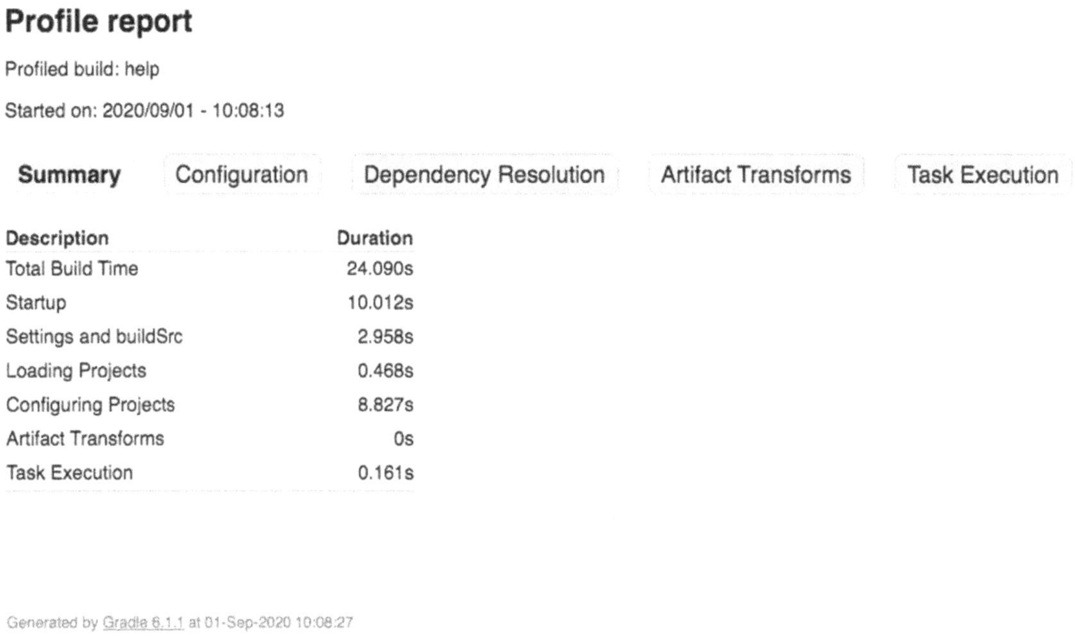

Profile report

Profiled build: help

Started on: 2020/09/01 - 10:08:13

Summary | Configuration | Dependency Resolution | Artifact Transforms | Task Execution

Description	Duration
Total Build Time	24.090s
Startup	10.012s
Settings and buildSrc	2.958s
Loading Projects	0.468s
Configuring Projects	8.827s
Artifact Transforms	0s
Task Execution	0.161s

Generated by Gradle 6.1.1 at 01-Sep-2020 10:08:27

***Figure 6-4.** Gradle profiling report*

Visit gradle.org to Learn More

There is a wealth of information online about Gradle, and the project's home page is a great place to start. Once you get a taste for what it can do, you'll find it becomes one of your go-to tools.

Managing Your Code with Source Control

Another large topic area that confronts many serious developers is how to manage their source code, projects, and associated resources over time. Source control is the concept of using a dedicated database that is adept at managing the file-based nature of software source – it is also sometimes known as version control – and solves two large problems simultaneously. First, as your development work grows, you will likely end up with dozens or even hundreds of projects, each with a wealth of files and related resources as you saw in Chapter 4. A source control system makes managing these sets of files far simpler and acts as a reliable backup and source of truth for your coding efforts. The second benefit from source control is the freedom it provides you to experiment, change, and make mistakes with your code and revert to earlier versions (usually, a version that was working) if the need arises.

Out of the box, Android Studio offers direct integration support for three different systems: Git, Mercurial, and Subversion. Each is popular for some section of the developer community, and if you have a preference, stick with it. To enable source control integration with your projects, open the VCS menu in Android Studio and choose the Enable Version Control Integration option. It will present the dialog shown in Figure 6-5 for you to select your chosen version control option.

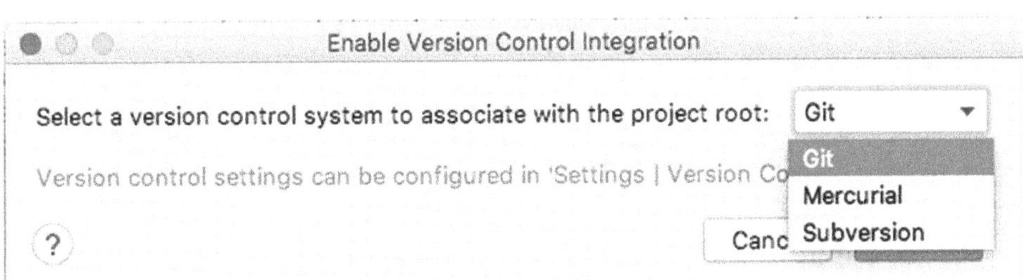

Figure 6-5. Enabling source control

With source control enabled, you will now see many more options available in the VCS menu, as well as from the context menu in any project view. The first time you attempt to use a feature, such as importing a Git branch or checking out a project from Subversion, you will be prompted for the URL and credentials needed to access your chosen system. From there, you'll be able to use a range of the features you see displayed in the menu in Figure 6-6.

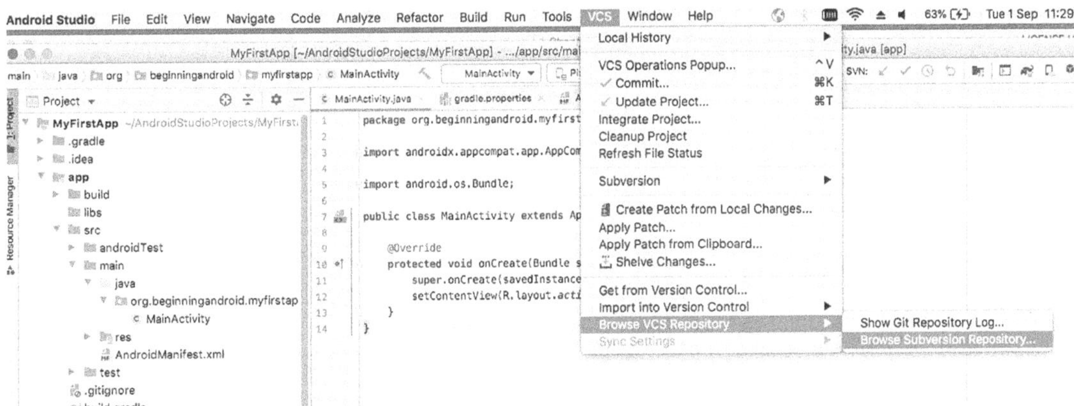

Figure 6-6. Source control features enabled in the VCS menu

Source control is a huge topic, and as you have already guessed, a large number of dedicated books and resources exist for these tools. If you're new to source control tools, I can recommend visiting `https://git-scm.com/`, `www.mercurial-scm.org/`, or `https://subversion.apache.org/` to get started with any of the systems Android Studio natively supports.

Completing Your Software Repertoire

As well as the tools and complementary systems for Android Studio I've already mentioned in this chapter, there are additional tools you might need or want in order to build various extra resources for your development. This can include things like images, animation, sound recordings, music, and more.

There are a lot of commercial tools that serve these purposes, and you may already know and use some of them. I'm going to highlight some key open source tools, which are strong competitors and in some cases leaders in their respective fields. I am a strong advocate for open source, which is why I tend to prefer open source tools where possible. You might not share that perspective, but the list that follows will outline what is available, even if you choose commercial alternatives.

Open source tools you should consider for your development environment include

Blender: For the top tool in all of 2D and 3D animation, you need look no further than Blender. It has a massive following in professional and amateur circles, is used in industries such as movies and TV, and is breathtakingly capable for almost any animation development you might have in mind. Find out more at `www.blender.org`.

GIMP (GNU Image Manipulation Program): A well-known image editing and manipulation tool, GIMP usually finds equal amounts of love and hate depending on who you ask. It is very capable for many common tasks, such as resizing, scaling, cropping, red-eye reduction, layer development/flattening, and more. Those who don't love it usually point to Adobe Photoshop as the gold-standard commercial product. These people aren't wrong – Photoshop is truly comprehensive and capable. But for an open source alternative, give GIMP a try (`www.gimp.org`).

Inkscape: Vector graphics can become a very large part of your Android development world, particularly if you venture into game development. Inkscape is a fantastic open source vector graphics program with a long history. Again, there are those who do say various commercial packages are better – and they might be right. Learn more about Inkscape at `https://inkscape.org`.

Audacity: Another application considered one of the best in its field, Audacity is one of the premier multi-track audio editing suites and supports all popular operating systems. Find Audacity at `www.audacityteam.org/`.

LAME: One of the original audio tools (and one that is embedded in many other tools mentioned in this chapter), LAME is a command-line tool and embeddable library that performs MP3 encoding of audio from a variety of sources (`https://lame.sourceforge.io`).

OpenShot: One of many open source video (and audio) editing suites, OpenShot has some great features including curve-based key frame animations, advanced timeline and frame-by-frame features, and cross-platform support. More details at `www.openshot.org`.

Olive: Another video editing tool, with an avid following (`www.olivevideoeditor.org/`).

DaVinci Resolve: Another immensely powerful video editing tool, which currently has the claim to fame of being one of the few tools to support very high-resolution video up to 8k. It also has strong support for collaboration across multiple users working on the same video projects. Learn more at `www.blackmagicdesign.com/`.

You will see some of these tools in action in Part 3 of the book, when we work with images, sound, video, and other resources in Android applications.

Summary

As you can see from the topics covered in this chapter, thinking through your hardware and software landscape can greatly aid you in your journey to becoming a dedicated Android developer. There is one more software topic that should be covered – Java and the JDK. This is a topic with literally hundreds of books written, and while we don't have that much space, we will devote an entire chapter to Java, starting on the very next page in Chapter 7!

Part II

Get the Android Development Know-how

Chapter 7

Introducing Java for Android Development

In this chapter, we'll explore how to get started with Java for developing Android applications, with a particular focus on how to tackle a topic as massive as Java without getting discouraged or daunted by its size. Those of you who already have some familiarity with Java development can skim most of the content, but there are some key points on Android specifics that I will recommend any reader review.

Learning Java to an expert level is a huge endeavor. Even learning it to a "happy beginner" level would take far more than a single chapter in this book or even a whole book in its own right. Literally "thousands" of books have been written on Java and its many aspects. Instead of providing an incomplete and ultimately less-than-useful introduction, we will focus on three key preparatory points to launch you on the path to learning Java with tools and resources beyond this book.

First, we'll review Java from a software perspective, including the Java Development Kit (JDK) and Java Runtime Environment (JRE), and the peculiarities of Android's use and adoption of Java's virtual machine environment – JVM – including its promise to enable run-anywhere software and the long history of Java versions.

Second, we will dive into a basic pure Java application that you can run on any machine with Java, starting you with one or two parts of the basics as a point from which to expand your understanding of Java and how that does (and doesn't) translate to Android applications.

Finally, we'll cover the key areas or themes in Java you should look to learn over time and links to some of the best free and commercial resources available to carry on your journey after this chapter.

G. Allen, *Android for Absolute Beginners*, https://doi.org/10.1007/978-1-4842-6646-5_7

OTHER DEVELOPMENT LANGUAGE CHOICES FOR ANDROID

Java has a long history with Android being (equal) first choice as the development language when Android launched. But it is not the only language supported for developing applications. Along with Java, Android has supported a "Native" form of development with C++ from its early days, via the "Native Development Kit," or NDK. In 2016, Google took the plunge and added Kotlin to the stable of supported languages and as of last year decided Kotlin would be the new first-choice language. Java is still the leading language in Android development in terms of application use, at nearly 90%. But many new applications mix Kotlin and Java or opt just for Kotlin. You can learn more about Kotlin development for Android in Apress' *Learn Kotlin for Android Development* (Späth, ISBN 9781484244661).

Java, Java, Everywhere

That catchy heading is one I mean in two ways – Java was meant to be a write-once, run-anywhere language. To quite a surprising degree, it has succeeded in that goal despite a lot of doubt, resistance, and even legal impediments. Java is also everywhere in the sense that it is the name of the programming language, but also often the shorthand name given to the software used to make that run-anywhere promise come true. The Java Virtual Machine (or JVM), and the way it is packaged for deployment on computers, is also often just referred to as Java. And as if that wasn't ample opportunity for confusion, once you become immersed in Java, you'll find yourself and other practitioners also referring to the core libraries that provide essential functionality as Java.

Naming complications are one issue you will adapt to as a Java developer, but Java has also had a torrid history when it comes to how that "run-anywhere" ability was actually delivered. JVMs are complemented by Java distributions as either a runtime known as Java Runtime Environment – JRE – or full developer tooling known as Java Development Kit, or JDK. How versions have been and are handled has been one of the most twisted tales in software, such that it is not uncommon to find systems trying to support five parallel major versions of Java at the same time – Java 6, Java 8, Java 9, Java 11, and whatever Java flavor was most recently released.

You are saved from some of the versioning headaches, thanks to Google's actions, where Android Studio took the plunge in its version 2.3 release to implicitly bundle a JDK and to fully manage this for you, so you never need to roll your own again. However, it can sometimes be useful to test out code outside of Android and also to learn more about Java in non-Android applications. Later in this chapter, we'll demonstrate how to do that if you are not already familiar with the approach and also use that as part of your springboard to learn Java – the language – if you are an absolute beginner in the space.

JAVA SECURITY

This topic isn't complete without discussing security. Whether it is as a stand-alone install or part of Android Studio, Java and its runtimes and JVMs have a very long, very troubling history of security issues. I won't delve into the thousands of vulnerabilities, bugs, and exploits that have been found – and fixed! – over the last two decades, but I will say this. Always patch your Java installs, including always keeping Android Studio up to date. Always!

To learn more about historic Java vulnerabilities that have affected Android, feel free to read more at www.beginningandroid.org.

Android's Java Time Warp

When first released, Google chose the then-current version of Java as the basis for Android, Java version 6 – or Java 1.6 as it was known at the time. As future versions of Android were released, Java releases were comparatively slow-moving, and there was significant upside in keeping Android compatible with Java 6. Over time, release patterns changed, particularly with Java, which, after slow releases for Java 7 and Java 8, picked up speed. We are now at Java 15 at the time of writing this book, but for a variety of technical and nontechnical reasons, Java compatibility got "stuck" in Android with Java 7 and partial support for Java 8. If you are learning Java for the purposes of writing Android applications, keep this in mind!

Concepts and features from Java 9 and beyond are simply not available for use when developing for Android. This means things such as modules introduced in Java 9, data class sharing introduced in Java 10, or the enhanced safety and utility of switch statements from Java 12 are not at your disposal. In practice, this doesn't present a huge impediment, but can take some time adjusting to if you are experienced with modern Java and have gotten used to the latest features it offers.

Using a JDK Installation for Learning Java

Thanks to Android Studio bundling the JDK with its installation, you have a ready-made "pure Java" environment to also use, on top of the great Android Studio IDE experience. To use the JDK on its own, you can look for the directory on disk where Android Studio places the JDK. You can find this directly from Android Studio itself, with any project open. Choose the `File` ➤ `Other Settings` ➤ `Default Project Structure` menu. You will see a dialog as shown in Figure 7-1, showing the JDK location.

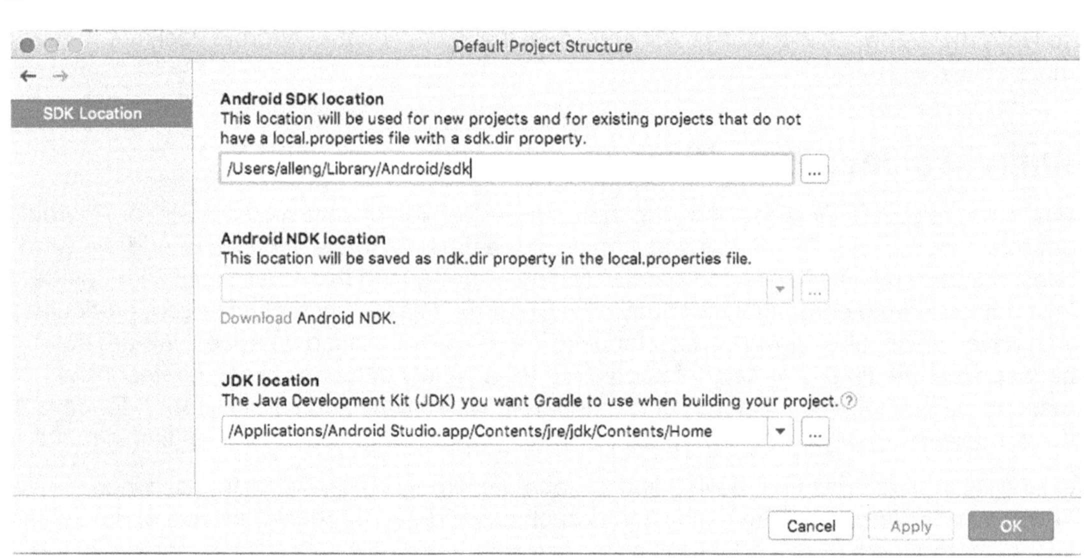

Figure 7-1. Android Studio showing the location of the JDK

To summarize for each supported operating system for Android Studio

> On macOS/OSX: The JDK is found at `/Applications/Android Studio.app/Contents/jre/jdk/Contents/Home`.
>
> On Linux: The JDK location can vary depending on where you instruct the Android Studio installer to place the IDE, but it is found in the `./android-studio/jre` folder under that location.
>
> On Windows: The JDK location can vary depending on where you instruct the Android Studio installer to place the IDE, but by default it is in `C:\Android\Android Studio\jre\bin`.

For the examples in this chapter that are pure (non-Android) Java, you can use a command prompt or shell to navigate to the directory via the "`cd`" command. You can also test to see if this directory is included in the `PATH` environment variable on your computer – which means your operating system will know where to find the JDK's key tools regardless of what directory you are working from. For example, the "`which javac`" command on macOS and Linux will return a path to the first installation of the `javac` binary, which is the Java compiler, if it is found in the directories specified in `PATH`. For instance, on my MacBook Air, I see the following:

```
$ which javac
/usr/bin/javac
```

What could be easier? Well, you might recall, in the prior heading about Java being everywhere, that it is common to have multiple versions of Java installed on the same machine and that those versions might be the full JDK, providing developer tools for Java, or just the JRE, which provides the runtime JVM and some supporting utilities, but not developer tools like the compiler.

If you want to be absolutely certain that you are using the compiler (javac binary) and JVM (java binary) that are bundled with Android Studio, use the full path to those programs when calling them. For instance, to be sure I'm using javac from Android Studio in the following example, I would invoke it as

```
$ "/Applications/Android Studio.app/Contents/jre/jdk/Contents/Home/bin/javac" somejavafile.
java
```

There are a lot of ways to interrogate which of the installed versions of Java you are using by default and to switch between them for various reasons – even within Android Studio itself. However, that's beyond the scope of this book. For beginners, I'd warn against tinkering with Android Studio's setting in this regard.

Your First Java Concepts in Code

It is traditional to start learning a programming language by writing a "Hello World" application. We're going to skip past that and go to a slightly more advanced example to show you the very basics of working Java code. Listing 7-1 shows the code for our sample non-Android Java application, FirstJavaDemo, which you can find in the Ch07/FirstJavaDemo.zip.

***Listing 7-1.** Source code from the FirstJavaDemo.java file*

```
import java.io.*;
import java.util.*;

public class FirstJavaDemo {
  public static void main(String[] args) {

    Console console = System.console();
    if (console == null) {
      System.out.println("Console not found");
      System.out.println("Please re-run from a command line, shell, or console window");
      System.exit(0);
    }

    System.out.print("Tell me something about yourself: ");
    String something = console.readLine();

    System.out.println("Interesting!  You said: " + something);
  }
}
```

In the following sections, we will step through what effect(s) individual pieces of this code have. At a slightly larger level, let's walk through the whole structure and explain in plain English what is happening. This will then allow you to cross-reference a layperson explanation, with the Java-specific aspects.

The first lines are import statements, instructing our program to use Java's library system (where other Java capabilities are bundled for you to use, without having to build them all from scratch yourself). The syntax looks a little weird, but at its heart we are instructing Java to bring in all aspects of the `java.io` library and `java.util` library. These libraries handle things like file and console input and output and other ubiquitous features you will often want or need.

We then have a `class` declaration. Classes are the central concept to the object-oriented (OO) design school of application development, and we talk more about them later in the chapter. Importantly, this is a class definition of my (or your) choosing. I chose the name `FirstJavaDemo`. The Java keyword "`public`" means that, if desired, other Java programs could look to import my class and reuse it.

The body of the class and other subblocks of logic are wrapped in curly braces – the { and } symbols you see. These curly braces are significant punctuation (tokens, in the parlance of programming and compilers) and must be used to group nested sets of logic – be it classes, their methods, inner logic blocks such as loops and conditional tests, and so on.

Next, we have the mandatory `main()` method, which we define as having a `void` return type, which in essence means on exit the program does not return any data from variables or other method calls, and taking a `String` array named `args` as (optional) parameter. In practice this approach is a long-term style in many programming languages, where parameters (or arguments) can be passed to a program when it first runs, to be used for any purpose the developer has in mind, such as to turn options on or off in the program or seed it with key startup data.

We then define and create an object named `console` (in lowercase), based on the `Console` object provided by the `System.console()` method, which itself is one of the utilities we have access to, thanks to importing the `java.util` library. That method hides away a whole host of operating system interaction between the `FirstJavaDemo` program and the JVM to hook up your program to a console – which is typically a shell or command prompt window or a similarly styled part of a more complex program like the console window in the Android Studio IDE.

KEY CONCEPTS: DATA TYPES AND VARIABLES

This example of a Console object and a working copy or container named "console" introduces two of the fundamental aspects of almost all programming languages, including Java. These concepts are variables and data types.

A variable can be thought of as a container or a placeholder for some as-yet unspecified value – just as in high school mathematics or algebra. In Java, a variable is first defined in such a way as to identify the kind of information it will contain, known as its data type.

A data type in Java is a specification of the kind of information or data used for a variable or in other circumstances. Data types come in two forms: The first are very simple data types known as primitives, which represent simple integer or floating-point numbers in several forms – int, short, long, float, and double – as well as simple character text known as char and boolean, which represents true or false values.

The second kind of data type is a more complex object, such as in our Console case. You can think of this more complex kind of data type as a compound collection of multiple primitive data types and the predefined logic that can be used to work with that data. This is the essence of a class in Java and other object-oriented programming languages.

Sometimes creating a console will fail for strange reasons – permissions issues are an example. We use Java's If-Then logic to introduce a logic test, represented by the == sign, to determine if our `console` exists or is undefined – `null` in Java parlance. If the `console` is undefined, we use the `System.out.println()` method that we have access to, thanks to the import of the `java.io` library, and write out some helpful literal string text that is meaningful to a human who might read it. We then exit the program at that point using the `System.exit()` method.

KEY CONCEPT: BRANCHING AND LOOPING STRUCTURES IN JAVA – IF, WHILE, FOR

The code in Listing 7-1 shows one of the main logic control structures in Java – the If statement. There are several other such structures that allow you to make decisions in your code based on testing a value and deciding on a suitable branch of logic or repeating actions based on testing a value until a condition changes. As well as the If statement, Java provides the For loop, the While loop, and the Do While loop. Each of these latter structures has many nuances, which we will explore later in this book, but about which you can learn more at `http://en.wikibooks.org/wiki/Java_Programming/`.

In the far more reliable and common scenario that all was well with creating the `console` object, we then use the `System.print()` method to print the text of a question in the console and the `System.readln()` method to accept a response typed by you and store that in a `String` variable named `something` we have defined as a place to hold your input text. Finally we use `System.println()` again with some `String` concatenation features provided by the + operator to respond to you.

That short description should help you understand what the `FirstJavaDemo` app does, but does not really give you a deep feel for the Java syntax, structure, or rules beyond a very cursory level. We'll build your understanding further in a moment. For now, let's practice compiling and running this program.

To compile the program, open a shell or command prompt, and if desired change directory to the JDK as noted earlier for your operating system. Note where on disk you have placed the `FirstJavaDemo.java` file from `Ch07/FirstJavaDemo.zip`. Then invoke the `javac` binary, passing it the full path and filename for `FirstJavaDemo.java`, for example, as follows on macOS or Linux:

```
$ javac <path-to-where-you-unzipped-code>/FirstJavaDemo.java
```

You should, after a brief moment, see the command or shell prompt return to your control. So what happened? The `javac` utility has processed the source code and generated an intermediary version of your code that the JVM can now understand and run. In your directory, you should see a new file, named `FirstJavaDemo.class`, which is the output of the `javac` command.

To run your code, use the `java` command (lowercase) and pass it the full path to the `FirstJavaDemo.class` file, but omit the file extension (the `.class` part) from the filename, for example:

```
$ java <my-path-to-the-file>/FirstJavaDemo
```

The output, once you answer the question prompt you should see on the screen, would then look like this:

```
$ java FirstJavaDemo
Tell me something about yourself: I program in Java
Interesting!  You said you: I program in Java
```

You did it! Using the Java-specific tools and some newly learned code, you've created a pure Java application. Read on to learn more about the Java language and how to get a deeper understanding for every word, line, and quirky punctuation mark in the `FirstDemoJava` application.

The Key Java Building Blocks for Android Development

All of the examples throughout the remainder of this book will rely on a certain level of knowledge of Java. In the remainder of this chapter, we will give you a master list of topics covering the fundamentals you'll need to at least follow along, but more importantly will also give you the starting point from which to further learn and educate yourself from the vast corpus of free and commercial sources available online, in bookstores, from schools and colleges, and so on for learning Java. We will link directly to some of these so your Java journey is not interrupted – I encourage you to follow some of these links as you work through this chapter, as it's never too early to go deeper on a Java topic!

To maximize your efficient learning of Java for Android Development, the following topics are key:

General software development knowledge:

- Structure and layout of code
- Object-oriented design and programming, including classes and objects
- Class methods and data members

Java-specific coding knowledge:

- Interfaces and implementations
- Threading and concurrency
- Garbage collection
- Exception handling
- File handling
- Generics
- Collections

Obviously this is not all of Java, but it is enough of a subset of Java to give you the building blocks to start on Android development immediately!

Structure of Code

Looking back at the FirstJavaDemo source code, you can appreciate how Java code is structured in the simplest case. Java can be thought of as an onion layering of the most basic constructs that build layer over layer to the most far-reaching and complex constructs. From simplest to most sophisticated, we have

Token: The smallest building block of Java, a token represents names of things like instances of objects that we have created, or that are system provided, such as the something String object in our FirstJavaDemo code, keywords from the Java language like "return," operators, punctuation characters like parentheses, and more.

Expression: One or more tokens along with operators like +, or method calls, that form a piece of logic. In our FirstJavaDemo example, we see an expression in "Interesting! You said: " + something, which is an expression to concatenate two strings with the + operator.

Statement: A complete set of logic built from tokens and expressions, delimited by a semicolon. This is often synonymous with one "line" of code, but it can actually span an arbitrary number of lines.

Method: A logical grouping of statements that form a coherent set of logic and can be invoked by use of a method's name. In our FirstJavaDemo code, we create the logic for the main method of our class, but we also reference methods from other classes, such as the readLine() method for reading text input at a console and the println() method to print back to a console.

Class: A representation of a conceptual object and all of the methods and data members that are used to represent that object and allow manipulation of it and its capabilities. The class concept is tied closely with the notion of object-oriented design, which we will touch on shortly.

Package: While not shown in our example, a package is a collection of classes and usually is used to bundle together those classes that support a specific related group of logic, for instance, file handling or graphics rendering.

There are many other structural aspects to Java code, but mastering the preceding will enable you to decipher, and exploit, more esoteric constructs based on your understanding of fundamentals.

ANDROID AND MAIN

No, that's not a street intersection, but it could be. In the FirstJavaDemo example, you will see we have one method defined, called main. Java's design stipulates that one of the few mandatory requirements of a Java program be that a method named main exist and that it will be the first method called by the JVM when running the program. Think of this as the Java equivalent of a large sign that reads "Start Here."

But take a look at the Android examples we've written already in prior chapters, like the MyFirstApp application. The MainActivity.java file is missing a main method. What's going on? Never fear. You application does have a main method, but it is buried away in the supporting scaffolding that Android Studio put in place. Rather than force you to juggle main methods and then all of the flow or event handling work that would provide the running application experience to your users, Android provides an activity lifecycle, with defined points around which you as the developer can focus, dealing with the points at which your activities are created, used, paused, and disposed. This activity lifecycle is covered in depth in Chapter 11.

If you look at the Android Java you've already written, including the `MyFirstApp` application, you can see many aspects of this hierarchy of the Java language in practice – without realizing it, you've already been exercising these concepts in your first applications.

Understanding Object-Oriented Design, Classes, and Objects

The Java programming language was designed from inception to embrace and express the notions of object-oriented design (sometimes abbreviated to "OO"). At its heart, object-oriented design uses the idea of expressing almost everything about the conceptual model you create in your applications with objects (or entities), such as "person" or "animal," and then using some strong design philosophy to shape how objects are defined, manipulated, extended, and refined. This is a huge topic, but you can begin with some excellent online material that builds over time to help you understand key OO concepts including encapsulation, inheritance, polymorphism, and more.

Working with Class Methods and Data Members

Part and parcel of adopting the object-oriented approach to coding is the concept that data about objects and instances of objects belongs to those entities, and to manipulate and interrogate that data, one should use the techniques offered (and prescribed) by the design of the class that generates those objects. In short, that means the methods (or functions) the class defines and offers to you the developer.

To those of you new to object-oriented development, this isn't as constraining as it first seems. It embodies one of the principles of object orientation, encapsulation. Everything you need for working with an object comes neatly wrapped up (encapsulated) with its class. There are a myriad benefits to this approach, which you can read about extensively in many object-oriented design texts such as Apress' *Interactive Object-Oriented Programming in Java* (Sarcar, ISBN 9781484254035) and in countless online web pages. Remember too that when you write your own classes, you have the freedom and liberty to make whatever class methods you wish available.

Developing Your Java-Specific Coding Knowledge

Learning all of Java is a huge effort, as I've conveyed already. Learning Java for Android is a little less daunting, but still covers a tremendous amount of the Java landscape. To get you started, here are the key areas to start mastering, with links to some of the best freely available resources online. While I will reference the Java Programming Wikibook, a free online resource, many other online sources are just as good. You can also hugely benefit from Android-specific Java books, such as Apress' *Learn Java for Android Development* (Späth and Friesen, ISBN 9781484259429).

Interfaces and Implementations

Understand how Java objects can build and extend others, and provide a template of what a derived version should do, with the mechanics of how to do it. See `http://en.wikibooks.org/wiki/Java_Programming/Interfaces`.

Threading and Concurrency

Particularly in our multicore CPU age, concurrency and threading provide ways to perform numerous streams of work simultaneously, so long as care is taken. See `http://en.wikibooks.org/wiki/Java_Programming/Threads_and_Runnables`.

Garbage Collection

Java was an early adopter of the approach to carefully managing resources like memory, which attempted to free the developer from having to track and manually dispose of resource allocations – an error-prone task to say the least! See the section on automatic memory garbage collection at `https://en.wikibooks.org/wiki/Java_Programming/Java_Overview`.

Exception Handling

When things do go wrong, providing safe, structured, and informative ways to gracefully deal with the problem is the goal. See `http://en.wikibooks.org/wiki/Java_Programming/Exceptions`.

File Handling

While our FirstJavaDemo app has the user entering data directly at the console by typing, it is far more common to consume and create data using files and the semantics that govern them. See `http://en.wikibooks.org/wiki/Java_Programming/BasicIO`.

Generics

Java is notionally a "strongly typed" language, which means it provides guardrails and protections to ensure that `Strings`, `integers`, and other types never exist with an incompatible data payload and that data of one type can't accidentally be placed in variables of another. This is a key protection mechanism, but can create inflexibility in some circumstances. Generics provide ways to maintain strong typing, but avoid needless duplication and excessive repetition when supporting the same general logic for data of different types. See `http://en.wikibooks.org/wiki/Java_Programming/Generics`.

Collections

Just as sets of primitive data types like integers can be grouped into arrays, so too can objects be grouped into convenient sets. Collections are one way (but not the only way) that Java supports manipulating groups of objects as sets. See `http://en.wikibooks.org/wiki/Java_Programming/Collections`.

Summary

No single chapter – or single entire book – could get you a complete beginner's guide to Java, but in this chapter we've attempted the next best thing. You're now armed with an understanding of Java the language, Java the software product, and what Java means to Android, along with a road map of what to learn and resources to help you grow your mastery of Java. I strongly encourage anyone new to Java to explore the other resources mentioned in the chapter and even more of the vast amount available commercially and for free online, before plowing on to the rest of this book. Even a little side reading and practice will reap huge rewards for your Android understanding.

Chapter 8

Introducing XML for Android Development

This chapter will tackle two topics. First, we'll take a look at XML from a beginner's perspective, for those of you who have never had to work with XML nor drill into its patterns of use, quirks, strengths, and issues. The second part of the chapter will cover the three main areas in Android development where you will commonly dip in to read, writing and editing XML:

- The application manifest, which we have already introduced
- Resource definitions, in particular constants like strings and so on
- Activity layouts, which are a huge topic but one that can be approached in a stepwise fashion

Getting Started with XML

Extensible Markup Language, or XML, is a subset of an older standard known as SGML, Standard Generalized Markup Language. The goal of XML is to convey data and information about that data – known as metadata – in a standardized structure that can be interrogated and used without any prior knowledge of what the data means or what rules exist for the structure. That is a fairly abstract definition, I know. An alternative definition is offered by Wikipedia:

> *Extensible Markup Language (XML) is a markup language that defines a set of rules for encoding documents in a format that is both human-readable and machine-readable.*
>
> —`https://en.wikipedia.org/wiki/XML`, July 2020

G. Allen, *Android for Absolute Beginners*, https://doi.org/10.1007/978-1-4842-6646-5_8

That's not much better as far as definitions go. A more pragmatic definition might be the following:

> *XML is a markup language that defines how to exchange data, and to describe the data being exchanged so that both humans and machines can make some sense of the data, and its structure and relationships to other data.*
>
> —Grant Allen, July 2020

Still not perfect, but getting there. Sadly, that comment can be applied to XML as a whole and not just my curt description. Perhaps a better way to build your understanding of XML is to actually delve into its structure and workings.

Some key points about XML. XML is not a programming language in the strict sense... Things written in XML don't "do" anything. XML is a markup language designed to convey meaning and structure to data, so that programs and programming languages can do things with that data.

When you create XML, you are placing text into a document with certain aspects governed by XML standards and rules – this is known as an XML document. No matter how complicated or convoluted an XML document becomes, you can always step back and consider it as just text – text with special meaning in places and agreed structures and rules around syntax, but text nonetheless.

XML has no set definition of what predefined components are required in an XML document. It does define the rules and syntax for how to define your own components in a document, using basic building blocks. The overall goal for XML and its rules is to allow a machine/program-independent way of describing and packaging data and to have the description and structure self-described in the XML document itself or an associated XML schema.

Let's look at the key XML building blocks.

XML Version and Encoding

There should be a special tag at the start of an XML document that indicates which version of the XML standard it follows and what character encoding is used for the text in the XML (ASCII, UTF-8, etc.). By default, and throughout almost all your Android development, this declaration will stipulate XML version 1.0 and UTF-8 encoding. The special tag takes the following form, using the special `<?xml` and `?>` opening and closing markers:

```
<?xml version="1.0" encoding="utf-8"?>
```

This helps any program reading and consuming your XML document understand how to interpret the text and the XML structure.

XML Elements

Elements are the fundamental building blocks of XML, being the "tags" that provide the meaning and structure for your data, but are themselves not data. XML elements are nested, such that your first, outermost element in your XML document is known as the root element, and it can contain (have nested within it) one or more child elements. There is only ever one root element in an XML document.

Element tags are enclosed in the < (greater than) and > (less than) symbols. For each element I define and use, I will require an opening tag and a matching closing tag with the same name, with a leading / (backslash) added to the element name in the closing tag. This approach must be used to make my XML syntactically correct – known as "well formed" in XML's jargon. For instance, I might decide to create an XML document for holding contact details for people in a data structure mimicking an address book and decide that my root element will be called `<addressbook>`.

My XML document would start out looking like this.

```
<?xml version="1.0" encoding="utf-8"?>
<addressbook>
</addressbook>
```

That includes the version and encoding special tag and the `<addressbook>` root element opening tag, properly closed with a matching `</addressbook>` closing tag. So far, so good.

I can include a child element for a person and child elements within a person for first and last names, as follows:

```
<?xml version="1.0" encoding="utf-8"?>
<addressbook>
  <person>
    <firstname>Jane</firstname>
    <lastname>Smith</lastname>
  </person>
</addressbook>
```

So far, so good. Remember, I am the one deciding what my element names are called and implicitly what purpose they serve.

> **Note** Closing tags for an element do not have to always be on a new line by themselves. In fact, no part of your XML has to have new lines at all. But it does make your XML more human-readable to do this. Commonly accepted norms for human-readable XML have opening tags appear on a new line and either have the closing tag at the end of the same line on which the opening element tag appeared – such as the preceding `<firstname>` and `</firstname>`– when there are no child elements for that tag, or have the opening and closing element tags on lines by themselves with any child elements nested within – such as the preceding `<person>` and `</person>` tags. Tags are also indented to denote that they are child elements, but again this is just convention for the ease of human readers.

If this were a real address book, I would have more than one person in it. But you might notice it would be hard to differentiate which person was which for a computer (or even human) reading this XML. If we did the following, any program trying to keep track of which person was which would have problems:

```
<?xml version="1.0" encoding="utf-8"?>
<addressbook>
  <person>
    <firstname>Jane</firstname>
    <lastname>Smith</lastname>
  </person>
  <person>
    <firstname>John</firstname>
    <lastname>Jones</lastname>
  </person>
</addressbook>
```

One solution to this in XML is to use attributes, which act like parameters for elements.

XML Attributes

Any XML element can have zero or more attributes associated with it. Attributes are distinct from the data provided in the element itself and appear within the < > markers of the element name, immediately following the tag name. Attributes take the form

```
attribute_name="value in double quotes"
```

Continuing our address book example, we could differentiate between different people in the XML data by adding an ID attribute to the `<person>` element, using numeric values to give each person a different ID. The result would be as follows:

```
<?xml version="1.0" encoding="utf-8"?>
<addressbook>
  <person id="1">
    <firstname>Jane</firstname>
    <lastname>Smith</lastname>
  </person>
  <person id="2">
    <firstname>John</firstname>
    <lastname>Jones</lastname>
  </person>
</addressbook>
```

Note that even though you and I might think of the ID value presented here as an integer and even have programs written to treat it like an integer, XML always places attributes in double quotes, making them appear to be strings.

If you have multiple attributes for an element, they are simply separated by a space. For instance, we might track the date we added someone to our address book using a dateadded attribute:

```
<?xml version="1.0" encoding="utf-8"?>
<addressbook>
  <person id="1" dateadded="2020-01-01">
    <firstname>Jane</firstname>
    <lastname>Smith</lastname>
  </person>
  <person id="2" dateadded="2020-01-31">
    <firstname>John</firstname>
    <lastname>Jones</lastname>
  </person>
</addressbook>
```

XML Values

The actual data packaged in XML documents are the values held within the open and closing element tags. In our ongoing address book example, our values are things like "Jane" for a `<firstname>` element and "Smith" for a `<lastname>` element. It may seem like overkill to have all of the XML syntax and element tags in place to convey this (and that verbosity is a common criticism of XML in general), but as a human reading the XML, it is nicely self-descriptive and also provides guarantees about structure, completeness, and so on.

Speaking of completeness, it is perfectly possible to have elements that don't themselves contain any data, just as what our very first address book XML document earlier in the chapter showed. There are options to allow your element to be present and not contain any data, both by using the opening and closing tag method you have already seen and by using the shorthand self-closing tag approach that only has the element tag name appear once, with a trailing / (backslash). Let's add a `<middleinitial>` element to our `<person>` structure, showing both options, as shown next:

```
<?xml version="1.0" encoding="utf-8"?>
<addressbook>
  <person id="1" dateadded="2020-01-01">
    <firstname>Jane</firstname>
    <middleinitial></middleinitial>
    <lastname>Smith</lastname>
  </person>
  <person id="2" dateadded="2020-01-31">
    <firstname>John</firstname>
    <middleinitial/>
    <lastname>Jones</lastname>
  </person>
</addressbook>
```

Both the `<middleinitial></middleinitial>` and `<middleinitial/>` forms are valid for an element with no data. Note that you cannot nest any child elements under a self-closing tag.

XML Namespaces

One of the huge strengths of XML is the way in which it makes exchanging data far easier for developers and systems that use data. Once you become accustomed to sharing data in XML format, it begins to feel like second nature. But you can run into issues with all of this ease of transfer and sharing. One particular issue is that because you define your own XML tags (potentially even defining your own XML schema), you might find that other people have developed their own schemata and used element names that conflict with yours. That's no big deal if you and they never share data, but the chances are if you become a practitioner sharing XML-formatted data, you'll run into name clashes at some point when trying to mix data from multiple sources. So what do you do?

The XML standard offers a two-part approach to help with this clash of names. First, you can prefix any element you like with an identifying string, which is a marker designating from which source a given element is considered to derive. So if we know that we're mixing data from our `<addressbook>` with our own definition for `<person>` with that of someone else who has a potentially totally different structure and set of elements, we can prefix our elements to differentiate them, for example:

```
<?xml version="1.0" encoding="utf-8"?>
<my:addressbook>
  <my:person id="1" dateadded="2020-01-01">
    <my:firstname>Jane</my:firstname>
    <my:middleinitial></my:middleinitial>
    <my:lastname>Smith</my:lastname>
  </my:person>
  <my:person id="2" dateadded="2020-01-31">
    <my:firstname>John</my:firstname>
    <my:middleinitial/>
    <my:lastname>Jones</my:lastname>
  </my:person>
</my:addressbook>
```

This prefix acts as the namespace for these elements, and items from the other XML document with a confusing version of person would have a different prefix for their namespace, for example:

```
<?xml version="1.0" encoding="utf-8"?>
<other:list_of_addresses>
  <other:person >
    <other:name>Judy</other:name>
    <other:surname>Walsh</other:surname>
  </other:person>
```

The XML standard requires that we provide a URI to act as the unique differentiator for our namespace – basically, an attribute that is guaranteed to be unique and reflect the XML structure we have defined for our document. This is specified with the xmlns attribute in the opening tag of an element – and typically you will see this in the root element of an XML document, as follows:

```
<?xml version="1.0" encoding="utf-8"?>
<my:addressbook xmlns:my="https://www.beginningandroid.org/XMLnamespaces/addressbook">
  <my:person id="1" dateadded="2020-01-01">
    <my:firstname>Jane</my:firstname>
    <my:middleinitial></my:middleinitial>
    <my:lastname>Smith</my:lastname>
  </my:person>
  <my:person id="2" dateadded="2020-01-31">
    <my:firstname>John</my:firstname>
    <my:middleinitial/>
    <my:lastname>Jones</my:lastname>
  </my:person>
</my:addressbook>
```

Other Parts of the XML World

There are other parts of the XML standard we won't cover in this chapter that might be of interest as your knowledge develops:

- CDATA: CDATA values are special XML values that are treated as verbatim data and are not processed or parsed to discover if there are further nested XML tags within. This might not make a lot of sense initially, but you will find this is often used to pass other forms of data markup, or presentation markup like HTML, as data with an XML document – it prevents XML parsers and programs looking to enforce XML standards from accidentally tripping up on things that look like they might be XML, but in fact are not – and certainly they don't follow XML rules.
- XML Path and XQuery: XML Path and XQuery provide ways to traverse an XML document, looking for data by navigating the hierarchy of tags, evaluating attributes, and so on. These tools aren't used in the basic design and build of Android applications by default, though you certainly can use them if you build Android applications that themselves manipulate XML-based data.
- XSLT and transformations: XSLT is the XML stylesheet transformation language, which is a programming language designed to interrogate and transform the structure and data of XML, creating derived data as an output. The output of an XSLT transformation is typically another XML document, though it can also be data in different formats.

There are literally thousands of websites that will help you learn more about XML, but now you know enough of the basics to dive into how Android uses XML and to start writing and editing your XML files for Android applications.

Using XML in Your Android Applications

As mentioned at the very start of this chapter, there are three main areas in which Android uses XML to help build and run applications. To recap, these are

- The application manifest, which we've already introduced
- Resource definitions, in particular constants like strings and so on
- Activity layouts, which are a huge topic but one that can be approached in a stepwise fashion

Reviewing the Android Manifest XML File

Regardless of your level of familiarity with XML – whether you've used it for years or taken the crash course outlined in the first half of this chapter – we can now explore the Android Manifest in detail. Listing 8-1 has the androidmanifest.xml content again for reference:

***Listing 8-1.** The androidmanifest.xml file revisited*

```
<?xml version="1.0" encoding="utf-8"?>
<manifest xmlns:android="http://schemas.android.com/apk/res/android"
    package="org.beginningandroid.myfirstapp">

    <application
        android:allowBackup="true"
        android:icon="@mipmap/ic_launcher"
        android:label="@string/app_name"
        android:roundIcon="@mipmap/ic_launcher_round"
        android:supportsRtl="true"
        android:theme="@style/AppTheme">
        <activity android:name=".MainActivity">
            <intent-filter>
                <action android:name="android.intent.action.MAIN" />

                <category android:name="android.intent.category.LAUNCHER" />
            </intent-filter>
        </activity>
    </application>

</manifest>
```

In Chapter 4, we highlighted some of the elements and other parts of this file, for instance, the use of a namespace to uniquely identify all Android resource elements with an `"android"` namespace, tied to the unique xmlns reference `xmlns:android="http://schemas.android.com/apk/res/android"`, and the use of <manifest> as the root element for an Android Manifest XML document. But we can now review some of the other elements and attributes.

> **Note** If you haven't already spotted it, Google tends to leverage attributes extensively across all uses of XML in Android development. At times many people highlight that this goes too far and that many attribute-heavy elements could be restyled to have child elements encompassing data values instead. It's a never-ending theoretical argument, which you will now be equipped to join!

There will typically be one `<application>` element tag in your manifest. Prominent attributes of this tag are the `android:icon` and `android:roundIcon` options and the `android:label` and `android:theme` attributes – this latter example acts as a name for a bundle of other style and design XML settings that you can adopt to give your applications a specific look and feel. You'll note that they all use a `"@path/detail"` form. The `"@"` notation is shorthand for referencing key resources within the `res/` hierarchy of your project – whether that's application icons controlled by the mipmap images, string values in the `strings.xml` file within the values hierarchy (discussed shortly), and so on.

We already briefly covered the `<activity>` element you see presented in Listing 8-1 and indicated how this specific entry links your `MainActivity` java activity to the `"MAIN"` action that is triggered when an Android application launches.

Your manifest can and will grow to include further `<activity>` elements, one for each of the activities you create for your application. Remember, there are no real limits to how many activities you might create for you application, so you can eventually see a lot of such elements.

We will return to build on your knowledge of the Android Manifest and its XML nuances as we progress through the book.

Using XML for Resource Definitions

Another major area where Android leverages XML is in the definition and use of constants or reference values, where a given piece of data is used in a read-only fashion in a range of use cases. There are a huge range of examples of how constant data can help streamline building your application and reduce the effort required in everything from ensuring a consistent look and feel in all activities and visual elements through to ensuring that key data value such as the height of Mount Everest (8848 meters), the name of your application ("MyFirstApp"), or other unchanging data values can be declared in one place but used in many others.

Some of the key resource definition files are

- colors.xml: A reference file for providing useful names, meaningful to you, for various Red-Green-Blue (RGB) hexadecimal representations of colors.
- strings.xml: A reference file for abstracting textual strings, such as simple words, phrases, sentences, and paragraphs, so that these can be referenced in various source code and other files without needing to copy the text into many places.

- styles.xml: A reference file for collecting sets of color definitions and other styling elements under the banner of a self-declared style, so that the style can be used as a common design theme throughout your application.
- dimens.xml: A reference file for providing abstract representations of different dimension and size settings, allowing you to control changes in density/size in one location rather than having to edit many values in many different files.

Those definitions of resource files are fine for a high-level conceptual understanding, but leave something to be desired to understand *how* they are used. Let's dive in and get our hands dirty mixing things up and adding new content to these resource files.

Changing Colors

The easiest XML file to tinker with is your `colors.xml` file. This file can contain as many aliases for colors as you desire. The default content is shown in Listing 8-2.

***Listing 8-2.** The default colors.xml file content*

```
<?xml version="1.0" encoding="utf-8"?>
<resources>
    <color name="colorPrimary">#6200EE</color>
    <color name="colorPrimaryDark">#3700B3</color>
    <color name="colorAccent">#03DAC5</color>
</resources>
```

Time to make some more changes to your `MyFirstApp` application. By altering the color element with the name attribute of `"colorPrimary"`, we can alter the look of your application wherever the layout references this color resource definition. You can see how this makes development easier when it comes to consistent color choice and color palette throughout an application's design.

Choose whatever RGB color representation appeals to you. Personally, I am quite fond of a nice forest green, so I would choose the hex value `#2F8800`, so your `colors.xml` definition would be updated as reflected in Listing 8-3.

***Listing 8-3.** Altering color definitions centrally via colors.xml*

```
<?xml version="1.0" encoding="utf-8"?>
<resources>
    <color name="colorPrimary">#2F8800</color>
    <color name="colorPrimaryDark">#3700B3</color>
    <color name="colorAccent">#03DAC5</color>
</resources>
```

Save these changes, and then run your `MyFirstApp` application again. You should see the color change take effect, as shown in Figure 8-1.

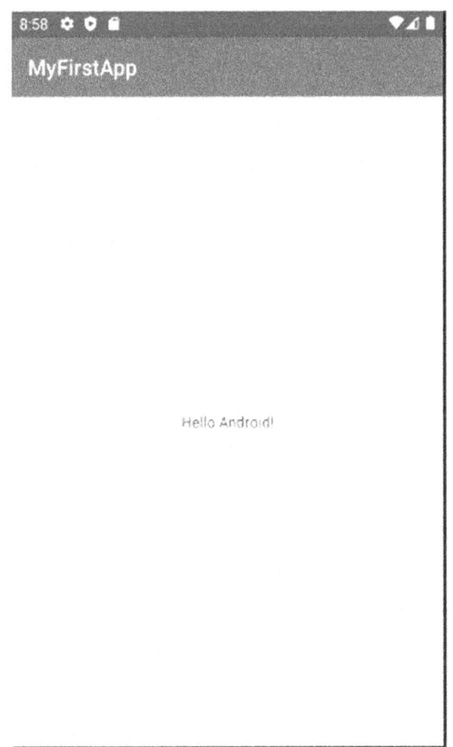

Figure 8-1. Changed colors in MyFirstApp

Compare this with the same app running using the Android defaults for your project, as shown back in Chapter 3 in Figure 3-19. The color differences should be apparent in your running application, even if they don't look so different printed in this book in black and white.

Getting Descriptive

The `strings.xml` file is a sleeping giant in the Android world. It is here that you can define all manner of constants, which are basically things that rarely change or at least start out in your application context as something with a fixed initial value. When you think about constants, you can go beyond the humorous examples I gave before (why limit yourself to the height of Mount Everest in meters – why not feet, rods, furlongs, or chains?!).

More seriously, you should keep a constant look out (no pun intended) for any time you are entering literal strings into your code and ask yourself if it wouldn't be better to instead place a single entry into the `strings.xml` file. There are literally decades of lessons learned by programmers the hard way that all boil down to the maxim "abstract literal strings out of your code – you will thank me later."

Let's add an entry to the `strings.xml` file, with the intention of replacing the on-screen text you see in your `MyFirstApp` application. There is more work to do than just defining the new reference value, but we will get to that in the next section. For now, open the `strings.xml` file, which should look a lot like Listing 8-4.

***Listing 8-4.** The default strings.xml file for MyFirstApp*

```
<resources>
    <string name="app_name">MyFirstApp</string>
</resources>
```

Add a new line, and create a `<string>` element entry with an attribute of name, equal to a text string named `welcome_text`. The value of the `<string>` element should be whatever text you actually want your user to see on-screen. Your `strings.xml` file should look something like Listing 8-5.

***Listing 8-5.** Adding a new <string> element to strings.xml*

```
<resources>
    <string name="app_name">MyFirstApp</string>
    <string name="welcome_text">Hello Android, from the strings.xml file!</string>
</resources>
```

Remember, this is XML. The value of the name attribute can be anything you like – `"welcome_text"`, `"look_at_my_great_string"`, `"text1"`, and so on. So long as you then reference this correctly in the future, you are reaping the "extensible" benefits of Extensible Markup Language! Let's see how we use this new string in the next section.

Defining Activity Layouts with XML

Perhaps the largest and most complex area in which Android relies on XML is in the definition and management of View layouts – that is, the definition and control of how the on-screen user interface is rendered for a user and how it is controlled programmatically by your application.

***Listing 8-6.** The default activity_main.xml layout file for MyFirstApp*

```
<?xml version="1.0" encoding="utf-8"?>
<androidx.constraintlayout.widget.ConstraintLayout
xmlns:android="http://schemas.android.com/apk/res/android"
    xmlns:app="http://schemas.android.com/apk/res-auto"
    xmlns:tools="http://schemas.android.com/tools"
    android:layout_width="match_parent"
    android:layout_height="match_parent"
    tools:context=".MainActivity">

    <TextView
        android:layout_width="wrap_content"
        android:layout_height="wrap_content"
        android:text="Hello Android!"
        app:layout_constraintBottom_toBottomOf="parent"
        app:layout_constraintLeft_toLeftOf="parent"
        app:layout_constraintRight_toRightOf="parent"
        app:layout_constraintTop_toTopOf="parent" />

</androidx.constraintlayout.widget.ConstraintLayout>
```

Our default `MyFirstApp` application was generated via the new project wizard, and by default this chose a default layout of "`ConstraintLayout`" for your `MainActivity` activity. This is one of many, many types of layout available for your activities, derived from the parent ***View*** class. We will delve into views, layout, and many of their permutations in the next few chapters. Right now, let's start working on your existing layout.

A `ConstraintLayout` is designed to give you very flexible control over the size and position of the other UI elements – known as widgets – that appear within it. From Listing 8-6, you can see we have only described one widget, which is a `TextView`. We'll get around to adding more widgets in the next two chapters. For now, let's make our on-screen greeting more flexible by using the power of the `strings.xml` reference value for our widget text, instead of a hard-coded value.

Let's update the layout XML to replace the hard-coded string "`Hello Android!`" with a reference to the `welcome_text` constant we defined in the previous section in the `strings.xml` file. Change the `android:text` attribute so that it references "`@string/welcome_text`", which is the name of the string alias created earlier. Your layout should now look like Listing 8-7, with the change shown in bold.

Listing 8-7. *Changing TextView text to reference strings.xml constant*

```
<?xml version="1.0" encoding="utf-8"?>
<androidx.constraintlayout.widget.ConstraintLayout
    xmlns:android="http://schemas.android.com/apk/res/android"
    xmlns:app="http://schemas.android.com/apk/res-auto"
    xmlns:tools="http://schemas.android.com/tools"
    android:layout_width="match_parent"
    android:layout_height="match_parent"
    tools:context=".MainActivity">

    <TextView
        android:layout_width="wrap_content"
        android:layout_height="wrap_content"
        android:text="@string/welcome_text"
        app:layout_constraintBottom_toBottomOf="parent"
        app:layout_constraintLeft_toLeftOf="parent"
        app:layout_constraintRight_toRightOf="parent"
        app:layout_constraintTop_toTopOf="parent" />

</androidx.constraintlayout.widget.ConstraintLayout>
```

> **Note** Somewhat annoyingly, while the reference value XML files are named in the plural – strings.xml, colors.xml, and styles.xml – when we actually reference the definitions they contain, we use singular references – @string, @color, and @style. Android Studio will help you out here with its prompting as you type.

With our layout XML changed to reference our strings.xml welcome_text value, it is time to run your application again to see the effect in action, as shown in Figure 8-2.

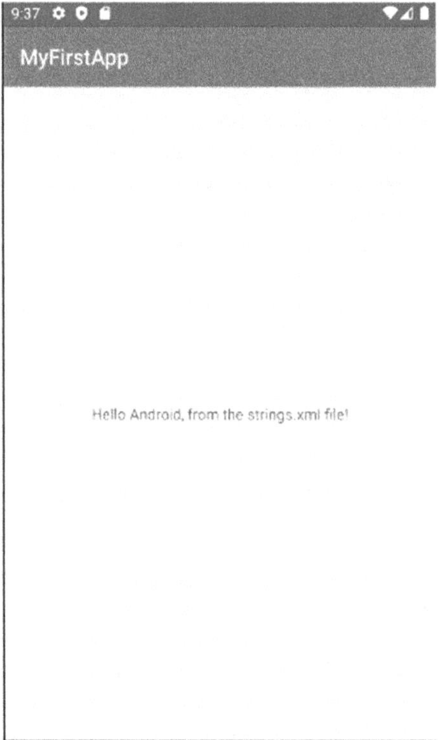

Figure 8-2. New welcome text in MyFirstApp controlled entirely through XML definitions

Voila! You have changed colors and welcome text in your application with just the XML definitions available to you. There's much more Android applications get out of using XML as a definition and control mechanism, and when combined with the power of Java to manipulate XML, the results can be astounding. But for now, you have the basics of XML you need to proceed with your Android journey.

Summary

You have had a whirlwind introduction to XML, and how Android leverages XML, in this chapter. XML is such a large topic that one chapter cannot do it justice, and I would encourage you to seek out more information online and in other books. One of the biggest advantages of XML in the Android development space is the ability to both use it to control application logic and control it through application logic. We will explore this in more depth in the next two chapters, where we get deeper into the world of Android layouts and widgets!

Chapter 9

Exploring Android Concepts: Core UI Widgets

In Part 1 of the book, you had a whirlwind tour of the steps required to create a new Android Studio project for your Android application and explored the structure, files, and purpose of the various parts of a default Android project. You delved into the initial steps of creating your own behavior with the XML configuration for your application's color scheme and leveraged the utility of text resources to personalize the welcome message in your application's main activity.

In this chapter, we will go beyond the surface changes from the earlier chapters and dive right into the major user interface elements you have available in all Android applications and those that will become the mainstay of many of the activities you develop and deploy for all of your future Android work. You will learn how to deploy, adapt, and control the many user interface widgets that are available to you as an Android developer and begin your journey crafting more sophisticated Android user experiences.

Everything Starts with View

In the Android world, every major element you can display on a user interface – an activity – inherits from a base class know as View. Any View-derived widget, be it a text box, button, pick list, or what have you, provides you with a range of common behaviors and benefits derived from this View lineage. These common behaviors and attributes include things like consistent ways to set and control fonts, colors, and other styling characteristics.

Over and above these common characteristics, a range of methods and attributes are available, thanks to the common View heritage all widgets have. We will cover these inherited characteristics next.

G. Allen, *Android for Absolute Beginners*, https://doi.org/10.1007/978-1-4842-6646-5_9

Key Methods Derived from View

Any widget derived from the View base class inherits a range of methods and properties that help manage things like basic state management, grouping with other widgets, parent and child objects in the layout, and so forth. The attributes you'll see include

- `findViewById()`: Finds the widget with a given ID, used extensively to link a widget defined in XML to control logic in Java (and Kotlin).
- `getParent()`: Finds the parent object, whether it's a widget or container.
- `getRootView()`: Gets the root of the tree provided from the activity's original call to `setContentView()`.
- `setEnabled()`, `isEnabled()`: Sets and checks the enabled state of any widget, for example, for things like checkboxes, radio buttons, and more.
- `isClickable()`: Reports whether this view (e.g., button) reacts to click or press events.
- `onClickListener()`: For views like buttons that can be clicked, defines a callback that will be triggered when the associated view is clicked. The callback implementation holds whatever logic you decide is needed.

Key Attributes and Properties Derived from View

Along with core methods from the View base class, all widgets also inherit some key properties. These properties include

- `android:contentDescription`: This is a text value associated with any widget that can be used by accessibility tools, where the visual aspect of the widget is of little or no help to the user.
- `android:visibility`: Determines if the widget should be visible or invisible at first instantiation.
- `android:padding`, `android:paddingLeft`, `android:paddingRight`, `android:paddingTop`, `android:paddingBottom`: Various approaches to pad values on all sides of the widget.

> **Note** Padding for a widget can also be set at runtime with the `setPadding()` method.

Introducing the Core UI Widgets in Android

There are a core set of UI widgets you will turn to again and again when building Android applications, as they provide many of the common user interface experiences users of computers, smartphones, and so on have learned to expect over the last few decades. Let's step through examples of each of these core widgets.

Labeling Things with TextView

Providing a readable text label is probably the most fundamental of all UI widgets, and you'll find a label or static text equivalent in almost every design toolkit ever invented. Android provides the TextView widget to carry out this function, letting you place a static string (or at least static to begin with, as the value of a TextView can be changed programmatically) anywhere on an activity's UI. The text of this string is entirely at your mercy, whether it's providing a description of an adjacent widget, a caption, some commentary, or notes – the choice is yours.

Android provides two major ways to define a TextView and indeed all UI widgets. The first approach is define your TextView entirely through the use of Java code, setting attributes like on-screen position, size, text payload, and so forth. Anyone who has prior experience developing nontrivial user interfaces will tell you this is a lot of work, it is error prone, and you will quickly see your code grow to unmanageable size. But there is a better way, and you've already used it!

It is far faster and easier to use Android's other methods for UI design, which is via declarative XML. In Chapter 3, you created your MyFirstApp application and took charge of the text within a TextView widget. In Chapter 7, you dabbled further with controlling the source of the TextView string and some other decorative attributes. You can add as many TextView widgets as you think make sense at any time, either directly through defining further <TextView> elements in the activity's XML definition file or by using the Graphical Layout Editor.

The Graphical Layout Editor lets you worry about the visual styling and automatically generates the necessary matching XML behind the scenes to describe your TextView widget. Let's put this through its paces right now. Even though your MyFirstApp app is perfectly fine, let's leave it out of the picture. In Android Studio, create a new project via the File ➤ New... ➤ New Project menu option. Just as we did in Chapter 3, give your project a meaningful name, such as TextViewExample, and choose the Empty Activity template. This will create your new project and place a TextView widget by default in the activity_main.xml file (just as happened when you created your MyFirstApp application). Your activity_main.xml content should look like Listing 9-1.

***Listing 9-1.** A fresh Android Studio application using the Empty Activity template*

```
<?xml version="1.0" encoding="utf-8"?>
<androidx.constraintlayout.widget.ConstraintLayout
xmlns:android="http://schemas.android.com/apk/res/android"
    xmlns:app="http://schemas.android.com/apk/res-auto"
    xmlns:tools="http://schemas.android.com/tools"
    android:layout_width="match_parent"
    android:layout_height="match_parent"
    tools:context=".MainActivity">

    <TextView
        android:layout_width="wrap_content"
        android:layout_height="wrap_content"
        android:text="Hello World!"
        app:layout_constraintBottom_toBottomOf="parent"
```

```
        app:layout_constraintLeft_toLeftOf="parent"
        app:layout_constraintRight_toRightOf="parent"
        app:layout_constraintTop_toTopOf="parent" />

</androidx.constraintlayout.widget.ConstraintLayout>
```

Rather than edit the XML here, invoke the Graphical Layout Designer by clicking the Design button on the far right-hand side of your Android Studio view. This should hide the XML content and instead present you with the equivalent graphical layout for your application as shown in Figure 9-1.

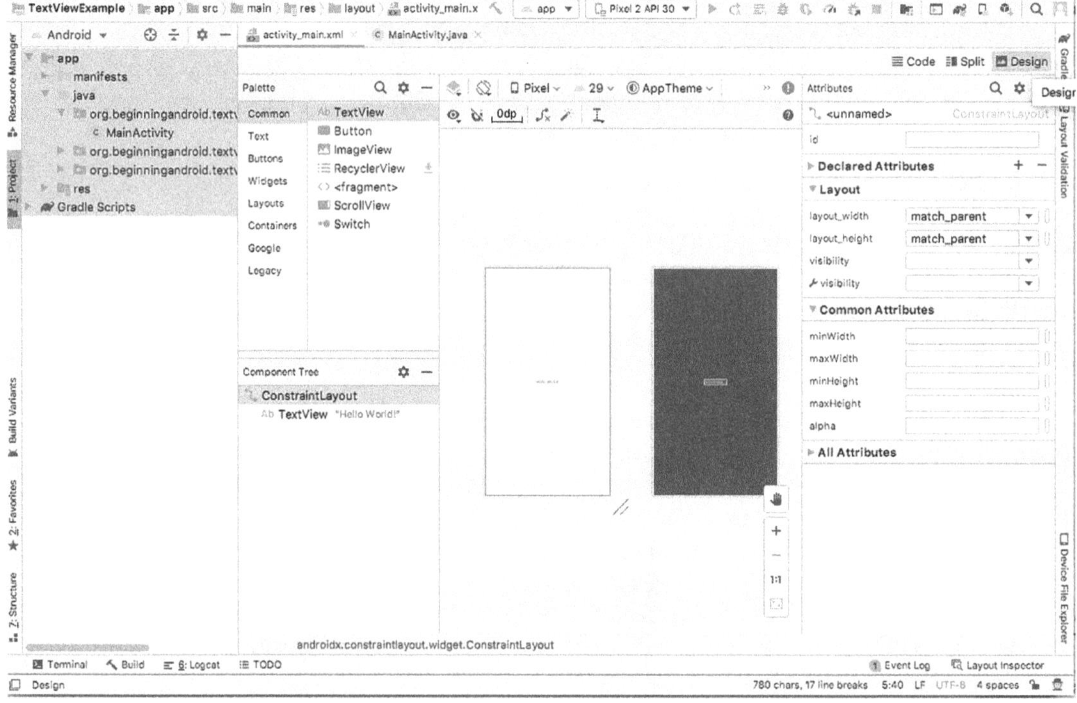

***Figure 9-1.** Invoking the Graphical Layout Designer*

There's a lot going on in this view, but the best way to learn is to experiment with each area in turn. Starting with the Palette section, you'll see a list of widget types – Common, Text, Buttons, and so on – and next to it a list of the actual widgets with a type. At the top of this list, you will see `TextView` as you can see in Figure 9-1. Click and drag this over the miniature screen depictions you see in the middle of the screen, and you should see a tiny floating label moving around, until you release the mouse button. Go ahead and do that anywhere that seems "right" to you.

A second `TextView` will now be in place, but you will see a red error flag – clicking that will inform you that you have not set "constraints" on the new `TextView`, so the position in which you've placed it will not be preserved if you actually build and run this application. Don't panic! We are going to fix that now, but in your XML definition, and learn more about `TextView` widgets in the process. Switch back to the code view of your layout by clicking the Code button on the far right.

Your activity_main.xml file will now resemble Listing 9-2, with a new <TextView> element and associated attributes added.

***Listing 9-2.** Your revised activity_main.xml file*

```
<?xml version="1.0" encoding="utf-8"?>
<androidx.constraintlayout.widget.ConstraintLayout
xmlns:android="http://schemas.android.com/apk/res/android"
    xmlns:app="http://schemas.android.com/apk/res-auto"
    xmlns:tools="http://schemas.android.com/tools"
    android:layout_width="match_parent"
    android:layout_height="match_parent"
    tools:context=".MainActivity">

    <TextView
        android:id="@+id/textView2"
        android:layout_width="wrap_content"
        android:layout_height="wrap_content"
        android:text="Hello World!"
        app:layout_constraintBottom_toBottomOf="parent"
        app:layout_constraintLeft_toLeftOf="parent"
        app:layout_constraintRight_toRightOf="parent"
        app:layout_constraintTop_toTopOf="parent" />

    <TextView
        android:id="@+id/textView"
        android:layout_width="wrap_content"
        android:layout_height="wrap_content"
        android:layout_marginStart="176dp"
        android:layout_marginLeft="176dp"
        android:layout_marginBottom="252dp"
        android:text="TextView"
        app:layout_constraintBottom_toBottomOf="parent"
        app:layout_constraintStart_toStartOf="parent" />

</androidx.constraintlayout.widget.ConstraintLayout>
```

We already worked on altering <TextView> attributes in earlier chapters, and now we're going to go to town a little! Let's introduce some new attributes that help you control TextView and other widgets:

- android:layout_marginStart
- android:layout_marginEnd
- android:layout_marginLeft
- android:layout_marginRight
- android:layout_marginBottom

As their names suggest, each of these helps set margins at various edges of a widget.

We are also benefiting from the default layout approach with our application, known as a ConstraintLayout. We will discuss layouts in more detail in the following chapters, but for now you can think of them as approaches to helping you with placing your widgets within an activity. Some layouts take care of lots of settings for you, at the expense of slightly less artistic freedom, whereas others give you carte blanche, but leave you needing to do more work. The ConstraintLayout is of the former sort, trying to help you as much as possible get good-looking layouts. Several key attributes that it brings to the layout of all widgets include

- app:layout_constraintTop_toTopOf
- app:layout_constraintBottom_toBottomOf
- app:layout_constraintLeft_toLeftmOf
- app:layout_constraintRight_toRightOf

There are many more combinations of layout_constraint*-style attributes that all serve the purpose of being able to specify how to align and size the widget based on proximity and relationship to another widget's top, bottom, left, or right edge, as well as its center, the positioning of any text in the related widget, and more!

We'll need these layout margin attributes and constraint attributes to provide predictable behavior for our new TextView, shown in bold:

```
<TextView
    android:id="@+id/textView"
    android:layout_width="wrap_content"
    android:layout_height="wrap_content"
    android:text="TextView"
    android:layout_marginStart="176dp"
    android:layout_marginLeft="176dp"
    android:layout_marginBottom="252dp"
    app:layout_constraintBottom_toBottomOf="parent"
    app:layout_constraintStart_toStartOf="parent" />
```

The actual values are fairly easy to understand. The three different margin attributes are setting the size of the margins in pixels around the TextView. The layout constraint attributes are tying the vertical and horizontal constraint defaults to something called "parent". In this instance, that means the parent activity itself. You can instead refer to the android:id of another widget to have it act as the guiding factor for constraining the widget.

With those changes in place, you should save your activity_main.xml file and then run your TextViewExample application to see that your new label is in place, positioned where you have instructed it to be, as shown in Figure 9-2.

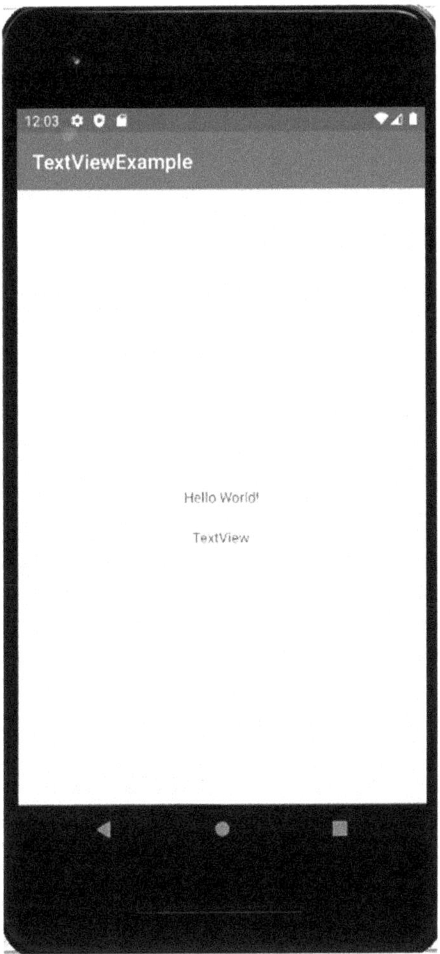

Figure 9-2. More TextView labels for your application

To complete the picture on `TextView` widgets, you should know that there are nearly 100 different attributes that can control behavior, style, size, color, and so forth for a `TextView` label. More examples include

- android:hint: A hint to display.
- android:typeface: Sets the typeface to use for the label (e.g., monospace).
- android:textStyle: Indicates what combination of bold (bold), italic (italic), and both (bold_italic) should be applied to the text.
- android.textAppearance: An omnibus property that lets you combine text color, typeface, size, and style in one go!
- android:textColor: Uses the common RGB notation in hexadecimal to choose the text color for the label. For example, #0000FF is blue.

You can find the code for this example in the `Ch09/TextViewExample` project folder.

It has been illustrative, and hopefully educational, up to this point to see what can be done with XML alone in Android, but the true power and flexibility in developing applications comes from the marriage of your chosen programming language and Android's XML powers. Once we move on to more sophisticated UI widgets, deploying your Java (or Kotlin) powers becomes both necessary and desirable, as you will see in the coming sections on other UI widgets.

Buttoning the Perfect UI

Buttons are a foundational piece of any UI development, harking all the way back to simulating real-world analogue buttons on electronics devices like TVs, radios (remember those?), and car dashboards. Android offers several types of button, the most straightforward of which is the `Button` widget from the android.widget package that includes simple text on the "face" of the button. Let's get stuck into creating a new application that uses a button and some Java logic to track and control the text that appears on the button. You can review this example in the `Ch09/ButtonExample` project folder.

First, create a new project using the Android Studio new project wizard, and choose the Empty Activity template as a starting point. Name your project `ButtonExample` (or something that you find equally descriptive). Once your project is created, open the activity_main.xml file and delete the default TextView element. Switch to the Design view in the layout editor, and from Palette choose the `Button` widget and place it on the screen. The exact positioning of the button doesn't matter, as we'll let it grow to fill our application activity entirely at a later point. You should see a layout similar in appearance to that shown in Figure 9-3.

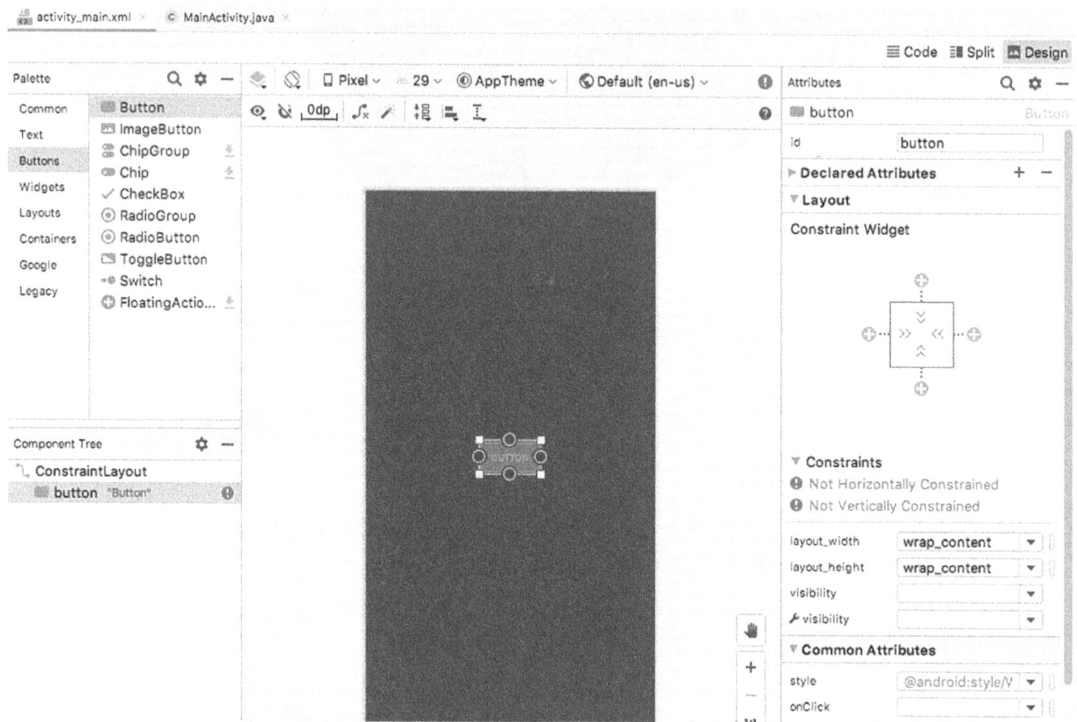

Figure 9-3. Adding a button to the design blueprint of ButtonExample

Note the two errors informing you that the button is unconstrained. This is because when you choose to use the ConstraintLayout layout to house other child UI widgets, each of those widgets requires at least one horizontal and one vertical "constraint," or instruction as to how they should be positioned in relation to the top, bottom, start, and end of the parent layout or another widget. To remedy this, use one of the two circles at the midpoint of each side, and click and drag the connector to the side of your design blueprint. This will set the horizontal constraint for the button to be the side of the activity, minus any margin. Then choose the circle in the center of either the top or bottom edge of the button, and click and drag the connecter to the top or bottom edge of the activity to set the vertical constraint. Switch to the code view of your `activity_main.xml` file, and it should look similar to that shown in Listing 9-3.

***Listing 9-3.** ButtonExample activity_main.xml file, showing Button definition*

```
<?xml version="1.0" encoding="utf-8"?>
<androidx.constraintlayout.widget.ConstraintLayout
xmlns:android="http://schemas.android.com/apk/res/android"
    xmlns:app="http://schemas.android.com/apk/res-auto"
    xmlns:tools="http://schemas.android.com/tools"
    android:layout_width="match_parent"
    android:layout_height="match_parent"
    tools:context=".MainActivity">

    <Button
        android:id="@+id/button"
        android:layout_width="wrap_content"
        android:layout_height="wrap_content"
        android:text="Button"
        tools:layout_editor_absoluteX="161dp"
        tools:layout_editor_absoluteY="341dp" />

</androidx.constraintlayout.widget.ConstraintLayout>
```

Next, we need to provide some oomph for our button, to have it actually do something. As such, open the `MainActivity.java` source file for `ButtonExample`, and replace its content with the Java code in Listing 9-4.

***Listing 9-4.** Modified Java code for ButtonExample*

```
package org.beginningandroid.buttonexample;

import androidx.appcompat.app.AppCompatActivity;
import android.os.Bundle;
import android.view.View;
import android.widget.Button;

public class MainActivity extends AppCompatActivity implements View.OnClickListener{

    Button myButton;
    Integer myInt;
```

```
    @Override
    protected void onCreate(Bundle savedInstanceState) {
        super.onCreate(savedInstanceState);
        myButton = new Button(this);
        myButton.setOnClickListener(this);
        myInt = 0;
        updateClickCounter();
        setContentView(myButton);
    }

    @Override
    public void onClick(View v) {
        updateClickCounter();
    }

    private void updateClickCounter() {
        myInt++;
        myButton.setText(myInt.toString());
    }
}
```

Breaking this code down section by section will help you understand what's going on and also demonstrate some of the common approaches you will use for all of your development, not just a button-clicking app!

The first few lines from the preceding listing introduce the package name and any desired or necessary Java class imports:

```
package org.beginningandroid.buttonexample;

import androidx.appcompat.app.AppCompatActivity;
import android.os.Bundle;
import android.view.View;
import android.widget.Button;
```

The package name will have been set for you based on the name you entered in the new project wizard. The class library imports for `androidx.appcompat.app.AppCompatActivity` and `android.os.Bundle` were also included by default by the new project wizard. I then explicitly added the `android.widget.Button` class, as that is the pre-built class that provides all of the common logic and behavior that I would want to wire up to the button I've placed in my layout. I lastly added the `android.view.View` class as it provides the pre-built ability to define listeners for events that happen on widgets derived from the View class – which means every widget we are discussing in this chapter. In particular, as shown in the next few paragraphs, I define and use an `OnClick` listener so the `ButtonExample` app can be notified of click events and trigger my desired logic.

You can see the first step of enabling `OnClick` listening by the change in the class definition for `MainActivity`. I have altered the default class declaration provided by the new project wizard, by also adding implements `View.OnClickListener`, as repeated in the following:

```
public class MainActivity extends AppCompatActivity implements View.OnClickListener{

    Button myButton;
    Integer myInt;

    // more code here
}
```

This modification to the class sets us up to provide the OnClick logic later – and Android Studio will prompt you to do this with a warning and also prompt you to add the android.view.View import if you haven't already done so. I define two handy variables next, a Button named myButton, which will be wired up to the UI widget, and an Integer named myInt, which I use as a counter to track how many times the button is clicked.

Next, the onCreate() method is enhanced to have it do the setup tasks we need when the activity is first run. We will delve into the four main lifecycle methods of an activity in Chapter 12, but for now you can rely on the fact that onCreate() is called only once, when your activity starts. In the ButtonExample code, we are defining and instantiating the myButton object, setting the OnClick listener for myButton, setting the value of myInt to 0 (zero) initially, and then calling the private method updateClickCounter().

Two very simple steps make up the entire updateClickCounter() method, as repeated in the following:

```
    private void updateClickCounter() {
        myInt++;
        myButton.setText(myInt.toString());
    }
```

First, the myInt value is incremented by 1. Subsequently, the .setText() helper method for the myButton object is called, and the String representation of the myInt value is passed to it, so that the text displayed on your button widget is updated to reflect the new value of myInt. In short, we increment the value of our click counter and have that displayed as the button text.

The final piece of the code that we skipped over is the onClick() method, which is invoked by the listener we defined any time the button is clicked. The logic within this method simply calls the private updateClickCounter() method, meaning that we reuse the same logic both at onCreate() time and in any subsequent button click.

Go ahead and run your code – or the Ch09/ButtonExample code from the book – and you should see a button-filled application, with an incrementing counter as the button label, similar to that shown in Figure 9-4.

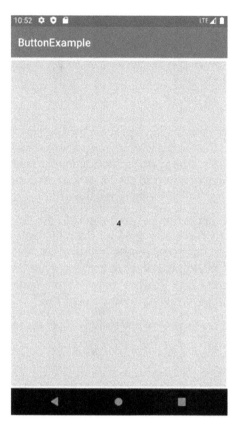

Figure 9-4. *The running ButtonExample application*

Getting the Picture with ImageView and ImageButton

If your Android applications only consisted of text and a few buttons, things would get very dull – with perhaps the possible exception of a crossword game. Images and pictures are a core part of UI design, and many applications don't just use them decoratively, but as part of the core application features such as photo albums, image editors, and so on.

Android has a pair of image-enabled equivalents to the `TextView` and `Button` you've already worked with – these are the `ImageView` and `ImageButton` widgets, and again they are derived from the base `View` class.

As with many of the widgets in this chapter, it is often best to use the layout editor in both blueprint/design mode and the accompanying code view, to define your `ImageView` or `ImageButton` in XML, rather than laboring away at programmatically defining these in Java.

Both `ImageView` and `ImageButton` introduce one additional attribute to their relative element XML definition, in the `android:src` value. The value of this attribute is a reference to an image resource you provide, whether that's a `.png` file, `.jpg/.jpeg` file, `.gif` file, or some other supported image format. In Chapter 4, I covered the project structure including the `res/drawable` hierarchy. It is in this folder you would place your image files for reference and where Gradle will look to find the referenced images for bundling into the application package at build time.

ImageButton differs from ImageView in supporting button-like behaviors that you have already seen earlier in this chapter for the regular Button widget. This means ImageButton widgets can (and should) have onClick listeners defined and subsequent logic built to handle whatever actions or behaviors you want your application to undertake when the ImageButton is clicked, just as you did for the Button widget.

If you remember back to our overview of the typical project layout in Chapter 3, you can likely guess that the default approach for specifying android:src values is to refer to graphics resources you have placed in your project's res/drawable directory (and/or density-specific variants thereof).

Listing 9-5 shows an example of an ImageView configured to reference an image in the res/drawable folder, which in this case is a photo I took of the Rosetta Stone in the British Museum.

***Listing 9-5.** Using an ImageView widget for the ImageViewExample layout*

```
<?xml version="1.0" encoding="utf-8"?>
<androidx.constraintlayout.widget.ConstraintLayout
xmlns:android="http://schemas.android.com/apk/res/android"
    xmlns:app="http://schemas.android.com/apk/res-auto"
    xmlns:tools="http://schemas.android.com/tools"
    android:layout_width="match_parent"
    android:layout_height="match_parent"
    tools:context=".MainActivity">

    <ImageView
        android:id="@+id/imageView"
        android:layout_width="wrap_content"
        android:layout_height="wrap_content"
        android:src="@drawable/rosettastone"
        android:contentDescription="The Rosetta Stone"
        tools:layout_editor_absoluteX="83dp"
        tools:layout_editor_absoluteY="144dp" />
</androidx.constraintlayout.widget.ConstraintLayout>
```

The running application can be seen in Figure 9-5.

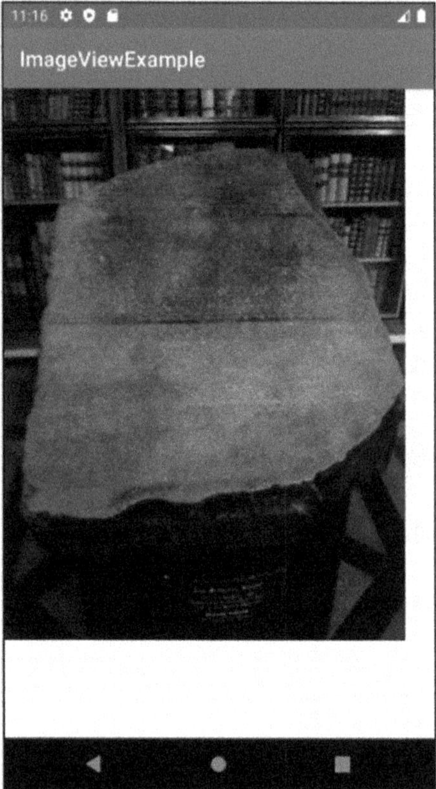

***Figure 9-5.** The running ImageViewExample application showing the ImageView with its resource*

You can find the code for this example in the `Ch09/ImageViewExample` folder.

Editing and Inputting Text with EditText

In your tour of Android widgets so far, you've seen static text labels, buttons that can trigger activity, and ways to display images. Nearly every application at some point needs input from the user, and that input is usually text. No widget set would be complete without some kind of editable form or field widget, and Android covers this need with the `EditText` widget.

`EditText` has a class hierarchy that sees it derived from the `TextView` class you already know and then ultimately the `View` class. Being a subclass of `TextView` means `EditText` inherits many of the capabilities, methods, and data members you have seen in use for `TextView`, such as `textAppearance`. `EditText` introduces a range of new properties and attributes as well, giving you fine-grained control over exactly how your text fields look and behave. These new attributes include

- android:singleLine: Manages behavior of the Enter key, determining if this should create a new line within the text field or shift focus to the next widget in your activity layout
- android:autoText: Manages the use of the built-in spelling correction features

- android:password: Configures the field to display password dots as characters are typed in
- android:digits: Restricts input to only accepting digits, hiding the alphabetic-typed characters

Android also offers a more nuanced – some would say sophisticated – approach to specifying field characteristics for `EditText`. The `inputType` property can be used instead, to bundle up all desired properties and attributes for an `EditText` field. We will cover `inputType` and related topics of keyboards and input methods in Chapter 10. Listing 9-6 shows `inputType` in action with other options.

Listing 9-6 shows an introductory use of the `android:inputType` attribute, in this instance flagging that the user's text should have the first letter of the first word automatically capitalized. We have also used the regular attribute `android:singleLine` set to false, enabling multiple lines of text within the `EditText` field.

***Listing 9-6.** Configuring EditText field behavior with XML properties*

```
<?xml version="1.0" encoding="utf-8"?>
<androidx.constraintlayout.widget.ConstraintLayout
xmlns:android="http://schemas.android.com/apk/res/android"
    xmlns:app="http://schemas.android.com/apk/res-auto"
    xmlns:tools="http://schemas.android.com/tools"
    android:layout_width="match_parent"
    android:layout_height="match_parent"
    tools:context=".MainActivity">

    <EditText
        android:id="@+id/myfield"
        android:layout_width="fill_parent"
        android:layout_height="fill_parent"
        android:inputType="textCapSentences"
        android:singleLine="false" />

</androidx.constraintlayout.widget.ConstraintLayout>
```

Listing 9-7 shows how to also work with an `EditText` field programmatically from your accompanying Java package. You can find this example in `Ch09/EditTextExample`.

***Listing 9-7.** The EditText widget can be manipulated easily from your code*

```
package org.beginningandroid.edittextexample;

import androidx.appcompat.app.AppCompatActivity;
import android.os.Bundle;
import android.widget.EditText;

public class MainActivity extends AppCompatActivity {

    @Override
    protected void onCreate(Bundle savedInstanceState) {
        super.onCreate(savedInstanceState);
        setContentView(R.layout.activity_main);
```

```
        EditText myfield=(EditText)findViewById(R.id.myfield);
        myfield.setText("Our EditText widget");

    }
}
```

Note that we have introduced the findViewById method in this listing. You can imagine that where you have any number of widgets, you need a programmatic way of finding which one you want to work with as part of your program logic. By using a resource ID reference, of the form R.id.named_id_from_XML_definition, you implicitly look for, and link to, the matching widget defined within your XML layout via the android:id attribute of that widget. So in this case, R.id.myfield finds and matches the android:id of your EditText, @+id/myfield.

You can see the results from the EditText example in Figure 9-6.

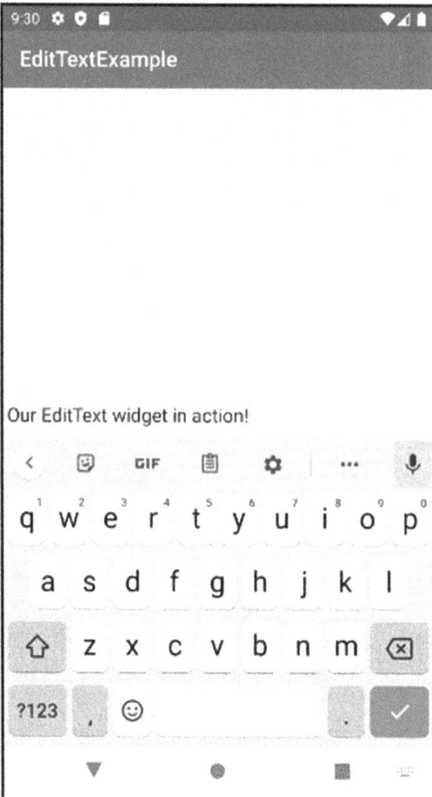

***Figure 9-6.** EditText widget in action, complete with editing text via the keyboard*

There are other typical signs that this is an editable field. The built-in dictionary and spelling checker are available – try misspelling a word, and it will be presented with red underlining. The blinking cursor is also evident when the field has focus for text input.

You can also help your users type more quickly by choosing the sibling widget known as the AutoCompleteTextView variant (again subclassed from TextView and View), which will prompt with auto-completed suggested words as the user types.

> **Note** You can get more sophisticated when working with EditText widgets, by using a layout known as a TextInputLayout, which wraps and extends the default EditText behavior with features like text hinting, highlighting, helper prompts, and so forth. You can find out more about TextInputLayout at developer.android.com.

Checking Out the CheckBox

Another classic UI widget included with Android is the CheckBox, providing a binary on/off, yes/no, or checked/unchecked widget. CheckBox is a subclass of View (you guessed it) and TextView (which might surprise you). This class ancestry means you get access to a range of useful properties via inheritance. The CheckBox object provides you with some Java helper methods to do useful things with your checkboxes:

- toggle(): Toggles the state of the CheckBox
- setChecked(): Checks (sets) the CheckBox regardless of current state
- isChecked(): A method to examine if the CheckBox is checked

In Listing 9-8, we have an example checkbox layout with simple accompanying Java logic you can find in the Ch09/CheckboxExample project.

***Listing 9-8.** A layout featuring a CheckBox*

```
<?xml version="1.0" encoding="utf-8"?>
<androidx.constraintlayout.widget.ConstraintLayout
xmlns:android="http://schemas.android.com/apk/res/android"
    xmlns:app="http://schemas.android.com/apk/res-auto"
    xmlns:tools="http://schemas.android.com/tools"
    android:layout_width="match_parent"
    android:layout_height="match_parent"
    tools:context=".MainActivity">

    <CheckBox
        android:id="@+id/check"
        android:layout_width="wrap_content"
        android:layout_height="wrap_content"
        android:text="The checkbox is unchecked" />

</androidx.constraintlayout.widget.ConstraintLayout>
```

While a mildly attractive CheckBox might look nice by itself, it really needs to *do* something for you or your users to be useful. We unlock the capabilities of a CheckBox by adding Java logic to partner our layout. Listing 9-9 is the Java package that demonstrates how to link logic to the checkbox.

***Listing 9-9.** Firing up a CheckBox with some programmatic logic*

```
package org.beginningandroid.checkboxexample;

import androidx.appcompat.app.AppCompatActivity;
import android.os.Bundle;
import android.widget.CheckBox;
import android.widget.CompoundButton;
import android.widget.CompoundButton.OnCheckedChangeListener;

public class MainActivity extends AppCompatActivity {
    CheckBox myCheckbox;

    @Override
    protected void onCreate(Bundle savedInstanceState) {
        super.onCreate(savedInstanceState);
        setContentView(R.layout.activity_main);

        myCheckbox = (CheckBox)findViewById(R.id.check);
        myCheckbox.setOnCheckedChangeListener(new OnCheckedChangeListener() {
            @Override
            public void onCheckedChanged(CompoundButton buttonView, boolean isChecked) {
                if (buttonView.isChecked()) {
                    myCheckbox.setText("The checkbox is checked");
                }
                else
                {
                    myCheckbox.setText("The checkbox is unchecked");
                }
            }
        });
    }
}
```

Clearly, there's a bit more going on here in the `CheckBox` code than earlier examples such as `EditText`. If you look first at the classes imported, you get a clue to what is happening. I have imported `OnCheckedChangeListener` and provided the implementation for the `onCheckedChanged()` callback method. This means we have set the `CheckBox` to be its own event listener for state change actions like being clicked.

When a user now clicks the `CheckBox` to toggle it, the `onCheckChanged()` callback is fired. The logic of our callback implementation tests the current state of the `CheckBox` after the toggle and updates the text of the checkbox with a written description of its new state. This is both a nice way to bundle up in one place all of the behavior of the widget and let us do things like form validation in the same logic flow during user entry, without needing to pass around a bag of user or data state. Your code and related runtime input checks are elegantly side by side.

Figures 9-7 and 9-8 show our CheckBoxExample app in both the checked and unchecked states.

Figure 9-7. The checkbox is unchecked

Figure 9-8. The checkbox is now checked

Switching It Up with a Switch

The `Switch` widget was introduced later in Android's development, but serves exactly the purpose its name implies. A `Switch` acts like a binary toggle, offering on/off-style state, which the user can activate by swiping or dragging with their finger as if they were toggling a light switch. A user can also just tap the `Switch` widget as if it were a `Checkbox` to change its state. Over several versions of Android, the Switch widget has been tweaked to deal with compatibility and other issues, so other variants like a "`SwitchCompat`" widget are sometimes used instead of the original `Switch` widget, but the overall purpose and handling is similar.

As well as the inherited properties from `View` and so on, a `Switch` widget provides the `android:text` property to display associated text with the `Switch` state. The text is controlled with two helper methods, `setTextOn()` and `setTextOff()`.

Further methods are available for a `Switch` widget, including

- `setChecked()`: Changes the current Switch state to on (just like Checkbox)
- `getTextOn()`: Returns the text used when the switch is on
- `getTextOff()`: Returns the text used when the switch is off

The `Ch09/SwitchExample` project provides a working example of a `Switch`. Listing 9-10 shows a simple switch layout.

***Listing 9-10.** The layout for SwitchExample*

```
<?xml version="1.0" encoding="utf-8"?>
<androidx.constraintlayout.widget.ConstraintLayout
xmlns:android="http://schemas.android.com/apk/res/android"
    xmlns:app="http://schemas.android.com/apk/res-auto"
    xmlns:tools="http://schemas.android.com/tools"
    android:layout_width="match_parent"
    android:layout_height="match_parent"
    tools:context=".MainActivity">

    <Switch
        android:id="@+id/switchexample"
        android:layout_width="wrap_content"
        android:layout_height="wrap_content"
        android:text="The switch is off" />

</androidx.constraintlayout.widget.ConstraintLayout>
```

> **Note** Don't try to have your `android:id` be "switch," as in `@+id/switch`. Java reserves the word `switch` for its case-like branch logic statement, so you will need to use something else as I have in this example.

The logic to configure the behavior of the switch lives in our Java code, shown in Listing 9-11.

Listing 9-11. Controlling switch behavior in code

```
package org.beginningandroid.switchexample;

import androidx.appcompat.app.AppCompatActivity;
import android.os.Bundle;
import android.widget.Switch;
import android.widget.CompoundButton;
import android.widget.CompoundButton.OnCheckedChangeListener;

public class MainActivity extends AppCompatActivity {
    Switch mySwitch;

    @Override
    protected void onCreate(Bundle savedInstanceState) {
        super.onCreate(savedInstanceState);
        setContentView(R.layout.activity_main);

        mySwitch = (Switch) findViewById(R.id.switchexample);
        mySwitch.setOnCheckedChangeListener(new OnCheckedChangeListener() {
            @Override
            public void onCheckedChanged(CompoundButton buttonView, boolean isChecked) {
                if (buttonView.isChecked()) {
                    mySwitch.setText("The switch is on");
                } else {
                    mySwitch.setText("The switch is off");
                }
            }
        });
    }
}
```

If that code structure and logic looks familiar to you, it should! Conceptually, a `Switch` and a `CheckBox` are almost identical, and your logic to operate on them is, at least at the entry level, almost interchangeable. You can see the switch in action, both on and off, in Figures 9-9 and 9-10.

Figure 9-9. The switch widget in the off position

Figure 9-10. The switch is on, and the logic has triggered to change its text

Choosing Things with Radio Buttons

Rounding out our detailed look at the core UI widgets of Android, it's time to introduce the RadioButton. Just as in most other widget toolkits, Android's RadioButton shares the two-state logic that you have already experienced with CheckBox and Switch widgets and gains many of the same features through also being a subclass of View and CompoundButton. Just as you've seen in earlier examples, you can set or test state through methods like toggle() and isChecked() and control text size, color, and so forth through styling attributes.

The Android RadioButton widget takes these capabilities further by adding a further layer of functionality to allow multiple radio buttons to be grouped into a logical set and then allowing only one of the buttons to be set at any time. That should sound familiar if you have used any other UI toolkit, web page, or smartphone application in recent years. To group multiple RadioButtons, each is added to a container element known as a RadioGroup, in the XML layout.

Just like other widgets, you can assign an ID to a RadioGroup via the android:id attribute, and using that reference as a starting point takes advantage of the methods available on the entire group of RadioButtons. These methods include

- check(): Checks/sets a specific radio button via its ID regardless of its current state
- clearCheck(): Clears all radio buttons in the RadioGroup
- getCheckedRadioButtonId(): Returns the ID of the currently checked RadioButton (this will return -1 if no RadioButton is checked)

Listing 9-12 shows the layout for a RadioGroup with RadioButtons.

***Listing 9-12.** RadioButton and RadioGroup layout*

```
<?xml version="1.0" encoding="utf-8"?>
<androidx.constraintlayout.widget.ConstraintLayout
xmlns:android="http://schemas.android.com/apk/res/android"
    xmlns:app="http://schemas.android.com/apk/res-auto"
    xmlns:tools="http://schemas.android.com/tools"
    android:layout_width="match_parent"
    android:layout_height="match_parent"
    tools:context=".MainActivity">

    <RadioGroup
        android:orientation="vertical"
        android:layout_width="fill_parent"
        android:layout_height="fill_parent" >

        <RadioButton android:id="@+id/radio1"
            android:layout_width="wrap_content"
            android:layout_height="wrap_content"
            android:text="Red" />
```

```
        <RadioButton android:id="@+id/radio2"
            android:layout_width="wrap_content"
            android:layout_height="wrap_content"
            android:text="Blue" />

        <RadioButton android:id="@+id/radio3"
            android:layout_width="wrap_content"
            android:layout_height="wrap_content"
            android:text="Green" />

        <RadioButton android:id="@+id/radio4"
            android:layout_width="wrap_content"
            android:layout_height="wrap_content"
            android:text="Yellow" />
    </RadioGroup>

</androidx.constraintlayout.widget.ConstraintLayout>
```

You can also intersperse and add other widgets into the RadioGroup structure, and these will render within the group per their constraint rules for ConstraintLayout or other placement rules for layouts we'll discuss in the next chapter. You can see the bare-bones RadioButtons in action in Figure 9-11.

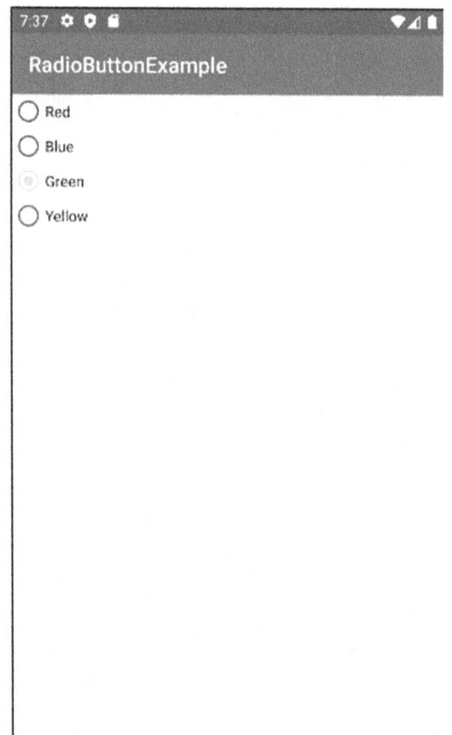

***Figure 9-11.** RadioGroup and RadioButton in action*

Learning Even More UI Widgets

There are always more widgets to learn or master with Android, and you can find out about additional examples on the website, at `www.beginningandroid.org`. Here, you'll find further examples for widgets such as

- Slider
- AnalogClock
- DigitalClock

We'll also look at more audio- and video-centric widgets in Chapters 13 and 14.

Summary

In this chapter, you have learned about many of the fundamental widgets – or views – that are available when building Android user interfaces. In the next chapter, we will take the user interface design concept further and introduce layouts that act as a container and framework for placing, organizing, and nesting your widgets in activities and other user interfaces.

Chapter 10

Exploring Android Concepts: Layouts and More

Understanding the various UI widgets available in Android definitely empowers you to make various design choices about how specific functions and behaviors in your application should present themselves, but there is more to activity design than picking a radio button or TextView. Layouts are Android's declarative mechanism that arms you with control over the complete on-screen landscape for your application.

Conceptually, a layout acts as both a container of the widgets you wish to use in an application or activity and the blueprint and scaffolding for how all of the widgets should appear, interact, and complement each other. As soon as you conceive of designs that use more than one or two widgets, you will want the power of layouts to help you avoid the tedium of manually controlling position, buffers and whitespace, grouping, and so on.

In the coming sections, we'll review some of the most useful, and most popular, layout types supported by Android, and the website contains further examples for some of the more specialized or rarely used layouts.

What Is Android Jetpack

Any cursory search or review of Android design will surface some interesting milestones, and some would say forks in the road, over Android's recent history. You will very likely see two terms of art crop up from any results from recent years. First, you will discover the term "Material Design," which is a styling and design philosophy Google introduced to the world in 2012 and which influences things like the default color palette, widget styling, and other design features in Android. The second term you'll encounter is "Android Jetpack," and you'll doubtlessly find commentary about it making design – including layouts – "easier," "better," and "new and different." Those claims are true, but they can lead to some confusion for a new developer. Am I using Jetpack? How do I even "get" Jetpack? And so on.

G. Allen, *Android for Absolute Beginners*, https://doi.org/10.1007/978-1-4842-6646-5_10

At the Google I/O developer conference in 2018, Google introduced Android Jetpack. Behind the headlines, it turns out that Jetpack is not something "different" per se, but rather a repacking of many disparate Android UI framework pieces and foundational elements and a revised and expanded approach to the Android Support Libraries. Jetpack is not a competing way of building things. Rather, Jetpack will filter through most of what you are doing, from referencing any library in the `androidx` namespace through managing backward compatibility and historic Android release support. In this way, you don't really "add" Jetpack to your design work. Instead, it implicitly and almost automatically steps in when you leverage features you would naturally reach for in building your application and using Android Studio to help you.

A quick view of what is considered under the auspices of Android Jetpack is provided by Google on the `android.com` website. The existing parts of Android placed under the Jetpack banner fall into four areas:

- Foundational components
- Architectural components
- Behavioral components
- UI components

Google provides the diagram shown in Figure 10-1 (source: android-developers.googleblog.com/2018/05/use-android-jetpack-to-accelerate-your.html) to demonstrate the specific parts of Android Jetpack in each of these four realms.

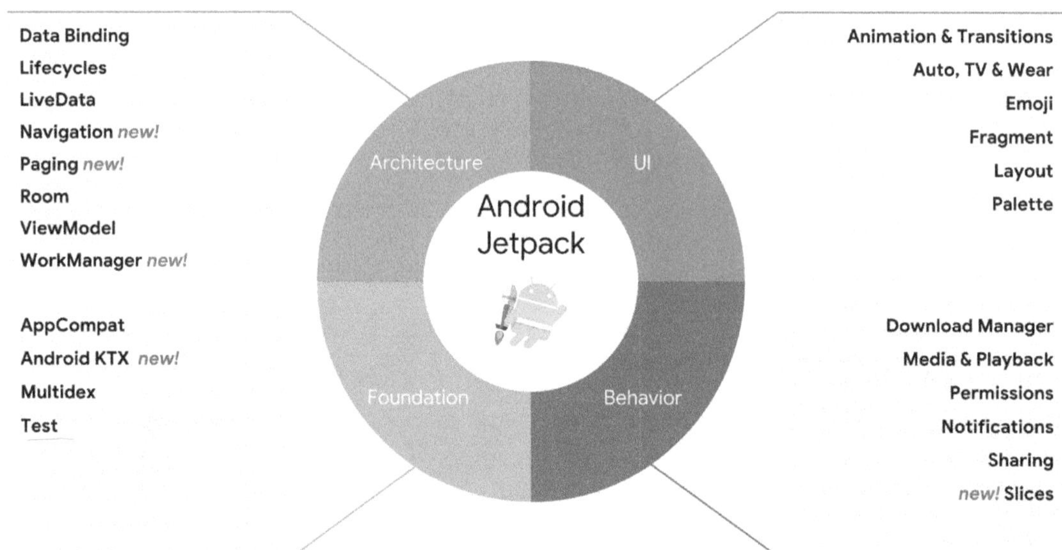

***Figure 10-1.** Understanding the Android Jetpack conceptual components*[1]

[1]Portions of this page are reproduced from work created and shared by the Android Open Source Project and used according to terms described in the Creative Commons 2.5 Attribution License. Source: `https://android-developers.googleblog.com/2018/05/use-android-jetpack-to-accelerate-your.html`

If you take one thing away from this section, it's that you needn't worry about asking yourself "Am I using Jetpack?" because you certainly are already! You may not be using all of the features and functional groups, but there's no need to try to do that.

Using Popular Layout Designs

We will cover the following major layout containers in the following sections:

- ConstraintLayout: The current default in Android for new projects, and part of Jetpack, where widgets are expressed with a minimal set of positioning constraints and no (or little) tree-style hierarchy.
- RelativeLayout: A default for many years following Android 4.0 until the introduction of Jetpack and `ConstraintLayout`, it uses a rules-guided approach for self-arranging UI elements.
- LinearLayout: The original default, commonly used in many early Android applications, this follows a traditional box model, imagining all widgets as boxes to fit within and around each other.

At the book's website, `www.beginningandroid.org`, you will also find extra material on other layouts Android offers, including

- TableLayout: A grid-like approach, similar to using an HTML table in web development.
- GridLayout: Deceptively similar to `TableLayout`, the `GridLayout` uses arbitrary-precision grid lines to split your display into successively more specific regions in which to house widgets.

After those topics, we'll turn to how to manipulate XML layouts from your Java code and embark on a modified version of the ButtonExample application to show how to find and work with your layouts in code.

> **Note** While we will spend lots of the chapter looking at XML for layouts, always remember that the Graphical Layout Editor has a design mode, letting you visually add widgets, place and arrange them, set relationships, and so forth. While you will likely always use a blend of both handwritten XML and the layout editor, it's worth jumping to the "other" one from time to time as you start favoring an approach. It's also a great way to learn more of the nuances of layout XML, by observing what Android Studio is doing in automatically generated XML when you use the Graphical Layout Editor.

Revisiting the Constraint Layout

You already got your hands dirty with very minimal `ConstraintLayout` designs in the earlier chapters, including your `MyFirstApp` and the many widget examples in Chapter 9. While you can continue to use `ConstraintLayout` as a simple container for widgets, providing constraint settings to Android so it can manage layout for you, there are more advanced features of ConstraintLayout that you should definitely know about and explore to take your activity design to higher levels.

There are a lot of very exciting features that ConstraintLayout offers, but I will flag three of the most recent and most useful.

Getting in the Flow

With the most recent updates to Android, ConstraintLayout has been expanded with an optional ability, to "flow" widgets on-screen in an activity as if pouring them across a screen and to wrap and shift widgets at runtime depending on the size and density of the interface of a given device.

In Flow parlance, you chain together sets of widgets in a virtual Flow layout that acts as a helper to the base ConstraintLayout. The Flow chaining of groups is specified in a <androidx.constraintlayout.helper.widget.Flow> element in your layout XML, and two key attributes then control Flow chaining and behavior.

The first attribute is the app:constraint_referenced_ids attribute, which takes a comma-separated string of widget IDs, instructing Android which parts of your interface are grouped into a specific virtual Flow layout.

The second attribute is app:flow_wrapMode, which takes one of three string values to instruct Android how to manage the flow of widgets in the Flow group. Possible values and related behavior for app:flow_wrapMode are as follows:

> none: Default approach – this creates a single logical chain of all the widgets in the group and overflows them if the widgets don't fit the dimension of the activity.
>
> chain: If an overflow occurs, add the overflowing widgets to a follow-on chain to contain them.
>
> align: Broadly similar to the chain approach, with the tweak that rows are aligned into columns.

Getting familiar with Flow options in ConstraintLayouts is very easy. Listing 10-1 shows the relevant layout XML file for the FlowExample project in Ch10/FlowExample.

***Listing 10-1.** Setting up Flow in your ConstraintLayout*

```
<?xml version="1.0" encoding="utf-8"?>
<androidx.constraintlayout.widget.ConstraintLayout
xmlns:android="http://schemas.android.com/apk/res/android"
    xmlns:app="http://schemas.android.com/apk/res-auto"
    xmlns:tools="http://schemas.android.com/tools"
    android:layout_width="match_parent"
    android:layout_height="match_parent"
    tools:context=".MainActivity">

    <TextView
        android:id="@+id/text1"
        android:layout_width="wrap_content"
```

```
        android:layout_height="wrap_content"
        android:text="Flow TextView 1"
        android:textSize="25dp"
        app:layout_constraintBottom_toBottomOf="parent"
        app:layout_constraintLeft_toLeftOf="parent"
        app:layout_constraintRight_toRightOf="parent"
        app:layout_constraintTop_toTopOf="parent" />

    <TextView
        android:id="@+id/text2"
        android:layout_width="wrap_content"
        android:layout_height="wrap_content"
        android:text="Flow TextView 2"
        android:textSize="25dp"
        app:layout_constraintBottom_toBottomOf="parent"
        app:layout_constraintHorizontal_bias="1.0"
        app:layout_constraintLeft_toLeftOf="parent"
        app:layout_constraintRight_toRightOf="parent"
        app:layout_constraintStart_toEndOf="@+id/text1"
        app:layout_constraintTop_toTopOf="parent"
        app:layout_constraintVertical_bias="0.499" />

    <TextView
        android:id="@+id/text3"
        android:layout_width="wrap_content"
        android:layout_height="wrap_content"
        android:text="Flow TextView 3"
        android:textSize="25dp"
        app:layout_constraintBottom_toBottomOf="parent"
        app:layout_constraintHorizontal_bias="1.0"
        app:layout_constraintLeft_toLeftOf="parent"
        app:layout_constraintRight_toRightOf="parent"
        app:layout_constraintStart_toEndOf="@+id/text2"
        app:layout_constraintTop_toTopOf="parent"
        app:layout_constraintVertical_bias="0.499" />

    <!-- Add/remove the androidx.constraintlayout.helper.widget.Flow spec to see Flow in
    action -->
    <androidx.constraintlayout.helper.widget.Flow
        android:layout_width="0dp"
        android:layout_height="wrap_content"
        app:layout_constraintStart_toStartOf="parent"
        app:layout_constraintEnd_toEndOf="parent"
        app:layout_constraintTop_toTopOf="parent"
        app:flow_wrapMode="chain"
        app:constraint_referenced_ids="text1, text2, text3"
        />

</androidx.constraintlayout.widget.ConstraintLayout>
```

The FlowExample layout is very straightforward. We have three TextViews, defined with constraints such that normally you would (attempt to) lay out with the text1 TextView first, then the text2 TextView to its right, and the text3 TextView to the right again of text2. I have deliberately chosen long text and large font size that make my point for me. At the bottom of the layout, you'll see the Flow defined in a <androidx.constraintlayout.helper.widget.Flow> element, where I specify my flow_wrapMode to chain and set the referenced IDs for the group to be "text1, text2, text3" – my TextView IDs.

If I omit the Flow virtual layout (see the comment in the XML layout that controls this), Android attempts to render the activity per the normal ConstraintLayout rules, with the result as seen in Figure 10-2.

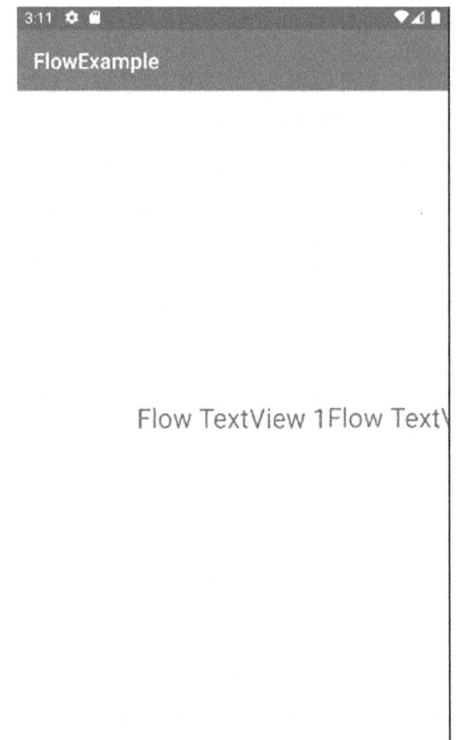

Figure 10-2. Without Flow, the ConstraintLayout renders widgets off-screen

You can see the problem straight away. I am deliberately using an AVD with a small virtual screen size. My text1 TextView rendered fine, and half of text2 made it onto the screen. But the rest of text2 is cut off, and text3 is nowhere to be seen. In reality, it is rendered, but not visible due to the layout having no way to adapt to the screen size with the layout lacking the Flow option. You can try running the example with the Flow element removed on a variety of AVDs with different screen sizes, to see how and where widgets get truncated or not displayed.

With the Flow element in place, rerunning the FlowExample application brings Flow's capabilities right to the fore. Figure 10-3 shows the same three TextViews, but this time with the Flow virtual layout power, Android has been able to follow the chain rule I specified and has flowed the widgets over to new rows to display everything in my layout specification.

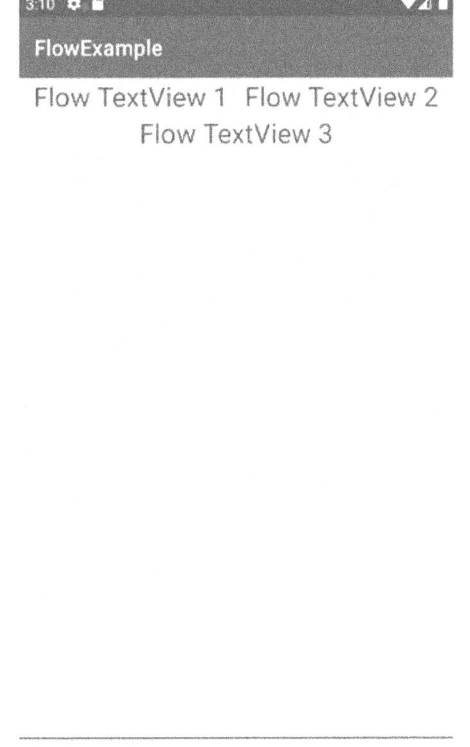

Figure 10-3. With Flow, the ConstraintLayout renders all

Flow is a super-easy new feature to master. You can take the FlowExample sample code and start adding more widgets, expand the Flow-referenced IDs set, and even change the flow_wrapMode, to see how Flow behaves.

Layering with Layer

Taking the ability to adapt widgets and views one step further is the Layer. The name Layer is very overloaded when it comes to interface design, so to be abundantly clear, a Layer does not directly lay out widgets or help build "stacks" of successive sets of UI components. A `ConstraintLayout` can be extended with a Layer to give you a single approach to rotate, translate, and scale a set of widgets and views with one mechanism.

As an example, you might be creating a graphical tile game and want to de-emphasize any picture tile a user isn't currently selecting. With a Layer, all other `ImageView` widgets could have the same layout change applied by having them added to a single Layer, and then the desired transformation could be applied once to the Layer, which it in turn would apply to its constituent widgets.

Moving with Motion

One much-heralded feature of the most recent releases of Android is the extension of `ConstraintLayout` known as MotionLayout. With `MotionLayout`, you can take boring, static views of any sort and build animated changes such as rotations, fade-in and fade-out, size changes, and more though defining and using `ConstraintSets`. Essentially, the constraints that describe how your widgets and views relate and position can themselves be treated as the variables that control motion and flow.

Building `MotionLayout`-based applications and the various `ConstraintSet` configurations they use can be very tedious to do by hand. With this tedium in mind, Google introduced the Motion Editor in Android Studio to give you an animation canvas with which to build compelling animated layouts.

To start using Motion and `MotionLayout` designs in the Motion Editor, Android introduced the `androidx.constraintlayout.motion.widget.MotionLayout` variant for `ConstraintLayout`. MotionLayout is still in its early days, with quite a few rough edges and manual steps required to set up and changes being made frequent with point releases of Android Studio. Layouts with motion effects also aren't best represented in a static book like this one.

So to ensure the most up-to-date walk-through of `MotionLayout` is available to you and that you have MotionLayout presented where you can see how the options play out in dynamic, moving layouts, a walk-through and `MotionExample` demo are available from the website at `www.beginningandroid.org`.

Using Relative Layouts

The `RelativeLayout` was a long-time default for Android and is still a very popular choice for activity and fragment design. As the term "Relative" implies, a `RelativeLayout` uses relationships between widgets, and the parent activity, to control the layout of widgets. The relativity concept is easy to grasp, for example, you can dictate that one widget is placed below another widget in relation to the relative's location or have its top edge align with a related widget and so on.

All of the relationship settings utilize a set of standardized attributes assigned to the widget XML definition in your layout XML file.

Placing Widgets Relative to the Parent Container

A good starting place for understanding `RelativeLayout` is to explore the attributes that allow you to position a widget relative to the parent. There are a core set of attributes you can use to anchor position based on a parent (e.g., activity) and its top edge, bottom edge, sides, and the like. These attributes include

- android:layout_alignParentTop: Aligns the widget's top edge with the top of the container.
- android:layout_alignParentBottom: Aligns the widget's bottom edge with the bottom of the container.

- android:layout_alignParentStart: Aligns the widget's start side with the left side of the container, used when taking account of right-to-left and left-to-right written scripts. For instance, in a US English left-to-right layout, this would control the widget's left-hand side.
- android:layout_alignParentEnd: Aligns the widget's end side with the left side of the container, used when taking account of right-to-left and left-to-right written scripts.
- android:layout_centerHorizontal: Positions the widget horizontally at the center of the container.
- android:layout_centerVertical: Positions the widget vertically at the center of the container. If you'd like both horizontal and vertical centering, you can use the combined layout_centerInParent.

When determining the final position of an edge for a widget, various other attributes are taken into account, including padding and margin widths. Be careful to allow for these if you delve into pixel-precise relative positioning.

Controlling Relative Layout Properties with IDs

The key to properly referring to widgets for `RelativeLayout` purposes is to use the identity of the referred widget, which you have already encountered: this is the `android:id` identifier of the widget in question. For example, in the `ButtonExample` project from earlier chapters, the button has the identifier `@+id/button`.

To further control the layout of widgets and describe their relative position to other widgets in the layout, you will need to provide the identity of the widget in the layout container. This is done by using the `android:id` identifier attribute on any widget that you want to refer to.

The first time you reference an `android:id` value, ensure you use the plus modifier (e.g., `@+id/button`). Any further references to the same identifier (widget) can omit the plus sign. Using the plus sign in the first reference to an identifier helps the Android linting tools detect identifier mismatches, where you have not correctly named a widget in a layout file. Think of this as the equivalent to declaring variables before using them.

With an id in place, our preceding example `@+id/button` could now be referenced by another widget, such as another button like `button2`, through the mechanism of referring to that id string in its own layout-related properties.

Note simplistic names like `button`, `button1`, and `button2` are fine for examples like these, but you will very much want to use meaningful widget identifiers and names in your applications.

Relative Positioning Properties

Now that you have a firm understanding of the mechanics of identifiers, you can appreciate the use of these six properties to control the position of widgets relative to each other:

- android:layout_above: Used to place a UI widget above the widget referenced in the property
- android:layout_below: Used to place a UI widget below the widget referenced in the property

- android:layout_toStartOf: Used to indicate the end edge of this widget should be placed at the start edge of the widget referenced in the property
- android:layout_toEndOf: Used to indicate the start edge of this widget should be placed at the end edge of the widget referenced in the property
- android:layout_toLeftOf: Used to place a UI widget left of the widget referenced in the property
- android:layout_toRightOf: Used to place a UI widget right of the widget referenced in the property

More subtly, you can also use one of numerous other properties to control the alignment of a widget in comparison to another. Some of these properties include

- android:layout_alignStart: Flags that the widget's starting edge should be aligned with the start of the widget referenced in the property
- android:layout_alignEnd: Flags that the widget's ending edge should be aligned with the end of the widget referenced in the property
- android:layout_alignBaseline: Flags that the baseline of any text, regardless of borders or padding, of the two widgets should be aligned (see in the following)
- android:layout_alignTop: Flags that the top of the widget should be aligned with the top of the widget referenced in the property
- android:layout_alignBottom: Flags that the bottom of the widget should be aligned with the bottom of the referenced widget in the property

Working with a RelativeLayout Example

You have enough coverage of the abilities and behaviors of RelativeLayout to dive into a working example. Listing 10-2 provides the layout XML using RelativeLayout from the `ch10/RelativeLayoutExample` project.

***Listing 10-2.** The XML layout for the RelativeLayoutExample application*

```
<?xml version="1.0" encoding="utf-8"?>
<RelativeLayout xmlns:android="http://schemas.android.com/apk/res/android"
    xmlns:app="http://schemas.android.com/apk/res-auto"
    xmlns:tools="http://schemas.android.com/tools"
    android:layout_width="match_parent"
    android:layout_height="match_parent"
    tools:context=".MainActivity">

    <TextView android:id="@+id/label"
        android:layout_width="wrap_content"
        android:layout_height="wrap_content"
```

```
        android:text="URL:"
        android:layout_alignBaseline="@+id/entry"
        android:layout_alignParentLeft="true"/>
    <EditText
        android:id="@id/entry"
        android:layout_width="match_parent"
        android:layout_height="wrap_content"
        android:layout_toRightOf="@id/label"
        android:layout_alignParentTop="true"/>
    <Button
        android:id="@+id/ok"
        android:layout_width="wrap_content"
        android:layout_height="wrap_content"
        android:layout_below="@id/entry"
        android:layout_alignRight="@id/entry"
        android:text="OK" />
    <Button
        android:id="@+id/cancel"
        android:layout_width="wrap_content"
        android:layout_height="wrap_content"
        android:layout_toLeftOf="@id/ok"
        android:layout_alignTop="@id/ok"
        android:text="Cancel" />

</RelativeLayout>
```

In this RelativeLayoutExample layout, we are building on your learning from earlier chapters to provide a richer understanding. To begin, you see the root element is <RelativeLayout>, which is the determining factor that this activity will use the RelativeLayout approach to layout and placement. On top of the normal boilerplate XML namespace attributes, three other attributes are introduced.

To ensure the RelativeLayout spans the entire width available on whatever sized screen is in use, the android:layout_width="match_parent" attribute is used. We can do the same for the height, but we can also tell the RelativeLayout to only use as much vertical space as is required to enclose the contained widgets – thus the use of the android:layout_height="wrap_content" attribute.

Leaning on the widgets we introduced in Chapter 9, we introduce four pieces for our activity: a TextView to act as our label, an EditText for our editable field, and the buttons OK and Cancel.

For the TextView label, the layout directs Android to place its left edge in alignment with the left edge of the parent RelativeLayout, using android:layout_alignParentLeft="true". We also want the TextView to have its baseline automatically managed once we've introduced the adjacent EditText, so we invoke the pixel-nudging perfection using android:layout_alignBaseline="@+id/entry". Note that we introduce the id with a plus sign because we haven't yet described the EditText, so we need to forewarn of its impending existence.

With the EditText, we would like this to sit to the right of the label and itself sit at the top of the layout consuming all the remaining space to the right of the TextView. We instruct it to lay out to the right using android:layout_toRightOf="@id/label" (which was already introduced, so no need to add the plus notation). We force the EditText to sit as high as possible in the remaining space of the RelativeLayout using android:layout_alignParentTop="true" and take the remaining space on the canvas to the right of the TextView by using android:layout_width="match_parent". This works because we know we also asked the parent to use the maximum available remaining space for width.

Finally, we tie the position of our two buttons to the widgets introduced earlier. We want OK placed below the EditText and aligned with its right side, so give it the attributes android:layout_below="@id/entry" and android:layout_alignRight="@id/entry". We then tell Android to place the Cancel button to the right of the OK button with the tops of the buttons in alignment, using android:layout_toLeft="@id/ok" and android:layout_alignTop="@id/ok".

Figure 10-4 shows our layout in action after we make these layout changes to a vanilla new Empty Activity project.

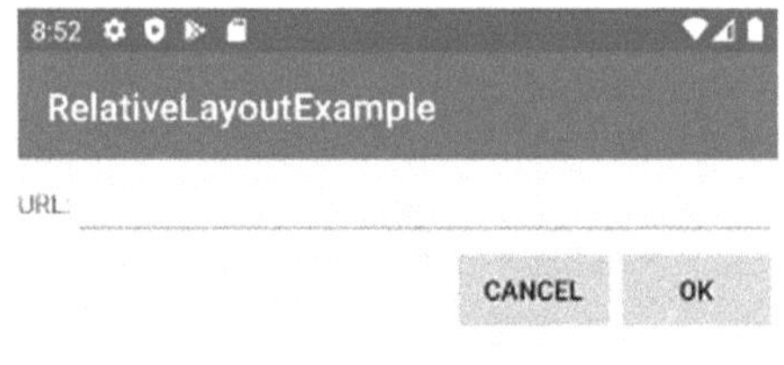

Figure 10-4. RelativeLayout in action

Overlapping Widgets in Relative Layouts

Each layout supported by Android provides you with specialized and unique features, and RelativeLayout is armed with some key capabilities, including the ability to have widgets overlap each other or appear as if one is in front of, or overlapping, another. This is achieved by Android tracking the child elements from the XML definition and applying a layer for each individual child element in the layout. This means that items defined later in the layout XML file will sit on top of older/earlier items if they use the same space within the UI.

There's nothing like seeing this in action to understand what this looks like and how this might help you in your application design. Figure 10-5 shows a layout with two buttons declared, the second of which will sit in front of, or over, the first.

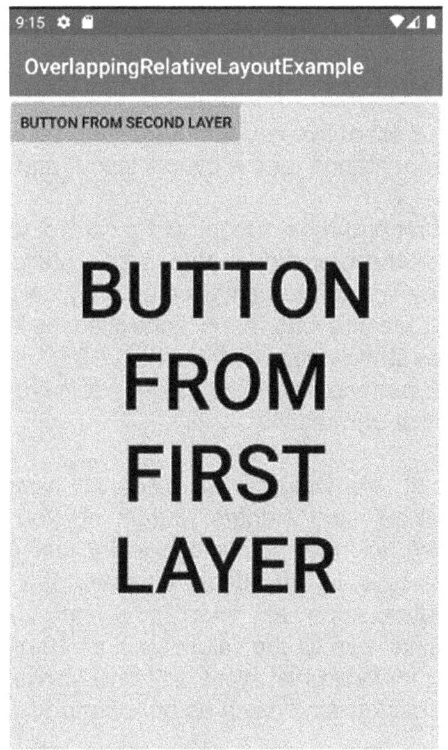

***Figure 10-5.** RelativeLayout's overlapping features in action*

The sky is the limit in terms of what types of widgets, and how many, you might want to overlay. You might also be wondering why anyone would want to overlay items in this way. As well as targeting some eccentric layout ideas, the overlapping possibility with RelativeLayout means it is possible to have widgets on-screen but unseen, still contributing to activity behavior.

Lining Up with Linear Layouts

There are times when designing layouts where you don't need or want the sophistication of constrained or relative widget positioning and instead you just want to rely on some of the age-old tested approaches to layout. Anyone familiar with the history of graphics design or interface design will have heard of the box model, where all the items (or widgets) that compose an interface are considered as elements that fall into rows and columns. The `LinearLayout` follows this model and was the original default used by early versions of Android. It may no longer be the layout of the day, but you can always rely on `LinearLayout` to be supported as a straightforward option for tweaking how your widgets are boxed, nested, and so on. What `LinearLayout` lacks is some of the clever, time-saving, or useful features we've talked about in ConstraintLayout and RelativeLayout, but at times simple solutions are all that's really required.

Mastering the Five Main Qualifiers for LinearLayout

When using a LinearLayout, a set of five key attributes help you control pretty much all aspects of placement and appearance for the overall layout and any contained widgets:

Orientation: The first and most fundamental control for a `LinearLayout` is to determine whether the box model should be considered one that is filled horizontally, line by line, or vertically, column by column. This is known as orientation for a `LinearLayout`, as is controlled by the android:orientation attribute, and takes string values of either `HORIZONTAL` or `VERTICAL`. Orientation can also be set at runtime from your Java code, with the `setOrientation()` method using similar parameters.

Margins: By default, any widgets you place will have no buffer or spacing between them and adjacent widgets. Margin lets you control this and add a buffer (or margin, as the name suggests) using attributes such as `android:layout_margin`, which affects all sides of a widget, or one of the one-sided attributes such as `android:layout_marginTop`. Any margin attribute takes a pixel size as the value, such as 10 dip. This is conceptually similar to padding for `RelativeLayout`, but only applies when the widget has a nontransparent background (such as on a button).

Fill method: We have already introduced the notions of `wrap_content` and `match_parent` for `RelativeLayout`. In the `LinearLayout` approach, all widgets must have specified a fill method, via the attributes `android:layout_width` and `android:layout_height`. These can take one of three values: `wrap_content`, which as per your earlier understanding instructs the widget to be only as large as needed to accommodate the text or image content; `match_parent`, taking the maximum amount of space the parent makes available; or a specific pixel value, measured in device-independent pixels, such as 125 dip.

Weight: When two or more widgets in a `LinearLayout` both specify `match_parent`, which one wins? How can they both take the maximum space the parent provides? The answer is the `android:layout_weight` attribute, which allows you apply a simple number value to each widget, for example, 1, 2, 3, 4, and so on. Android will sum all of the weights present in the LinearLayout and then provide UI space to a widget based on its fraction of the total weights of all widgets in the layout. So, for instance, if we have two TextViews both configured to match_parent, with android:layout_weight of 5 for the first TextView and 10 for the second TextView, then the first button will get one-third of the available space (5/(5+10)), and the second button will get two-thirds. There are some further methods for setting weights, but none are as intuitive as the android:layout_weight approach.

Gravity: When using a LinearLayout, the default layout approach Android takes is to align all widgets from the left if using HORIZONTAL orientation and all widgets from the top if using VERTICAL orientation. From time to time, you might want to override this behavior to force a bottom-up or right-sided bias to your layout. The XML attribute android:layout_gravity allows you to control the behavior, as does the method setGravity() at runtime. Acceptable values for VERTICAL orientation for android:layout_gravity are left, center_horizontal, and right. For HORIZONTAL orientation, Android will default to aligning with respect to the invisible base of the text of your widgets. Use the value center_vertical to have Android use the notional center of the widget instead.

A LinearLayout Example

Reviewing the theory of LinearLayouts is somewhat overwhelming to begin with, so it makes sense to start exploring some of the concepts to help build an intuitive grasp of how, when, and where to work with the key LinearLayout levers.

All of the LinearLayout options can be daunting when thinking in purely theoretical terms. The dynamic example in Listing 10-3 shows how many of these options work.

***Listing 10-3.** Demonstrating the options provided by LinearLayout*

```
<?xml version="1.0" encoding="utf-8"?>
<LinearLayout xmlns:android="http://schemas.android.com/apk/res/android"
    xmlns:app="http://schemas.android.com/apk/res-auto"
    xmlns:tools="http://schemas.android.com/tools"
    android:layout_width="match_parent"
    android:layout_height="match_parent"
    tools:context=".MainActivity">

    <RadioGroup
        android:id="@+id/orientation"
        android:orientation="horizontal"
        android:layout_width="wrap_content"
        android:layout_height="wrap_content"
        android:padding="5dip">
        <RadioButton android:id="@+id/horizontal"
            android:text="horizontal"/>
```

```
        <RadioButton android:id="@+id/vertical"
            android:text="vertical"/>
    </RadioGroup>
    <RadioGroup
        android:id="@+id/gravity"
        android:orientation="vertical"
        android:layout_width="fill_parent"
        android:layout_height="wrap_content"
        android:padding="5dip">
        <RadioButton android:id="@+id/left"
            android:text="left"/>
        <RadioButton android:id="@+id/center"
            android:text="center"/>
        <RadioButton android:id="@+id/right"
            android:text="right"/>
    </RadioGroup>
</LinearLayout>
```

The example uses two straightforward building blocks to help us with understanding orientation and gravity. I have defined two separate RadioGroup widgets, such that the first has a set of RadioButtons to control orientation and the other a set of RadioButtons to control gravity. To give us a starting point, we use the XML definition for vertical orientation by choosing android:orientation="vertical", which will place the RadioGroups one above the other and the RadioButtons within them in vertical fashion as well.

I then override the vertical stacking of the two radio buttons in the initial RadioGroup, switching them to horizontal layout using android:orientation="horizontal". While I wanted to inherit the other attributes from the parent RadioGroup, I flexed the ability to override specific attributes in the child RadioButtons. Lastly, we set padding around all of our widgets of 5 dip and set the wrap_content option.

Running this example code with no supporting Java logic – just the layout – shows these initial settings in action, although there's no other behavior yet to change what you see, but that will follow in a moment. The layout is shown in Figure 10-6.

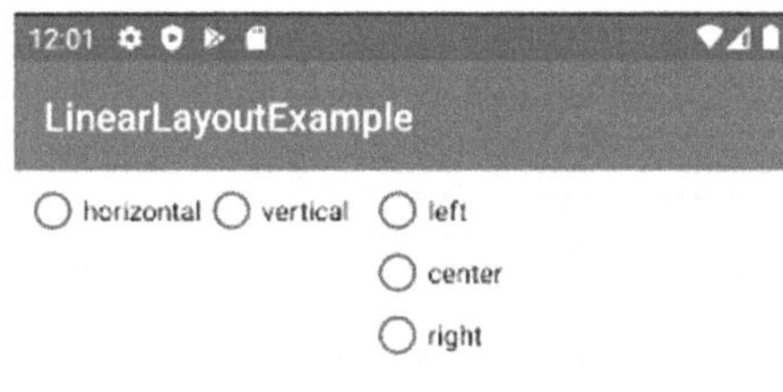

Figure 10-6. Setting up the orientation and gravity examples

It's nice to see the layout rendered, but really it would be better to get some Java logic written to actually alter the orientation and gravity in accordance with the radio button settings. That's exactly what Listing 10-4 shows.

Listing 10-4. Java logic to implement orientation and gravity changes based on UI selection

```
package org.beginningandroid.linearlayoutexample;

import androidx.appcompat.app.AppCompatActivity;
import android.os.Bundle;
import android.view.Gravity;
import android.widget.LinearLayout;
import android.widget.RadioGroup;

public class MainActivity extends AppCompatActivity implements RadioGroup.OnCheckedChange
Listener {
    RadioGroup orientation;
    RadioGroup gravity;

    @Override
    protected void onCreate(Bundle savedInstanceState) {
        super.onCreate(savedInstanceState);
        setContentView(R.layout.activity_main);
```

```
        orientation=(RadioGroup)findViewById(R.id.orientation);
        orientation.setOnCheckedChangeListener(this);
        gravity=(RadioGroup)findViewById(R.id.gravity);
        gravity.setOnCheckedChangeListener(this);
    }

    public void onCheckedChanged(RadioGroup group, int checkedId) {
        switch (checkedId) {
            case R.id.horizontal:
                orientation.setOrientation(LinearLayout.HORIZONTAL);
                break;

            case R.id.vertical:
                orientation.setOrientation(LinearLayout.VERTICAL);
                break;

            case R.id.left:
                gravity.setGravity(Gravity.LEFT);
                break;

            case R.id.center:
                gravity.setGravity(Gravity.CENTER_HORIZONTAL);
                break;

            case R.id.right:
                gravity.setGravity(Gravity.RIGHT);
                break;
        }
    }
}
```

Understanding what the Java code is doing is very easy. To begin, during the application's `onCreate()` call, we register listeners for clicks on either `RadioGroup` using `setOnCheckedChangedListener()`. We implement `OnCheckedChangeListener` in the activity, which means the activity itself becomes the listener.

When you click any of the `RadioButtons`, the listener triggers the callback `onCheckChanged()`. In the definition for that callback method, we determine which `RadioButton` was clicked of the five rendered. Once we know which `RadioButton` it was, our logic calls either `setOrientation()` to toggle from vertical to horizontal layout flow or `setGravity()` to the relevant left, right, or center gravity value. Two of the six possible outcomes are shown in Figures 10-7 and 10-8.

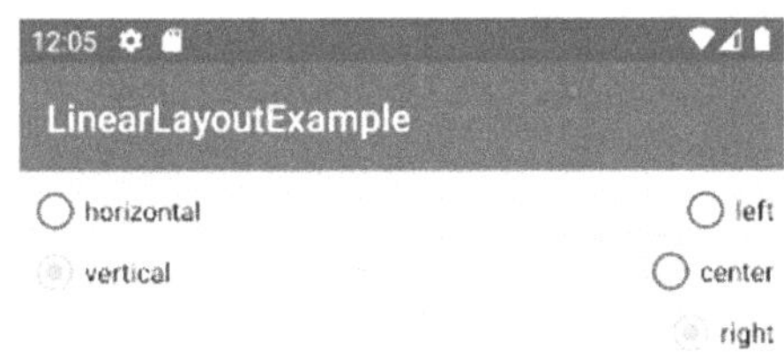

Figure 10-7. Up, down, and all around with orientation and gravity

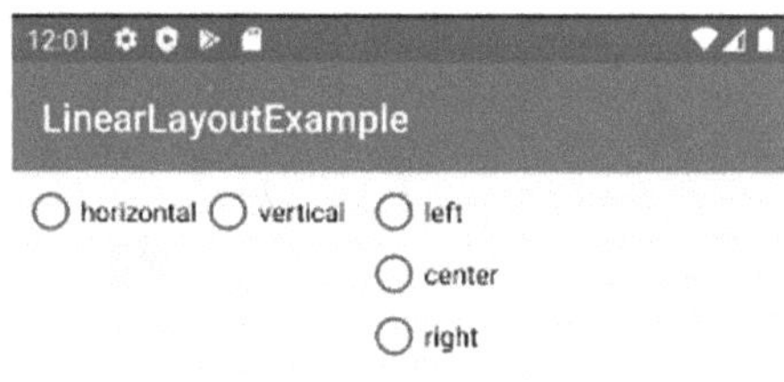

Figure 10-8. Another orientation and gravity example

Even More Layout Options

There are a range of further layout types available with Android, many of which have risen and fallen in popularity with successive Android releases. Here are the main ones to know about – further examples for these layouts are available from the website at `www.beginningandroid.org`.

Table Layouts

Back in the early days of the Internet, web page designers often used the humble HTML table to place content on a page. While web design has leapt forward, the concepts of table-based layout are still useful, and Android adopted them in the `TableLayout` container.

Just as with HTML, `TableLayout` in Android is quick to use and relies on the notion that a `TableLayout` has `TableRow` child elements to control size, placement, and more. One more similarity with the old HTML approach for web pages is that the high-fidelity precision is hard to perfect.

Grid Layouts

If the idea of TableLayout has your imagination racing, then you will love GridLayout. A close cousin to TableLayout, GridLayout places its children widgets and UI elements onto a grid of infinitely detailed lines, which separate the area rendered by your activity into cells. The secret to GridLayout's precise control is that the number of cells, or grid lines used to describe the cells, has no limit or threshold. Simply add more grid lines to carve up your UI into ever-finer subcells for placing widgets.

Mastering XML-Based Layouts with Java Logic: The Best of Both Worlds!

As you become more familiar with XML layouts and Java-managed layouts, you will eventually realize you can have the best of both worlds and that you can always change your mind. You might prefer to prototype in XML and reach for the Graphical Layout Editor, or you could prefer to try really nuanced runtime layout selections using Java. Regardless of the approach, you can at any time change your mind with a bit of code or tweaked XML. To illustrate, Listing 10-5 lists the counting Button code from your ButtonExample application, converted into an XML layout file. You can find this code in the Ch10/ButtonAgain sample project.

***Listing 10-5.** Flexing XML layouts and controlling them with Java logic*

```
<?xml version="1.0" encoding="utf-8"?>
<androidx.constraintlayout.widget.ConstraintLayout
xmlns:android="http://schemas.android.com/apk/res/android"
    xmlns:app="http://schemas.android.com/apk/res-auto"
    xmlns:tools="http://schemas.android.com/tools"
    android:layout_width="match_parent"
    android:layout_height="match_parent"
    tools:context=".MainActivity">

    <Button
        android:id="@+id/button"
        android:layout_width="fill_parent"
        android:layout_height="fill_parent"
        android:layout_alignParentBottom="true"
        android:layout_alignParentLeft="true"
        android:layout_alignParentRight="true"
        android:layout_alignParentTop="true"
        android:text="" />

</androidx.constraintlayout.widget.ConstraintLayout>
```

In Listing 10-5, you should spot the XML equivalents of the pieces we put together for the ButtonExample application, including the following:

- Setting ConstraintLayout to be the root element
- Defining the button that acts as the clicker and counter display and assigning an android:id so the we can reference it from our code and perform our click counting in Java
- androind:layout_alignParentBottom, androind:layout_alignParentTop, androind:layout_alignParentLeft, and androind:layout_alignParentRight, each contributing to the "parental" alignment of the button
- android:layout_width and android:layout_heigh, setting the button to consume the entire screen, as we did with ButtonExample
- android:text, the text to be displayed on the button, which initially will be the empty string

While this is a very simple example to convert to XML, the core concepts are what's important, and they stay the same. More complex examples will have multiple widgets expressed in XML and sublayouts and branches to control complexity. As I tend to lean to XML-based layouts, you will see plenty more of these throughout the latter half of the book.

Connecting XML Layout Definition in Java Code

As you embrace the XML layout approach and start polishing widget positioning and more, a very important question crops up: How does one determine from within Java logic which layout to use – even if we only have one layout for our activity? The solution is based on a single method call designed exactly for this purpose, which is typically invoked in your activity's `onCreate()` callback, to make the perfect marriage between Java and XML: the `setContentView()` method.

The redux of the `ButtonExample` application has its layout in the normal default location in `res/layout/activity_main.xml`, though the technique works regardless of custom naming for your activity XML files. To complete the hookup from your code to your layout, invoke `setContentView()` like this:

```
setContentView(R.layout.activity_main);
```

If you look at the original version of `ButtonExample`, you will note that `setContentView()` was called there as well. So what has changed? In `ButtonAgain`, we are passing a reference to the XML-based view we've defined, based on the AAPT utility built into Android Studio having parsed your XML and generated the `R` Java class for you. You benefit from the `R` class in being able to make simple code references to the XML layout and parts within it. It does not matter how many layouts you have nor how complex they are, AAPT will package them all into an omnibus Java class and make them available in the `R.layout` namespace. You reference any layout using the calling convention `R.layout.<your_layout_file_name_without_the_XML_extention>`.

To find widgets within a layout returned by `setContentView()`, you invoke the `findViewById()` method and pass it the numeric reference for your widget. Read that sentence again, and you will spot the "gotcha." What do I mean by numeric reference? There's been no XML visible that claims to be a numeric identifier or reference for widgets. This is a mystery easily solved.

At packaging time, AAPT will identify each widget you have in your layout(s) and assign them an ID number and include it as member data in the `R.java` file. Check for yourself by opening the `R.java` file any time you like. But don't bother trying to memorize things this way. You can have Android resolve the ID number for any widget you want to reference using the `R.id.<widget_android:id_value>` parameter. You can use this to resolve the ID for any widget subclassed from the base View class (which is pretty much everything).

With the mechanics out of the way, you should be able to see the tremendous power you get from a combination of AAPT packaging things neatly into `R.java` based on your layouts and the `setContentView()` and `findViewById()` methods. For instance, different activities can be passed different instances of a `View`, and more intriguingly, you could change the `View` based on some program logic, enabling you to, for instance, use a different layout when you detect a different style of device.

Revisiting MyFirstApp via ButtonAgain

In the original `ButtonExample` example, the button's display would show the number of times the button had been pressed. The counter began at 1 for when the button was loaded via `onCreate()`. The majority of the existing logic, such as the code for counting clicks, still works in our modified `ButtonAgain` version. The main difference from the `ButtonExample` code is shown in Listing 10-6, where we substitute the previous Java calls in our activity's `onCreate()` method with the definition from the `ButtonAgain` app XML `ConstraintLayout` layout.

***Listing 10-6.** ButtonAgain Java code, linking seamlessly to the layout XML*

```
package org.beginningandroid.buttonagain;

import androidx.appcompat.app.AppCompatActivity;
import android.os.Bundle;
import android.app.Activity;
import android.view.View;
import android.widget.Button;

public class MainActivity extends AppCompatActivity implements View.OnClickListener{

    Button myButton;
    Integer myInt;

    @Override
    protected void onCreate(Bundle savedInstanceState) {
        super.onCreate(savedInstanceState);
        setContentView(R.layout.activity_main);
        myButton=(Button)findViewById(R.id.button);
```

```
        myButton.setOnClickListener(this);
        myInt = 0;
        updateClickCounter();
    }

    public void onClick(View view) {
        updateClickCounter();
    }

    private void updateClickCounter() {
        myInt++;
        myButton.setText(myInt.toString());
    }
}
```

You can now see the changes clearly, by reviewing the `onCreate()` method. First, we use `setContentView()` to the automatically generated `R` Java class for our specified XML layout. Then we use the `findViewById()` method, asking it to find the widget that has the `android:id` value of "`button`". We are returned the reference we need in programmatically driving the button's behavior, including changing its label to reflect our calculated click counter value.

Putting all of the code and XML together results in a `ButtonAgain` application that looks and acts surprisingly similar to the ButtonExample application, as shown in Figure 10-9.

***Figure 10-9.** The ButtonAgain application, combining Java logic and XML layout perfectly*

Summary

With a whirlwind tour of layouts and some of their features complete, you should now be imagining where you might start using some of the containers and layout styles in this chapter. You can also play the game of "guess what layout style your favorite app uses." This isn't the end of our layout journey, and we will revisit more concepts throughout the remainder of the book.

Chapter 11

Understanding Activities

Your introduction to activities up until now has been focused primarily on using them as a vessel in which to learn about UI widgets and layouts, in the knowledge that they are computationally "cheap," the fundamental building block of Android UIs, and designed so that you can make and use as many as you like in your applications in full knowledge that Android the operating system will happily reclaim resources and keep your activities manageable.

That's all well to say in theory, but what about some practice? In this chapter, we'll delve into "how" Android manages activities through the activity lifecycle, experiment with the various phases of activity life, and then expand your baseline for constructing compelling user interfaces by introducing the activity's partner in crime, fragments. You can think of fragments as the compositing technique used to decide when and how to leverage different combinations of activities and activity components for larger screens, or screens with extremes of dimensions.

Delving into the Android Activity Lifecycle

All of the examples in the book so far have used one activity, even though you've read multiple times now that your application can have as many as you like. Regardless of how many activities you have, each one's use is governed by a lifecycle, wherein activities are selected to run; are created, used, paused, and/or resumed; and are ultimately stopped and disposed of. With a plain English description of the stages of the lifecycle helping you appreciate what's going on, let's look at the actual technical aspects of lifecycle states and the callback methods Android uses to trigger state transitions. Figure 11-1 shows the big picture of these lifecycle states and accompanying callback methods.

G. Allen, *Android for Absolute Beginners*, https://doi.org/10.1007/978-1-4842-6646-5_11

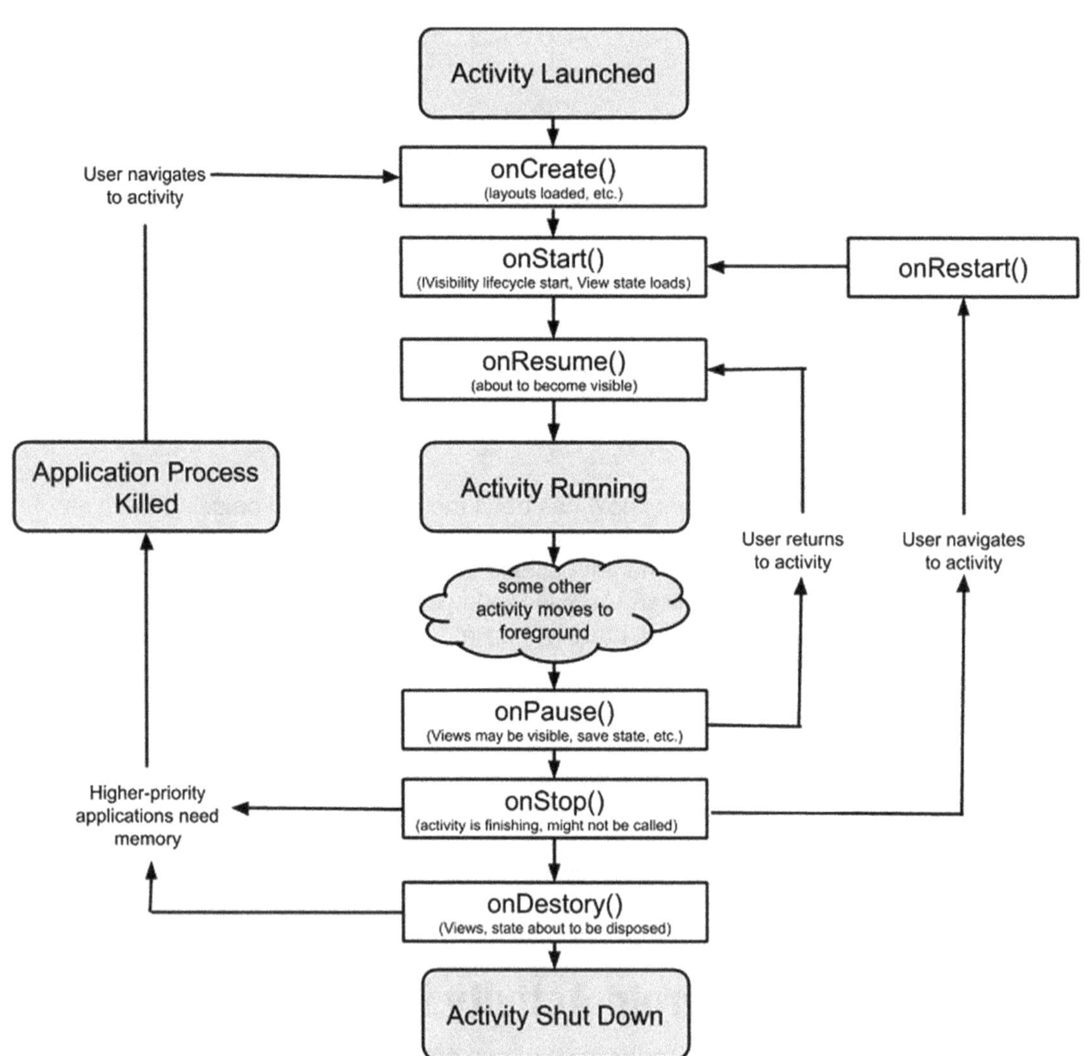

***Figure 11-1.** The Android activity lifecycle with callback transition methods*

An application typically exists in one of four main states:

- Launched: The initial state of an application once some action – usually, a user triggering it – has instructed the Android operating system to run said application.
- Running: The first moment (and ongoing state) at which a user sees your application and can interact with it. Typically this is after a range of preparatory steps have been conducted after launch.
- Killed: The state an app moves to after the Android operating system is signaled with the notification that the application is no longer needed, either because a user closed it or some resource-induced reaping has occurred.

- Shutdown (and, implicitly, any app not in the Launched, Running, or Killed state): The final state in which all persistent data, view hierarchy, cached data, and so on are expunged from the operating system's memory.

Each of those states is quite self-explanatory. What gets an application to move between states is where the fun begins, in the realm of lifecycle callback methods.

Understanding Activity Lifecycle Callback Methods

Each of the lifecycle methods shown in Figure 11-1 comes with specific behaviors and uses with which you should become familiar. You might not need to suddenly start adding custom logic to these lifecycle stages for your applications straight away, but knowing where to add things will set you up for rapid advancement as an Android developer in the future. We will step through each method one at a time, to highlight their specific uses.

Each of the methods has common characteristics with the others, such as the near-universal use of the respective parent class' equivalent method as the first action when any of the callback methods is invoked. For example, you see in earlier examples in the book the first act of the `onCreate()` method is to call `super.onCreate()`, which invokes the parent's version. There are exceptions when you don't want to automatically have the parent called, but I will flag those cases as we encounter them. For now, assume a default good behavior is to follow the "parent calling" practice.

onCreate()

Every activity starts life in the `onCreate()` method. Whether your user has tapped the icon on the Android home screen to start your application or a configuration change has triggered the need to recreate the display, `onCreate()` is called. The method takes a Bundle object to account for these later cases of recreation, as the Bundle will be the store of any previous state, data, and resources that are needed to bring the activity to life – collectively known as instance state.

You should consider the following actions for any `onCreate()` method for your activities:

- Load into the content view all of the layouts you plan to use, so that Android can create the UI prior to displaying it when the onStart() method is called.
- Initialize any activity-level variables you have defined within the activity class definition.

You might also need to do any work to use global resources or variables you might have created as part of your application. We will return to this topic of global resources shortly when we discuss `onRetainNonConfigurationInstance()` and also explore more example uses when we cover preferences later in this chapter and the remainder of the book.

onStart()

The work of `onStart()` begins once `onCreate()` has completed the task of building all the objects from your layout definitions, along with any other initialization work. It is the job of `onStart()` to actually render the resulting UI to the user on-screen. The `onStart()` method is also called on the path following `onRestart()` in the preceding lifecycle model.

There are not many cases where you will need to override `onStart()` and provide your own logic. Even if you are tempted to, you need to be aware that if your activity is following the `onRestart()` path, instance state is still not fully restored at this point and won't be until the subsequent call to `onRestoreInstanceState()` is made.

One corner case where implementing your own `onStart()` override is useful is when you have some custom resource that is long-lived, that you have cleanly frozen or paused based on your activity going out of view – being a good citizen and not using resources when you don't have to. Should you choose to set up such resource management, then the `onStart()` method would be where you would resume or defrost such a custom resource. Be sure to call the `super.onStart()` method to invoke the parent's equivalent, even if you know there is no override code in the parent. Android itself still needs to do its own internal work in this case.

onRestoreInstanceState()

If a user ends an activity, either by using the back button or via some other path that shifts them from your activity to another, they have signaled that they are finished with the original activity and all of the state associated with it. This would indicate to you, as the application developer, that you can also dispense with the activity, other than any long-lived resources you need to maintain. When Android itself terminates an activity, the circumstances are usually different. Primarily, Android terminates an activity due to a configuration change, and it does need to concern itself with what is needed to recreate the activity to meet the user's needs. That means recreating not just the visual display of the activity, but all of its instance state.

You might want to perform any custom instance state recovery here, and remember that instance state is not the same as long-term storage. Other mechanisms exist to handle that, including preferences, which we will cover later in the book. Where you want to persist more complex or larger types of data than those for which the preference system is designed, then fundamental computing concepts such as files and databases are the best approach, and we will cover those in Chapter 18.

onResume()

The `onResume()` method is the moment of truth when it comes to Android UIs. The `onResume()` method is the key method that makes the fully rendered and inflated layout visible, shifting all of the accumulated objects, logic, and so forth into the foreground. Together with `onPause()`, the transitions to and from foreground will trigger multiple times in the life of your activity, as other activities and applications preempt it, jump to focus, are closed by the user, and so on.

The only logic you should normally consider adding to `onResume()` is related to the real-time visual aspects changing your activity, including

- Animation
- Video
- Custom view transition effects

In all other respects, you should avoid any other custom logic in `onResume()`.

onPause()

Android is designed from the ground up to support many applications running simultaneously and relies on applications being able to simply and easily pause their activity in order to free resources for other activities that the user has decided to use. To support this, applications will frequently move from foreground state to background state. Immediately prior to this, the `onPause()` method will be called.

The most important tasks to consider during the `onPause()` call include saving any state not yet placed in the Bundle for your activity and taking care of any custom animation, video, audio, or other real-time aspects of your logic. Additionally, the `onPause()` call also acts as the threshold past which Android can unilaterally terminate your activity and reclaim its resources. This means that once the `onPause()` call exits, there is no guarantee your process and activity will ever receive an event again – so save what you need and don't assume your activity state persists without your intervention beyond this point.

onStop()

If `onStart()` governs activities moving to the foreground, you can think of `onStop()` as the reverse: in charge of shifting your activity to the background. After `onStop()` completes, your activity is no longer visible, even though the related view hierarchy and properties remain intact.

Under Android's zealous resource management approach, you should always keep in mind that `onStop()` may never be called for your activity, so it isn't wise to rely on custom logic here. The one area where you might consider overriding the default is for any interaction with an Android service where foreground interactivity is not normally required anyway.

onSaveInstanceState()

Both the name of the `onSaveInstanceState()` method and its position in the lifecycle diagram in Figure 11-1 give a very good indication of its purpose. The role of this method is to save activity state for any activity that is about to be destroyed by the `onDestroy()` method, thus avoiding the situation where a user finds important state has gone missing without them realizing their activity has potentially ended and been recreated. This happens frequently under any configuration change event, so the experience for users needs to make this transparent and automatic.

> **Note** There is a trend to start favoring the concept of a `ViewModel` and to save any transient state using that technique. However, the `onSaveInstanceState()` method is still fully supported. You can read more about ViewModel at `developer.android.com`.

onRestart()

The `onRestart()` method is called each time an activity moves from the stopped state to the started state. The method gives you the flexibility to handle freshly started versions of your activity differently from those that were stopped and have now restarted, such as by having a preserved view hierarchy in the restarted case that you can leverage to speed up some initialization activity.

onRetainNonConfigurationInstance( )

This is a very long, strange name for a method, and close inspection of the lifecycle diagram shows you it isn't there either! The reason for this is that `onRetainNonConfigurationInstance()` is not strictly tied to an activity's lifecycle. Rather, its purpose is to provide the callback mechanism to invoke whenever an Android system undergoes a configuration change.

"What is a configuration change?" you might ask. There are several prominent actions that Android considers a change in the entire device's configuration that all running applications must then be notified about and perform any necessary steps to accommodate such a change. These configuration change actions include

- Rotating the device from landscape to portrait or vice versa
- Connecting the device to a USB power source
- Docking the device in a cradle
- Adding or removing an SD-style storage device
- Changing the input or display language for the Android operating system

Your activity might need to deal with some or all of these events. The most obvious example is needing to redraw (or, strictly, recreate) the layout based on new orientation of the device. In these instances, Android will have preserved all resources from the prior incarnation of the activity, and a call to the `getLastNonConfiguationInstance()` companion method will return a reference to these, enabling you to perform any further change handling you might need.

This approach is less common in contemporary application development, with the advent of headless fragments. We will cover fragments next in Chapter 12.

onDestroy()

We've reached the end of the lifecycle methods, and fittingly it is the `onDestroy()` method, which itself is all about ending activities. We know that activities are cheap and plentiful and should be used and then discarded whenever desired as you build your application.

The core logic you could consider adding to an override of `onDestroy()` is any activity-centric cleanup. As there is no guarantee that `onDestroy()` is ever called for your activity, you should not rely on it nor expect to interact with other resources or services.

Appreciating the Objectives of the Activity Lifecycle

For new developers, mastering the whole notion of callbacks is crucial to a wider mastery of messages and event-based development. However, if you only think of your Android applications as activities in certain states, waiting to jump when signaled by a callback, you miss some of the bigger ideas at play.

Overall, the single biggest goal of cheap, easily manipulated activities and the neat packaging of callback methods that mean each activity carries its own instructions on how to get "there" from "here" is the appearance to your users of one seamless application that is responsive to their input and desires. This user-centric view is vital to providing a cohesive experience, as your users will tend to think of your applications as sets or hierarchies of screens and not as a loose affiliation of activities that are created and destroyed easily and often.

As you start composing applications with ever greater numbers of activities, it will serve you well to keep the following principles in mind:

- **Activities should have a focus**. Each activity you create should help serve a single (but not necessarily simple) purpose or outcome, rather than being a catch-all of unrelated options, actions, and outcomes.
- **Save state, and then save it again.** Users are unpredictable, and they will do the darndest things when using your application – everything from shutting down the phone to repeatedly switching in and out of your application and beyond. To give your users the confidence that your application intuitively handles any surprises, it is important to save state often. Think of it as a natural safety net that is both cheap and effective.
- **Give every view an ID**. Each widget, each view, and each ViewGroup should be annotated with an android:id attribute. This helps you help yourself, as saving instance state becomes so much easier when every view has an ID.
- **Applications and activities can disappear**. There are circumstances beyond your control, particularly where no matter how efficient and lightweight you make your application, your users decide to install it side by side with other applications that are memory hogs and resource villains. If the user pauses your app in such an environment, the Android OS could come knocking to kill your running application to free up much-needed memory.

Managing Activity Configuration Changes

Through the descriptions earlier in this chapter, I highlighted that the normal activity lifecycle has at least one exception, being an activity configuration change. A configuration change is typically defined as an event that affects the entire application, user space of Android, or entire Android device. This might make you think I'm talking about seismic events – an Android earthquake perhaps. The reality is a little more mundane. The kinds of events that are classed as a configuration change include changing the interface language of the device, plugging the device into a power source, pairing with another device, or simply rotating the device from portrait to landscape or vice versa.

Working with the Default Approach to Configuration Change

First, the good news: Android tracks all configuration changes that happen to the device for you, through the use of a notification callback to all running applications to inform them of a particular change. Together with this base notification, Android then goes to great lengths to avoid burdening you with excessive work to determine how the configuration change should manifest in your application. Android does this through leveraging existing structures in your program.

One of the most valuable actions Android takes on your behalf is to monitor any configuration change that has occurred and to refer to all of the available layouts you have created for your application and perform all of the layout work required to recreate your activity with the layout that matches the result of the configuration change, whether that is matching a rotation to the relevant portrait/landscape layout, a language change from left-to-right to right-to-left, and so on.

With layout behavior and recreation done for you, that leaves only needing to take care of any resource you have created or acquired for a given activity. You need to save and restore these as part of a configuration change, as Android destroys the prior activity and recreates it. Your activity gets the chance to cleanly save its current state and resources, so that when recreated your new activity can restore them to bring the activity state back to the equivalent of the pre-destruction state. The following callbacks cover the flow that allows you to save and restore state and resources across a configuration change:

- `onSaveInstanceState()`: When any configuration change is triggered, a call to `onSaveInstanceState()` is made immediately prior to Android destroying the current activity. That is the time to save any transient or in-use resources or data you need to keep. Create and use a Bundle object to hold all of the items you wish to keep, ready to then use in subsequent activity recreation. If you look back at the examples already shown throughout the book, you can see where a Bundle object is used at `onCreate()` time (more on that shortly). The `onSaveInstanceState()` superclass ancestor also performs a range of very helpful work for you behind the scenes, including saving view state for any object – widget, UI element, and so on – that has been declared with an ID, ready for recreation when needed.

- `onCreate()`: When it is time for an activity to come to life, it is either created afresh, or in our current discussion, it is passed the desired Bundle object so that resources and other data saved away can be restored. You don't need to do anything more sophisticated than ensuring you call the parent class `super.onCreate()` method. You can always choose to add custom state and save it during `onSaveInstanceState()`– you would need to then provide your custom restore logic to `onCreate()` as well or to the next method called when (re)creating an activity, `onRestoreInstanceState()`.
- `onRestoreInstanceState()`: Your Bundle object is also passed to this method, and you can optionally retrieve and restore any further resources you wish at this time. One advantage of waiting until this point in the activity lifecycle is that you can be sure your activity's layout has been inflated, and the content view set, such that all visual aspects of your activity are in place.

Summary

You now have a firm grounding in the activity lifecycle and the importance of the callback methods that you have available and can override when needed. We continue discussing lifecycles in Chapter 12 when we introduce fragments and will then present a consolidated example application that shows how and where to use lifecycle callback method overrides in real life.

Chapter 12

Introducing Fragments

In our tour of Android layout fundamentals up to now, we've covered the essential View-based UI widgets and introduced activities and their lifecycle. For many years, this was all there was to creating applications in the Android world – design your activities, add the logic you desired for your application, and create and dispose of the resulting inflated (or rendered) activities as users moved through the features of your application.

Around 2011, things exploded. Or, more specifically, screen sizes exploded with the emergence and popularity of tablets and their larger displays. Fast-forward a few years, and we have tablet-like displays in cars, giant TV screen displays, and more, all driven by Android. Using the sudden available screen real estate to maximum advantage drove Google to rush out one of the biggest changes to the Android UI world since its inception: fragments.

Fragments solve many problems. From ensuring there are no vast areas of wasted space to overcoming brute-force scaling tricks that just look terrible, fragments give you the mechanism to compose UIs from multiple related sets of widgets and then flexibly show fragments in activities and thus be able to show more content, or provide more functionality, in one screen.

Starting with the Fragment Class

With the advent of large screens and user experiences that typically see much more device rotation – for example, reading in portrait mode, followed by watching a movie in landscape mode – developers have to choose between creating many more activities or a better way to reuse the activity collection already built for an application. Fragments are biased toward the latter reuse paradigm and introduce an intermediary layer between activities and the layout containers in which they are rendered and the UI widgets used for functionality. This helps reduce complexity while dealing with the nearly endless proliferation in screen sizes. Some aspects of working with your application change, in particular the lifecycle of your activities. We will cover that in detail next.

G. Allen, *Android for Absolute Beginners*, https://doi.org/10.1007/978-1-4842-6646-5_12

FRAGMENTS AND BACKWARD COMPATIBILITY

Fragments were introduced way back with the Android 3.0 release (known as Honeycomb). You can rely on good support in even older releases via Jetpack or the older Android compatibility library.

Using Fragment-Based Design for Your Applications

Before diving into fragment-centric design, you should know that using fragments is entirely optional. If you now love the idea of designing lots of activities, there is no need to move away from that approach. But if you would prefer to leverage the benefits fragments offer, read on.

To design with fragments in mind, think of your existing layouts and where the various widgets like TextView, Button, RadioGroup, and other views have been placed. Anywhere you have a subset of widgets that are conceptually related and sit together – such as a TextView acting as a label alongside an EditText – then you can consider that subset ripe for wrapping in a fragment. To present this visually, Figure 12-1 shows this kind of grouping, with the fragment intermediary layer between the widgets and the overall activity.

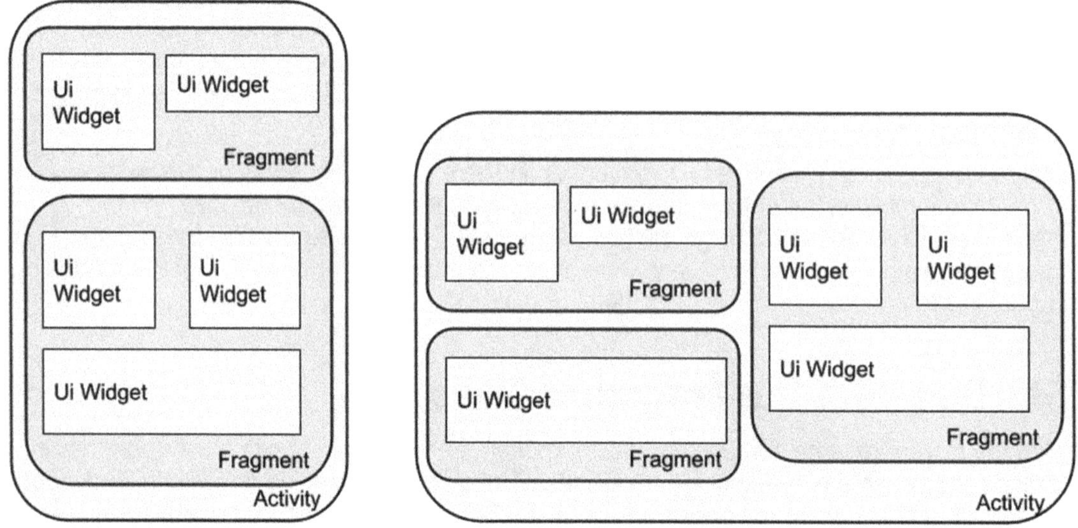

Figure 12-1. Fragments as the intermediary group between widgets and activities

With this model, you can see how the fragment groupings can be moved around, and potentially more fragments and their contained widgets displayed, on larger screens and in different orientations. You still maintain the ability to show a well-polished UI on a smaller phone screen, without having to compromise at either end of the scale.

To achieve this feat, fragments start by adding XML to your layouts using `<fragment>` element blocks. You will see this in practice in the example that follows. The rest of your layout definitions remain mostly unchanged, meaning all that you have learned up to this moment is still 100% useable in a fragment setting. This lets you continue to use hierarchies of views and have those inflated to create the resulting screens a user interacts with, just as before.

Using fragments also introduces an additional case where you use a Bundle object, providing for initialization, saving of state, and recreation, in much the same way as with activities discussed earlier in Chapter 11. There are other features of fragments that are worth knowing, including the following:

- You can subclass the base fragment class and add your own custom logic, but you must provide a constructor for the derived class.
- When using fragments, a Fragment Manager will be created by Android to handle bidirectional interplay between your fragments – you don't need to code for this.

The other major change to be aware of is how the overall activity and fragment lifecycle changes.

Working with the Fragment Lifecycle

A lot of shared behavior and concepts exist between the fragment lifecycle and the activity lifecycle I introduced earlier in Chapter 11. As with the activity lifecycle, a visual diagram of the fragment lifecycle helps conceptualize the states and transitions. The full fragment lifecycle is shown in Figure 12-2.

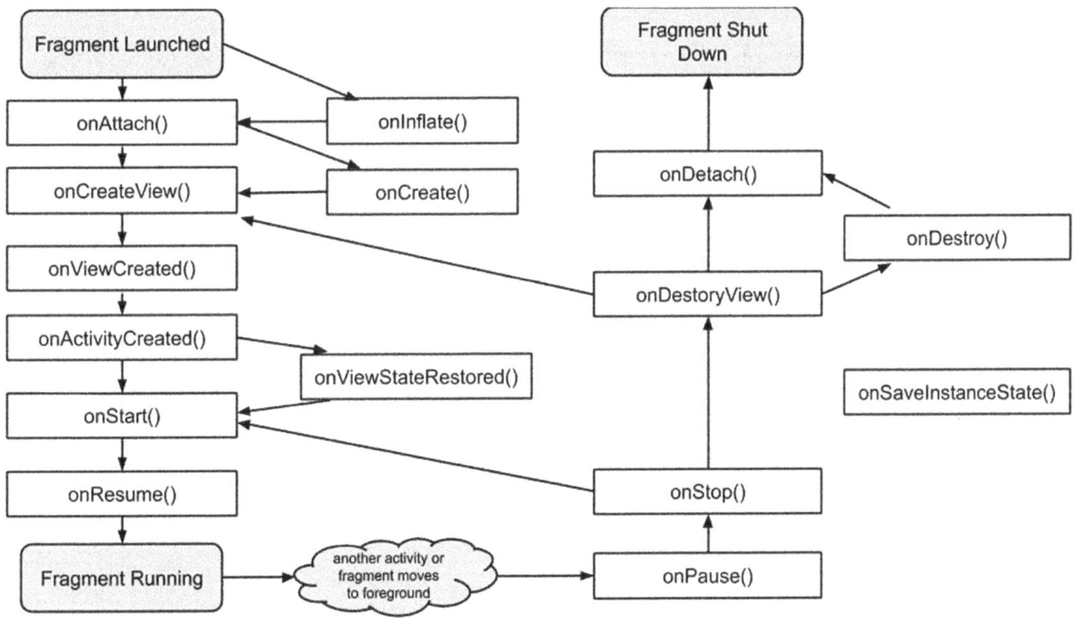

Figure 12-2. The fragment lifecycle

The primary differences between the original activity lifecycle and the fragment lifecycle are related to the interaction of host activities with constituent fragments. There can be added complexity and more than one event transition for a fragment when compared to the parent activity's single state transition.

Reviewing the Fragment Lifecycle Callback Methods

Many of the fragment lifecycle callback methods share names with ones you saw for activities, but you should take care to note this doesn't mean they do exactly the same thing. The following list presents the key differences, as well as the fragment-only callback methods.

onInflate()

The `onInflate()` method is called in order to inflate into the on-screen UI the layout of fragments defined in your layout XML files using the `<fragment>` element. You can also directly call `onInflate()` if you explicitly create new fragments programmatically in your code via the `newInstance()` call. Parameters passed to this include the reference activity in which the fragment will live and an AttributeSet with any additional XML attributes from the `<fragment>` tag. At this stage, Android is determining what your fragment will look like when rendered, even though it is not currently going to display it. That step happens during the `onAttach()` callback.

onCreate()

The `onCreate()` for fragments is similar to that for activities, with a few minor tweaks. The main change is that you cannot rely on any activity view hierarchy being in place to reference in the `onCreate()` call. If you think about it, this makes sense, as the activity with which the fragment is associated is transiting through its own lifecycle, and just when you think you can start relying on it, it may well cease to exist or undergo a configuration change or another event that causes the view hierarchy to be destroyed or recreated.

onAttach()

The `onAttach()` callback happens immediately following Android's determination of which activity the fragment is attached to. This is the point at which you can do things with the activity relationship safely, such as get and use context for other operations. Any fragment has an inherited method `getActivity()` that will return the activity to which it is attached. Your fragment can also use the `getArguments()` method to fetch and work with any initialization parameters.

onCreateView()

The `onCreateView()` callback provides you the mechanism to return your selected view hierarchy for your fragment. It takes a `LayoutInflater` object, `ViewGroup`, and the `Bundle` of instance state and then relies on Android to choose a suitable layout based on all the usual screen size and density attributes, inflate it with the .inflate() method of the LayoutInflater, modify layout in whatever way you think necessary, and then hand back the resultant view object for rendering.

onViewCreated()

Immediately after onCreateView() returns, onViewCreated() is triggered. It can perform further post-processing work before any saved state is used to modify the view.

onViewStateRestored()

The onViewStateRestored() method is called in the cases when your fragment's view hierarchy has all of its state restored. This is handy for differentiating cases of new creation vs. resumption after a configuration change and so on.

onStart()

The fragment's onStart() callback is directly associated with the parent activity's equivalent onStart() and is called immediately after the fragment is displayed in the user's UI. Any logic you thought of placing in an activity-level onStart() callback should instead be placed into the relevant fragment onStart() method.

onResume()

The fragment onResume() method is also closely mapped to the equivalent activity onResume() method. It is the last call made before the user takes full control of the activity and its fragments.

onPause()

The onPause() callback is also closely matched with the overall activity's onPause() method. Should you move logic to your fragments, then the rules from the activity variant about pausing audio or video, halting or releasing other actions and resources, and so on all apply here.

onSaveInstanceState()

The fragment version of onSaveInstanceState() is identical to the activity equivalent. You should use onSaveInstanceState() to persist any resources or data you want to keep between fragment incarnations via the Bundle object for the fragment. Do not go overboard saving huge amounts of data and state – remember that you can user identifier references for long-lived objects outside the fragment itself and just refer to, and save, those.

onStop()

The onStop() method is equivalent to the same method for an activity.

onDestroyView()

onDestroyView() is called as the fragment moves to the end-of-life stage. When Android has detached the view hierarchy associated with the fragment, onDestroyView() is then triggered.

onDestroy()

Once the fragment is no longer in use, the onDestroy() method is called. The fragment is still attached to and associated with its activity at this point, even though it is soon to be sent to the scrap heap!

onDetach()

The final step in terminating a fragment comes when it is detached from its parent activity. This also marks the moment when all other resources, references, and other lingering identifiers should be destroyed, removed, or released.

Starting Simple with Fragment Lifecycle Events

The preceding set of lifecycle stages and associated callback methods for fragments might have left your head spinning, and you might be worried you have to code for all of those methods immediately in order to use and benefit from fragments. You need not worry! Just as with the introduction to the activity lifecycle, you do not have to override all of the stub methods with your own logic. Only if there is something you need or want to do at a particular state transition do you need to provide supporting code. You can start with the bare minimum of providing an override for the onCreateView() method and call it quits.

In the following ColorFragmentsExample code, I do just this, keeping the callback logic to an absolute minimum.

Creating a Fragment-Based Application

It is time to see fragments in action! I will use a simple set of color-themed widgets and activities to illustrate the ease with which you can start using fragments.

Creating Fragment Layouts: The Color List

Listing 12-1 shows the fragment-based layout that will be used within the parent activity to show a list of colors.

Listing 12-1. *Fragment layout for displaying a list of colors*

```
<fragment xmlns:android="http://schemas.android.com/apk/res/android"
    xmlns:tools="http://schemas.android.com/tools"
    android:id="@+id/color_list"
    android:name="org.beginningandroid.colorfragmentsexample.ColorListFragment"
    android:layout_width="match_parent"
```

```
    android:layout_height="match_parent"
    android:layout_marginLeft="16dp"
    android:layout_marginRight="16dp"
    tools:context=".ColorListActivity"
    tools:layout="@android:layout/list_content" />
```

This definition incorporates the `<fragment>` XML element and in turn relies on the stock list_content layout to show `TextView` entries in a list. We will use this fragment for all the different possible display sizes and orientations, whether it is for a single-pane view on a phone screen or a multi-pane view layout on a giant screen.

Creating Fragment Layouts: The Color Detail

I will use a `TextView` widget to show details of a color, which will then be placed within the fragment, and that fragment will be placed in a parent activity. The simple layout for the `TextView` is available in the fragment_color_detail.xml file in the `Ch12/ColorFragmentExample` project. Listing 12-2 shows the contents.

***Listing 12-2.** The TextView layout used to show color details*

```
<TextView xmlns:android="http://schemas.android.com/apk/res/android"
    xmlns:tools="http://schemas.android.com/tools"
    android:id="@+id/color_detail"
    style="?android:attr/textAppearanceLarge"
    android:layout_width="match_parent"
    android:layout_height="match_parent"
    android:padding="16dp"
    android:textIsSelectable="true"
    tools:context=".ColorDetailFragment" />
```

The Single-Pane Parent Activity for Color Details

When running on a small-screen device, we will lay out our `TextView` in an activity suited for such as size. The only task for the activity is to create the fragment housing the `TextView`, and you can see this code in Listing 12-3.

***Listing 12-3.** The activity_color_detail.xml layout*

```
<FrameLayout xmlns:android="http://schemas.android.com/apk/res/android"
    xmlns:tools="http://schemas.android.com/tools"
    android:id="@+id/color_detail_container"
    android:layout_width="match_parent"
    android:layout_height="match_parent"
    tools:context=".ColorDetailActivity"
    tools:ignore="MergeRootFrame" />
```

This is a simple `<FrameLayout>` with some basic flourishes. The `TextView` will be placed within this layout via a fragment.

The Dual-Pane Parent Activity for Color Details

When we move to a much larger screen, a more appropriate layout will place all of the fragments and UI widgets on the screen at once, maximizing the use of space.

The `activity_color_twopane.xml` layout file might strike you as yet more work to do, but on closer inspection, you will see that that it really is just a composition that includes the `<fragment>` and `<FrameLayout>` that we pulled into separate layouts for smaller screens. Listing 12-4 shows this XML.

***Listing 12-4.** The activity_color_twopane.xml layout*

```
<LinearLayout xmlns:android="http://schemas.android.com/apk/res/android"
    xmlns:tools="http://schemas.android.com/tools"
    android:layout_width="match_parent"
    android:layout_height="match_parent"
    android:layout_marginLeft="16dp"
    android:layout_marginRight="16dp"
    android:baselineAligned="false"
    android:divider="?android:attr/dividerHorizontal"
    android:orientation="horizontal"
    android:showDividers="middle"
    tools:context=".ColorListActivity">

    <fragment android:id="@+id/color_list"
        android:name="com.artifexdigital.android.colorfragmentsexample.ColorListFragment"
        android:layout_width="0dp"
        android:layout_height="match_parent"
        android:layout_weight="1"
        tools:layout="@android:layout/list_content" />

    <FrameLayout android:id="@+id/color_detail_container"
        android:layout_width="0dp"
        android:layout_height="match_parent"
        android:layout_weight="3" />

</LinearLayout>
```

The only differences when compared to the separate layouts concatenated together are the android:layout_weight values, which will be used to manage the comparative screen space used by the two fragments when presented together in a single activity. By selecting a 1:3 ratio, this will give the master list fragment a quarter of the space and the detail fragment the remaining three-quarters.

Selecting Which Layout to Inflate

How does your Android application decide which layout to use and what arrangement of fragments to display? The answer lies in the use of multiple refs.xml files sitting in your `res/` resource folder hierarchy for your project. In our example, we have a refs.xml file in each of the `res/values-large` and `res/values-sw600dp` folders.

When our code runs, Android will check at runtime for any size-specific XML resources across all of the different size-specific `res/` directories (and there can be more than two, as you saw in our exploration of the Android project structure earlier in the book). There is only one child element in refs.xml for large- and sw600dp-sized screens, as follows:

```
<item type="layout" name="activity_color_list">@layout/activity_color_twopane</item>
```

Any screen that Android categorizes as "large" or meeting sw600dp resolution standard will trigger Android to use the `activity_color_twopane` layout from the XML file of the same name.

Coding for Fragments

There are very few differences to concern yourself with when writing code for a fragment-based application. The primary areas that do differ are the lifecycle-related callbacks we covered earlier in Chapter 11 and that your UI-centric logic and any related data handling would move to the fragment level. Your activities still remain, and their logic for handling activity lifecycle events and functionality that spans fragments also stays in place.

Our `ColorListActivity` is an excellent example of the low burden for coding when using fragments. Listing 12-5 shows the full logic for our application, including handling whether our application ends up displaying as one or two fragments within the parent activity.

***Listing 12-5.** The code for the ColorListActivity*

```
package org.beginningandroid.colorfragmentexample;

import android.content.Intent;
import android.os.Bundle;

public class ColorListActivity extends FragmentActivity
        implements ColorListFragment.Callbacks {

    private boolean mTwoPane;

    @Override
    protected void onCreate(Bundle savedInstanceState) {
        super.onCreate(savedInstanceState);
        setContentView(R.layout.activity_color_list);

        if (findViewById(R.id.color_detail_container) != null) {
            mTwoPane = true;

            ((ColorListFragment) getSupportFragmentManager()
                    .findFragmentById(R.id.color_list))
                    .setActivateOnItemClick(true);
        }
    }
```

```
    @Override
    public void onItemSelected(String id) {
        if (mTwoPane) {
            Bundle arguments = new Bundle();
            arguments.putString(ColorDetailFragment.ARG_ITEM_ID, id);
            ColorDetailFragment fragment = new ColorDetailFragment();
            fragment.setArguments(arguments);
            getSupportFragmentManager().beginTransaction()
                    .replace(R.id.color_detail_container, fragment)
                    .commit();
        } else {
            Intent detailIntent = new Intent(this, ColorDetailActivity.class);
            detailIntent.putExtra(ColorDetailFragment.ARG_ITEM_ID, id);
            startActivity(detailIntent);
        }
    }
}
```

Overall, the logic is very straightforward. As `onCreate()` is called, we inflate the `activity_color_list` layout into the UI. Next, we test to determine if the color_detail_container view object has been instantiated (regardless of whether or not it is displayed). This gives us a proxy to determine if the application is running within the activity_color_twopane layout, based on the screen detection rules in Android and our `refs.xml` rules. If we are running in this state, we set a Boolean `mTwoPane` value to true and, using the `getSupportFragmentManager()`, set up click handling via the `setActivateOnItemClick()` method.

The `onItemSelected()` override then takes on the task of determining what to do when a user clicks a color. Should we create an additional fragment using the `color_detail_fragment` layout and associated code in `ColorDetailFragment.java`, or should we fire off `startActivity()` with the intent explicitly calling for the `color_detail_activity` layout and associated `ColorDetailActivity.java` code?

The source code in `Ch12/ColorFragmentExample` also reveals the mechanism for showing color details and the supporting `ColorContent` class, which is just a Java packaging approach of an item set for colors and some management functions (remember, Android's Java support has not progressed past Java 8, so more modern approaches like data classes are not available). Other options that could have provided this list are a Content Provider or another data source.

ColorFragmentExample in Action

With the application logic, layouts, and fragments complete, let's run the application!

To see the power of fragments in action, we will need the two different-sized emulators already set up from earlier examples. Figures 12-3 and 12-4 show the color list and color detail fragments within separate activities on a small device – I used my Pixel 2 AVD for this example.

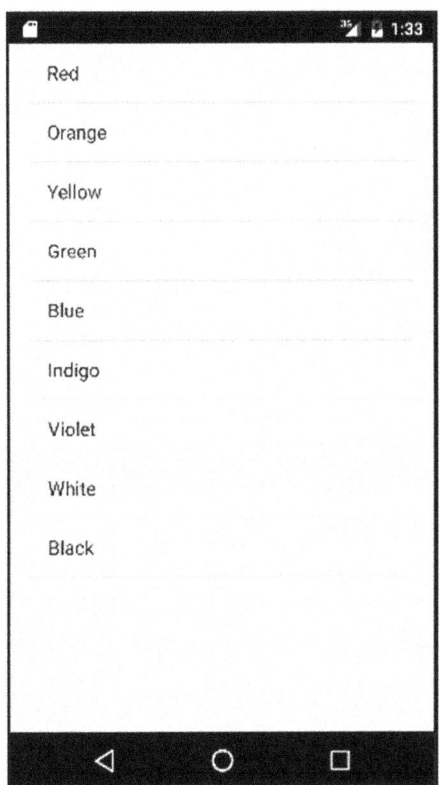

Figure 12-3. The color list fragment showing on a Pixel 2 emulator

Figure 12-4. Showing the color detail fragment by triggering a new activity

You can see the difference when running the same application on a much larger screen. Figures 12-5 and 12-6 demonstrate the power of fragments, with the application running on a Pixel C emulator.

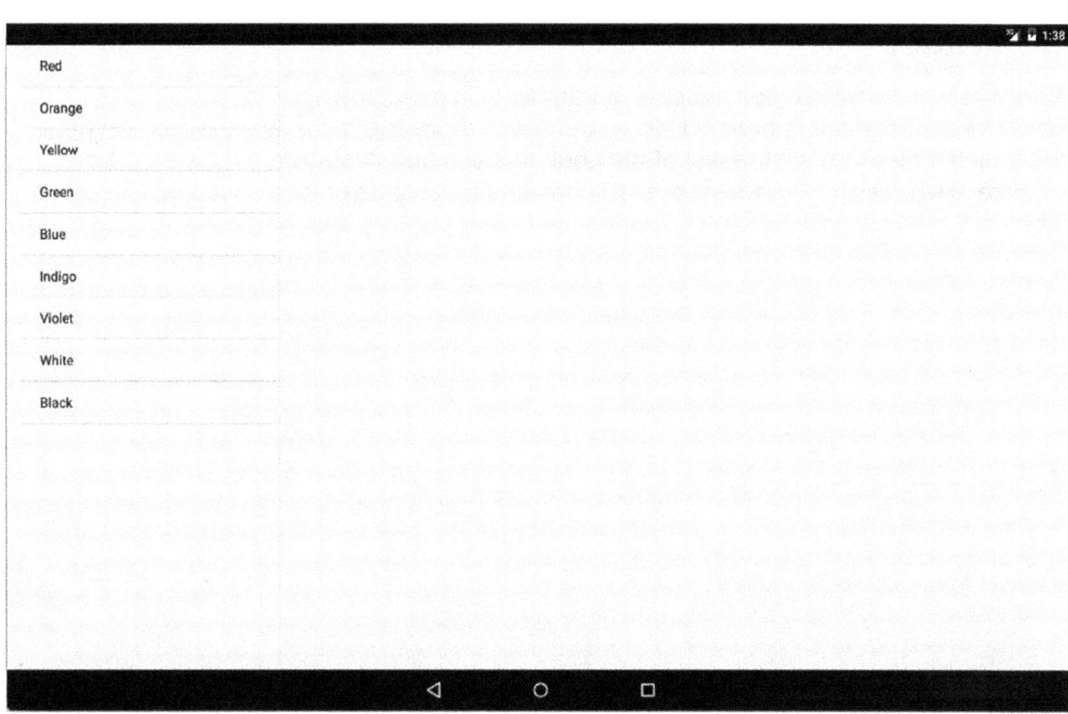

***Figure 12-5.** ColorListActivity initial display with one fragment on a Pixel C*

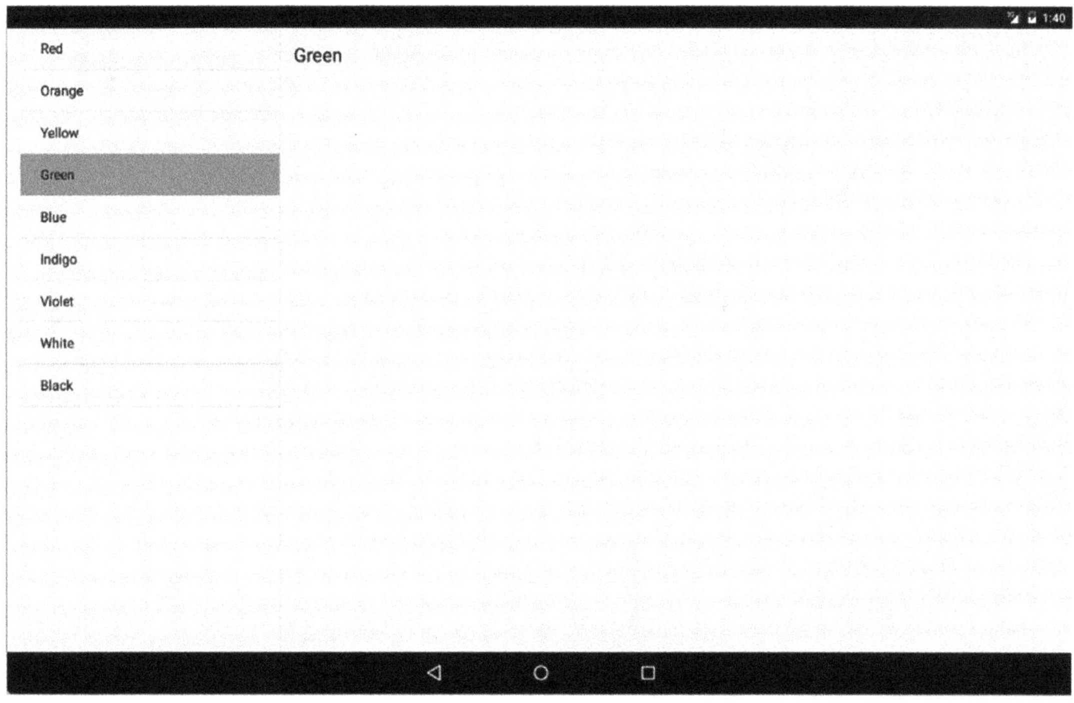

***Figure 12-6.** After detecting the large screen, the second fragment is added to the activity*

Summary

Now that you have the core concepts of fragments in mind, the best way to explore the full power of the fragment approach is to practice with more and more applications. We have further examples through the rest of the book that use fragments and more on the book website at `www.beginningandoid.org`. You can find thousands of more examples across the Web.

Part III

Get Sophisticated

Chapter 13

Working with Sound, Audio, and Music for Android

It is time to move on to some of the more involved and interesting aspects of developing applications for Android. Over the next few chapters, we will explore adding audio, video, and still images to your applications and the mechanisms to both create and record these media types, as well as display and use them.

Let's get started with a tour of audio capabilities. One caveat for the remainder of this chapter: A printed book cannot really provide audio examples (though the online version can). To get the most out of the sample code in this chapter, you should absolutely try to run these applications on a device or AVD.

Playing Back Audio

Android provides a wealth of ways in which to access and use audio in your applications. In fact, the number of ways has grown so much over time that the choices can be almost too much. Never fear. Android has also built a well-structured method to help manage all of these different approaches – known as the Media package – which we will come to shortly.

Choosing Your Audio Approach

First, let's look at the major ways to harness audio playback in Android. Depending on your needs and from where you are planning to source your audio, each of these different methods provides benefits and options to you.

G. Allen, *Android for Absolute Beginners*, https://doi.org/10.1007/978-1-4842-6646-5_13

Using Raw Audio Resources

A raw audio resource is a sound file or audio source that is packaged as a file and bundled with your application in its `raw` folder. The raw approach means that you can guarantee the audio you wish to use is available at all times, and this approach is very commonly used for audio such as sound effects in games, notifications, and so forth. The drawback of the raw approach is that changing audio packaged with the application's APK can only be done by replacing (upgrading) the whole application.

Using Audio Assets

Audio assets are also packaged with your application, so have the same benefits and disadvantages of the raw approach. The additional benefit the asset approach provides is making your audio available via a URI naming scheme, for example, `file:///android_asset/some_URL`. This benefits you when using any API that expects or needs a URI, of which there are many across Android.

Using File Storage for Audio

Not for the faint-hearted, the file storage approach is even more basic than the raw approach. You use the on-board or removable storage of the device to hold the audio file. Access is via file I/O APIs (which we cover later in the book). While this is more of a burden to manage, it means you can in theory download new files, change files, and remove files without having to upgrade the application.

Accessing Audio Streaming Services

If you want to dispense with the need to worry about storing audio at all, streaming is the answer. You can stream audio from other on-device services or Android Content Providers (that may themselves stream from elsewhere) or directly stream from an Internet-based service. Streaming frees you from worrying about storage, file management, space requirements, or upgrades. It replaces those worries with connectivity anxiety – you can only stream when you have a working data connection.

Working with the Media Package

The wealth of options for dealing with audio can be a blessing and a curse. There is a mechanism to suit your every whim, but with choice comes complexity. Fortunately, Android comes equipped with the multitalented Media package to help simplify your life as a developer while preserving the options you have available.

The Media package provides two key classes for your use, the MediaPlayer for playing audio, which we will deal with first, and the MediaRecorder for on-device recording, which we deal with later in the chapter.

Creating an Audio Application

To bring the Media package – and MediaPlayer class – to life, we are going to create an iconic application that you would almost certainly be familiar with. If you've ever owned an iPod, smartphone, or the like, you have likely played MP3 audio files of your favorite music, podcasts, or similar. It's time to make your own MP3 player application.

Choosing Between Assets and Resources

As outlined earlier in the chapter, you have options as to which method to use to manage audio files to make them accessible to your application.

If we wanted to use a raw audio resource, we would first need to create a raw folder within our project to host audio files. This can be done in Android Studio, by navigating to the res folder in the hierarchy and choosing the menu option `File` ➤ `New` ➤ `Directory`. Name the directory "raw," and your raw folder will now be in place.

If we wanted to use the asset-based approach, we would have the same initial need to create the assets folder for our application. To create an assets folder in Android Studio, highlight the app parent-level folder in your project hierarchy, and then choose the `File` ➤ `New` ➤ `Folder` ➤ `Assets Folder` menu option in Android Studio, which will prompt for the creation of an assets folder for your project, as shown in Figure 13-1.

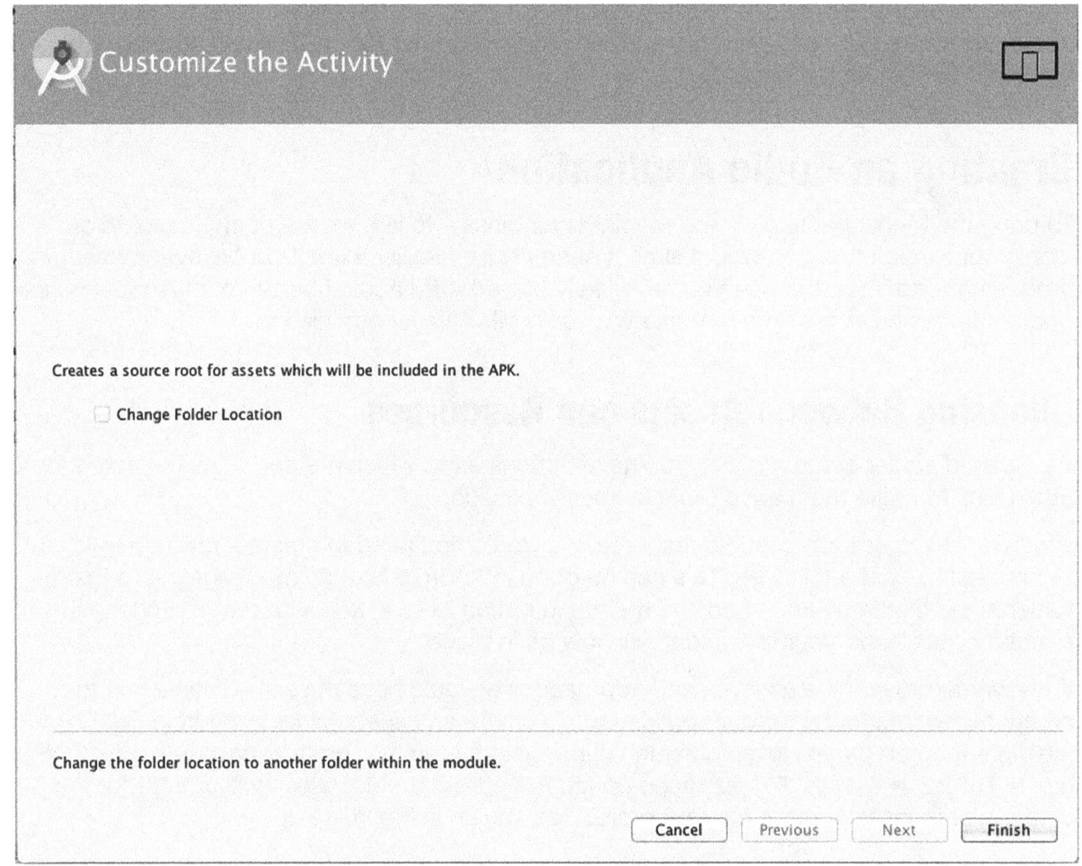

***Figure 13-1.** Prompt to add an assets folder to your project in Android Studio*

The corresponding file system location for your Android Studio assets folder within your project is `./app/src/main/assets` (or `.\app\source\main\assets` under Windows).

If you want to continue using the traditional raw folder, you can find (or create) it under the `./app/src/main/res` folder of your project.

Writing the Code for Audio Playback

In the spirit of learning MediaPlayer and the fundamentals of how all of the parts of putting an audio player together work, we are going to sidestep some of the other goodies that are part of the Media package, including bundle special on-screen widgets and other attractive assets that would give you a great-looking media player quickly, but rob you of any chance to learn how and why it works.

We will start simply and build things up over the next few chapters, exploring successive parts of the Media framework as we go.

Playing Back Audio the Simple Way

For our initial exploration of the Media framework for audio playing, we will use a very simple initial interface as shown in Figure 13-2. Don't worry. We will expand and improve this over the next few chapters.

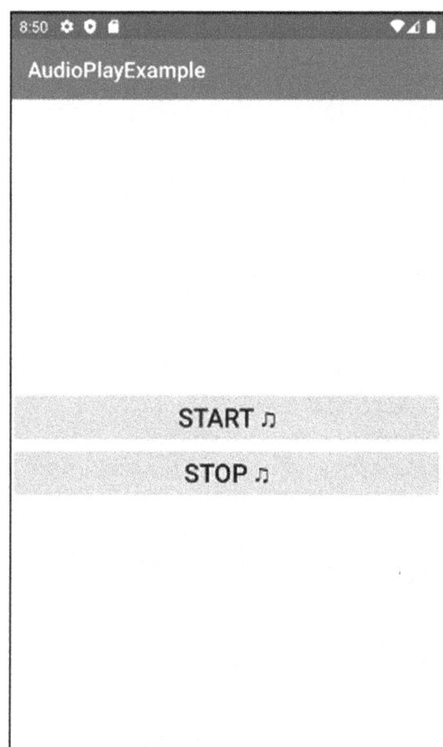

***Figure 13-2.** The initial simplistic audio player interface*

While this austere design is not fancy, it lets us explore the mechanics of starting playback and stopping it. The layout XML is shown in Listing 13-1 and is available as part of the `Ch13/AudioPlayExample` project.

***Listing 13-1.** The layout for the AudioPlayExample project*

```
<?xml version="1.0" encoding="utf-8"?>
<androidx.constraintlayout.widget.ConstraintLayout    xmlns:android="http://schemas.android.
com/apk/res/android"
    xmlns:app="http://schemas.android.com/apk/res-auto"
    xmlns:tools="http://schemas.android.com/tools"
    android:layout_width="match_parent"
    android:layout_height="match_parent"
    tools:context=".MainActivity">
```

```
    <Button
        android:id="@+id/startButton"
        android:layout_width="match_parent"
        android:layout_height="wrap_content"
        android:layout_above="@+id/stopButton"
        android:layout_marginTop="268dp"
        android:onClick="onClick"
        android:text="Start &#9835;"
        android:textSize="24sp"
        app:layout_constraintTop_toTopOf="parent"
        tools:layout_editor_absoluteX="-16dp" />

    <Button
        android:id="@+id/stopButton"
        android:layout_width="match_parent"
        android:layout_height="wrap_content"
        android:layout_alignParentStart="true"
        android:layout_alignParentLeft="true"
        android:layout_centerVertical="true"
        android:onClick="onClick"
        android:text="Stop &#9835;"
        android:textSize="24sp"
        app:layout_constraintTop_toBottomOf="@+id/startButton"
        tools:layout_editor_absoluteX="0dp" />
</androidx.constraintlayout.widget.ConstraintLayout>
```

Briefly, the layout provides for the two buttons, labeled “Start” and “Stop” with a Unicode symbol for a musical note appended. Importantly, each of the two buttons adds the `android:onClick` attribute, which enables us to wire up a method to invoke when the buttons are clicked. We’ve used the same target method name for each button – `onClick`. This method will be invoked when either button is clicked, and we’ll use the `android:id` values to drive the logic in that method to determine what to do.

Coding the Java Logic for AudioPlayExample

Our Java logic for the AudioPlayExample is shown in Listing 13-2 and is also available in the `Ch13/AudioPlayExample` project.

***Listing 13-2.** The Java code supporting the AudioPlayExample application*

```
package org.beginningandroid.audioplayexample;

import androidx.appcompat.app.AppCompatActivity;
import android.media.AudioManager;
import android.media.MediaPlayer;
import android.os.Bundle;
import android.view.View;
```

```
public class MainActivity extends AppCompatActivity {
    private MediaPlayer mp;

    @Override
    protected void onCreate(Bundle savedInstanceState) {
        super.onCreate(savedInstanceState);
        setContentView(R.layout.activity_main);
    }

    public void onClick(View view) {
        switch(view.getId()) {
            case R.id.startButton:
                doPlayAudio();
                break;
            case R.id.stopButton:
                doStopAudio();
                break;
        }
    }

    private void doPlayAudio() {
        mp = MediaPlayer.create(this, R.raw.audio_file);
        mp.setAudioStreamType(AudioManager.STREAM_MUSIC);
        mp.start();
    }

    private void doStopAudio() {
        if (mp != null) {
            mp.stop();
        }
    }

    public void onPrepared(MediaPlayer mp) {
        mp.start();
    }

    @Override
    protected void onDestroy() {
        super.onDestroy();
        if(mp != null) {
            mp.release();
        }
    }
}
```

Before we delve into the code, step back and look at how many lines of code there are. Very few, and many of those are the lifecycle callback method boilerplate you would expect to see. As you'll see, that's because even using MediaPlayer in a low-level way is still very efficient to code.

As well as the expected imports of `view.View` (for all the standard Android widgets and others) and `os.Bundle`, we import the key Media framework packages for audio playback:

- `Android.media.AudioManager`: The AudioManager provides a range of support functions to make audio handling of all sorts of audio easier. You use AudioManager to flag that an audio source is a stream, voice, machine-generated tone, and so on.
- `Android.media.MediaPlayer`: The workhorse of the Media package, MediaPlayer gives you total control over preparing and playing back audio from local and remote sources.
- `Android.media.MediaPlayer.OnPreparedListener`: The key to asynchronous playback, OnPreparedListener is the interface that enables callbacks to playback music after off-thread preparation has been done.

The `onCreate()` callback implementation does the very familiar work of inflating our layout into the UI for the application. It then cedes control to the other methods in response to user interaction with the buttons.

From the description of the layout XML earlier, you know that `onClick()` is implemented to determine action based on the `View` that is passed to it. When the user decides to click either of the `startButton` or `stopButton` buttons, Android passes a reference to the respective `View` representing the clicked button to the `onClick()` method. A Java switch statement detects which `View` was passed to the method and by implication which button was clicked. If the `startButton` was clicked, the `doPlayAudio()` method is invoked. Alternatively, if it was the `stopButton`, we call the `doStopAudio()` method.

When a user clicks the "Start" button and thus invokes the `startButton` logic, a range of expected and not-so-expected things happen. Things begin with the creation of a `MediaPlayer` object, to which we bind our audio file. The `R.raw.audio_file` notation is conceptually similar to the layout inflation notation you've already seen, such as `R.layout.activity_main`. Android will traverse the raw folder packaged with the application in the `.apk` file and try to find an asset named `audio_file` with any supported audio extension (e.g., mp3, m4a, etc. – the filename of `audio_file.m4a` in our example).

With the file determined, we then use the AudioManager class for the first time, through the `mp.setAudioStreamType()` method. AudioManager can do many things for you, one of which is to set the stream type for the given audio resource. Android supports a range of audio stream types, allowing it to provide the best support for volume, fidelity, and so on for the audio in question. We use the `STREAM_MUSIC` stream type, signaling we want things like the highest dynamic range the device supports and so forth. Other options include `STREAM_DTMF` for DTMF tones – and Android filters any streams marked this way to conform to the DTMF standard – and `STREAM_VOICE_CALL` stream type, which triggers Android to invoke or suppress various echo-canceling techniques on voice audio.

As we are working directly with a raw asset, we can move immediately to call `mp.start()` in `doPlayAudio()`. This triggers the MediaPlayer object to start actually playing the file and sending audio to the speaker or headphones.

A user clicking "Stop" triggers the `doStopAudio()` method, which is largely self-explanatory. We first call the `stop()` method on the `MediaPlayer` object if it is instantiated. We use the `if{}` block testing structure for instantiation to check we don't try to stop anything if the user has never clicked Start (e.g., if they open the application and click Stop as their first action by mistake).

Next is the `onPrepared()` callback method. This method links to the package definition where AudioExample implements the `OnPreparedListener` interface. Technically, we don't use the `onPrepared()` callback in this first pass of the AudioExample application, but it is included here to highlight that there are times where you cannot immediately begin playback after the `MediaPlayer` object is instantiated and the `AudioManager` has been invoked to set the stream type. When and why to use `onPrepared()` will be covered further in the streaming playback example.

We conclude with the `onDestroy()` callback to release the MediaPlayer object if it has been previously created.

With the code covered, you're now ready to try it out for yourself. Fire up an AVD image, and run the example, or your variant if you have modified the `Ch13/AudioPlayExample` code, to satisfy yourself that the final working product actually makes some noise!

Using Streaming for Audio Playback

While playing back MP3 files and other stored audio was considered all the rage at the dawn of the iPod and other music players, obviously times change, and it would be remiss of Android not to keep up. Android provides full support for streaming media, including audio, from other services both on the device and remotely. Once again the Media framework handles things for you.

Figure 13-3 shows our modified AudioPlayExample, as a new and improved AudioStreamExample. I will save you the XML being repeated here in the text – feel free to view it in `Ch13/AudioStreamExample`.

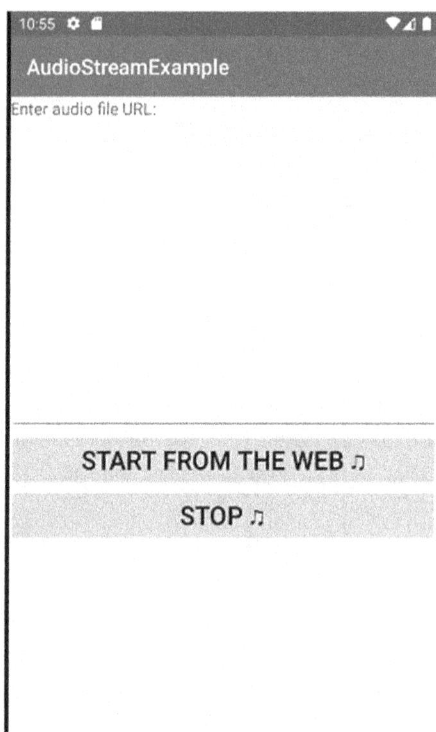

Figure 13-3. The AudioStreamExample UI

To source and play audio as a stream, a little more work is required from our Java code, which you can see in Listing 13-3.

Listing 13-3. *AudioStreamExample logic*

```
package org.beginningandroid.audiostreamexample;

import androidx.appcompat.app.AppCompatActivity;
import android.media.AudioManager;
import android.media.MediaPlayer;
import android.media.MediaPlayer.OnPreparedListener;
import android.os.Bundle;
import android.view.View;
import android.widget.EditText;

public class MainActivity extends AppCompatActivity implements OnPreparedListener {
    // useful for debugging
    // String mySourceFile=
   //        "https://ia801400.us.archive.org/2/items/rhapblue11924/rhapblue11924_64kb.mp3";
    private MediaPlayer mp;
```

```
    @Override
    protected void onCreate(Bundle savedInstanceState) {
        super.onCreate(savedInstanceState);
        setContentView(R.layout.activity_main);
    }

    public void onClick(View view) {
        switch(view.getId()) {
            case R.id.startButton:
                try {
                    EditText mySourceFile=(EditText)findViewById(R.id.sourceFile);
                    doPlayAudio(mySourceFile.toString());
                } catch (Exception e) {
                    // error handling logic here
                }
                break;
            case R.id.stopButton:
                doStopAudio();
                break;
        }
    }

    private void doPlayAudio(String audioUrl) throws Exception {
        mp = new MediaPlayer();
        mp.setAudioStreamType(AudioManager.STREAM_MUSIC);
        mp.setDataSource(audioUrl);
        mp.setOnPreparedListener(this);
        mp.prepareAsync();
    }

    private void doStopAudio() {
        if (mp != null) {
            mp.stop();
        }
    }

    // The onPrepared callback is for you to implement
    // as part of the OnPreparedListener interface
    public void onPrepared(MediaPlayer mp) {
        mp.start();
    }

    @Override
    protected void onDestroy() {
        super.onDestroy();
        if(mp != null) {
            mp.release();
        }
    }
}
```

Our code has evolved from the first AudioPlayExample in two ways, which you can see in the doClick() and doStartAudio() methods. The doClick() method has changed to take the URL entered by the user in the EditText object, mySourceFile, and treat this as the chosen audio file to play. We use the String value of the EditText to pass to the modified doPlayAudio() method in the subsequent call. The try-catch block is in place to cover the exceptions that doPlayAudio() can now throw, for instance, if the URL is not found or does not return a stream.

The doPlayAudio() method now eschews the direct file access. Instead, we simply create the new mp MediaPlayer object. We invoke the AudioManager package and declare that the eventual data source will be STREAM_MUSIC. Subsequently, we call setDataSource() using the URL passed (this method also has many other useful options, but we will leave those for a later discussion).

To successfully use the setDataSource() call, we need to grant our application the android.permission.INTERNET permission in the manifest file so it can fetch the source (music) stream. We cover permissions in depth in Chapter 19, but for now all you need to do is add the following to your project's AndroidManifest.xml file:

```
<uses-permission android:name="android.permission.INTERNET" />
```

Lastly, a call is made to .prepareAsync() on the MediaPlayer object.

SYNCHRONOUS VS. ASYNCHRONOUS PLAYBACK

There are pros and cons to trying to immediately playback audio – regardless of its source. In brief, as a developer, you need to answer the question: What happens in the interval between the user clicking Play (or the equivalent) and the music actually being ready and available to play through the device? Do you block all activity and wait or let other things continue? This is a deeper topic that has a range of nuances, and you can read more on the book website at www.beginningandroid.org.

Playing the Music Stream

With those changes all mastered, our AudioStreamExample will finally receive the callback to onPrepared() so that the music (or voices, birdsong, or what have you) will start playing. The logic for onPrepared is unchanged from the previous example.

Exploring Other Playback Options

Using the Media package and MediaPlayer objects is not the only option you have for working with audio and music under Android. Other options include the following:

- SoundPool: A lean version of MediaPlayer, SoundPool simplifies the approach to dealing with on-device sound files. It dispenses with any streaming or service-provided audio and leverages file/resource access using a FileDescriptor to access audio files packaged with the application's .apk file via simple methods including .load() and .getAssets().openFd().

AsyncPlayer: MediaPlayer provides some support for asynchronous preparation of audio playback, but much of the mechanics for actual playback as you've seen in the AudioPlayExample application are synchronous. AsyncPlayer uses a completely asynchronous two-step approach. First, an AsyncPlayer object is instantiated and, then its `.play()` method is invoked with the URI of the audio to play. Sometime thereafter, the audio will begin to play, but the time involved is nondeterministic given the asynchronous nature of this approach.

JetPlayer: At the other end of the complexity spectrum is JetPlayer. With JetPlayer, you use an external tool bundled with the Android SDK and APIs to package and manage audio for your application and present access to it via the MIDI standard. From there, your Android application then uses the audio and has access to some quite sophisticated manipulation options that are beyond the scope of this book.

ExoPlayer: The newest, and increasingly popular, approach to playback. ExoPlayer is an open source offering from Google, released outside the normal Android mechanisms, and offers experimental or novel features like SmoothStreaming adaptive playback. It is specifically designed to be extended and modified by developers like you. See `https://github.com/google/ExoPlayer` for more details.

There is a wealth of documentation on each of these alternatives for audio available on the `android.com` website.

Recording Audio

With the first fundamentals of audio playback covered, it is time to turn our attention to recording audio and sharing those sounds. Just as playback has many alternative approaches, recording audio also has a diverse set of possibilities in Android.

Recording Audio with MediaRecorder

The complement to the `MediaPlayer` introduced at the beginning of the chapter, `MediaRecorder` provides a broad set of tools for recording sound in a range of circumstances. The best way to learn what it has to offer is to dive in with an example, and we will do exactly that by extending our earlier example to incorporate recording features in the `Ch13/AudioRecordExample` code. In Figure 13-4, you see the extended – though still simple – user interface that adds recording buttons to the existing playback example you've already seen.

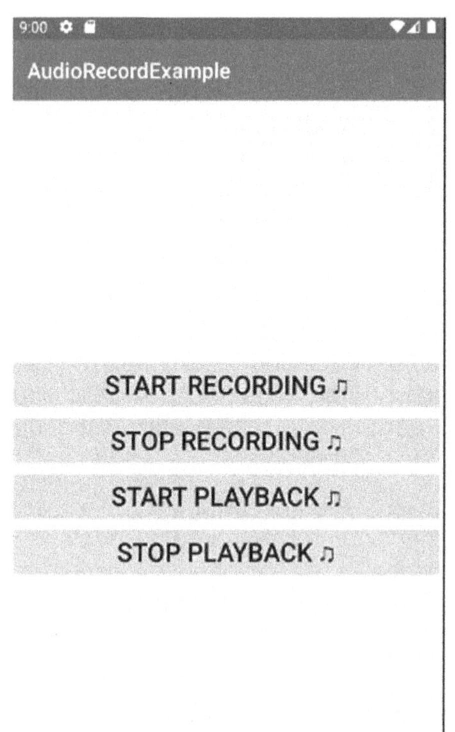

***Figure 13-4.** Recording buttons added to the UI for AudioRecordExample*

The AudioRecordExample layout XML is shown in Listing 13-4. The most notable point is to observe that per the previous pattern, all of the buttons will trigger the `onClick()` callback method, which means recording and playback (and the stopping of both) will be handled in the complementary Java code.

***Listing 13-4.** AudioRecordExample layout XML*

```
<?xml version="1.0" encoding="utf-8"?>
<androidx.constraintlayout.widget.ConstraintLayout
xmlns:android="http://schemas.android.com/apk/res/android"
    xmlns:app="http://schemas.android.com/apk/res-auto"
    xmlns:tools="http://schemas.android.com/tools"
    android:layout_width="match_parent"
    android:layout_height="match_parent"
    tools:context=".MainActivity">

    <Button
        android:id="@+id/startRecordingButton"
        android:layout_width="match_parent"
        android:layout_height="wrap_content"
        android:layout_above="@+id/stopRecordingButton"
        android:layout_marginTop="236dp"
        android:onClick="onClick"
```

```
        android:text="Start Recording &#9835;"
        android:textSize="24sp"
        app:layout_constraintTop_toTopOf="parent"
        tools:layout_editor_absoluteX="0dp" />

    <Button
        android:id="@+id/stopRecordingButton"
        android:layout_width="match_parent"
        android:layout_height="wrap_content"
        android:layout_alignParentStart="true"
        android:layout_alignParentLeft="true"
        android:layout_centerVertical="true"
        android:onClick="onClick"
        android:text="Stop Recording &#9835;"
        android:textSize="24sp"
        app:layout_constraintTop_toBottomOf="@+id/startRecordingButton"
        tools:layout_editor_absoluteX="-16dp" />

    <Button
        android:id="@+id/startButton"
        android:layout_width="match_parent"
        android:layout_height="wrap_content"
        android:layout_below="@+id/stopRecordingButton"
        android:onClick="onClick"
        android:text="Start Playback &#9835;"
        android:textSize="24sp"
        app:layout_constraintTop_toBottomOf="@+id/stopRecordingButton"
        tools:layout_editor_absoluteX="0dp" />

    <Button
        android:id="@+id/stopButton"
        android:layout_width="match_parent"
        android:layout_height="wrap_content"
        android:layout_below="@+id/startButton"
        android:onClick="onClick"
        android:text="Stop Playback &#9835;"
        android:textSize="24sp"
        app:layout_constraintTop_toBottomOf="@+id/startButton"
        tools:layout_editor_absoluteX="0dp" />

</androidx.constraintlayout.widget.ConstraintLayout>
```

The AudioRecordExample layout has self-explanatory buttons for starting and stopping both record and playback. One significant difference from our earlier examples sits behind the scenes. In order to access the recording features of any Android device, your application will need permission. It will also need permission to write what it records to storage (assuming you want to store what you record). We will cover permissions and security in detail in Chapter 19, but for now the following two permission declarations should be added to the AndroidManifest.xml file:

```
<uses-permission android:name="android.permission.RECORD_AUDIO" />
<uses-permission android:name="android.permission.WRITE_EXTERNAL_STORAGE" />
```

One extra permission step will be required at runtime, with the user prompted to allow writing to external storage. With the relevant permissions set, your code can now access recordings and store them away. Listing 13-5 shows the Java logic for AudioRecordExample.

***Listing 13-5.** The AudioRecordExample code*

```
package org.beginningandroid.audiorecordexample;

import androidx.appcompat.app.AppCompatActivity;
import android.media.AudioManager;
import android.media.MediaPlayer;
import android.media.MediaRecorder;
import android.os.Bundle;
import android.view.View;
import java.io.File;

public class MainActivity extends AppCompatActivity {
    private MediaRecorder mr;
    private MediaPlayer mp;
    private String myRecording="myAudioRecording";

    @Override
    protected void onCreate(Bundle savedInstanceState) {
        super.onCreate(savedInstanceState);
        setContentView(R.layout.activity_main);
    }

    public void onClick(View view) {
        switch(view.getId()) {
            case R.id.startRecordingButton:
                doStartRecording();
                break;
            case R.id.stopRecordingButton:
                doStopRecording();
                break;
            case R.id.startButton:
                doPlayAudio();
                break;
            case R.id.stopButton:
                doStopAudio();
                break;
        }
    }
```

```
private void doStartRecording() {
    File recFile = new File(myRecording);
    if(recFile.exists()) {
        try {
            recFile.delete();
        } catch (Exception e) {
            // This code can be extended to deal with errors in recording here.
        }
    }

    mr = new MediaRecorder();
    mr.setAudioSource(MediaRecorder.AudioSource.MIC);
    mr.setOutputFormat(MediaRecorder.OutputFormat.DEFAULT);
    mr.setAudioEncoder(MediaRecorder.AudioEncoder.DEFAULT);
    mr.setOutputFile(myRecording);
    try {
        mr.prepare();
    } catch (Exception e) {
        // do exception handling here
    }
    mr.start();
}

private void doStopRecording() {
    if (mr != null) {
        mr.stop();
    }
}

private void doPlayAudio() {
    mp = new MediaPlayer();
    try {
        mp.setDataSource(myRecording);
    } catch (Exception e) {
        // do exception handling here
    }
    mp.setAudioStreamType(AudioManager.STREAM_MUSIC);
    try {
        mp.prepare();
    } catch (Exception e) {
        // This code can be extended to deal with errors in playback here.
    }
    mp.start();
}

private void doStopAudio() {
    if (mp != null) {
        mp.stop();
    }
}
```

```
    @Override
    protected void onDestroy() {
        super.onDestroy();
        if(mr != null) {
            mr.release();
        }
        if(mp != null) {
            mp.release();
        }
    }
}
```

The code for AudioRecordExample should look broadly familiar, as it models the control logic we have previously used with the onClick() method. In onClick(), we switch based on the button clicked by the user, with the playback start and stop basically mimicking the earlier code of AudioPlayExample and the doStopRecording() method being almost identical to doStopAudio() with only the basis of MediaRecorder and MediaPlayer objects changing respectively. This parallel between the two classes is intended, where common objectives are served by conceptually matched methods.

The major new logic in our code is with the doStartRecording() method. To begin, doStartRecording() ensures the File object, myRecording, is newly created, deleting any previously existing object if necessary. We make use of the java.io.File package to provide the file handling capabilities in this case – strictly, this is vanilla Java in action, accessing a standard Java library, and outside the guide rails of Android. We will cover more of the capabilities of using standard Java libraries later in the book.

We then create a MediaRecorder object, named mr, and invoke its .setAudioSource() method to signal that the application wants to access the microphone (MIC) so that it can record sound. This is the logic that mandates the RECORD_AUDIO permission in our manifest file.

Having given our application access to the microphone, we are able to set the desired output container format for the audio and the desired codec to use to encode the sound that will be recorded and placed in the container. These are the .setOutputFormat() and .setAudioEncoder() calls. In our example, we use the DEFAULT option in each case, which in practice chooses a container and audio codec based on the particular support offered by the hardware device and version of Android in use.

Key output formats supported by Android include

- AAC_ADTS: The container popularized by Apple and AAC audio format.
- AMR_NB: The AMR narrow band container type is recommended when you would like maximum portability across Android devices.
- MPEG_4: The MPEG-4 container format is one of the most venerable, but also the most likely to be misinterpreted on older platforms and devices. Use with caution.

- THREE_GPP: Another recommended container format for broad Android support.
- WEBM: The container used for both Google's WEBM format and then patent-unencumbered Ogg encoded file format.

The topic of container formats and audio and video codecs is wide and filled with a lot of history and industry intrigue. It would make for a great book in itself, but alas, we don't have space to explore it in-depth here. To help you as you start writing Android applications that leverage audio, here is a list of the more popular codecs used for audio (and video) encoding in Android:

- AAC (and also AAC_ELD and HE_AAC): Audio codecs for the Advanced Audio Coding standard. Widely supported by Apple and other devices and platforms.
- AMR_NB: The actual audio encoder for AMR narrow band. While not widely used outside Android, this codec provides broad support across Android versions and devices.
- VORBIS: The Ogg Vorbis audio codec format.

If you look again at the `.doStartRecording()` method, the `.setOutputFile()` call configures the Java File object we created earlier, as the repository for the audio stream the user will record.

Finally, we get to the normal two steps of calling `.prepare()` and `.start()` for our `MediaRecorder` object. Just as the `MediaPlayer` object has to cope with a range of potential delays, so too does the `MediaRecorder`. These delays could be nonresponding remote services, slow on-board storage, or what have you. Whatever the situation, `.prepare()` takes care of the work to allow your recording to be stored and returns control to the caller (your application) once all is in place. It is at this point that the call to `.start()` actually begins capturing the audio input.

The best way to experience all of this in action is to run the example `Ch13/AudioRecordExample` for yourself on your chosen device or AVD.

Expanding Your Developer Audio Toolset

Having introduced you to the first aspects of audio and sound under Android, there are other parts of bringing audio content into an Android application that are worth knowing. These areas include some of the fundamentals around audio for computers and mobile devices, as well as the kinds of tools outside of Android Studio that are vital to making the best use of sound and audio in your applications.

Digital audio – that is, audio captured or created in digital form for reproduction and use on computers, phones, and other digital devices – is a huge topic. The remainder of the chapter will give you starting points from which to explore further.

Understanding Key Audio Aspects

When it comes to assessing how "good" audio is, there are a lot of subjective opinions – I will spare you my music preferences, as good as they are! But there are also some objective aspects of audio that you should familiarize yourself with so that you can first understand what properties contribute to audio quality and then how you can go about affecting those qualities to make "better sound."

Audio Sampling and Frequency

Your Android device and its audio playback, the sound applications you write, the computer you use to listen to music, and most modern electronics audio equipment are based on digital encoding of audio or sound. This encoding is produced in one of two ways: either by directly creating the digital values or more typically (at least historically) by sampling a continuous audio source or signal and using enough samples taken frequently enough that a good approximation of the audio signal is created in digital "snapshots."

This is the basic tenet of audio sampling. Things get more complicated as you consider how often you should sample an analogue signal to get enough of a digital snapshot to provide some fidelity – something that when replayed sounds nearly indistinguishable from the analogue original. Sampling frequency is the term used here, and typically for audio you will see sampling rates at 44100 times per second – for example, 44.1 kHz. There are other higher and lower rates possible, with the choice affecting both the quality of the final audio and the amount of data used to represent it.

Audio Resolution

If we are sampling audio at 44.1 kHz, what exactly are we capturing when we sample the analogue signal? The answer is bits of information regarding the amplitude (size) of the sound wave at the sample's point in time. The more space made available for storing a sample, the more we can cover both absolute highs and lows in the signal amplitude, but more importantly the more we can finely differentiate between small steps in the signal. This is also known as the "bitrate" for the audio sample.

Some historic examples of well-known audio resolution bitrates include compact disks (CDs), which used an 8-bit bitrate in the CD standard. This allowed for decent sample fidelity and resulted in data of approximately 44 kB per second of sampling at 44.1 kHz sample rate. DVDs upped the game for bitrate allowing for up to 16-bit audio, and contemporary "HD" audio is typically considered anything with a bitrate of 24 bits of higher. This all contributes to better data capture and in theory better quality and fidelity for the sound, but the price is more and more storage required to hold the resulting data. It was these storage considerations that led to the proliferation of formats that save space in a trade-off with quality – the realm of codecs.

Encoding, Decoding, and Data Loss

The desire to find ways of encoding the audio such that required space was greatly reduced followed many paths. Briefly, a range of research and techniques were developed in a number of research and commercial settings that saw the sampled audio processed to drop or remove data that represented sounds, or aspects of sounds, that people mostly did not notice were missing once dropped. The most famous example is the standard developed by the Fraunhofer Institute in Germany, MPEG-1 Audio Layer 3 – better known as MP3. This used frequency clipping techniques and other methods to capture far smaller amount of data that could still be used to create a reasonably high-fidelity reproduction of the original audio.

This approach to encoding the audio is known generally as "lossy" compression or encoding, because some of the data is lost. The alternative is "lossless" encoding, where no source data is discarded. Encoding standards including WAVE (or WAV, a form of pulse code modulation) and FLAC are lossless formats. You will often hear all of these approaches referred to as codecs, which is a portmanteau of two abbreviations: code from the word encode and dec from the word decode.

For your work in developing Android applications using audio, you can see how the choice of codec and lossy vs. lossless capture will directly affect the size and quality of the audio you use.

More Audio Theory

There is a great deal more to learn and understand about audio theory, which an Android book lacks the space to convey. Topics such as sequency, synthesis, and more have entire libraries of books written about them, and there is also a wealth of information online about all of these topics. A good starting point is Wikipedia, and for practice and tutorials on experimenting with sampling, bitrate, encoding formats, and more, look at the tools introduced in the next section.

Choosing Further Audio Tools

Playing back already-created audio is a nice addition to your applications, whether it is music, a podcast, or sound effects for your application. At some point, you are likely to need to move beyond using other people's audio assets and want to either create your own or mix and adjust other prerecorded sounds. Audio recording and editing software is a big field, but to get you started, you won't go wrong looking at some of the popular (and free!) options that might be available to you.

Introducing Audacity

There are a few software fields where free and open source software have a strong presence, and even dominate, and audio editing is one of them. Audacity has been a popular audio editing suite for over a decade, and in the words of its about page from the Audacity website

> *[Audacity] is a free, easy-to-use, multi-track audio editor and recorder for Windows, macOS, GNU/Linux and other operating systems. The interface is translated into many languages.*

Audacity has a huge range of features, but the most important can be summarized as follows:

- Recording live audio – from any input source available to your computer
- Recording playback on computer – capturing the audio from other systems you might be running
- Full editing capabilities and support for all key audio formats, including MP3, WAV, AIFF, FLAC, Ogg Vorbis, and more (obviously, this covers almost all Android-supported formats – a bonus!)
- Other formats editable through a rich add-on library system, such as M4A and WMA
- Full tools for copying, cutting, splicing, mixing, pitch and tempo adjustment, and speed alteration
- Support for 16-bit, 24-bit, and 32-bit quality and full spectrum of sample rates
- Advanced features such as spectrogram analysis and other powerful options

I could go on with even more features and capabilities, but you can read more for yourself at Audacity's own excellent documentation website, at `https://manual.audacityteam.org`.

At the time of writing this book, Audacity is at version 2.4.2. As it is open source and freely available, I highly recommend you at least download and install it to give Audacity a tryout. There are very accessible tutorials at `https://manual.audacityteam.org/man/tutorials.html`, including the two that I recommend everyone new to being an audio buff starts with: editing an audio file and creating a new recording. You'll be creating assets for your Android application in no time.

Working with WavePad

Another strong contender for capable audio editing tool is WavePad, which has grown in prominence in recent years. WavePad boasts a feature set at least as strong as Audacity's and in some cases goes even further.

One key area of wider capability for WavePad is it has support for even more esoteric and rare audio file formats, such as VOX. Perhaps the most intriguing part of WavePad is that it has mobile versions of itself, including an Android version. That means that you could be using your own mobile device to create, edit, and perfect the audio you need for new applications you are writing for that very same device.

WavePad uses a "Freemium" model, providing some features for free, but others require a paid-for license. You can find more about WavePad at `www.nch.com.au/wavepad/index.html`.

For Apple Mac Owners, There Is GarageBand

For those of you in possession of a Mac computer, there is one more option worth considering. Every Mac for the last decade or more has shipped with GarageBand, Apple's own music editing and creation software.

GarageBand has a lot of great features and a very strong community around it. Obviously, as GarageBand is bundled with Macs, there's no download for me to point you to, and if you have a Mac, GarageBand was included in the price you paid for your machine – so there's no marginal expense to start using it.

Summary

In this chapter, we've introduced some of Android's core audio and sound handling capabilities, including the Media package and MediaPlayer plus MediaRecorder. We've seen a variety of ways of playing back and recording sound and briefly touched on the alternative packages Android provides for audio, including SoundPool and JetPlayer.

We will pick up from this topic in the next chapter when we look at video and see again the power of the Media package.

Chapter 14

Working with Video and Movies for Android

One of the biggest boom areas of mobile use in recent years has been video. Whether it is streaming Netflix shows to watch while commuting, catching up on cat antics on YouTube, or using video-based chat and messaging applications, video has never been more front and center when it comes to Android. Adding video capabilities to your application is remarkably simple, though there are also some strange and unexpected aspects to video under Android that you should know.

In this chapter, we will look at the easiest way to add video content to your application and then spend time on the wider video toolset you should master if you plan to get serious about video for Android. Later in the book, we will also mention options for video using Android's Content Provider mechanism.

Playing Back Video

Just as with audio and sound, Android provides a range of ways to bring video playback into your applications. Some of these ways are, in fact, the same classes and frameworks you have already worked with in the previous chapter such as the Media framework.

There are aspects to playing back video that are unique to it, and the foremost of these is the use of a dedicated widget, the VideoView, used to actually display video and control some aspects of how the video behaves during playback, as well as some of the control users have over video while playback happens.

Working with video can be remarkably straightforward in Android. While you can build up layers of sophistication and complexity, starting with the bare essentials is a good way to understand the mechanics of what is going on during video playback and also to familiarize yourself with the fundamental building blocks that the more sophisticated methods hide away from you.

G. Allen, *Android for Absolute Beginners*, https://doi.org/10.1007/978-1-4842-6646-5_14

We will start exploring video playback by walking through an example application, which you can find in the Ch14/VideoPlayExample project folder.

Designing a VideoView-Based Layout

In order to display video for playback, we need a suitable activity with a VideoView object. Listing 14-1 shows the layout for the VideoPlayExample application, which has just such a VideoView.

Listing 14-1. *Layout XML including VideoView object for VideoPlayExample*

```
<?xml version="1.0" encoding="utf-8"?>
<androidx.constraintlayout.widget.ConstraintLayout
xmlns:android="http://schemas.android.com/apk/res/android"
    xmlns:app="http://schemas.android.com/apk/res-auto"
    xmlns:tools="http://schemas.android.com/tools"
    android:layout_width="match_parent"
    android:layout_height="match_parent"
    tools:context=".MainActivity">

    <VideoView
        android:id="@+id/video"
        android:layout_width="match_parent"
        android:layout_height="match_parent"
        app:layout_constraintTop_toBottomOf="@+id/stopButton"
        tools:layout_editor_absoluteX="0dp" />

    <Button
        android:id="@+id/startButton"
        android:layout_width="match_parent"
        android:layout_height="wrap_content"
        android:layout_above="@+id/stopButton"
        android:onClick="onClick"
        android:text="Start Video &#127910;"
        android:textSize="24sp"
        app:layout_constraintTop_toTopOf="parent"
        tools:layout_editor_absoluteX="16dp" />

    <Button
        android:id="@+id/stopButton"
        android:layout_width="match_parent"
        android:layout_height="wrap_content"
        android:layout_alignParentStart="true"
        android:layout_alignParentLeft="true"
        android:layout_centerVertical="true"
        android:onClick="onClick"
        android:text="Stop Video &#127910;"
        android:textSize="24sp"
```

```
        app:layout_constraintTop_toBottomOf="@+id/startButton"
        tools:layout_editor_absoluteX="16dp" />

</androidx.constraintlayout.widget.ConstraintLayout>
```

Reviewing our layout, you will note we have three widgets as follows:

- A "Start Video" button, with the `android:id` of `startButton` and an `android:onClick` attribute set to "onClick"
- A "Stop Video" button, with the `android:id` of `stopButton` and an `android:onClick` attribute set to "onClick" just as `startButton` has
- A `VideoView` widget, with an `android:id` of `video`

We are using a `ConstraintLayout` layout and have set the `startButton` to be constrained to the top of the parent (so top of the activity window). The `stopButton` is constrained to align to the bottom of the `startButton`, and the video `VideoView` is constrained to align to the bottom of the `stopButton`. The resulting layout – prior to showing any video – looks much like the image in Figure 14-1.

***Figure 14-1.** The visual layout of the VideoPlayExample application*

The layout is deliberately very straightforward, so that the logic of accessing video files, playing them, and so on is more approachable. You might already be able to guess at the basic structure, given the use of `android:onClick="onClick"` attributes for both buttons.

Controlling Video Playback in Your Code

Looking at the Java logic that accompanies our layout, you will immediately spot a pattern that parallels the examples I introduced for audio and sound in Chapter 13. Just as we saw with the AudioPlayExample and AudioStreamExample applications, much of the control logic centers around the use of the onClick() method to drive the activity behavior. Our Java code looks as follows, in Listing 14-2.

***Listing 14-2.** The Java logic for video playback*

```
package org.beginningandroid.videoplayexample;

import androidx.appcompat.app.AppCompatActivity;
import android.net.Uri;
import android.os.Bundle;
import android.view.View;
import android.widget.MediaController;
import android.widget.VideoView;

public class MainActivity extends AppCompatActivity {
    private VideoView vv;
    private MediaController mc;

    @Override
    protected void onCreate(Bundle savedInstanceState) {
        super.onCreate(savedInstanceState);
        setContentView(R.layout.activity_main);

    }

    public void onClick(View view) {
        switch(view.getId()) {
            case R.id.startButton:
                doPlayVideo();
                break;
            case R.id.stopButton:
                doStopVideo();
                break;
        }
    }

    private void doPlayVideo() {
        vv =(VideoView)findViewById(R.id.video);

        mc = new MediaController(this);
        mc.setAnchorView(vv);
```

```
        vv.setMediaController(mc);
        vv.setVideoURI(Uri.parse("android.resource://" + getPackageName() + "/" + R.raw.
        video_file));
        vv.requestFocus();
        vv.start();
    }

    private void doStopVideo() {
        if (vv != null) {
            vv.stopPlayback();
        }
    }
}
```

> **Note** This code example uses a video file, named "video_file.m4a." If for any reason you need access to the original video file, it is available from the `beginningandroid.org` website.

Starting with our `MainActivity`, you will observe we create two objects. The first is the `VideoView` object, named vv, which will be used later to bind to the inflated layout's `<VideoView>` element. The second is a `MediaController` object, `mc`, which we will talk about shortly. The `onCreate()` override performs the basics of inflating out the layout, and that's about it.

Next, you will see the `onClick()` method, which, just as in the audio examples, takes a `View` as a parameter and then uses a `switch` statement based on the view's `android:id` to determine which button was clicked: `startButton` or `stopButton`. This is pretty much the same pattern used throughout the examples in Chapter 13 – you can tell it is one I find valuable repeatedly!

If the `startButton` is detected as the `View` (button) clicked, then the `doPlayVideo()` method is called. This method starts by ensuring the vv `VideoView` object is bound to the `VideoView` UI widget, using the by-now-familiar technique of invoking `findViewById()` and using the `R.id.video`-style representation of the android:id of "video" held by the `VideoView` in the layout.

Next, we instantiate the new `MediaController` object, `mc`, and then immediately call the `setAnchorView()` method. This binds the `MediaController` and allows it to present a set of floating controls that will appear over the `VideoView` object when in use in the application. You will be able to see some of these controls when you run the `VideoPlayExample` application. Likewise, we indicate to the `VideoView` that the `mc MediaController` is responsible for managing some aspects of playback in any video shown in the vv `VideoView`.

The call to `vv.setVideoURI()` builds a compliant URI referencing a video named `video_file.m4v` that has been placed into the raw folder of the project. To see what the fully formed URI looks like, you can debug the code and set a breakpoint in Android Studio.

With the video's URI passed to the VideoView, we invoke requestFocus() to ensure the widget has focus and then start playback by invoking the start() method. Assuming all works as described, you should see the video begin to play, as shown (at least as a still capture) in Figure 14-2.

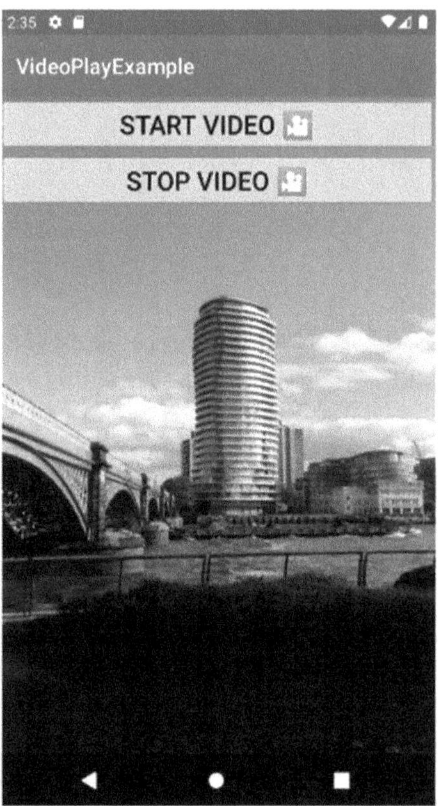

***Figure 14-2.** The VideoPlayExample showing video during playback*

The last part of our logic is the doStopVideo() method, which is called in response to the onClick() method detecting the user clicking the stopVideo button. In doStopVideo(), we first check to ensure the VideoView object vv has been instantiated and then call its stopPlayback() method.

As well as our very rudimentary, explicit controls, you will also be able to see the MediaController's floating UI elements appear over the video if you touch anywhere within the bounds of the VideoView during playback. The MediaController playback controls will appear as shown in Figure 14-3.

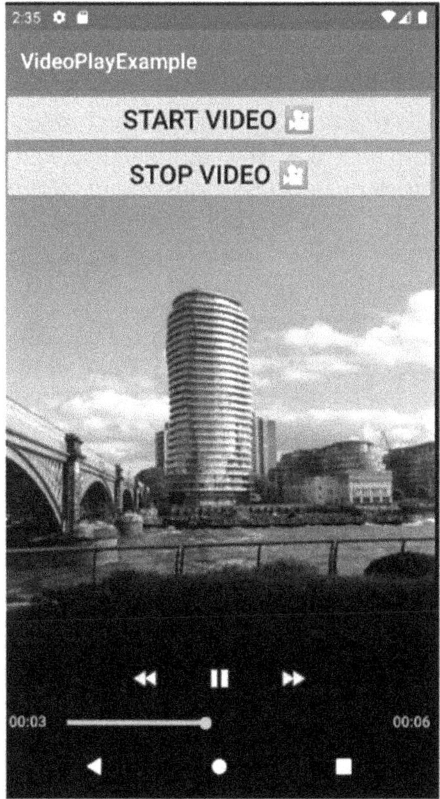

Figure 14-3. The MediaController controls in view during playback

Understanding Key Video Concepts

With the basic mechanics of video playback mastered, there are several paths you can follow to start expanding your repertoire of video skills. You can try further combinations of activities and the VideoView and MediaController view objects to lay out exactly the kinds of video interfaces you desire. And you can combine video snippets into more complex activities, such as a video cut-scene opening sequence for an application or game.

The other path you can and should take in parallel is to ensure you have a good grounding in the fundamental aspects of digital video, so that you can make good choices about content, its size, quality, and uses, when it comes to building your Android applications. Next up, we will cover the key concepts you should know about.

Bitrate

We introduced the concept of bitrate when talking about audio in Chapter 13. Conceptually, bitrate represents the same facet of video – being the amount of data available to represent aspects of the video, or frame of a video, at any given instant. The bitrate of video is usually calculated as a combination of (at least) two factors. First, what is the resolution of the video, or in other words the horizontal and vertical density of pixels governing the actual physical height and width of the video frame? Second, how many bits of information are used to describe the color, hue, and saturation of each given pixel in the overall resolution?

In general, as we saw with audio, a higher bitrate means better fidelity, which typically results in perceived better quality from a person viewing the video. The trade-offs are also the same: a higher bitrate takes more storage, because more bits of information are encoded for each video frame. This then leads us to a discussion of frame rate.

Frame Rate

The frame rate for a video is almost self-explanatory. At what rate are frames of images shown such that human persistence-of-vision effects kick in to trick us to think that the pictures are moving? Most of the video codecs (discussed in the following) supported by Android default to 30 frames per second. There is some support for lower and higher frame rates, but you will typically only use these in special circumstances.

Codecs

In stark contrast to the audio world, where Android supports a vast range of audio codecs, in the video realm, there exists a modest list of supported video codecs and video container formats for Android devices. The reasons for this are a rabbit hole of vested interests, patent law, industry cartels, and questionable priorities from vendors and license holders that almost never place the user first.

I will provide my opinion on a range of these motivating factors and constraints shortly, but here is the objective view of video codec support in Android at the time of writing. Modern Android devices, and the Android operating system, natively support playback of video in the following codec:

> H.263: Developed by the Video Coding Experts Group, it was designed to be a low-bitrate compression format.
>
> H.264 (baseline and main profiles): Designed to increase quality over H.263 while also reducing bitrate and therefore file size, H.264 has dominated the video codec scene in recent years.
>
> H.265: The successor to H.264, H.265 is also known as HEVC, or the High-Efficiency Video Encoding scheme. Its designers assumed it would succeed H.264 to be the most popular codec, but its patent encumberance meant that many online, media, and technology companies sought a different path, focusing on codecs like AV1 (discussed in the following).
>
> MPEG-4 SP: This is a specific kind of codec, not to be confused with the container format MPEG-4. You will find files declaring themselves as MPEG or MPEG-4 that in fact have H.263, H.264, or H.265 encoded video. They are claiming to be MPEG or MPEG-4 based on the container format (its full name is MPEG-4 part 14), not the video codec. More on this distinction in the following.

VP8: Created by On2 Technologies, this was specifically designed as a more efficient codec for modern use. When On2 Technologies was acquired by Google, the codec was rereleased as an open, royalty-free codec.

VP9: The successor to On2 Technologies' VP8 codec, providing increased performance for encoding and decoding.

AV1: A recent collaboration by many companies in the technology and media field. AV1's greatest claim is that it available as an "unencumbered" format, meaning royalties do not need to be paid to patent holders for its use.

That might seem like a wide-ranging list of video codecs. In truth, it is a very useful set and will enable you to work with all kinds of video. However, there are many more video codecs in use today, including many very popular, many container formats of which Android again only supports a subset. Most of the limitations and incompatibilities have nothing to do with technology and everything to do with patents and licensing regimes and the capricious nature of some of the interested parties from industries like electronics, cinema, and entertainment.

Understanding the Complex World of Video Containers and Child Codecs

To better prepare you for future video-focused development, it is definitely worth delving into the world of video containers, formats, codecs, and subtitles, so you are aware of what a video really is and what is and is not included in the media content you might use and distribute.

What you might think of as a video file – that is, a file with a suffix like `.mp4, .m4v, .avi, .mov, .mkv`, and so on – is a representation of potentially many video, audio, and subtitle resources, packaged into a container. The container nomenclature is used to indicate a proprietary, industry-standard, or open format for the file, which means consumers of the file can work out where the video content, audio content, and subtitles exist within the file.

Figure 14-4 gives you a visual overview of a video container format and its contained media.

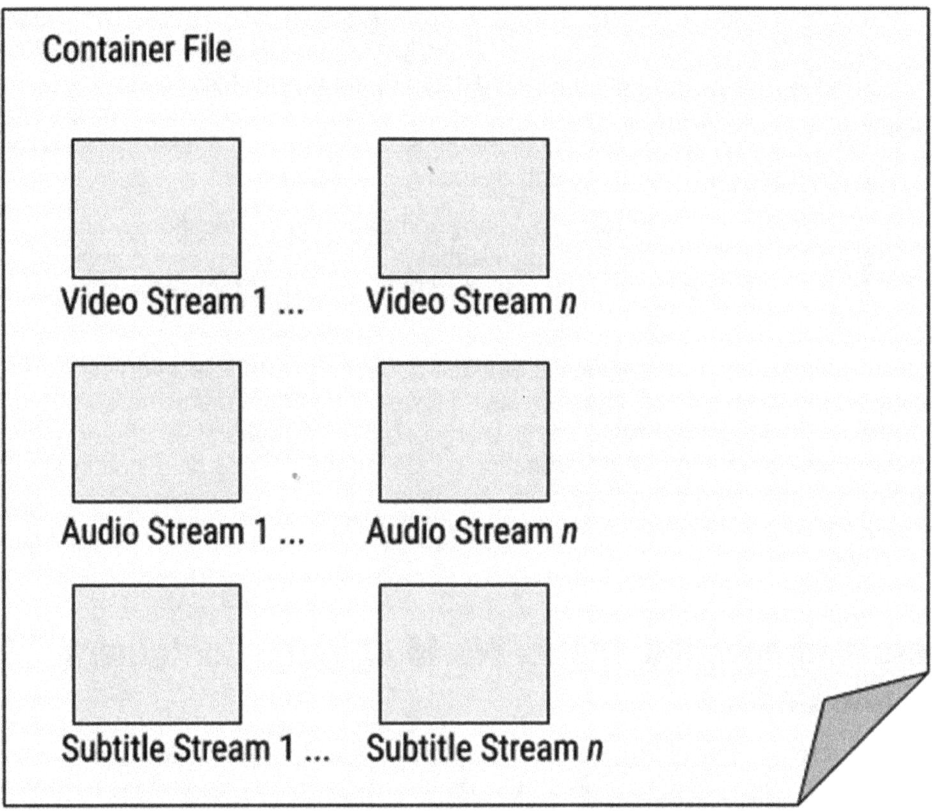

Figure 14-4. Conceptual view of a video container format

As you can see, your video file is really a combination of the four aspects shown:

- The overall container format, for which Android supports MPEG-4 part 14, Matroska, 3GPP, and WebM – but not other popular containers such as AVI
- One or more videos encoded using a supported codec (as outlined earlier in this chapter)
- One or more audio streams encoded using a supported audio codec (as outlined in Chapter 13)
- One or more subtitle/caption resources

Those factors in combination make your life as an avid video-focused developer a little more complex. If that's where the complexity ended, you would probably feel happy to work with these factors. But there is one more complication, and that revolves around the combination of video and audio codecs Android supports inside a given container format. Things are unfortunately not universally plug-and-play, where you could work with any permutation of the options outlined here. Instead, you should always reference the currently supported combinations for Android in the Android developer reference documentation, which you can find at `https://developer.android.com/guide/topics/media/media-formats`.

So what do you do when presented with great video material you want to use in your application that happens to be in an unsupported container or when you want to use unsupported codecs or combinations of container formats and codecs? I'm glad you asked! In the next section, we will walk through a great range of tools you can consider adding to your developer toolkit to advance your video content creation, editing, and management skills.

Expanding Your Developer Video Toolset

As an avid Android developer, you will realize quickly that tools like Android Studio are designed primarily around coding, layout, and the workflow of turning code into working applications. Android Studio doesn't come equipped with advanced tools for things like graphics or video creation or editing, which means to build your options as a developer, you should look at tools to complement your IDE that do excel at things like video editing.

Reviewing the Range of Video Editing Tools Available to You

When it comes to the field of video production, video editing, and video content management, there is a surprisingly vast array of software options from which you, as a developer, can choose. These include both traditional installed software and hosted/cloud versions of some quite powerful tools.

In deciding what tool or tools to adopt and use, you will want to ask yourself a few questions about how you plan to use video in your applications, as this will skew the choice of tools accordingly. Some of the key questions to ask are as follows:

- Will I be embedding video in my application – and therefore including it as raw or asset files – or will I stream from an online source?
- Will I be creating and recording my own videos or using other sources of videos and simply incorporating whatever I source that way?
- Will I need to manage a library of videos or video content, or do my videos total a very small set of content that I can manage in an ad hoc fashion?
- Will I want to edit, change, or otherwise alter video for inclusion in my application?

Thinking through those questions can help you avoid choosing tools that don't have strengths in the areas you need, not to mention potentially helping you avoid cost in monetary terms and developer time by picking better tools for what you seek to do.

I have outlined in the following a range of contemporary, popular, free, and commercial tools that you should explore for yourself, and judge what tool or tools will match your needs the best. Then I walk through using HandBrake – a very popular, free, open source tool – for one of the most common video workflows you will encounter as an Android developer: editing an existing video for playback on Android.

Popular Open Source Video Editing Suites

This list of open source tools is not exhaustive, but touches on a range of popular video editing tools:

FFmpeg: A fantastically powerful library and set of command-line tools for all forms of video editing, transcoding, and more. FFmpeg is also commonly found as the engine doing the hard work within some of the other tools mentioned in this book and elsewhere.

VideoLAN VLC: A video playback, editing, and general jack-of-all-trades tool, VLC benefits from being available on every conceivable operating system platform, including Android itself.

HandBrake: A single-purpose, very powerful tool. HandBrake's main goal is to provide the best possible tools to transcode video. It does this very well – in fact, we'll explore its use later in the chapter.

Kdenlive: A very competent editing and management suite for video and also one of the most mature.

OpenShot: Newer than Kdenlive, but targeting the same comprehensive video editing and management toolset.

Popular Commercial Video Editing Suites

Adobe Premiere: As a long-time user of Premiere, I can tell you it has a wealth of features and works reasonably well with other Adobe products. It's pricing often leaves hobbyists or early-stage developers looking elsewhere.

Final Cut Pro: Apple's major commercial offering, a very capable tool but one clearly designed for the macOS community.

Lightworks: A serious tool for serious video editing and management, Lightworks was born in the movie industry and is the de facto standard in that space.

DaVinci Resolve: A newer and very interesting product, Resolve is offered under a "Freemium" model, where the entry level is free (and very good) and more sophisticated features and capabilities are offered in the paid-for versions.

Apple iMovie: If you are an owner of a Mac machine, then your purchase included the bundled iMovie software. While this is targeted at home and consumer use, it is actually a great product that can do a lot for your initial movie editing and management needs. Obviously Mac-only.

Introducing HandBrake for Video Editing

To get you familiar with the workflow of video editing, let's review the most straightforward task you will likely undertake, which is to transcode an existing video from some arbitrary container format and video codec into a supported container and codec for use in your Android applications. One of the stand-out tools for this kind of work is HandBrake, which is akin to a Swiss Army knife of video transcoding. Other tools can also do an admirable job of transcoding, but HandBrake is one of the easiest in which to gain proficiency.

Downloading and Installing HandBrake

One of the reasons I am a fan of HandBrake is that it is available for every major operating system. Whether you are using macOS, Windows, or Linux, you will be able to run a native version of HandBrake on your system.

Head to the HandBrake website at `https://handbrake.fr/` and download the package or package configuration appropriate for your operating system. In the examples that follow, we'll be using the Ubuntu (Debian) Linux installation, which includes the extra step of configuring package management to download HandBrake for you. The steps after that will be basically identical regardless of your platform.

On Debian or Debian-based systems, add the handbrake repository to your repository configuration, as outlined in the instructions on the website, and then run

```
sudo apt install handbrake-gtk
```

You can also optionally install the command-line version at the same time, for example:

```
sudo apt install handbrake-gtk handbrake-cli
```

For RPM-based Linux systems like Fedora, CentOS, Red Hat, and so forth, use the equivalent `yum` package management commands. For Windows users, use the downloadable installer to install HandBrake. For macOS users, download the HandBrake `DMG` image, and mount this by double-clicking it. Then drag the HandBrake application to your Applications folder.

Running and Using HandBrake

Start HandBrake as appropriate for your operating system, and you should see the home screen as shown in Figure 14-5.

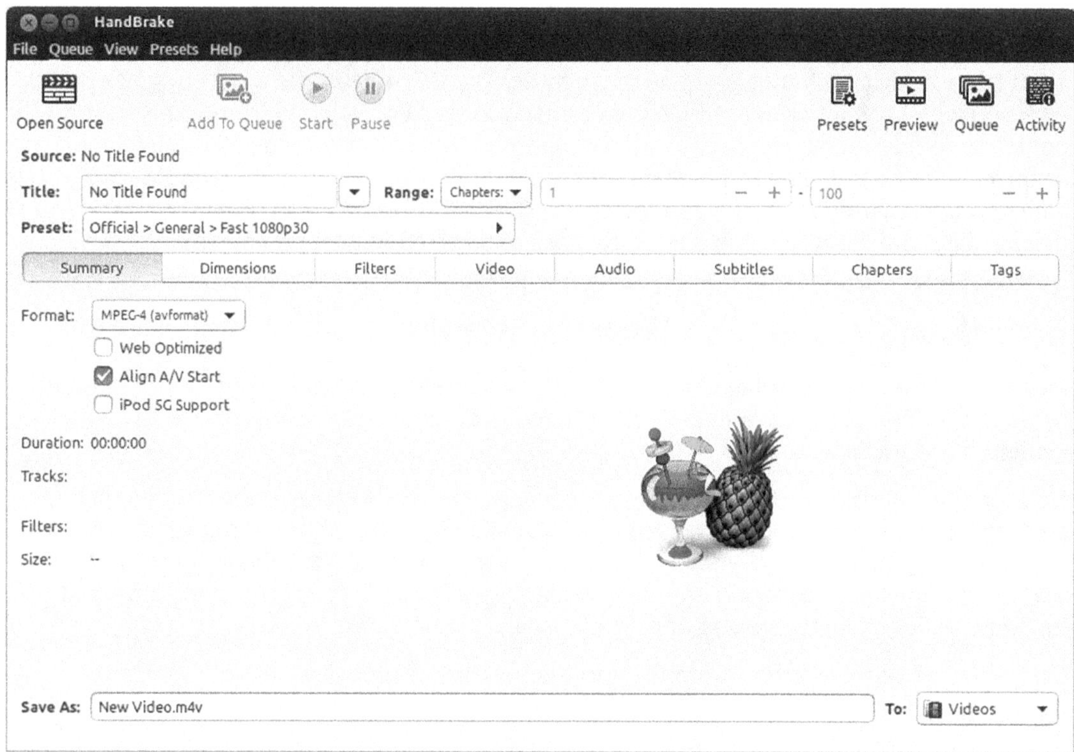

***Figure 14-5.** The home screen for HandBrake*

As you would expect, there are many options you can explore from the starting point of the home screen. To demonstrate the key features of HandBrake, we will select an existing video file so that we can transcode it to a suitable format for Android use. To select the file, click the Open Source button in the top left of the HandBrake window. In my case, I'm going to choose a file that I have captured on another device, which in my case is called `IMG_9111.MOV`. The file selector is shown in Figure 14-6 – if you are following these instructions with your own video file, obviously your own source filename will differ.

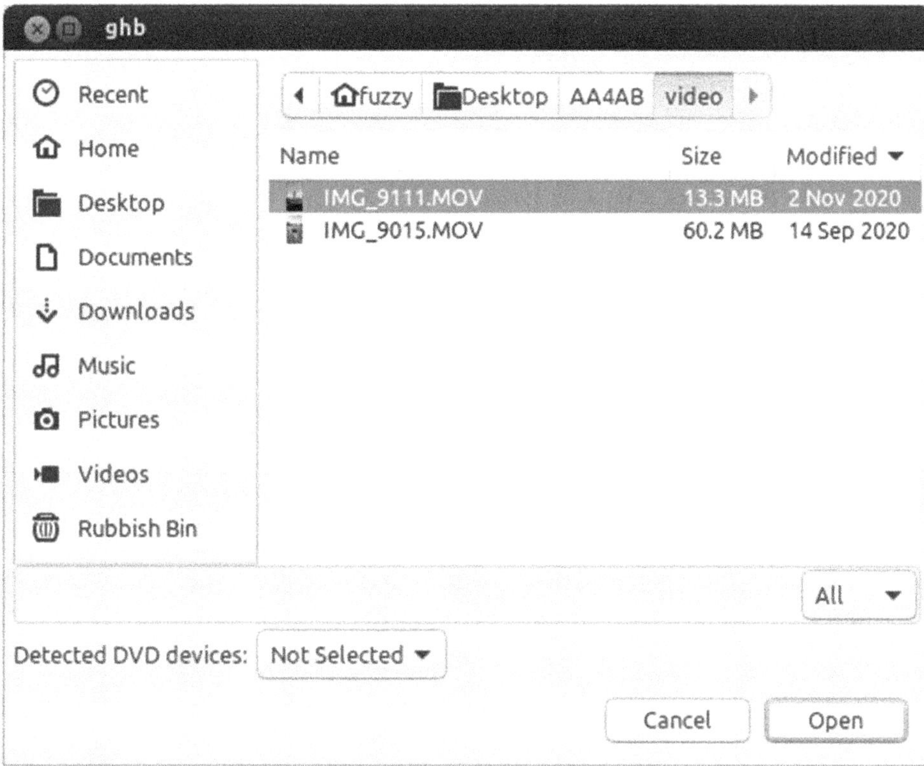

***Figure 14-6.** Selecting a source video file to transcode in HandBrake*

One of the best features of HandBrake is its ability to determine the source file's container format, codecs for video and audio, and so on. You will not be asked to specify any of these input parameters – though you can override things in HandBrake as your expertise dictates.

Having selected a source file, your main concern will be to instruct HandBrake to transcode the video into a format based on a codec Android supports and to package it within a container format that is also supported. HandBrake shines in this regard, coming prepackaged with a range of existing options that you can choose with a few clicks to meet the format and codec support requirements that Android dictates.

To have HandBrake use a pre-configured target format for Android, click the right-pointing arrow on the right-hand side of the `Preset` field. This will pop up a menu with options including `General, Web, Devices`, and so on. Choose the `Devices` sub-menu, and a further sub-menu will display, similar to the one shown in Figure 14-7.

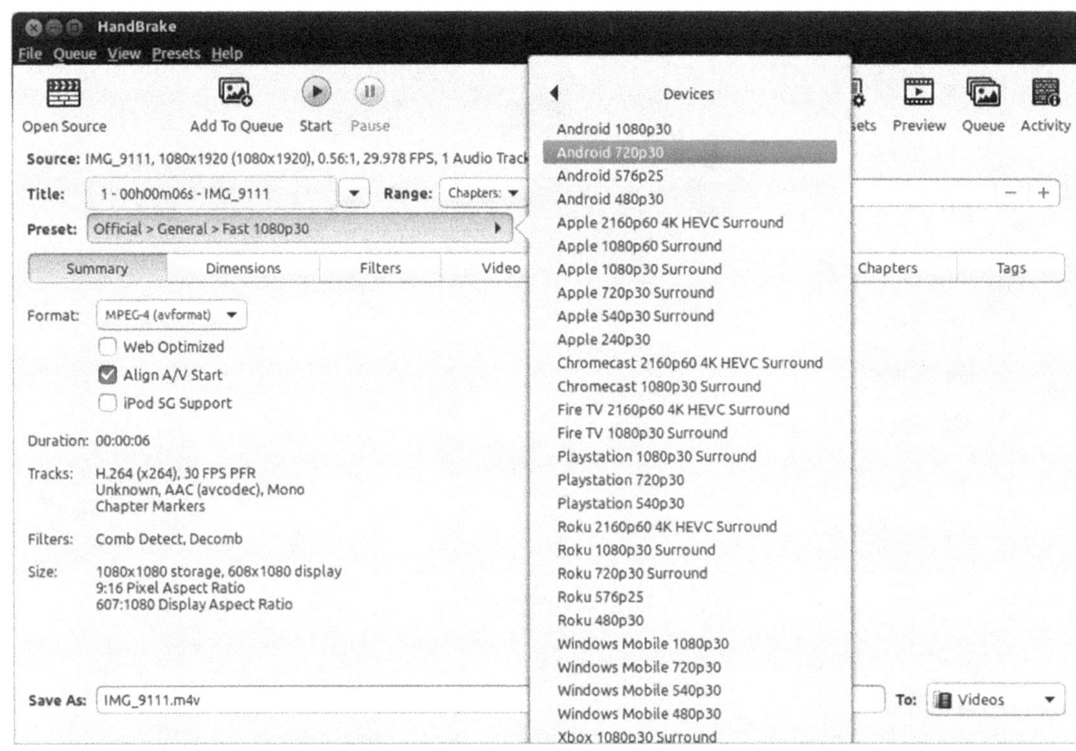

***Figure 14-7.** Pre-configured options in the Devices sub-menu in HandBrake*

There are many pre-configured options shown, as you can see, for many devices, not just Android ones. We are interested in a good compromise between overall resolution and frame rate to ensure our resulting transcoded video is not too large. In my example, I've selected the `Android 720p30` pre-configured option, which will automatically set these qualities for my transcoded video:

1. Android-supported container format: In this example, this will be the MPEG-4 container format.
2. Android-supported video codec: The `Android 720p30` pre-configured settings use H.264 as the video codec.
3. Android-supported audio codec: AAC will be used as the audio codec.
4. Resolution: This will allow a maximum of 720 "progressive" scan lines per frame of the video (thus the shorthand 720p).
5. Frame rate: 30 frames per second.

I will specify a target file to save the resulting transcoded video, which in this case is called `IMG_9111.m4v`. Click the Start button to have your transcoding begin, and when it's complete, HandBrake will show a cheeky message telling you to put down your coffee because your converted video is ready.

The final product in my case was a video file of 1.1 MB in size and still in very good quality when playing back on an Android device. This compares very favorably to the 14 MB original video file.

Going Further with Video for Android

You can see for yourself how good my example video transcode looks and the basic mechanics of video playback by reviewing the VideoPlayExample application introduced at the start of the chapter. I encourage you to do more with this example to get a feel for video's strengths and challenges under Android. First, try substituting your own videos, including ones you edit and transcode with HandBrake or other tools. You can start judging for yourself what approaches work for your applications by using `VideoPlayExample` as a simple test harness for all kinds of video experiments.

The second thing to do is convert `VideoPlayExample` to use a URI and stream its source file. Copy the logic from the audio streaming examples in Chapter 13, or check out the book's website at `www.beginningandroid.org/` for more example code for video stream playback.

Summary

In this chapter, we have introduced the world of video for Android applications and shown how basic video playback can be added to your applications. You've also seen how adding other video editing and creation software to your developer toolkit greatly expands what you can do with video.

Chapter 15

Introducing Notifications

Just about every operating system in history has invented a mechanism to alert you to interesting, important, or emergency notices. From counting "likes" to low power warnings, notifications are a ubiquitous part of almost every device experience. Android provides a contemporary notification ecosystem and takes the basics further with some very useful abilities in its notification framework.

Every Android device, from phones to tablets to in-car entertainment systems, possesses a range of notification mechanisms, and we will explore these in this chapter. If you have used an Android device, you will be familiar with the tray icons that appear at the top of the screen or on the lock screen. You will also have seen pop-up dialog notifications, which have their pros and cons.

On top of the notification capabilities of software, Android serves up various hardware options that can come to the party to help with notifications. Whether it is vibrating to add impetus to an incoming notification or haptic feedback to ensure your user gets in-the-moment tactile feedback, Android presents a united front for your notification needs via a comprehensive framework.

Configuring Notifications

In the normal course of using an application, it has a lot of ways to present new or important information to grab the user's attention. There are times when something notable has happened, but the user has navigated away from the application, or it's in the background or paused. For applications like services with no UI, there's no normal user-facing visibility, so an extra hurdle exists in those circumstances when trying to be noticed.

Android handles these cases and more via its `NotificationManager` system service. The `NotificationManager` is available to you through your application via the passing of an appropriately structured parameter to a `getSystemService()` method call. This can be as simple as the following code snippet:

```
getSystemService(NOTIFICATION_SERVICE)
```


G. Allen, *Android for Absolute Beginners*, https://doi.org/10.1007/978-1-4842-6646-5_15

The call to getSystemService() will provide you with a resulting NotificationManager object, and you then have access to notification management methods it provides. Some of the most common methods you will use with the NotificationManager object are

- notify(): As the name suggests, this is the method used to activate a notification according to whatever trigger or circumstance you think warrants the user's attention. It takes a Notification object as a parameter, which carries the details of your notification – text, images, and so on – in the payload, and the chosen ways in which you want the Android notification infrastructure to alert the user.
- cancel(): Use this method to dismiss a notification. Android can also cancel notifications in response to certain user actions, including gestures like "swipe to dismiss."
- cancelAll(): The nuclear option! When you simply want all notifications that a NotificationManager object has active to go, invoke cancelAll().

Customizing Notifications with the Notification Object

Default notification behavior in Android is quite capable of doing most of the things you want when it comes to notifying users. But there are times when you want to go the extra mile and really seek the user's attention. The Notification object has methods to enhance and customize your notification.

Understanding Old and New Ways of Enhancing Notifications

Notifications have evolved over time with Android, such that there is the original (old) way of enhancing notifications using individual additional methods to tweak and amplify your effort and the more recent method of using a NotificationBuilder object to tackle all of the customization in one go. I will show both approaches and flag that if you are targeting older builds of Android prior to version 7, the older method is more likely to be reliable for your needs.

Adding Sounds to Your Notification

Let's start our notification exploration with the older/traditional approach and in particular Android's support of sound for many different types of notifications. By leveraging a range of user-configurable sounds at the base Android level, you can avoid having to manage audio resources if you prefer not to. You can have your Notification object leverage the device's default sound (whether or not configured by the user) by invoking its .defaults() method as follows:

```
Notification myNotification = new Notification(...);
myNotification.defaults = Notification.DEFAULT_SOUND;
```

You can take the extra step of providing your own sound by using a Uri reference to an audio resource, whether it is a raw or assets-managed file you have provided or a reference to one of the many sounds that come bundled with Android.

An example of using the stock Android "Kalimba" sound is shown in the following, using the Uri for this resource via the ContentResolver class and assigning the sound accordingly:

```
Notification myNotification = new Notificiation(...);
myNotification.sound = Uri.parse(ContentResolver.SCHEME_ANDROID_RESOURCE +
                                 "://" +
                                 getPackageName() +
                                 "/raw/kalimba");
```

As there are multiple mechanisms to triggering a notification, it is important to know there is a hierarchy of priorities. Any sound notification assigned with `.sound()` – or other notification form for that matter using its own relevant method – will be overridden by any equivalent set with the `.defaults()` method if such a call includes a parameter for the notification type, such as the flag `DEFAULTS_SOUND` for sounds. This will happen regardless of the order in which you call these methods.

In the newer world of notifications in Android, you set properties like the sound you wish to use by building up a `NotificationBuilder` object and then finally having the `Notification` use the `NotificationBuilder` when you've set all of your desired properties. The equivalent effort to set a sound using the newer approach would look as follows:

```
Notification.Builder myBuilder = new Notification.Builder(this, ...)
myBuilder.setSound(Uri.parse(ContentResolver.SCHEME_ANDROID_RESOURCE +
                             "://" +
                             getPackageName() +
                             "/raw/kalimba"));
```

Using Device Lights for Your Notification

It's rare to find an Android phone or tablet that lacks a built-in LED light as part of the front-facing display. This light can be put to many uses, including acting as another vector for notifying users of notifications (and not just keeping me, your trusty author, awake at 3:00 a.m.). The built-in light for an Android device can be controlled in several ways by configuring based on your Notification object's configuration:

- The .lights() method activates the LED when passed a Boolean TRUE value.
- You can change the color of the LED, on supported devices, via the ledARGB parameter and the matching hex code for the RGB-based color you wish to use.
- Blink and cycle the light using the ledOnMS and ledOffMS values, expressing on and off times in milliseconds.

The equivalent approach for newer Android builds using `Notification.Builder` is the `.setLights()` method. You can probably start to guess how to infer the new methods using the builder approach from the old methods using a base Notification object directly and vice versa.

> **Note** The Notification.Builder() approach was introduced with Android 8 and the older notification style deprecated. With API levels beyond 24, you should always use Notification.Builder() and let Android's compatibility libraries deal with behavior on older versions.

As well as the particular notification flourish you wish to use, be sure to set the `Notification.flags` field to include the `Notification.FLASH_SHOW_LIGHTS` flag. On basic devices with monochromatic LEDs, you might find your color choice isn't applicable, and instead the device will vary the brightness of the LED. For devices that have LEDs supporting multiple color output, there will be a small subset of cases where this also happens if the manufacturer hasn't included the necessary smarts for the Notification class to be able to control color.

There is also the case of devices where there is no LED for notification use, including things like TVs, Android Auto systems, and some embedded uses of Android. Given this varied device landscape, you should consider flashing LED notification as a bonus, rather than a critical method of gaining attention.

Shaking It!

Your users have more senses than just sight and hearing that you can use to attract their attention. When blinking lights and catchy sounds aren't enough, you can move (pun intended) on to vibration. Android's original notification model includes a default flag to allow use of the device-wide default for shaking things up:

```
myNotification.defaults = Notifcation.DEFAULT_VIBRATE;
```

The newer approaches to notification use the `.setVibrate()` method on the Builder object to the same effect.

To have any vibration-based notifications actually trigger physical vibration, you will need the following permission in your manifest:

```
<uses-permission android:name="android.permission.VIBRATE" />
```

When the default vibration is not enough, you can perform custom vibration via `.vibrate()` and `.setVibrate()` methods, providing a `long[]` value in milliseconds, for example:

```
new long[] {1000, 500, 1000, 500, 1000}
```

is a valid sequence that would trigger three one-second-long vibrations, with a half-second gap between each vibration.

Adding Icons for Notifications

The notification methods we've covered so far seek to grab the user's attention in the moment. Android also offers the ability to use graphics, in the form of icons, to provide more information and context to the user about a notification.

Icons are image files and therefore considered drawables for Android's resource management purposes. You need to provide a `contentIntent` value, which is passed as the `PendingIntent` when the user actually taps the icon you provide in a notification. This `PendingIntent` acts as a placeholder and time-delay function allowing an Intent to be prepared, so that it can later be triggered by an activity or another technique.

UNDERSTANDING PENDINGINTENT

A PendingIntent is a mechanism Android uses to pass a token, or permission in advance, to another application or service running on the device. With a PendingIntent, the receiving application can run a chosen piece of code from your application at some future point – whether or not your application itself is running – and use the permissions of your application to do so.

As well as being able to add your chosen icon and related `contentIntent`, you can also add a brief text description with the `tickerText` attribute. This text should be used for the most important part of the notification text you want the user to see, such as the name of a contact sending a message, the subject of an email message, the caption of a social media post, and so on. The `setLatestEventInfo()` method allows you to specify all three of the `icon`, `contentIntent`, and `tickerText` in a single call.

This `PendingIntent` approach is applicable regardless of the notification model you are using – old or new.

Icon Sizes for Different Android Versions

Adding icons allows you to tailor icons to your desired level of artistry, but there are considerations for the various versions of Android you need to keep in mind, as these affect the resolution of icon images supported.

To maximize the range of Android devices you can support and their related notification styles and sizes, you should create at least four drawables representing your icon:

- A 12-pixel by 19-pixel bounding box, housing a 12-pixel square icon, for use on low-density screens. This icon would be placed in the res/drawable-ldpi-v9 project folder.
- A 16-pixel by 25-pixel bounding box, housing a 16-pixel square icon, for use on medium-density screens. This icon would be placed in the res/drawable-mdpi folder.

- A 24-pixel by 38-pixel bounding box, housing a 24-pixel square icon, for use on high-density, extra-high-density, and extra-extra-high-density screens. This icon would be placed in the res/drawable-hdpi-v9, res/drawable-xhdpi-v9, and res/drawable-xxhdpi-v9 folders.
- A 25-pixel square for all Android versions prior to 2.3 (and regardless of actual screen density on those old devices). This would be placed in the res/drawable resource folder.

These variations change over time, as does Android's suggested approach to supporting different resolutions, so be sure to check the details on icon styling at the Android developer site. The site includes some useful information on upscaling and downscaling drawables where you decide you won't, or can't, provide any of the expected fidelity levels for your application. Don't panic if you skip one of these icons, but be aware that Android will attempt to scale another of your icons to fill the gap, and the resulting on-screen image might not be fantastic.

Floating Numbers for Added Information

There is one last twist to notifications you may have already seen and possibly have relied on. This is the "number" overlaying a launcher icon for an application, which provides a count of similar notifications, or unread/unresponded notifications, for that given application.

The floating number tweak is achieved by using a public data member named `number` of the `Notification` object, which you can set to any arbitrary number you wish. It will be displayed as an overlay to your application's launcher icon in the top-right or top-left corner of the icon (depending on locale and right-to-left or left-to-right convention on the device). By default this value is not set and is ignored by Android unless and until you set a value for number.

Introducing Notification Channels in API Level 26

With the advent of API 26, Android dispensed with the notion of a common notification space for all applications and services and introduced the concept of channels. The goal of channels is to allow users (and implicitly applications) to group and partition notifications into different groups and then treat those groups differently.

A classic use case for this is to have some notifications be considered informational and show up at "normal" times, but to be hidden when the user specifies a do-not-disturb period. Other notifications could be assigned to channels for "urgent attention" or "emergencies" and be handled in different ways.

As Google is constantly adjusting and shifting the notification landscape, the channels concept has patchy use in real life. However, as a developer, you need to consider this if you are using any form of notification on newer devices with Android releases 9.0, 10.0, 11.0, or higher.

The `NotificationBuilderExample` later in the chapter shows how simple it is to define and use a channel and handle behavior on old and new Android devices with old and new API level support.

Notifications in Action

You have now covered the original, and still useful, notification concepts that Android has relied on for many releases. Let's take a look at notifications in use in the `NotificationBuilderExample` app, which you will find in the `ch15/NotificationBuilderExample` project folder.

I am using a straightforward layout, so will omit its XML here to save space. You can see the UI in Figure 15-1.

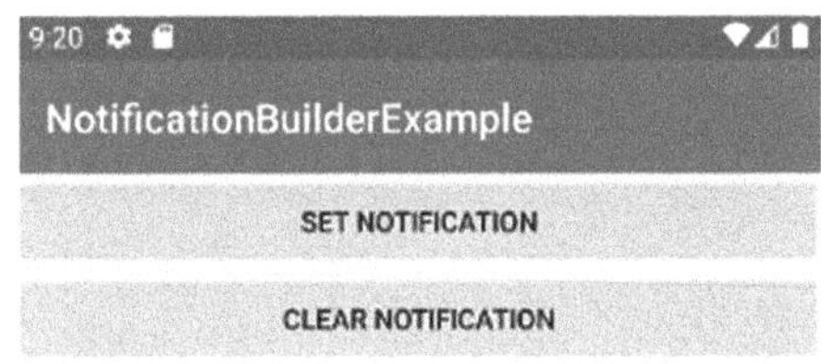

Figure 15-1. The basic NotificationBuilderExample layout, with no notifications showing

Supporting Logic to Create the Notifications

The heart of the `NotificationBuilderExample` is the code that brings to life user notifications when interacting with the UI, shown in Listing 15-1.

Listing 15-1. *Implementing the code for NotificationBuilderExample*

```
package org.beginningandroid.notificationbuilderexample;

import androidx.appcompat.app.AppCompatActivity;
import androidx.core.app.NotificationCompat;

import android.app.Notification;
import android.app.NotificationChannel;
import android.app.NotificationManager;
import android.app.PendingIntent;
import android.content.Intent;
import android.os.Build;
import android.os.Bundle;
import android.view.View;

public class MainActivity extends AppCompatActivity {
    private static final int NOTIFICATION_ID=12345;
    private static final String MYCHANNEL = "";
    private int notifyCount = 0;
    private NotificationManager myNotifyMgr = null;

    @Override
    protected void onCreate(Bundle savedInstanceState) {
        super.onCreate(savedInstanceState);
        setContentView(R.layout.activity_main);
        myNotifyMgr = (NotificationManager)getSystemService(NOTIFICATION_SERVICE);
        if (Build.VERSION.SDK_INT>=Build.VERSION_CODES.O &&
                myNotifyMgr.getNotificationChannel(MYCHANNEL)==null)
                  { myNotifyMgr.createNotificationChannel(new NotificationChannel(MYCHANNEL,
                          "My Channel", NotificationManager.IMPORTANCE_DEFAULT));
                    }
    }

    public void onClick(View view) {
        switch(view.getId()) {
            case R.id.notify:
                raiseNotification(view);
                break;
            case R.id.clearNotify:
                dismissNotification(view);
                break;
        }
    }
```

```
    public void raiseNotification(View view) {
        Intent myIntent = new Intent(this, NotificationFollowon.class);
        PendingIntent myPendingIntent = PendingIntent.getActivity(MainActivity.this, 1,
        myIntent, 0);

        NotificationCompat.Builder myNotifyBuilder = new NotificationCompat.
        Builder(MainActivity.this, MYCHANNEL);

        myNotifyBuilder.setAutoCancel(false);
        myNotifyBuilder.setTicker("Here is your ticker text");
        myNotifyBuilder.setContentTitle("An Android Notification");
        myNotifyBuilder.setContentText("Notice This!");
        myNotifyBuilder.setSmallIcon(R.drawable.wavinghand);
        myNotifyBuilder.setContentIntent(myPendingIntent);
        myNotifyBuilder.build();

        Notification myNotification = myNotifyBuilder.getNotification();
        myNotifyMgr.notify(NOTIFICATION_ID, myNotification);
    }

    public void dismissNotification(View view) {
        myNotifyMgr.cancel(NOTIFICATION_ID);
    }
}
```

While there is a reasonable amount of code there, and in the companion `NotificationFollowon` class, much of it should already be familiar to you. Setting up the activity in `onCreate()` does the normal tasks of restoring or creating state and inflating the layout, plus the work of creating the `myNotifyMgr` object to bind to the system notification infrastructure. The `NotificationBuilderExample` class itself also sets up a fictitious ID for the notification and a counter to track how many pending notifications there are. Note that you could easily decide to have multiple different types of notifications from your application. If you decide to do this, be sure to use a different ID to distinguish each type.

The other major piece of logic in `onCreate()` performs the necessary SDK (API) level check to see if the use of notification channels is necessary in order to show the user the desired notification. If the SDK version is at or above the level where channels are mandated, we check if `MYCHANNEL` exists (the `null` comparison), and if it doesn't yet exist, we instantiate it ready for use. If it does exist, no extra work is required – for example, if we have already used the application and left it running after triggering notifications at least once.

The `onClick()` method is the familiar pattern I use for grouping button click handling together – though again in this example you could just as easily have had each button call the relevant `raiseNotification()` and `dismissNotification()` methods directly. It is the implementation of those methods that houses our interesting notification logic.

Within the `raiseNotification()` method, we perform almost all of the optional configuration and customization described at the start of the chapter. First, we create a `PendingIntent` pointing at the `NotificationFollowon` activity. This will be triggered if a user decides to click the waving hand icon in the notification drawer.

Next, the Notification (or in this case NotificationCompat) Builder object is created, and we allocate any resulting notifications generated from this builder instance to the MYCHANNEL channel set up in the onCreate() method.

Then we get into the meat of using the myNotifyBuilder object, adding lots of notification bells and whistles for the final Notification object we will build:

- .setTicker() is called to provide some ticker text.
- .setNumber() is called to increment the number of times the notification has been raised.
- .setSound() is called and given the pop.mp3 sound as a resource from the raw folder.
- .setVibrate() is called with a cadence of 1 second on and half a second off of vibration.
- .setAutoCancel() is called to disable the auto-cancel option.

With all of the options configured, I finally pass the current state of the build to the myNotification object and then pass the Notification and NOTIFICATION_ID to the NotificationManager for presentation to the user.

Seeing Notifications from the User's Perspective

Running the NotificationBuilderExample application on a virtual device gives most of the experience of notifications (vibrations tend to be the one thing AVDs handle poorly). Figure 15-2 shows the notification appearing in the icon bar of the home screen.

Figure 15-2. Notification triggered in the top-left corner – the small waving hand icon

If you look closely, you will see the small waving hand icon at the top of the screen. If it is hard to see on the printed (or on-screen) page, be sure to try running the example for yourself to see it appear in your own virtual device. Depending on the API levels supported by your AVD, you may or may not see the additional status text associated with the Notification object.

Clicking the Clear Notification button makes the icon disappear, and if you are fast enough to click it while the pop sound is still playing or a real device is still vibrating, those additional customizations will also stop.

The notification endures throughout the lifecycle of the `NotificationBuilderExample` activity and even after you have sent it to the background in favor of using other applications or returned to the launcher home screen. Try it for yourself, and you should still see the notification icon as in Figure 15-3.

Figure 15-3. Notification icon persists even after leaving activity

Once the notification has fired, and at any point thereafter, the user can access the notification drawer that collects all the notifications from all the applications on the device (and potentially groups them via channel if using a sufficiently recent API level and compatible device). In Android you open the notification drawer by "grabbing" the bar at the top of the screen and dragging all the way to the bottom. In Figure 15-4, you can see the example notification with the additional details I added, including the notification title and additional text.

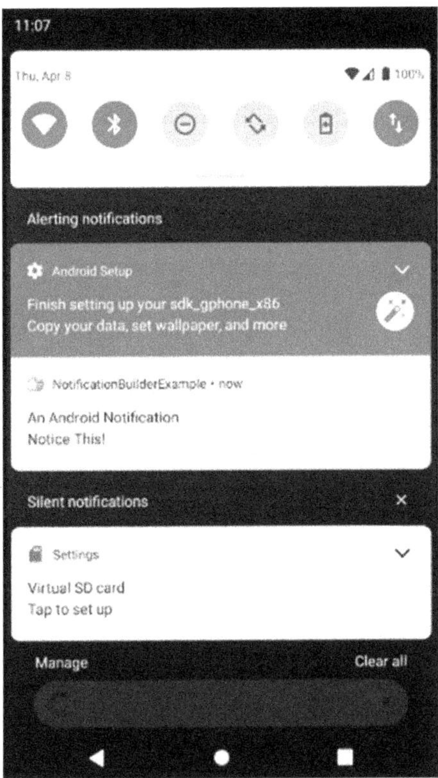

***Figure 15-4.** The notifications drawer open, showing our notification*

What you see in the notification drawer depends directly on the release of Android in use. The examples in the preceding figures are from an Android 10.0 AVD instance, with our icon chosen from the appropriate screen density resource or scaled from the nearest available resource packaged with the application. Our 25-by-25-pixel waving hand is far more recognizable in the notification drawer. The title and additional text are shown, along with the timestamp passed to the `Notification` object at creation time.

You will also notice the number value presented in the notification drawer of newer Android releases, instead of as an overlay on the icon in the icon bar. Google made this change to Android to deal with the clutter that was starting to creep into icon displays on smaller phone screens. By shifting the number to the notification drawer, people's launcher screens grew a little less overwhelmed.

The user can click the icon to trigger the follow-on activity or simply dismiss the notification – just as if they had clicked the Clear Notification button on the activity home screen. On recent versions of Android, you will see the three slightly offset horizontal bars below the notifications, which are the Dismiss All option. Even newer versions of Android will show the "Clear All" and "Manage" options at the bottom of the notification drawer. In our example, whichever clearing technique you choose will trigger the `cancelAll()` method on all active NotificationManager objects, completely clearing the notification drawer in the process.

A completely clear notification drawer then looks like the depiction in Figure 15-5.

***Figure 15-5.** All notifications cleared from the device*

Note that clearing notifications in this fashion will not necessarily clear the notification count you might have been tracking in your application. Remember, even though you have switched away from the application, Android hasn't necessarily triggered `onDestroy()` or reaped the application for its resources.

Summary

You now have a firm grounding in the notification system available with Android and experience of using notifications. There are more advanced topics that expand notifications and their uses, which you can find on the book's website at `www.beginningandroid.org`. These advanced notification topics include timeline notifications, bundled notifications for groups or sets of related notifications, expandable notifications, and specialized notification types for Wear OS and embedded uses of Android such as Android Auto.

Chapter 16

Exploring Device Capabilities with Calls

With all of the ideas we have already covered in the book, and will still cover in later chapters, it is easy to delve headlong into all kinds of application development that only deal with the great software platform Android provides. It is so easy, in fact, that often you overlook one of the other tremendous opportunities you have as an Android developer: working with the Android hardware as well.

In this chapter, we will very briefly look at how to start using device capabilities – specifically, calling and sensors. This will be super-brief, but should give you the start to continue learning more about hardware capabilities independently.

Calling the Shots

Android has come a long way from the early days when it was all about phones. With the explosion in devices and form factors that now use Android – as I outlined in Chapter 1 – it can be worth thinking in advance about how and why your application might want to add telephony support and how it might adapt to circumstances and devices where there is "no phone."

Specifying Telephony Support

To flag to Android that your application requires access to the hardware features associated with telephony, you should add the following hardware requirement entry to your `AndroidManifest.xml` file:

```
<uses-feature android:name="android.hardware.telephony" android:required="true" />
```

The android.hardware.telephony feature indicates that your application requires cellular access and support and means that users can be guided in advance about whether the

G. Allen, *Android for Absolute Beginners*, https://doi.org/10.1007/978-1-4842-6646-5_16

application is suitable for their device, such as when searching or downloading applications on Google Play.

Making Telephony Support Optional

If it strikes you that it's a bit extreme to hang an entire application on whether or not it has cellular access granted, you would be right. Where you are considering building an application where telephone access is a bonus, but not a hard requirement, then you can make use of techniques to check for telephony support in your application logic at application runtime and handle both cases of having and not having access to the cellular hardware.

Android uses the `PackageManager` class to help detect all manner of hardware, from accelerometers and microphones all the way through to the capabilities around phone hardware. The most common approach is to use the `hasSystemFeature()` method, as shown in the pseudo-code snippet in Listing 16-1.

***Listing 16-1.** A code fragment showing detection of cellular hardware access*

```
PackageManager myDevice = getPackageManager();
if (myDevice.hasSystemFeature(PackageManager.FEATURE_TELEPHONY) {
    // the user's device has telephony support
    // add your call-related logic here
} else {
    // the user's device lacks telephony support
    // do something that doesn't require making calls
};
```

You can also check for other useful aspects of telephony support, such as network type and voice implementation, for example, VoLTE, LTE, GSM, CDMA, and so on.

Making Calls

Now that you have the mechanism in place to determine either the requirement or desirability of having device call support, you can start leveraging that for interesting uses in your application. Thankfully, Android makes this very straightforward, thanks to its roots in being a smartphone operating system – the emphasis is on the phone.

Android's very helpful approach to making calls and other aspects of telephony easy to access and use centers on the `TelephonyManager` class. As its name suggests, TelephonyManager takes care of a range of call management and associated tasks, including things like call handling, call state, network details, and more. You will typically find yourself using these methods:

- `getPhoneType()`: Returns details about the phone and network, including radio support for GSM, LTE, and so on.
- `getNetworkType()`: This method provides details of the data capabilities from the currently connected cellular network. This is helpful in understanding classes of network, such as LTE, 4G, 3G, and other variants.

- getCallState(): A very handy method to help you determine if the phone is idle (not engaged in a call), in call setup mode, or currently in a call – known as being "off the hook" or "offhook."

To actually dial a number and start a call, you would invoke one of the ACTION_DIAL or ACTION_CALL intents. The use of, and differences in, these approaches will be covered shortly. Both approaches share a starting point of an intent that takes a Uri representing the number your user wishes to call, as a string in the format tel:*nnnnnnnn*. In the Uri string, *nnnnnnnn* represents the digits of the phone number to call. Seeing the process in action will help make the steps in calling a number clear.

> **Caution** It is good practice to examine the current call state before initiating any new calls. Android has a range of options to deal with multiple incoming and outgoing calls simultaneously, but that topic is firmly in the realm of advanced cellular wrangling and beyond the scope of this book. For now, make good use of the getCallState() method and base your actions on the results it delivers.

Laying Out the CallExample Application

The working example of a call-making application can be found in the Ch16/CallExample project. This project uses a very straightforward layout to allow you to focus on the calling and dialing options it exposes. To begin with, you can see the layout used in Listing 16-2.

***Listing 16-2.** The layout of the CallExample application*

```
<?xml version="1.0" encoding="utf-8"?>
<LinearLayout xmlns:android="http://schemas.android.com/apk/res/android"
    xmlns:tools="http://schemas.android.com/tools"
    android:layout_width="match_parent"
    android:layout_height="match_parent"
    android:orientation="vertical"
    tools:context=".MainActivity" >

    <TextView
        android:layout_width="wrap_content"
        android:layout_height="wrap_content"
        android:text="Phone Number:" />

    <EditText
        android:id="@+id/phonenumber"
        android:layout_width="match_parent"
        android:layout_height="wrap_content"
        android:inputType="number" />
```

```
    <Button
        android:id="@+id/usedialintent"
        android:layout_width="match_parent"
        android:layout_height="wrap_content"
        android:text="Call with ACTION_DIAL"
        android:onClick="callWithActionDialIntent" />

    <Button
        android:id="@+id/usecallintent"
        android:layout_width="match_parent"
        android:layout_height="wrap_content"
        android:text="Call with ACTION_CALL"
        android:onClick="callWithActionCallIntent" />
</LinearLayout>
```

Looking at the fields specified in the layout, you see a combination of `TextView` and `EditText`, which acts as the input field for the user to specify the number they wish to call. There are then two buttons, `"Call with ACTION DIAL"` and `"Call with ACTION_CALL`," which, as you can guess, trigger the respective methods to fire the intent of each type and thus make the phone call.

You can see the resulting rendered layout in Figure 16-1.

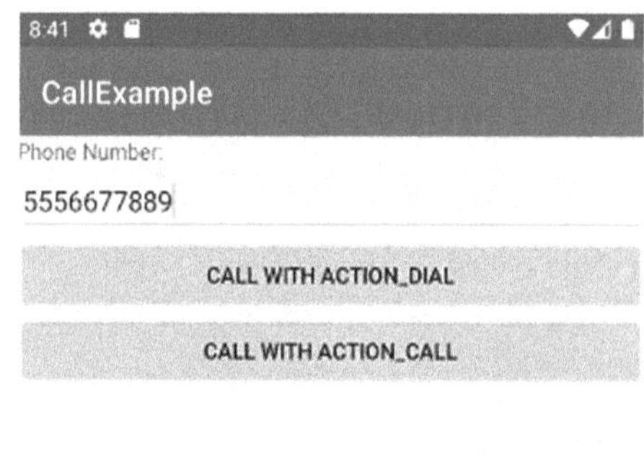

***Figure 16-1.** The CallExample layout for calling a number specified by the user*

I have deliberately chosen a few new features to include in this layout, beyond just the parts needed to showcase calling features – let's get those out of the way first. For a little variety, I have based this layout on a `LinearLayout`. You will see the `EditText` view with the id `phonenumber` has an attribute of `inputType="number"`. This will trigger Android to modify the Input Method parameters for this view so that input is only provided for digits and some limited punctuation. You can see the effect of this when running the application, as the virtual keyboard – or Input Method Editor (IME) – shown for input will look like a phone dialing pad rather than a full-blown keyboard.

THE ANDROID INPUT METHOD FRAMEWORK

Android provides a very powerful abstraction layer for dealing with user input, so that it can work flexibly with physical keyboards, soft keyboards that appear on-screen, and even handwriting recognition hardware and software. This is the Input Method Framework.

Whenever you use a view that triggers user input, you implicitly work with the framework by being presented one of the default editor views – an IME. You can live with the defaults and configure them as we have done in the phone dialing example, as well as for other common cases such as date input. You can also customize any IME to add or restrict what "keys" or values appear in the editor for the user to "press". You can read more about the Input Method Framework and IMEs on the book's website, at `www.beginningandroid.org`.

The `usedialintent` and `usecallintent` buttons have those IDs to give a strong hint of what is to come when each one is clicked. Using the first button "`Call with ACTION_DIAL`" will follow the code path that triggers the `ACTION_DIAL` intent, and the "`Call with ACTION_CALL`" will similarly trigger an `ACTION_CALL` intent. We will cover intents in more detail in Chapter 17, but for now, what is the difference between the two?

With an `ACTION_DIAL` intent, Android is notified that it needs to show an IME to the user, to confirm (or adjust) the number to be called before initiating the telephony magic behind the scenes. You can see this in Figure 16-2 further on in this chapter. In the alternative scenario, triggering an `ACTION_CALL` intent immediately initiates the call with the number provided in the Uri, without any further user interface or confirmation.

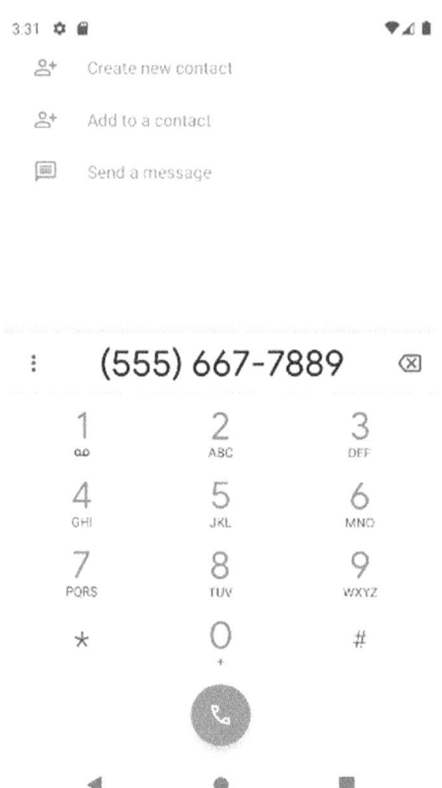

Figure 16-2. The CallExample application triggering ACTION_DIAL

There are many reasons for these two different approaches, but the main one is to do with ensuring the user is aware that a call is about to be initiated and to provide them control over the process, with `ACTION_DIAL`. This is very important when you consider that this is one of the built-in parts of Android that can cost the user real money. Making calls is cheap in some locations, but in many countries and areas is still something considered a nontrivial expense.

Because `ACTION_CALL` moves immediately to make a call without the confirmation step offered by `ACTION_DIAL`, Android offers a measure of protection for `ACTION_CALL` by requiring any use of it in an application to have the `CALL_PHONE` permission in its manifest before a `startActivity()` call with `ACTION_CALL` intent will work. Note also that the CALL_PHONE permission is considered to be in the highest category of permissions due to the potential for misuse, and therefore not only must you have this permission in your application manifest, but at runtime your users will also be prompted to allow the application to make calls. Defense in depth, so to speak.

Working Logic for the CallExample Application

With the options for calling understood and a straightforward layout ready to present to our users, it is time to look at the logic to bring calling to life. Listing 16-3 shows the Java code to plumb in the logic for our `CallExample` application.

***Listing 16-3.** Java logic for the CallExample application*

```
package org.beginningandroid.callexample;
import androidx.appcompat.app.AppCompatActivity;

import android.content.Intent;
import android.net.Uri;
import android.os.Bundle;
import android.view.View;
import android.widget.EditText;

public class MainActivity extends AppCompatActivity {

    @Override
    protected void onCreate(Bundle savedInstanceState) {
        super.onCreate(savedInstanceState);
        setContentView(R.layout.activity_main);
    }

    public void callWithActionDialIntent(View view) {
        EditText targetNumber=(EditText)findViewById(R.id.phonenumber);
        String dialThisNumber="tel:"+targetNumber.getText().toString();
        startActivity(new Intent(Intent.ACTION_DIAL, Uri.parse(dialThisNumber)));
    }

    public void callWithActionCallIntent(View view) {
        EditText targetNumber=(EditText)findViewById(R.id.phonenumber);
        String callThisNumber="tel:"+targetNumber.getText().toString();
        //the following intent only works with CALL_PHONE permission in place
        startActivity(new Intent(Intent.ACTION_CALL, Uri.parse(callThisNumber)));
    }
}
```

In a shift away from my normal approach of using a single onClick() method to guide subsequent execution with a switch statement on a view passed as a parameter, in this example instead, we have the methods callWithActionDialIntent() and callWithActionCallIntent() called directly from the layout configuration for each button, respectively.

Each method does some similar processing, by first determining into which View (in our case, the EditText) the user has entered the desired phone number. Then the Uri string is created with the appropriate formatting, and then startActivity() is called, with the desired intent and the Uri as parameters.

Making an ACTION_DIAL Call

In Figure 16-2, you can see the result of the user clicking the useDialIntent button. The digits (if any) from the EditText field have been constructed into a Uri behind the scenes in our callWithActionDialIntent(), and the ACTION_DIAL intent has been triggered.

The dialer you see in Figure 16-2 looks close to, but not exactly like, the IME shown in Figure 16-1. Key differences that you should spot include not just the slightly different styling of the numbers, the color scheme, and so on, but also the addition of options such as the ability to add this number as a contact. You can probably already guess that this is achieved by firing yet another intent.

You will also see formatting differences in the number and any associated punctuation marks like hyphens and parentheses. These will all be styled according to the location and language setting of the device. My AVD used for the view shown in Figure 16-2 uses a US locale and English as the language, thus the formatting you see with the first three digits treated as an area code and placed in parentheses and the hyphenation of the number as is idiomatic to the United States and Canada.

The final, and most important, addition is the green phone soft key at the bottom of the display, which you can guess is used to actually trigger the call.

Making an ACTION_CALL Call

Triggering a call with the `usecallintent` button shows you – well, it shows you – the dialing screen in Android and not much else. The dialer from the previous example is not triggered, and therefore there is little else to show or explain. Your users will go straight to the "actually making a call" dialing screen, as shown in Figure 16-3.

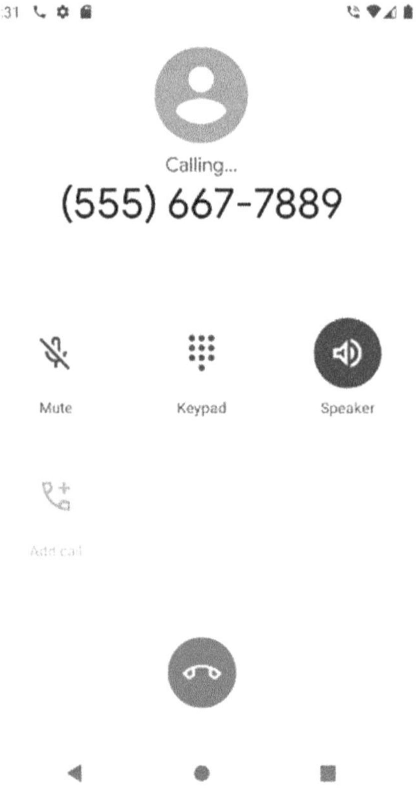

Figure 16-3. Calling in action, with ACTION_CALL

Handling Incoming Calls

Working with an incoming call is quite a bit more complex than receiving one and beyond the scope of this book. But taking full responsibility for an incoming call isn't always needed, and you can have your application do other useful things when a call is received, even if your application isn't the one dealing with the main task of managing the conversation.

The principal method to have a secondary application respond to an incoming call is to register a broadcast receiver for the broadcast intent ACTION_PHONE_STATE_CHANGED in your AndroidManifest.xml file. We will explore broadcast receivers in more depth in the next chapter. For now, it is enough to know that the ACTION_PHONE_STATE_CHANGED intent is fired by the TelephonyManager framework when a call is received. Listing 16-4 illustrates the receiver declaration in your manifest file.

***Listing 16-4.** Setting the receiver for incoming calls in AndroidManifest.xml*

```
<receiver android:name="MyPhoneStateChangedReceiver">
    <intent-filter>
        <action
            android:name="android.intent.action.PHONE_STATE"  />
    </intent-filter>
</receiver>
```

As a call is made to the device, the TelephonyManager fires the intent, and any receiver - including yours - is notified through use of a callback to the respective method specified. The ACTION_PHONE_STATE_CHANGED intent can also include two optional pieces of data that you can use to drive your logic. One is a state value for the call, such as CALL_STATE_OFFHOOK or CALL_STATE_RINGING, indicating the call has been answered or is still triggering the ringer waiting to be answered. If the CALL_STATE_RINGING value is used, there is also an optional additional value of EXTRA_INCOMING_NUMBER, which provides the caller ID, if the network has provided it.

Listing 16-5 is an example Java method for the MyPhoneStateChangedReceiver class to give you an idea when you can do with the callbacks.

***Listing 16-5.** A Java method fragment for working with an incoming call*

```
public class MyPhoneStateChangedReceiver extends BroadcastReceiver {
    @override
    public void onReceive(Context context, Intent intent) {
        String deviceCallState = intent.getStringExtra(TelephonyManager.EXTRA_STATE);
        if (deviceCallState.equals(TelephonyManager.EXTRA_STATE_RINGING) {
            // The phone is still ringing and might have the caller ID
            String callerID =
              intent.getStringExtra(TelephonyManager.EXTRA_INCOMING_NUMBER);
            // Try to display the number, etc.
        } else {
            // do something else
        }
    }
}
```

As with other hardware features, working with incoming calls is considered a sensitive task and requires explicit security permissions. Your application will need the READ_PHONE_STATE permission in the manifest file in order to receive the ACTION_PHONE_STATE_CHANGED intent.

Part IV

Get Together

Chapter 17

Understanding Intents, Events, and Receivers

As you are well into the latter half of this book, you have already been exposed to many techniques for designing and building activities. You have a firm grasp of the activity lifecycle and the callbacks triggered at various points as an activity starts, waits, pauses, and ultimately ends. Most of the example applications shared to this point have consisted of but one, single activity. How does that align with the comments I made at the start of the book that activities are cheap to create, use, and dispose of and that you should be prolific in your use of them?

I'm glad you asked! We want to ensure you can easily use and deploy multiple activities. While the earlier examples of video players, phone dialers, and more were good examples, each of those example applications launched its single activity when the application was launched, by having the activity specified in the AndroidManifest.xml file with several intriguing attributes within a child element known as <intent-filter>. That gives a little clue as to what might happen with more than one activity, but where and how do we specify second and subsequent activities, and how do we launch them when needed, if not when the application starts? Let's resolve these mysteries now.

Introducing Android Intents

The answer to the riddle about using multiple activities in your application lies in Android's equivalent to an event-based or message-based system, which is known as "intents." Just as with many other operating systems like Linux, Windows, and macOS, which base themselves on sending and responding to events, Android uses many similar concepts with intents including triggering and responding to actions that call for different activities to be presented to an application. There are some nuances to how this works in Android, so read on!

G. Allen, *Android for Absolute Beginners*, https://doi.org/10.1007/978-1-4842-6646-5_17

In its simplest form, an intent is a message sent from an application or service on Android, indicating that the user of the application or service wants to do something. That "something" could be a very well-known action, such as knowing exactly which activity to show a user based on their actions. But Android also offers the possibility of using other activities available from the base platform and other applications, from within your own application. In these circumstances, you might not have control over what other activities might be available nor which ones a device's user might prefer if there are multiple ways to satisfy their intent. Android has both the known and unknown options covered by using the matching part of the messaging system, known as receivers.

The job of a receiver – whether it is one you have written or from another application – is to listen out for intents and, if the receiver is capable of handling the kind of requested intent, to respond in a variety of ways. We will touch on receivers later in the chapter, after we have introduced the mechanics of intents. Both intents and receivers join to form the central mechanism for triggering successive activities and wiring together all of the activities you want in your application to create the final experience. As a bonus, this same mechanism is what allows you to harness other applications' activities where that makes sense for your application.

Understanding Intent Behavior

The two fundamental parts to the anatomy of an Android intent are the desired action the user or application has and the context in which that desired action is triggered. When we talk about desired actions, we mean such simple concepts as "view this thing," "make a new one of these," and so on. We will cover a more exhaustive list of actions shortly. When it comes to context, that can be more varied and is best be thought of as a range of supporting data that helps make sense of the intent, and any nuances or special circumstances, so it can be directed appropriately and serve the resulting activity.

This notion of support data takes the form of a `Uri`, such as `content://contacts/people/4`, which is `Uri` notation for the fourth set of contact details in Android's contact storage. If you take that `Uri` and pair it with an action like `ACTION_VIEW`, you have all the basic ingredients for an intent. Android interprets this intent and will find an activity able to show the user (or provide to a view for population) a set of contact details. If instead you make the action something like `ACTION_PICK` on a `Uri` that points to a collection – `content://contacts/people` – Android will look for any activity that can present multiple contacts as well as provide the ability to pick from them.

While a `Uri` bundled with an action is the simplest form of an intent, that's not the limit of what can be included. There are four additional aspects you can include in any intent you form, to expand the intent payload and help improve what Android and applications can do with the intent and its data payload. Each of these forms part of an Intent object:

> Intent category: The category for an intent helps define what activity can satisfy its base action. As an example, the "main" activity where you intend your users to start interacting with your application will be of category `LAUNCHER`. In this way, you signal to Android that the activity is suitable for inclusion on the Launcher menu (your Android home screen). Other activity/intent categories include `DEFAULT` and `ALTERNATIVE`.

MIME type specification: At times it will not be possible to know or have defined a specific Uri for a collection of items such as contacts or photos. To help Android find a suitable activity that can deal with sets of data in these circumstances, you can specify a MIME type, for instance, image-jpeg for an image file to help when dealing with sets of photos.

Component nomination: One of Android's strengths is the ability to leverage activities at runtime that you don't know about when building your application. But at other times, you know exactly which activity you want to invoke with your intent. One way to do this is to specify the class of the activity in the (desired) component of the intent. In this way, you don't need to add other contextual hints in the hope you trigger the right intent, with the trade-off being taking on the risk of assumed knowledge about the implementation of the component class. This goes against the tenet of object-oriented programming known as encapsulation.

Extras: There are times when you have other contextual clues and data that you would like to make available to the receiver for a variety of reasons. When this doesn't fit neatly into a `Uri` naming scheme, extras come to the rescue. This is a simple Bundle object that can include anything else you would like. The one caveat is that providing such a Bundle is no guarantee the receiver will make use of it.

An Intent Action for Every Occasion

You can find a full list of intent actions and categories provided with the Android documentation at `https://developer.android.com/reference/android/content/Intent#constants_1` so I won't duplicate that here. Instead, let's look at the most common and interesting actions, to inform us for the forthcoming examples in this chapter and the remainder of the book:

- ACTION_AIRPLANE_MODE_CHANGED: The user of the device has toggled the airplane mode setting from on to off or vice versa.
- ACTION_CAMERA_BUTTON: The camera button (hard button or soft button) was clicked.
- ACTION_DATE_CHANGED: The date has changed, meaning any application logic you have written that uses timers, elapsed time, and so forth might be affected.
- ACTION_HEADSET_PLUG: The user of the device has attached or removed headphones to or from the headphone socket.

As you can see, intent actions cover all kinds of things happening in your application and also the entire device environment.

Caution: Google adds new actions to the set available for intents with each new release of Android. It also deprecates (and later removes) some older actions it deems no longer useful. As you maintain your application over time, you should check to see if actions on which your application depends have been deprecated or removed.

Understanding Intent Routing

You might have thought that component nomination, mentioned earlier in the chapter, would ordinarily be a great way to invoke any and all activities you desire, whether those of your own writing or others. The reality is a little different.

If you have an activity's class that you have written and understand how and why it is the best recipient for an intent, then it is perfectly OK to do so. But when working with activities from other applications, it is not reliable and at times is unsafe and can result in poor, unexpected, or downright incorrect behavior.

The programming principle of encapsulation is at the core of this warning. Think for a moment about letting other developers rely on your own classes and their internal implementation. As you mature as a developer, you will constantly tweak and adjust code and classes, and this introduces the very real likelihood that someone's assumption about the internals of a class will wind up wrong, because you have changed the logic. The same is true in reverse, and you shouldn't rely on implementation logic staying unchanged (or even staying in existence at all) in others' applications.

To safely target the application or service of your choice with the intent model, prefer instead the use of Uris and MIME types. If we can peek into the innards of other people's applications, how then do we direct Android to the preferred activities or receivers (such as a service) to receive the intent? The answer lies in Android's implicit routing scheme, which passes intents on to all of the activities and so forth that should receive them, based on a set of eligibility rules.

The rules for the implicit routing scheme are as follows:

1. The activity must indicate its ability to handle the intent, through the appropriate manifest file entry (discussed in the next section).
2. If a MIME type is part of the intent context, the activity must support the MIME type.
3. Every category in the event context must also be supported by the activity.

These rules help narrow down the possible set of matching activities that can receive your intent to only those that will do a faithful job of acting on the intent in a way suitable for your use.

Including Intents in Your Manifest

Android uses your `AndroidManifest.xml` file as the location to hold intent filters, indicating which components in your application can be notified and respond appropriately to given intents. If your component's manifest entry doesn't list the intent action, then it won't be chosen to receive notification of such an intent via the implicit routing mechanism. You can think of this as the opt-in approach to components handling intents, building a list of the intents you do wish to consume.

When you create a new Android project, Android Studio creates your first intent filter as part of the skeleton AndroidManifest.xml file. You have already seen this in action for all of the example applications so far in the book. As a refresher, Listing 17-1 is the manifest from your very first application, MyFirstApp, in Chapter 2. In bold you can see the activity MainActivity and its specified intent file.

Listing 17-1. *Example intent filters from an AndroidManifest.xml file*

```
<?xml version="1.0" encoding="utf-8"?>
<manifest xmlns:android="http://schemas.android.com/apk/res/android"
    package="org.beginningandroid.myfirstapp">

    <application
        android:allowBackup="true"
        android:icon="@mipmap/ic_launcher"
        android:label="@string/app_name"
        android:roundIcon="@mipmap/ic_launcher_round"
        android:supportsRtl="true"
        android:theme="@style/AppTheme">
        <activity android:name=".MainActivity">
            <intent-filter>
                <action android:name="android.intent.action.MAIN" />
                <category android:name="android.intent.category.LAUNCHER" />
            </intent-filter>
        </activity>
    </application>

</manifest>
```

Two parts of the intent filter are key to its operation. First, we specify the MainActivity activity is of the category LAUNCHER, meaning any intent that triggers it must also be of that category. Second, we also specify the action android.intent.action.MAIN, which is used to designate that any intent looking for a MAIN-capable activity could be accepted. You can have more possible actions for your MainActivity as well as more categories, signifying it has more capabilities that you are supporting via whatever logic you have written for the activity's class.

Any other activities for your application would not use the MAIN/LAUNCHER combination for action and category – in almost all circumstances, you only use one such designation in your manifest. While there are many categories and actions from which to choose, you will very frequently end up using the DEFAULT category, particularly with any view- or edit-style actions, together with a <data> element describing the mimeType that an activity can deal with for viewing or editing. For example, Listing 17-2 shows an intent filter for a notes-style application.

Listing 17-2. *An intent filter for an example secondary activity in your application*

```
<activity
    android:name=".MyNotesActivity"
    <intent-filter>
```

```
        <action android:name="android.intent.action.VIEW" />
        <category android:name="android.intent.category.DEFAULT" />
        <data android:mimeType="vnd.android.cursor.dir/vnd.google.note" />
    </intent-filter>
</activity>
```

The activity defined in the preceding includes an intent filter that describes how it can be launched to deal with an intent from any application asking to view content using the Uri for content with a `vnd.android.cursor.dir/vnd.google.note mimeType`. This intent could come from your own application, such as following a user action from your launcher activity, or from any other application that can create a well-formed `Uri` for this activity and use that as the payload for an intent it fires.

Using Android's Verified Links

An additional feature for dealing with the Uris of intents is the mechanism of auto-verified links, which deals specifically with Uris that are also valid URLs (so website addresses). With a verified link, you can add to your code an explicit rule to make the link between URLs from a specific website and the companion application 100% verified and the preferred way of dealing with intents that have a matching URL. This includes behind-the-scenes mechanisms to enable seamless authentication if needed and avoid the traditional "website or application" picker dialogs that Android historically used.

Seeing Intent-Launched Activities in Action

Armed with the knowledge of the theory and structure of intents, you are ready to dive into an example that illustrates their power and convenience. I have mentioned multiple times the philosophy of Android in having many activities to support the array of functionality you desire for your application, such as a photo album application having a given activity to view individual pictures, another activity to view groups or albums (perhaps using the `GridView`), and even more activities for tagging, sharing on social media, and so on.

There is one last thought to consider before we delve into implementing a multiactivity application. If your application launches an activity, via an intent, from a given activity, what information about the state of the launched activity should the invoking activity be concerned with? Does your launching activity need to know anything about the second (or subsequent) activity, such as when it completes or what work it achieves, and be passed some result?

Deciding on Activity Dependency

To deal with the dependency vs. no dependency issue, Android provides two primary ways to invoke an activity with an intent.

The first approach is the `StartActivity()` method, which is used to flag that Android should find the activity best matched to the payload of the intent – including action, category, and MIME type. The "winning" activity is started, and the payload from the intent will be passed for any use the activity might make of it. The calling activity will continue its lifecycle and will not receive any update or notification about the called activity's work, lifecycle events, data changes, and so forth.

Relying on a lottery, or something approaching one, might not sound the greatest way of influencing which activity should be chosen to deal with an intent. You need not worry, as there is a second approach known as the `startActivityForResult()` method. In `startActivityForResult()`, more than just a well-formed intent is used to influence which activity is triggered; it also includes a specific reference to the desired activity and a unique calling number to the activity invocation. A notification is sent back to the calling activity when the called activity ends, which means you can mimic a traditional user experience of a parent window or screen opening a child window or screen, for things like processing a login request or selecting an option from an available list. In detail, the callback includes

- The unique calling number associated with the activity specific to this call and the original `startActivityForResult()` method. In this design, you would opt to use a switch pattern to determine which of your child activities had completed and continue with your application logic appropriately.
- A numeric result code from the stock Android-provided results of `RESULT_OK` and `RESULT_CANCELED`, along with any custom data or results you care to provide of the form `RESULT_FIRST_USER, RESULT_FIRST_USER + 1`, and so on.
- (Optionally) A `String` object with any data your called activity should return, such as the item chosen from a `ListAdapter`.
- (Optionally) A `Bundle` containing any additional information that doesn't fit neatly into the first three options.

Armed with the choice between `startActivity()` and `startActivityForResult()`, your main concern should be determining which is best to use at application design time. It is possible to dynamically determine this at runtime, but juggling all the emerging possibilities among potentially dozens or hundreds of activities can become overwhelming.

Creating an Intent

With the knowledge of how to invoke activities using your desired method, what remains is for you to create the `Intent` object to use as the payload from which to trigger its launch. Should you want to launch another activity from within the realm of your own application, then the most direct approach is to create your intent directly and explicitly state the component you wish to activate. This would have you create a new Intent object like this:

```
new Intent(this, SomeOtherActivity.class);
```

Here, you explicitly reference that you want to invoke your `SomeOtherActivity` activity. For this style of direct invocation, you don't need to construct an intent filter in your `AndroidManifest.xml` file – your `SomeOtherActivity` will be started whether it likes it or not!

Obviously it is your responsibility as the developer to ensure your SomeOtherActivity can respond accordingly.

I outlined in the earlier sections of this chapter the elegance and preference for using a Uri and matched set of criteria to feed to Android so that it can find appropriate activities for your uses. Android has a range of supported Uri schemes, and you are free to create a Uri matching any one of them. As an example, here is a snippet creating a Uri for a contact in the contacts system:

```
Int myContactNumber = 4;
Uri myUri = Uri.parse("content://contacts/people/"+myContactNumber.toString());
Intent myIntent = new Intent(Intent.ACTION_VIEW, myUri);
```

We are using the number for the fourth contact and then constructing the Uri string to reference that contact. We can then pass that Uri to the Intent object.

Starting the Intent-Invoked Activity

You have built your intent, so it is time to choose which of startActivity() or startActivityForResult() to call. There are some more advanced options you could consider, but they are beyond the scope of this book. If you are interested, the Android documentation has more to say on options including startActivities(), startActivityFromFragment(), and startActivityIfNeeded().

Listing 17-3 shows a sample layout from the ch17/IntentExample project, using a very simple layout with one label, one field, and one button.

***Listing 17-3.** A layout to demonstrate intents*

```
<androidx.constraintlayout.widget.ConstraintLayout
    xmlns:android="http://schemas.android.com/apk/res/android"
    xmlns:app="http://schemas.android.com/apk/res-auto"
    xmlns:tools="http://schemas.android.com/tools"
    android:layout_width="match_parent"
    android:layout_height="match_parent"
    tools:context=".MainActivity">

    <TextView
        android:id="@+id/textView1"
        android:layout_width="wrap_content"
        android:layout_height="wrap_content"
        android:layout_alignBaseline="@+id/myContact"
        android:layout_alignLeft="@+id/button1"
        android:layout_alignBottom="@+id/myContact"
        android:text="Contact Number:"
        tools:layout_editor_absoluteX="41dp"
        tools:layout_editor_absoluteY="31dp" />
```

```
    <EditText
        android:id="@+id/myContact"
        android:layout_width="wrap_content"
        android:layout_height="wrap_content"
        android:layout_alignParentTop="true"
        android:layout_toRightOf="@+id/textView1"
        android:ems="10"
        android:inputType="number"
        app:layout_constraintStart_toEndOf="@+id/textView1"
        tools:layout_editor_absoluteY="19dp">

        <requestFocus />
    </EditText>

    <Button
        android:id="@+id/button1"
        android:layout_width="match_parent"
        android:layout_height="wrap_content"
        android:layout_below="@+id/myContact"
        android:onClick="viewContact"
        android:text="View Contact"
        app:layout_constraintTop_toBottomOf="@+id/myContact"
        tools:layout_editor_absoluteX="16dp" />

</androidx.constraintlayout.widget.ConstraintLayout>
```

> **Note** In this ConstraintLayout example, I have deliberately left the EditText and TextView not fully constrained vertically and/or horizontally. You will see warnings in Android Studio that by not having these constraints, the widgets will "jump" to default positions without them. In this design, this still produces the desired layout, but you can add constraints to these views if you prefer when you run the example.

If you look at the View-based widgets in the layout, you see the button will invoke a `viewContact()` method. To give the user the experience they expect, we'll need to code the creation of a contact `Uri` as explained in the preceding section and use it to create the `Intent` object that will start an activity to (hopefully) display a contact. The example code is shown in Listing 17-4.

***Listing 17-4.** Java logic for our intent-triggering contact application*

```
package org.beginningandroid.intentexample;

import androidx.appcompat.app.AppCompatActivity;
import android.content.Intent;
import android.net.Uri;
import android.os.Bundle;
import android.view.View;
import android.widget.EditText;
```

```
public class MainActivity extends AppCompatActivity {
    private EditText myContact;

    @Override
    protected void onCreate(Bundle savedInstanceState) {
        super.onCreate(savedInstanceState);
        setContentView(R.layout.activity_main);
        myContact=(EditText)findViewById(R.id.myContact);
    }

    public void viewContact(View view) {
        String myContactNumber=myContact.getText().toString();
        Uri myUri = Uri.parse("content://contacts/people/"+myContactNumber);
        startActivity(new Intent(Intent.ACTION_VIEW, myUri));
    }
}
```

The logic used here is purposefully very simple and very direct. This lets you focus on exactly what we have discussed in the chapter.

> **Note** To see this example work in practice, you will need to have used your AVD or device to create a few contacts and preserve the state of the AVD so that they are not lost when restarting the AVD. In this way, there will be contacts to actually display when the intent fires!

Running the `IntentExample` project will result in the `IntentExample` activity showing as in Figure 17-1.

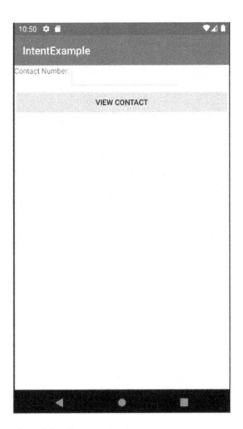

Figure 17-1. The main IntentExample activity showing after launch

The reason you see this activity first is because the automatic project setup from Android Studio (or any other IDE that you are using) has added it with the necessary attributes and data value of the LAUNCHER category in your manifest file.

Enter a number for a contact in the EditText field, and click the View Contact button, and intents and receivers will do their magic. Your contact Uri is bundled up into your intent, and the call to startActivity() sends Android off to sift through all the activities from all the applications on the device, to find the most appropriate activity to handle the ACTION_VIEW action for your intent. You can see the result in Figure 17-2.

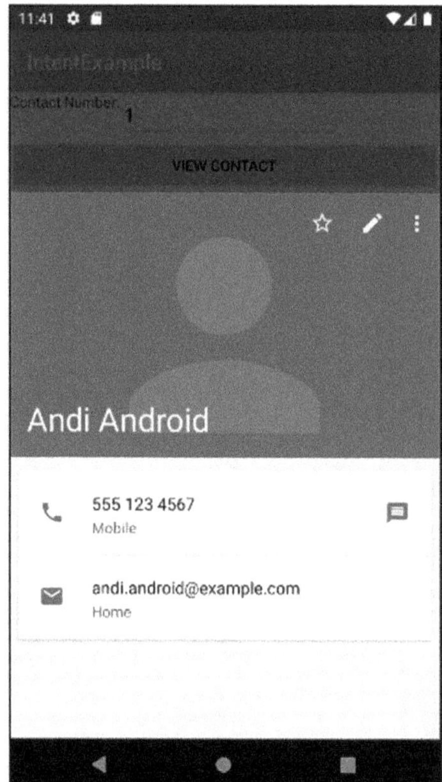

Figure 17-2. The contact activity selected to satisfy our intent

What you see in the screen shown in Figure 17-2 is the current Android-native contact view activity, rather than anything I have coded in the `IntentExample` project. You would consider this a safe invocation of an activity from outside your application as we took the right steps to provide a `Uri`, and we can safely expect Android itself to find the right activity to fulfill our intent. There was no brute-force attempt to demand a specific activity using the component-naming method.

Introducing Receivers

Throughout this chapter, we have explored how to use intents to create and activate multiple activities within your application, with the goal of handling a broad variety of actions in your application in response to your user's interaction and desire. But not every response to the user's wish, or the intent triggered, needs to be handled in the scope of (yet another) activity. There are a number of real-world examples of satisfying an intent where you really do not need all of the features and sophistication of an activity, lightweight as they are. Some examples include data manipulation, performing calculations, and so forth where the calculation or result can be determined without the involvement of any UI or wanting to direct the intent at an Android service rather than any end user–facing application. For instance, you may want to build a music sharing service that sends all music to a cloud storage provider for backup, without any user interaction. There are also more advanced circumstances where you won't know if a full-blown UI activity is required until runtime, which means you need to plan and design for activity-driven and "activity-less" approaches simultaneously.

Using Receivers When No UI Is Needed

To deal with these "activity-less" situations, Android provides the `BroadcastReceiver` interface and the concept of receivers. You're now familiar with the lightweight nature of activity-based UI screens for rapidly dealing with user interactions, and receivers are a complement to this that provide lightweight objects that are created to receive and process a broadcast intent and can then be discarded.

The Android documentation shows you that there is only one method in the definition for a BroadcastReceiver, called named `onReceive()`. The `onReceive()` method can be thought of as the "Get to it!" method for your receiver. It is up to you to implement any desired logic in a receiver and ensure it works with the associated intent in the way(s) you have in mind.

Implementing `BroadcastReceivers` starts in the same way as activities, with a declaration in your `AndroidManifest.xml` file. Use the element name <receiver>, with an `android:name` attribute of the class that implements `BroadcastReceiver`, for example:

```
<receiver android:name=".ReceiverClass" />
```

Any receiver you implement is ephemeral, existing only for the time it takes to execute the logic you create to implement its `onReceive()` method, following which it is then discarded for garbage collection. There are restrictions to receiver behavior, some expected and some a surprise. As you would expect from an approach designed for when UIs are needed, you cannot invoke any UI elements in your receiver logic. Less expected, but still important, is the restriction that you cannot issue any callbacks. These restrictions are relaxed a little for receivers implemented on a service or an activity (an allowed combination), where in these cases the receiver lives for the lifetime of the related object.

You cannot create receivers via the manifest for services or activities. You can dynamically generate receivers for these circumstances using `registerReceiver()` within `onResume()` to flag that your activity is able to receive intents of particular actions/categories/mime-type combinations. If you use this approach, you must also perform housecleaning by calling `unregisterReceiver()` during the `onPause()` callback.

Working with Receiver Limitations

There is one additional limitation of receivers you should know about, in addition to the ones noted in the previous section. The mechanics of intents and broadcast receivers described so far might lead you to think you can use both in combination as a general approach to messaging for you application. The "spanner in the works" to this idea is the activity lifecycle. In particular, when activities are paused, they will not receive intents.

The inability to receive intents when paused means you open up the problem of missed messages (intent broadcasts), and you will need to avoid receivers bound to activities, instead preferring declarations via the `AndroidManifest.xml`. You will also need to think about “re-messaging” and retry logic to be able to recover from any missed messages or look to use a more sophisticated third-party message bus system or similar approach.

Summary

In this chapter, I have introduced all of the mechanisms you need to expand your applications from single-activity programs to the realm of activities galore! You have a good foundation in the intent and broadcast receiver mechanics of Android and should be able to expand your use of activities in the applications you plan to write.

Chapter 18

Introducing Android Services

Thanks to its Linux operating system heritage, Android is blessed with many platform features that bring the power of Linux to an entirely new user base. Part of this rich heritage includes a particular group of applications that run in the background, without a user interface, which offer their capabilities to all other programs running on Android. These are known in Android as services, similar to the daemon concept in Linux and the services concept in Microsoft Windows.

This chapter will explore some of the fundamentals of Android services, showing you the steps to create, start, and operate with services. To add to this exploration, we will also look at a range of simple service examples to broaden your understanding using services.

Services Background

The rationale for services comes from many needs, in particular those that arise when functions or tasks need to be performed by one or several applications, but where those tasks don't need any form of UI interaction or user-facing activity to be displayed. On any Android device, there are hundreds of services that run at any point in time, including ones that

- Provide a local interface to control a remote API such as a location service or mapping applications.
- Maintain long-lived connections for messenger and chat applications that have "conversations" running over days, weeks, months, or more.
- Continue to process a task or piece of work once invoked by a user, without further interaction. A great example is downloading updates for Android applications from Google Play store and other locations.

These are just some of the examples you can find right now on an Android device, and there are obviously many more. For example, think back to our audio and video examples and the Media framework, where the tasks of actual audio and video playback relied on background services.

G. Allen, *Android for Absolute Beginners*, https://doi.org/10.1007/978-1-4842-6646-5_18

You are not obliged to use services when building applications, but you can think of them as helpers that stand by ready to help you if needed – both the services you might write and the default services provided by the Android platform.

Using WorkManager as an Alternative to Services

While the balance of this chapter focuses on the tried and tested service approach to the needs outlined in the preceding section, Android does offer other approaches. One of these is the WorkManager, which is part of the Jetpack libraries introduced earlier in the book. WorkManager allows you to have work performed in the background even after your application is terminated. You can think of WorkManager as the simple, handheld way of having work performed asynchronously outside of your application.

WorkManager has its strengths, and you can learn more about them at `https://developer.android.com/topic/libraries/architecture/workmanager/basics`. The universal capabilities of services, and their power and utility, make for a compelling subject to master and add to your developer toolset, and we will delve into that for the rest of this chapter.

Starting with Your Own Service

Defining and creating your own service application is remarkably similar to what you have already learned in making normal activity-based Android applications. The steps to create an Android service should appear familiar to you:

- Using an Android-provided base class, extend it and add any necessary class inheritance to create your own custom service.
- Determine which callback methods you need to override, and then write the code to implement your desired logic.
- Add the necessary `AndroidManifest.xml` entries to provide permissions, definitions, and links into the wider Android platform so that your service can run and serve other applications.

We will explore each of these areas to give you a full understanding in the following section.

Implementing Your Service Class

Within the default Android development framework, the `Service` class is provided as a foundation from which to build your own services. The `Service` class also provides several useful subclasses out of the box that match common service patterns many developers have, though you are free to start with the `Service` class itself or any of the helper subclasses depending on your needs. Of these, by far the most useful and commonly adopted is the `IntentService` subclass.

The basic code outline for a simple service is shown in Listing 18-1.

Listing 18-1. Outline of a service application in Android

```
package com.artifexdigital.android.serviceskeleton

import android.app.service
//more imports here

public class SkeletonService extends Service {
    //overrides and implementation logic here
}
```

Managing the Service Lifecycle via Callbacks

There are a range of callbacks provided by the `Service` class and its subclasses, designed for you to override with your own logic implementing service control behavior. The `Service` callback and lifecycle notions are very similar to the `Activity` and `Fragment` lifecycles we explored in Chapters 11 and 12, with the main difference being there are fewer states in which a service will find itself. This simplicity means there are only five main callbacks for you to consider when dealing with service behavior when coding your supporting logic:

- `onCreate()`: Very similar to the `onCreate()` method for activities, the service's `onCreate()` method is invoked when any trigger for service activity happens.
- `onStartCommand()`: When the related `startService()` method is called by a client application, the `onStartCommand()` method is invoked and its logic processed.
- `onBind()`: When client applications attempt to bind to the service with a `bindService()` call, the `onBind()` method is invoked each time.
- `onTrimMemory()`: As part of Android's attempt to manage resources in an assertive fashion, services selected for resource reclamation while the device is under memory shortage will have their `onTrimMemory()` method called. This gives the service a more controlled way to try to return memory, before more drastic measures are taken.
- `onDestroy()`: When performing a normal graceful shutdown, `onDestroy()` is invoked. Just as with normal activities, graceful shutdown is not guaranteed, and therefore neither is a call to `onDestroy()` guaranteed.

Your understanding of lifecycle management from activities and fragments stays the same. That means your service should create what it needs during its `onCreate()` call and clean up and dispose of any lingering resources during `onDestroy()`, if not before.

One thing that differs between activities and services is that for services, there are no `onPause()` and `onResume()` equivalents. Your service is either running or it's not. That means there is no need to provide background transition methods when a service is considered always in the background. This absence of pause/resume means you always should be mindful to minimize any state held by the service or use preferences or other storage where appropriate to survive unexpected service termination. Not only can Android terminate a service at any time for resources – bypassing any call to onDestroy() – but users can also kill your services via the application management systems' setting Activity. Services with clients bound to them become more complicated to manage in this regard, and we will explore this in the examples in a moment.

Providing Manifest Entries for Your Service

To declare your service application, you will need to make appropriate declarations in the AndroidManifest.xml file. This begins with the core definition of a <service> element as a child of the <application> element. Listing 18-2 shows the basic entry for a service, including the required android:name attribute, which in this case is "Skeleton".

***Listing 18-2.** A minimal service definition in the AndroidManifest.xml file*

```
<?xml version="1.0" encoding="utf-8"?>
<manifest xmlns:android="http://schemas.android.com/apk/res/android"
    package="com.artifexdigital.android.skeletonservice" >

    <uses-permission android:name="android.permission.INTERNET" />

    <application
        android:allowBackup="true"
        android:icon="@mipmap/ic_launcher"
        android:label="@string/app_name"
        android:theme="@style/AppTheme" >

        <!-- any other application child elements would go here -->
        <service android:name="Skeleton">
    </application>
</manifest>
```

You are free to mingle the definitions for a service and activities in the same project and therefore in the same AndroidManifest.xml file. You will find this commonly done for applications that are developed in conjunction with their own services. When you do create services, you don't always want to allow just any application to bind to them and use them. In these cases, you can use an android:permission attribute in your <service> element to restrict access.

Service Communication

Defining your new service is no more complicated than the steps already outlined in this chapter. Once you have your service created, controlling how client applications such as activities and other services interact with your service is a little more involved.

Clients (activities or services) communicating with a service take either of two possible paths: starting commands or binding. When it comes to your service communicating back to clients, things expand to quite a few options from which you as the developer can choose.

Client-to-Service Communication

When a client of any kind wants to work with a service, whether that client is an activity, fragment, or some other service, there is one central question that will guide you in choosing which of the two communication approaches is best suited to the task. Is this a one-time, never-to-be-repeated request for a service to do something for the client? In these single-interaction cases, the command approach to service communication is best. If the client needs to work with the service over a sequence of actions, maintaining ongoing interaction with the service, then service binding is the way to go.

Invoking Commands with startService()

The easiest way to have your service carry out tasks for a client application, whether it's an activity or some other source, is a call to the `startService()` method. In Chapter 17, we introduced the `startActivity()` method that can trigger an arbitrary activity by taking an intent and some parameters, and in a similar way, the `startService()` method also accepts an intent and a set of intent extras as parameters to let you pass a context-specific payload to the receiving service. The most basic form of calling `startService()` is as follows:

```
startService(someSignatureIntent);
```

This basic form of calling `startService()` provides the intended Intent class as the sole parameter. Calling `startService()` is asynchronous, and your application's main thread – which manages the primary UI – will not block waiting for a response and instead will continue immediately with its normal lifecycle.

Calling `startService()` will trigger Android to start the service if it is not started, and in both the started and to-be-started flows, Android then passes the intent from the first parameter to the `onStartCommand()` method. Your service implementation can inspect and use the intent, and optionally the data payload in a second parameter, as you desire in the logic you code for the `onStartCommand()` method.

Whereas the calling application is not blocked by the service invocation, your service will process the `onStartCommand()` method in its main thread, so you should take care not to undertake too much heavy processing, blocking external calls, or any other time-consuming work that might prevent a speedy response. Where you do need to perform such long-running work as part of your service logic, you can explore adding further threads with the java.util.concurrent package and its executor and related abilities to carry out this work off the main service thread.

The fire-and-forget nature of using `startService()` means that it will not return payloads or a response in the normal sense to the calling application. For those circumstances where this is desired, the service-to-client communication approach is more appropriate and covered later in the chapter. The `startService()` call does return a value to signal whether the call completed successfully or was killed for resource starvation or other reasons. This return value is from a small predefined set, from which you will commonly see the following:

- START_STICKY: Restart the service once Android has enough free memory to do so, but don't worry about the triggering intent, and pass a null intent instead.

- START_NON_STICKY: Don't automatically restart the service at all, even if Android resource pressure drops to a low enough level to allow it. Implicitly this means the service will not be started until your application or some other explicitly calls `startService()` or otherwise invokes the need for the service again.
- START_REDELIVER_INTENT: Restart the service once Android has enough free memory, and also attempt to redeliver the original Intent object passed to the service when the original (failing) call was made.

Once a service starts, whether from a `startService()` invocation or otherwise, it will run indefinitely, barring any low-resource conditions on the device that might see Android kill it as part of wider resource management. This is in keeping with the notion that once your client has what it wants, it doesn't really care what happens to the service afterward. From a developer standpoint, you might consider from time to time whether your service is doing anything useful, and for want of client demand determine that it has nothing to do and to gracefully shut down. There are two main options for a service to terminate itself, as follows:

- Use the `stopService()` method. Analogous to `startService()`, you call `stopService()` with a parameter of the same intent used to start the service or an intent of a derived class. The service will be stopped and all resources released and state destroyed. As Android does not track the origin or number of `startService()` calls to a service, it similarly doesn't differentiate as to which client sends the appropriate `stopService()` call. Only one `stopService()` command is required, regardless of how many `startService()` calls were received in the service's lifetime.
- Code your service with a `stopSelf()` call. Your service can control its own demise, and you might look to do this as part of some logical culmination to the work your service performs, such as when a music track has finished playing or a file download completes.

When building your own services, feel free to explore both approaches to managing their termination. Alternatively, you can leave this to Android's general service cleanup capabilities. If you choose to use service binding as the method for working with a service, the cleanup and shutdown mechanisms are very different.

Using the Bind Approach with Services

The single-shot approach of using `startService()` for one-time interaction with a service is a very useful mechanism. There are times where you will want to interact with a service multiple times or in more complex situations that need more than a single to-and-fro, such as sending successive commands or exchanging data in both directions so your application can perform some useful work for its user.

This is where the binding approach with `bindService()` steps in. Binding to a service sets up a two-way communication channel so your application can access the service's API via its Binder. A Binder is the object returned to the calling application from the `bindService()` call and is then used for all subsequent activity. A client using the bind approach can signal to Android that it wants the service started if it is currently stopped, by using the

BIND_AUTO_CREATE flag. One difference from the startService() approach is that once a client releases the bind with the service, the service will be marked as capable of being shut down. We will cover the mechanics of shutdown in these circumstances later in the chapter.

> **Caution** When invoking a service that may not be running, if you do not provide the BIND_AUTO_CREATE flag as part of the bindService() call, then you risk the method returning false (and not providing you a Binder object) if the service was not already running. The lesson here is to not rely on hunches or assumed state for the service. Instead, always practice clean exception handling and always check for bindService() failure regardless of the circumstances.

When Android is under memory pressure, it can help to signal that you can cope with a sudden shutdown of the service you are working with, using the BIND_ALLOW_OOM_MANAGEMENT flag. This flag signals that your application's binding is not considered critical and it can tolerate the sudden disappearance of the service terminating in out-of-memory circumstance. At its simplest, you are flagging that you are happy to sacrifice your binding (and Binder object) for the greater good of the device and all the other applications running on it.

An application's call to bindService() is an asynchronous call, which includes the intent used to identify the service and optionally the BIND_AUTO_CREATE flag. Because bindService() is asynchronous, you will not know the results and subsequent state of the service until the ServiceConnection object is interrogated and the resulting Binder object is returned from onBind(). Once you confirm these have been instantiated and are available, you can start calling the Binder methods and actually interact with the functionality of the service. It's normal for you to subclass the Binder methods to actually implement whatever logic you intend your service to have.

Your application can keep the ServiceConnection object – and the implicit connection to the service – in existence for as long as you like. When you have completed working with the service, you call the unbindService() method to indicate that your service binding can be released, and the ServiceConnection object and associated resources are freed. This unbinding eventually leads to onServiceDisconnected() being called, along with the Binder object falling out of scope, meaning any custom logic you've built and presented via its API-like methods should no longer be invoked. Should any other applications have bound to the service, your call to unbindService() will not cause the service to be stopped. In practice, the last client application to unbind is the one that will trigger Android to then shut down the service.

Service-to-Client Communication

As we have explored services so far in this chapter, you can see how client-to-service communication is well supported by the command approach and the bind approach. When it comes to communicating from a service to a client, there are a range of options to cover almost any scenario you can imagine. Let's explore the main options and keep in mind that these approaches are not quite as structured as the startService() and bindService() options for client-to-service communication.

Using bindService() Methods for All Communication

When considering how services communicate back to their interested clients, the first option to consider is having interaction happen via `bindService()` and the methods you create for clients to use. The advantage of the bind approach is that you control exactly what the client receives by the returned objects and information from your service methods and get guarantees that the client actually gets what it asks for because the only way for the client to receive what it wants is to call your API methods.

The clear disadvantage to this approach is that clients not using `bindService()` to set up a durable duplex channel with your service won't be able to receive anything – any client that interacts via `startService()` calls is just out of luck! That might sound acceptable now, but it's good practice to design your service to accommodate many different client use patterns.

Intents and Broadcast Receivers

In Chapter 17, we introduced Android's foundational approach to communicating between applications, in the intent and broadcast receiver mechanisms. As introduced, you experimented with examples that broadcast an intent from your code. Services are also at liberty to use this approach!

In practice, you leverage intents and receivers by registering a `BroadcastReceiver` object using the `registerReceiver()` method in your client application and use that to capture component-specific broadcasts from the service imperative that you would document, so that the client can correctly identify the broadcast intents and process them as needed.

Taking an intent approach has benefits, but does come with the drawback that the intent must be action-orientated, rather than relying on some activity to volunteer to act on it. You are also assuming that the client activity itself is still running with its receiver and that it hasn't been paused or chosen for termination due to resource pressure or other on-device events.

Use PendingIntent Objects

Android provides the `PendingIntent` object to signal an intent with associated action that needs to be performed. When it comes to services, your client would call `onActivityResult()` to deal with the downstream logic once the service performs its work. The client passes the `PendingIntent` object to the service, through `startService()` calls' ability to take an extra payload, and the service would then signal the client by calling the `send()` method on it.

There is extra work required to make this approach effective, as you will need client code to interpret and identify which of the variety of `send()` method invocations has been used.

Use Messenger and Message Objects

Should PendingIntent objects not be enough by way of alternatives, Android additionally provides the Messenger object for inter-context communication, such as from services to activities. An individual activity comes with a Handler object, which can be used for the activity to send messages itself. However, the Handler is not exposed for activity-to-service or intra-activity interaction. This is where the Messenger object saves the day. It can send messages to any Handler and thus can be used to bridge the gap and reach any activity.

To make use of Messenger objects, you add one as an extra to your intent prior to invoking the service. The service receives the intent in typical fashion and can extract the Messenger object, and when the time comes to communicate to the client, the service should create and populate a Message object and then call the Messenger's .send() method to pass the Message as a parameter back to the client. On your client side, you receive this via the Handler and its handleMessage() method.

While this is conceptually very neat, there are the extra steps to create and exchange Messenger and Message objects. There is also a potential performance impact as you must deal with the handleMessage() method in the main application thread of your activity – so keep such handling lightweight!

Use Independent Messaging

As well as the various Android-native and on-device methods we've covered in the preceding sections, you have further options via external messaging or pub/sub systems to deal with service-to-client communication. This is more and more popular as options like Google Cloud Messaging and its clones develop more and more useful features. The times when it makes sense to use this kind of third-party approach are typically when your use case can tolerate asynchronous messaging.

For more details on Google Cloud Messaging, check out the documentation at the developer website at https://developers.google.com/cloud-messaging/android.

Create Callbacks and Listeners

The Messenger and PendingIntent examples in the earlier sections demonstrate how easy it is to attach objects to the intent extras that are passed to a service. Using this approach requires that your object is "Parcelable," and you can create your own objects to satisfy this need, including callbacks or listeners of your own.

Taking this approach requires you to define your listener objects and at runtime have the client and service coded deploy and dispose of listeners when communication is needed. You would also be responsible for registering and retracting listeners, so that you aren't left with any orphans and the attendant resource waste/loss that would entail.

Use Notifications

A service has no direct UI itself, but it can interact with another application's UI. Think back to the topic of notifications we introduced in Chapter 15, and you can see how this could be leveraged by a service to present information and responses directly to the user.

Services in Action

We've covered the many aspects of services, client communication, and overall behavior with Android, so now it's time to build and run your own example service and client application. For the purposes of having a useful example that doesn't take an entire chapter to cover itself, we will create a simple photo sharing service and simple client example to put service theory into action. This won't be an Instagram or Flickr clone – the goal is simplicity so you can focus on engineering a service.

Choosing the Service Design

A simple photo sharing application is a perfect scenario for using the `startService()` model of service interaction, where we will send a "please share this" instruction to a service and not need to do any follow-up that would require binding to the service. We shall device our service from the base `Service` class and then implement the `onStartCommand()` method and the `onBind()` method (even though it is not used by our example client, we still need to do this to correctly extend the Service base class).

We could have chosen another Service subclass such as `IntentService`, which offers to cover much of the implementation for you such as neatly calling `stopService()`, `startService()`, and so forth, but as we do not want or need some of those helpers, we'll stick with the preceding approach. In particular, I want the service to live on after the `startService()` call so that we can later stop sharing if we want to.

Which photos you choose to share is not that important to the example, so I have stubbed those out in the example. You can tinker with this and add images or other resources if you wish.

Creating the Java Logic for the Service

The `ServiceExample` implementation is quite straightforward, focusing on the core parts of the implementation of overrides expected from the base `Service` class, plus my custom service-specific logic for photo sharing. Listing 18-3 has the full service implementation from the example in `ch18/ClientExample`.

***Listing 18-3.** Service implementation for ServiceExample.java*

```
package com.beginningandroid.clientexample;

import android.app.Service;
import android.content.Intent;
import android.os.IBinder;
import android.util.Log;
```

```
public class ServiceExample extends Service {
    public static final String EXTRA_ALBUM="EXTRA_ALBUM";
    private boolean isShared=false;

    @Override
    public IBinder onBind(Intent intent) {
        // We need to implement onBind as a Service subclass
        // In this case we do not actually need it, so can simply return
        return(null);
    }

    @Override
    public int onStartCommand(Intent intent, int flags, int startId) {
        String album=intent.getStringExtra(EXTRA_ALBUM);
        startSharing(album);
        return(START_NOT_STICKY);
    }

    @Override
    public void onDestroy() {
        stopSharing(); }

    private void startSharing(String album) {
        if(!isShared) {
            // Simplified logic - you might have much more going on here
            Log.w(getClass().getName(), "Album successfully shared");
            isShared=true;
        }
    }

    private void stopSharing() {
        if(isShared) {
            // Simplified logic - you might have much more going on here
            Log.w(getClass().getName(), "Album sharing removed");
            isShared=false;
        }
    }
}
```

We don't have any service-specific setup that needs to be performed at service startup, so we can omit extra logic in an `onCreate()` call and rely on the parent class taking care of this. We implement `onStartCommand()` so that we can take the desired action when the client calls `startService()`. That means we want to examine the intent used to designate the service and interrogate the extras the `ServiceExample` wants, such as the name of the photo album for sharing. Once we have the album name, we then call `startSharing()` as implemented for this specific service.

I have stubbed out most of the follow-on pieces of the startSharing() method as mentioned. One useful thing we can implement in this example is using Android's logging infrastructure to emit relevant information at various points to inform us the service is alive and working, even though it lacks a UI. This technique would also help you with all kinds of debugging, usage metrics, and so on in a real service. From the example application and service, you'll be able to tell it's running and moving through parts of its service logic by the output in Logcat. This is also useful if you see nothing – no logging gives you a clue that something has gone wrong.

I have implemented the onDestroy() method, which for now just calls our service's stopSharing() method. Just as with startSharing(), this is mostly stubbed out, with some logging to help you confirm the service code is working when invoked.

As mentioned earlier, even though we don't plan to use the binding approach, we still need to implement onBind() based on our subclassing from Service. It can return null in this instance. A future enhancement could allow other clients to bind and do more sophisticated things like create a photo montage, show the thumbnails of the album, and so on.

Creating an Example Client to Use the Service

For completeness' sake, it is good to see a client actually use the service, rather than just rely on my promise that the service does what it says. Listing 18-4 gives a simple layout for a client to drive the ServiceExample service.

***Listing 18-4.** The layout for the ClientExample application*

```
<?xml version="1.0" encoding="utf-8"?>
<RelativeLayout xmlns:android="http://schemas.android.com/apk/res/android"
    xmlns:tools="http://schemas.android.com/tools"
    android:layout_width="match_parent"
    android:layout_height="match_parent"
    tools:context=".MainActivity">

    <Button
        android:id="@+id/startSharing"
        android:layout_width="match_parent"
        android:layout_height="wrap_content"
        android:text="Start Sharing"
        android:onClick="onClick" />

    <Button
        android:id="@+id/stopSharing"
        android:layout_width="fill_parent"
        android:layout_height="wrap_content"
        android:text="Stop Sharing"
        android:layout_below="@id/startSharing"
        android:onClick="onClick" />

</RelativeLayout>
```

You can see I have created a very simple UI, as the `ClientExample` application has just two buttons, one labeled "Start Sharing" and one labeled "Stop Sharing." Remember, the goal here is understanding service mechanics, not UI aesthetics.

As we are using the command-style `startService()` approach to interacting once with the service, our Java logic is quite straightforward as well. Listing 18-5 shows the full client logic.

***Listing 18-5.** Java code for the sample ClientExample application*

```
package org.beginningandroid.clientexample;

import androidx.appcompat.app.AppCompatActivity;
import android.content.Intent;
import android.os.Bundle;
import android.view.View;

public class MainActivity extends AppCompatActivity {

    @Override
    protected void onCreate(Bundle savedInstanceState) {
        super.onCreate(savedInstanceState);
        setContentView(R.layout.activity_main);
    }

    public void onClick(View view) {
        switch(view.getId()) {
            case R.id.startSharing:
                startSharing(view);
                break;
            case R.id.stopSharing:
                stopSharing(view);
                break;
        }
    }

    public void startSharing(View view) {
        Intent myIntent=new Intent(this, ServiceExample.class);
        myIntent.putExtra(ServiceExample.EXTRA_ALBUM, "My Holiday Snaps");
        startService(myIntent);
    }

    public void stopSharing(View v) {
        stopService(new Intent(this, ServiceExample.class));
    }
}
```

You will be very familiar by now with the rudimentary `onCreate()` method, which in `ClientExample` just inflates the layout. The `onClick()` implementation follows the pattern for checking which button was clicked by the user by interrogating the view passed and triggers either the `startSharing()` or `stopSharing()` method as needed.

If startSharing() is invoked, it instantiates an intent for the service, passing a very believable album name for the set of photos we want to share. The service is called with startService() passing the intent. Our stopSharing() implementation basically calls the stopService() command with a new intent of the appropriate type, matching the original service call, and thus targets our service for shutdown.

Testing the Service in Action

You can go ahead and test running the service and watching the results. Be sure to add the <service> entry to your manifest, for example:

```
<service android:name=".ServiceExample" />
```

When you run the ClientExample application, it triggers the calls to the ServiceExample service enabling you to see entries in Logcat as follows:

```
...org.beginningandroid.clientexample.ServiceExample: Album successfully shared
...org.beginningandroid.clientexample.ServiceExample: Album sharing removed
```

Summary

You have now explored all of the basics of services and are ready to include them in your future application designs. Be sure to try building your own service variants that use the different service-to-client communication methods we explored in this chapter.

Chapter 19

Working with Files in Android

In this chapter, we will explore files in detail, including Android's methods for storing, retrieving, and managing data for your applications. In the following chapter, we will deal with the complementary tools around databases, which together with files represent a wealth of options for data management in your applications. We will also contrast these with Content Providers, Android's more sophisticated model for data access and management.

The examples in this chapter focus on two broad approaches offered by Android for file-based data. Approach 1 can be considered the "application-embedded" model, which uses raw resources and assets packaged with your application. Approach 2 is the "Java I/O" approach, which leverages the near-famous java.io package to manipulate files, data streams, and so on just as you would with Java-based file management on any other operating system.

Each approach has merits and drawbacks, which we will cover, and you can rest assured there is no best approach – just the best for the problem at hand.

Using Assets and Raw Files

In Chapters 13 and 14, we introduced audio and video examples that relied on some of Android's features dealing directly with files. Use of the raw and asset locations such as we explored in the examples in those chapters isn't limited to just media files like audio, images, and video. You can put pretty much any type of file in those locations, so long as you take on the developer responsibility for knowing how to access and manipulate their content. As an example, you could store a .csv file for holding some useful data.

Android provides easy access to files via the Resources class and its `getResources()` method. With a raw resource file, you present its content through an `InputStream` by a call to the `openRawResources()` method. Your task as a developer is to know what the data in the `InputStream` means. Before we look at an example, there are some important pros and cons to working with data sources from raw or asset files to know.

G. Allen, *Android for Absolute Beginners*, https://doi.org/10.1007/978-1-4842-6646-5_19

Advantages of the raw-based approach include the following:

- Your files can be packaged with your application, thanks to the Android Asset Packaging Tool, AAPT.
- You can co-locate resources in a library project, so you can access them from many applications when needed.
- Files are private by default, with external access requiring full knowledge or the package name and resource name to reference or appropriate library or API calls, as well as file access permissions granted in the manifest file or at runtime.
- Read-only and static data can be packaged in common formats, like JSON or XML.

To balance the advantages, there are some key disadvantages to be aware of in this approach:

- Read-only by default. Editing existing resources packaged with the application is not straightforward.
- Sharing is nontrivial, for other applications or service users.
- Static nature imposes issues keeping information up to date.

Armed with those benefits and disadvantages, you can make an informed choice of whether this is the right approach for your application and desired functionality.

Populating Lists from Resource Files

Understanding the benefits and drawbacks of file management is best demonstrated with an example. For this example, we will introduce the `ListView` UI widget and adapter logic and use them as the mechanism with which to read data from an XML file and populate a list of values from the file's data dynamically at application runtime. Listing 19-1 shows a simple layout providing a `ListView` to ultimately display the data from our XML resource file.

***Listing 19-1.** The layout for the RawFileExample*

```
<?xml version="1.0" encoding="utf-8"?>
<RelativeLayout xmlns:android="http://schemas.android.com/apk/res/android"
    xmlns:app="http://schemas.android.com/apk/res-auto"
    xmlns:tools="http://schemas.android.com/tools"
    android:layout_width="match_parent"
    android:layout_height="match_parent"
    tools:context=".MainActivity">

    <TextView
        android:id="@+id/mySelection"
        android:layout_width="match_parent"
        android:layout_height="wrap_content" />
```

```
    <ListView
        android:id="@android:id/list"
        android:layout_width="match_parent"
        android:layout_height="match_parent"
        android:drawSelectorOnTop="false" />

</RelativeLayout>
```

For this example application, we will have our ListView show the names of colors and take those color names from the XML file colors.xml we provide in the ch19/RawFileExample project. You can see the content of the file colors.xml in Listing 19-2.

Listing 19-2. *The colors.xml file content*

```
<colors>
    <color value="red" />
    <color value="orange" />
    <color value="yellow" />
    <color value="green" />
    <color value="blue" />
    <color value="indigo" />
    <color value="violet" />
    <color value="black" />
    <color value="white" />
</colors>
```

You can see that the colors.xml file is very simple, which is intentional. Our focus is the logic required to actually open this file, read and parse its content, and use the resulting data in an appropriate data structure for our application, rather than XML complexity. Listing 19-3 shows the logic for a straightforward ListActivity-based application that will display the color names from the colors.xml file in a list and then let the user click to choose a particular color.

Listing 19-3. *RawFileExample Java logic for processing the XML resource file*

```
package org.beginningandroid.rawfileexample;

import android.app.ListActivity;
import android.os.Bundle;
import android.view.View;
import android.widget.ArrayAdapter;
import android.widget.ListView;
import android.widget.TextView;

import org.w3c.dom.Document;
import org.w3c.dom.Element;
import org.w3c.dom.NodeList;

import java.io.InputStream;
import java.util.ArrayList;
```

```
import javax.xml.parsers.DocumentBuilder;
import javax.xml.parsers.DocumentBuilderFactory;

public class MainActivity extends ListActivity {

    private TextView mySelection;
    ArrayList<String> colorItems=new ArrayList<String>();

    @Override
    protected void onCreate(Bundle savedInstanceState) {
        super.onCreate(savedInstanceState);
        setContentView(R.layout.activity_main);
        mySelection=(TextView)findViewById(R.id.mySelection);

        try {
            InputStream inStream=getResources().openRawResource(R.raw.colors);
            DocumentBuilder docBuild= DocumentBuilderFactory
                    .newInstance().newDocumentBuilder();
            Document myDoc=docBuild.parse(inStream, null);
            NodeList colors=myDoc.getElementsByTagName("color");
            for (int i=0;i<colors.getLength();i++) {
                colorItems.add(((Element)colors.item(i)).getAttribute("value"));
            }
            inStream.close();
        }
        catch (Exception e) {
            e.printStackTrace();
        }

        setListAdapter(new ArrayAdapter<String>(this,
                android.R.layout.simple_list_item_1, colorItems));
    }

    public void onListItemClick(ListView parent, View v, int position,
                                long id) {
        mySelection.setText(colorItems.get(position).toString());
    }
}
```

Reviewing the code for `RawFileExample`, you will immediately notice the number of external Java libraries we are importing to handle file I/O and XML parsing. This is the power of the Java heritage for Android in action. Even if you choose to move on to Kotlin as your preferred programming language, the huge breadth of Java libraries are available to help you with functionality.

The `onCreate()` method first creates an `InputStream` object, and then we call `getResources().openRawResource()` to perform the act of finding the file within the `.apk`, allocating its file descriptor, associating them with the `InputStream`, and finally readying the system for subsequent use of the data stream from our file. From that point on, the remaining logic is what's needed to interpret what is in the file.

Following the initial file handling, we use a DocumentBuilder object to parse the content of the file and store the resulting representation in a Document object, named myDoc. Using DOM semantics, we call getElementsByTagName() to collect all of the <color> elements into our NodeList object. This might seem excessive given our file's simplicity, but imagine a more complicated XML schema with other elements, child elements, and so on, and you can see how this does the sifts to find our desired elements efficiently.

Finally, we use a for loop, iterating through the NodeList <color> entries, to extract the value attribute's text – which is the actual color name string we want to present in the ListView. With our NodeList populated, we can then inflate the ListView with the ArrayAdapter configured to use the list of color names, asking it to render the result using the default simple_list_item_1 built-in XML layout.

The logic for handling the user clicking a color retrieves the color string and populates the TextView with the user's chosen entry.

Running the application shows the data from the colors.xml file rendered in our ListView, as shown in Figure 19-1.

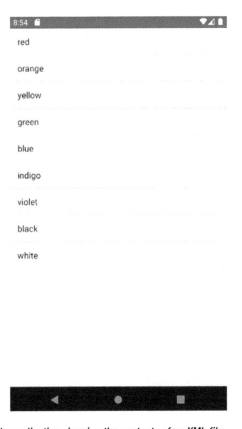

Figure 19-1. The RawFileExample application showing the contents of an XML file

Working with Files from the File System

If you have any prior experience with file I/O with general Java applications on traditional file systems, then the Android approach will be very familiar to you. For those of you not familiar with Java-based file reading and writing, here is a quick introduction.

From a Java point of view, files are treated as streams of data, and two objects become central to any reading or writing of files: `InputStream` and `OutputStream`. These streams are provided by invoking the `openFileInput()` and `openFileOutput()` methods from your code. With a stream in hand, your program logic is then responsible for actions such as reading from the `InputStream` or writing to the `OutputStream`, as well as cleaning up all of the resources when you are done.

Android's File System Model

Thanks to Android's history and Google's overly paternalistic thoughts on whether people should have full access to their own device, you as a developer will be confronted with two concepts when dealing with local file storage on a device. All storage will be divided between "internal" and "external," but those terms have a skewed meaning. In contemporary Android, "internal" mostly means what you think, but "external" means both traditional external storage like SD cards and a portion of the on-board storage that ordinary people would consider internal, but that Android calls external to indicate you have more liberal access to it for traditional file I/O.

As well as using the "internal" area for system-related purposes, there are also other differences in thinking about file systems under Android that represent advantages and disadvantages to both internal and external storage.

Internal storage is as follows:

- Is found on every Android device and is always in place.
- Files that form part of your application designated to be placed on internal storage are considered an integral part of your application. The files are installed when the application is installed and removed when the application is removed.
- The default security boundary for internally saved files is private to your application. Sharing requires explicit additional steps.
- Is usually significantly smaller than the available external storage, and users can see this storage fill up and present space management problems, even when ample external storage is available.

External storage is different, as follows:

- Android provides a USB abstraction layer and interface for external storage. When in use as a USB device, applications on the device cannot access external storage.
- The default security boundary is to make all files on external storage world-readable. Other applications can read your externally stored files without developer or user knowledge or permission.

- Depending on the save method invoked, externally stored files might not be removed when your application is uninstalled.

Now that you're aware of those aspects of both internal and external storage, read on!

Permissions for Reading and Writing Files

If you choose to use internal storage, then your application always has permissions to write to, and read from, the portion of internal storage reserved for it. To find the details of any internal storage for your application, call `getFilesDir()`. You can also use `getDir()` to return a named (sub)directory for you to use, creating it in the process if it doesn't already exist.

You can open a file for output streaming – otherwise known as writing – through a call to `openFileOutput()`. If the file doesn't already exist, it will be created for you. The `openFileInput()` method performs file opening for an `InputStream` to satisfy your reading requirements, thought note that for this call your specified file must already exist.

Both `openFileOutput()` and `openFileInput()` accept a number of `MODE_*` options that control the file and stream behavior. The most commonly used `MODE_*` options include

MODE_APPEND: None of the existing data in the file is changed, with the data from the string appended to the existing content in the file.

MODE_PRIVATE: Permissions on the file are set to only allow the application that creates it (and any other that runs as the same user) to access the file. This is the default.

MODE_WORLD_READABLE: Opening permissions for reading to all applications and users on the device. This is considered poor security practice, but is often seen when using Content Providers or services is considered overkill.

MODE_WORLD_WRITABLE: Even more dangerous than world-readable is world-writable. Any application or user can write to the file. Just because other developers use this doesn't mean you should!

For your application users, no specific permissions are needed to create, open, or write to an internal file within the application's allocated internal file system space. The simplest example of creating a file stored within the internal device storage is as follows:

```
FILE myFile = new FILE(context.getFilesDir(), "myFileName");
```

The situation differs when you start working with external storage. Different methods are at your disposal, and the permission model strictly enforces appropriate controls and safeguards. In order to write to external storage, your Android Manifest will need to include the privilege `android.permission.WRITE_EXTERNAL_STORAGE`, just as we saw in the audio and video examples in Chapters 13 and 14.

Older versions of Android, up to Android Marshmallow, allow your application to read freely from external storage without specifying or requiring any particular permission. For more recent versions of Android, you need to include `android.permission.READ_EXTERNAL_STORAGE` in your manifest. As there is no impact in including this for old versions, you should simply default to adding this regardless of your plans for version support.

The methods available for external storage access closely match in name the previously introduced methods for internal storage, but tend to add the word “external” or “public.” The `getExternalStoragePublicDirectory()` method is designed to allocate well-structured directories and files into which you can store documents, audio, pictures, video, and more. The method takes an enum signifying one of the predefined application directories and a filename of your choosing.

Android has dozens of application directories, including

> DIRECTORY_DOCUMENTS: For storing traditional text or other editable documents created by the user.
>
> DIRECTORY_MUSIC: A place to keep all kinds of music and audio files.
>
> DIRECTORY_PICTURES: For storing still image files such as photos, drawings, and so on.

All of these predefined locations are helpful, with reassuring predictability for those circumstances where they are a good fit, but there will be occasions when you have distinctly different types of files you want to store. For these situations, the general-purpose `getExternalStorageDirectory()` method is used, providing similar functionality to the `getFilesDir()` noted earlier in the chapter for internal storage.

Examining External Files in Action

With a bunch more theory digested, it’s time to explore external files with a working example. The `ExternalFilesExample` app, found in `ch19/ExternalFilesExample`, walks through the mechanics of saving a file and reading back its content.

Figure 19-2 is the layout used to provide a text entry field, buttons for file writing and reading, and a text reading field. The corresponding layout XML file is in the `ch19/ExternalFilesExample` project, but we will save some space by not repeating it here.

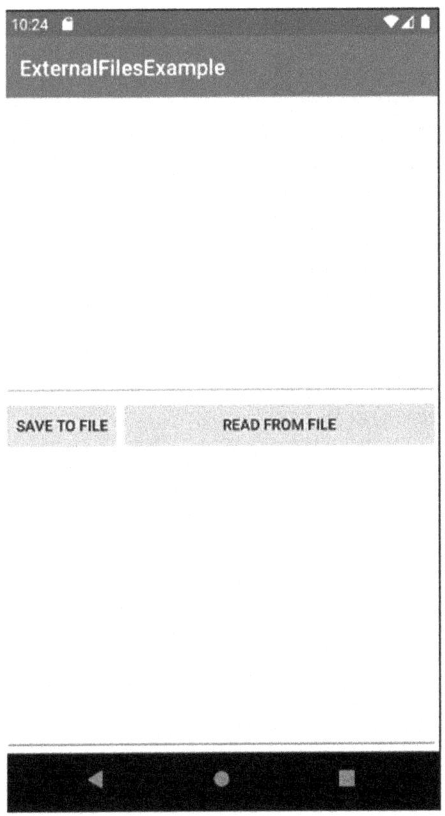

Figure 19-2. An activity with fields and buttons for testing external file management

The supporting logic for our application follows the pattern I have used several times, with a central `onClick()` method receiving the button clicks, switching to the appropriate method based on which view (button) the user chooses at runtime. The code is shown in Listing 19-4.

Listing 19-4. The ExternalFilesExample Java code

```
package org.beginningandroid.externalfilesexample;
import androidx.appcompat.app.AppCompatActivity;

import android.content.Context;
import android.os.Bundle;
import android.view.View;
import android.view.inputmethod.InputMethodManager;
import android.widget.EditText;

import java.io.BufferedReader;
import java.io.IOException;
import java.io.InputStream;
import java.io.InputStreamReader;
import java.io.OutputStreamWriter;
```

```
public class MainActivity extends AppCompatActivity {
    public final static String FILENAME="ExternalFilesExample.txt";

    @Override
    protected void onCreate(Bundle savedInstanceState) {
        super.onCreate(savedInstanceState);
        setContentView(R.layout.activity_main);
    }

    public void onClick(View view) {
        switch(view.getId()) {
            case R.id.btnRead:
                try {
                    doReadFromFile();
                }
                catch (Exception e) {
                    e.printStackTrace();
                }
                break;
            case R.id.btnSave:
                doSaveToFile();
                break;
        }
    }

    public void doReadFromFile() throws Exception {
        doHideKeyboard();
        EditText readField;
        readField=(EditText)findViewById(R.id.editTextRead);
        try {
            InputStream inStrm=openFileInput(FILENAME);
            if (inStrm!=null) {
                // We will use the traditional Java I/O streams and builders.
                // This is cumbersome, and we'll return with a better version
                // in chapter 20 using the IOUtils external library

                InputStreamReader inStrmRdr=new InputStreamReader(inStrm);
                BufferedReader buffRdr=new BufferedReader(inStrmRdr);
                String fileContent;
                StringBuilder strBldr=new StringBuilder();

                while ((fileContent=buffRdr.readLine())!=null) {
                    strBldr.append(fileContent);
                }
                inStrm.close();
                readField.setText(strBldr.toString());
            }
```

```
        }
        catch (Throwable t) {
            // perform exception handling here
        }
    }

    public void doSaveToFile() {
        doHideKeyboard();
        EditText saveField;
        saveField=(EditText)findViewById(R.id.editText);
        try {
            OutputStreamWriter outStrm=
                    new OutputStreamWriter(openFileOutput
                            (FILENAME, Context.MODE_PRIVATE));
            try {
                outStrm.write(saveField.getText().toString());
            }
            catch (IOException i) {
                i.printStackTrace();
            }
            outStrm.close();
        }
        catch (Exception e) {
            e.printStackTrace();
        }
    }

    public void doHideKeyboard() {
        View view = this.getCurrentFocus();
        if (view != null) {
            InputMethodManager myIMM=(InputMethodManager)
                    this.getSystemService(Context.INPUT_METHOD_SERVICE);
            myIMM.hideSoftInputFromWindow
                    (view.getWindowToken(), InputMethodManager.HIDE_NOT_ALWAYS);
        }
    }
}
```

What Goes into Saving and Reading Files

Exploring the `ExternalFilesExample` project, we see two key methods. First is the `doSaveToFile()` method, which performs some preparation and housekeeping with a call to `doHideKeyboard()` (covered in a moment), followed by creating the local `saveField` variable and binding it to the `EditText` view in the layout. This is done so we can eventually reference the text in the UI for saving.

The main try/catch block follows, defining the output stream to be used to stream the text to the file nominated by the variable `FILENAME`. We then invoke the `.write()` method to attempt to actually write out the text through the stream to the file.

It probably won't escape your notice that there are many nested layers of exception handling in the `ExternalFilesExample` code. Writing to files can run into many, many issues, from full storage through to users spontaneously removing an SD card to which you were writing in the midst of the writing process! In short, taking extra care with exceptions is always prudent around file access.

Second, to read from the file, we use the `doReadFromFile()` method, following similar setup work as we used with the `doSaveToFile()` method. We call `doHideKeyboard()` first (covered in the following), and then local variable `readField` is created and bound to the `editTextRead` widget. This will be used to show the contents of the file once read.

Next, we add a `try/catch` block that encompasses some textbook Java file handling. We use a stream reader to access the file and pass that buffer to allow consumers to control access to the data. The buffer is used to access the stream line by line with the while block, and we gradually build up the full content of the file in the string builder. With all of the lines read from the stream (and, therefore, the file), the stream is closed, and we then transfer everything from the buffer via the strBldr object to the `readField EditText` widget in our layout.

There are more streamlined, modern ways to accomplish all of the preceding, but crucially they hide the fundamental mechanics of what is happening. In the `ExternalFilesExample` code, you see the messy details of how Java I/O happens at the lowest level, to build an appreciation of both the objects and work required and also all the points where things can go wrong! No one in their right mind would expose a programming pattern for file access like this today – they'd hide it away, even though under the hood all of these steps would still be happening.

Helping Streamline IMEs

Our code deviates a little from strict file handling with the `doHideKeyboard()` method. This is a helper method you'll find useful again and again, and it helps reduce the steps required of your users when entering text and proceeding with their desired action. When your user types text in the `EditText` field, the IME is triggered and presents the soft keyboard for the user to enter their desired text. We could customize the IME to add a "Done" button using the IME "accessory button" option, but that's an additional key press to ask of your users.

Instead I have crafted the layout to ensure the save (and read) button will be visible even when the IME is active, which means the user can type away and then immediately click the save button. The call to `doSaveToFile()` invokes `doHideKeyboard()`, which determines first which `View` the user interacted and whether or not the Input Method Framework is active and presenting a keyboard. If one is shown, we invoke `.hideSoftInputFromWindow()` to hide the keyboard. While the user doesn't see all of these mechanics, they benefit from the simplicity gained in the user experience – one less key press to have their file saved!

Saving and Reading Files in Action

Now that you have an understanding of the ExternalFilesExample example, it is time to see it come to life. Figure 19-3 shows how the display initially looks for the application when the user first starts to enter text into the top field.

Figure 19-3. Entering text to be saved to an external file

As I promised, the IME (keyboard) appears in the lower half of the screen, but our buttons are still accessible. In this example, this is more of a hack – it is not the burnished UI a fully fledged application would use, but shows the file I/O we care about. The user can click the "Save to File" button at any point, triggering the `doSaveToFile()` method. As outlined earlier in the chapter, this calls the `doHideKeyboard()` method, and our UI will appear as shown in Figure 19-4 at this point.

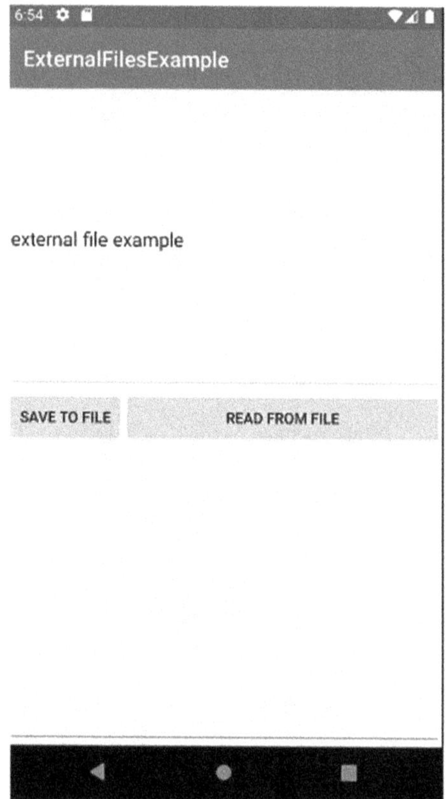

***Figure 19-4.** The IME is hidden along with saving the file*

The text that is entered into the `EditText` field is saved in a file named `ExternalFilesExample.txt`. The contents of `ExternalFilesExample.txt` can be recalled at any time by hitting the "Read from File" button. This triggers the contents of the file to be read and then displayed by the `doReadFromFile()` method. Figure 19-5 shows the results of this file retrieval.

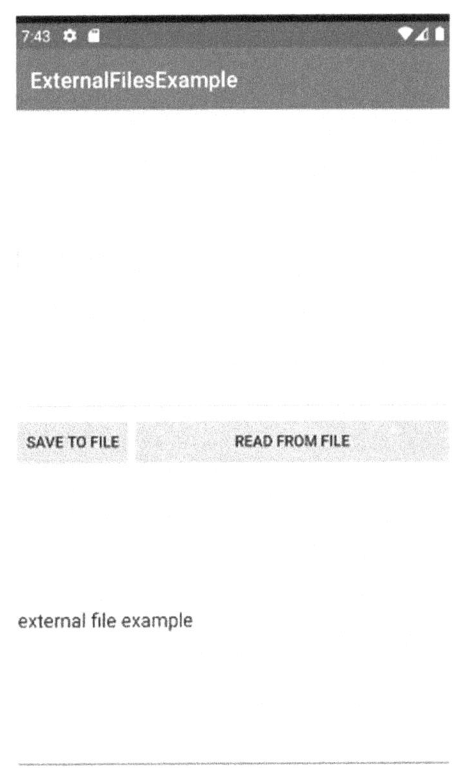

Figure 19-5. Recalling the contents of the external file

Ensuring External Storage Is Available When Needed

When I introduced using external storage earlier, I outlined some of the potential drawbacks, including the uncertain nature of whether you can rely on it being there when needed. Your users can do crazy things, like physically removing SD cards from their devices, and even for those devices that are mimicking external storage via an internal memory partition, Android still allows that external storage to be mounted as a USB device elsewhere, which implicitly cuts of access to the storage from other applications.

Your goal as a developer should be to create well-behaved applications, even when your users are not! This means it is prudent to perform sanity checks on the presence and availability of your external storage before your application attempts to use it.

To this end, Android provides some useful environment methods, the most useful of which is `Environment.getExternalStorageState()`, which returns a string from a predefined enum that describes the current state of the external storage. You can use this state to determine the availability, health, and so on of external storage. Common values returned include

> MEDIA_BAD_REMOVAL: This state indicates the physical SD card was removed before being unmounted, possibly leaving files in an inconsistent state due to cached pages not being flushed (see the file system discussion later in this chapter).

MEDIA_REMOVED: This value is returned when no external storage is mapped from the on-board device and no SD card is present.

MEDIA_SHARED: When the device has its external storage mounted as a USB device to some other external platform, this is the value returned to indicate that external storage is not available to be used at this time, even though it is present in the device.

MEDIA_CHECKING: When an SD card is inserted, checks are performed to determine if the card has been formatted and if so with which file system. This is the value returned while these processes take place.

MEDIA_MOUNTED: The normal state for external storage that can be used.

MEDIA_MOUNTED_READ_ONLY: Typically seen when the SD card's physical switch is set to the read-only position, meaning that no writing to that part of external storage can be performed.

The Android documentation at developer.android.com has the full list of all the possible external storage state values.

Other Considerations with Android File Systems

Now that you are familiar with a variety of approaches to working with files in Android, there are a few subtle and not-so-subtle management considerations to think about to ensure the long-term viability of using files on the file system.

Android File Systems Throughout History

Over Android's history as a smartphone operating system, it has supported a range of file system standards for on-board storage. The three main formats across that history are

- YAFFS, or Yet Another Flash File System: The original file system for NAND-based storage, it offered a number of useful benefits, including wear-leveling support so that the decay over time of flash storage from multiple writes was managed and to some extent hidden from the operating system and applications, as well as file system–level garbage collection tools to help move bad regions of storage to a "dead pool," not to be used for meaningful storage.
- YAFFS2 and evolved and tweaked version of YAFFS: Providing better long-term health management for underlying storage.
- EXT4, the file system popularized by Linux: With all of the "grown-up" management features of a mature file system, including per-file locking semantics, permissions, and so on.

One issue with older YAFFS and YAFFS2-based file systems, and the devices that use them, is lack of file-locking semantics. In short, neither provides you the option, as a developer, to lock a single file (e.g., when making an edit to a shared file), and instead you rely on locking the "entire file system" to ensure consistent access. This has a bunch of downsides, from blocking other applications that might be trying to write to the file at the same time to impeding efficient UI behavior if file I/O is happening on the main thread.

Your main problem as a developer is just not knowing what file system a user's device might employ. You are likely to get the blame for poor performance from I/O locking and blocking issues, even when it might be Android itself that is causing the issue.

Avoiding UI Issues with File I/O

There are a range of techniques you can use as a developer to mitigate locking and contention issues with `YAFFS` or `YAFFS2` file systems. These techniques can also assist in general with other types of I/O to network endpoints as well.

Using StrictMode to Profile an Application

The Android ecosystem comes with a range of tools available to help with performing application behavior and performance. The StrictMode policy tool is one such tool and helps with any I/O delay issues by profiling the operation of all of your code looking for issues defined in its policies.

StrictMode has a range of policies available, though you will likely find yourself using two of its original offerings. The first policy is the Virtual Machine policy that covers generally poor behavior or practices across an entire application, such as leaking database connection objects. The second set of policies are the Thread policies, and these look in particular for poorly behaved code happening on the main UI thread. This can help spot code – both yours and Android's – that is going to slow or interrupt a user's smooth experience with the UI.

You can activate a StrictMode policy by calling the static `StrictMode.enableDefaults()` method from your onCreate() callback. Invoking this call will report a range of useful information in your Logcat output regarding UI thread issues including file I/O concerns. You can also define your own policies if you desire – the specifics are beyond the scope of this book, but the Android documentation has more detail should you be interested.

> **Caution** As useful as StrictMode policies can be, never leave them defined in your final shipped code and applications. Leaving StrictMode in place will create a very large volume of log data on your users' devices, consuming the very file system space you have carefully been trying to manage.

Moving Logic to Asynchronous Threads

The preceding discussion on StrictMode opens up the world of moving logic away from the main UI thread and interface for your application. At almost all times, it is worth thinking about whether there is other logic in your application that doesn't need to happen on the critical path, such as background lookup of data from an online service, messaging or pub/sub-style notifications, cached items, and so forth.

Anything that could happen off the critical path should be considered for asynchronous operation, and that is where Android's `AsyncTask` shines, being able to spawn additional threads to take on any logic you throw at it. This is well worth mastering as part of your Android learning, as most developers use it as the workhorse for managing threading across their applications.

The AsyncTask class is provided in a form that means you, as the developer, must subclass it to create specific implementations for the work you want to do. This makes sense, as Android can't know the details of your application in advance nor cover the millions of tasks developers around the world would want it to handle. To use AsyncTask, you take its provided doInBackground() method and implement the actual logic you want performed on another thread. There are optional additional methods you can implement to provide pre- and post-execution logic, interact with the UI in a controlled way, and so on.

Listing 19-5 gives you a stub showing the subclassing of AsyncTask to illustrate how it can be used to perform file saving operations. There are countless other ways this could be implemented, but you will appreciate the overall idea.

***Listing 19-5.** An example AsyncTask subclassing*

```
private class SmartFileSaver extends AsyncTask<Void, Void, Void> {

    protected void onPreExecute() {
        // This method will fire on the UI thread
        // Show a Toast message
        Toast.makeText(this, "Saving File", Toast.LENGTH_LONG).show();
    }

    protected void doInBackground() {
        // This method will spawn a background thread
        // All work happens off the UI thread
        // create output stream
        // call .write()
        // catch exceptions
        // etc.
    }

    protected void onPostExecute() {
        // This method will fire on the UI thread
        // Show a Toast message
        Toast.makeText(this, "File Saved", Toast.LENGTH_LONG).show();
    }
}
```

Using the SmartFileSaver.execute() method will invoke our various onPreExecute(), doInBackground(), and onPostExecute() methods with Android managing the related thread lifetime and UI interaction.

Summary

You now have a firm introduction to the basic mechanics of file I/O under Android and in particular a low-level understanding of the file systems, file handling, and stream and file content mechanics that are part of any approach to working with files.

Chapter 20

Working with Databases in Android

Files are not the only way to store information from your application onto an Android device. Android provides two more major approaches to information management: a fully fledged relational database option based on SQLite and the Android Content Provider framework. In this chapter, we will explore the SQLite database – for those of you interested in Content Providers, you can learn more on the book's website at `www.beginningandroid.org`.

If you are familiar with SQLite, you realize it represents a rock-solid database engine shipped as a single include or library for any kind of application. SQLite recently chalked up 25 years as a shipping product, proving itself one of the all-time mainstays of software development.

Working with SQLite: The World's Most Popular Database!

Any of you who have worked in the field of databases will be familiar with SQLite, but as popular as it is, those of you from other fields may have never heard of it. Without a word of hyperbole, SQLite is "the most popular" relational database technology on the planet. That's a bold claim, so let me provide some supporting evidence.

To give you an idea of how universal and popular SQLite is, I've compiled this short list of data points to help.

SQLite is

- The default and core relational database offered on every smartphone operating system. We're obviously talking about Android in this book, but every other smartphone OS you've ever heard of – like iOS – and OSs you maybe haven't, like Symbian, all use SQLite as the default database for almost all their internal needs.

G. Allen, *Android for Absolute Beginners*, https://doi.org/10.1007/978-1-4842-6646-5_20

- Chosen by every web browser as the key technology for local caching, bookmarks, and more. Whether you use Chrome, Safari, Opera, Edge, or Internet Explorer (remember that?!), you are using SQLite every day.
- Included in "millions" of commercial and open source products. I'm not exaggerating when I say millions!

One of my favorite ways of illustrating exactly how popular SQLite has become is to frame it as follows. You, dear reader, have used or benefited from SQLite every day since the first day you bought a smartphone. Even if you didn't realize it, you are a walking, talking SQLite beneficiary!

> **Note** To delve further into the world of SQLite, I can recommend *The Definitive Guide to SQLite*, Second Edition, ISBN 9781430232254. In the interests of full disclosure, I am one of the co-authors of that book.

Many of you will not be familiar with SQLite at all. You will not have explored SQLite's capabilities under Android or leveraged its benefits. That's completely expected and why this chapter exists. From here on, we will walk through the fundamentals of using SQLite as a database and core capability of Android, and we'll build a working database-driven example application to hone your skills.

Quickly Learning SQLite for Android Development

SQLite is targeted very much as a straightforward database library providing all the core things you might want from a relational database query and transaction engine. This means you get access to a fully compliant Structured Query Language, or SQL, interface, though it is always important to remember what level of SQL – such as SQL-92 and SQL-99 – is introduced in any feature you might be interested in. This is doubly important, as the version of SQLite shipped with a user's device usually trails the latest release by several years.

SQLite supports the normal SQL commands like `SELECT`, `INSERT`, `UPDATE`, and `DELETE`, but may not support some key features of later SQL evolutions depending on the version. This can include

- Only supporting a subset of ANSI outer join syntax
- Minimal alter table support, allowing you to rename and add columns, but not drop columns or morph data types
- Support for row-level triggers, but not statement-level triggers
- Views being read-only
- No support for window functions and common table expressions, even though these were added to SQLite in version 3.25 – only devices supporting Android SDK level 29 or higher will provide a version of SQLite that supports window functions

You might worry about those missing features, but in reality they are mostly at the higher end of database usage and not a daily requirement for most uses of a small embeddable database library. You still get the tremendous power of SQL even without those more recent features.

Creating SQLite Databases for Your Applications

When it comes to kick-starting your application with a SQLite database, you have two approaches from which you can choose:

1. Create a SQLite database file as part of your development environment, or source it externally and copy it as a resource into your Android project.
2. Have your Android application create the database it needs and optionally populate with any beginning data.

Each approach has benefits and drawbacks. By packaging a premade SQLite database, you sign yourself up to keeping the database schema and code development in sync – though this is a problem not unique to Android. Having your application create the database spares you this burden, but depending on the kind and amount of data your SQLite database might need, it could place a heavy startup burden on your application. Android can help with this, as it provides a range of SQLite setup assistance options.

Android provides the `SQLiteOpenHelper` class, designed for you to subclass in your application. `SQLiteOpenHelper` takes care of all the initial setup of a SQLite database and deals with future changes and upgrades. Your job is to implement (at least) three of the methods from the parent `SQLiteOpenHelper` class, with a fourth method for downgrades also available as an option.

Your first job is for you to add logic to the `SQLiteOpenHelper` constructor, calling that parent constructor as a basis. The parent class takes care of checking to see if the nominated database file already exists and creates the file if needed. The constructor also performs a version check against the provided version and can call the `onUpgrade()` and `onDowngrade()` methods as necessary, as well as some other more esoteric tasks beyond the scope of this introduction.

Second, you must implement the logic for the `onCreate()` method. This is where you build and execute the Data Definition Language (DDL) SQL commands to create your tables, indexes, views, and so on, according to your database schema design. Following object creation in the SQLite database, you should then populate any data you need via insert and update statements.

Finally, you will need to implement `onUpgrade()` (and optionally the `onDowngrade()` method). These methods handle the DDL that implements schema changes and any related data changes you wish to make as you upgrade your application and decide the SQLite database structure needs to change to support your desired application behavior.

With the theory of using SQLite in your application covered, it's time to explore an example application that will help bring the concepts to life.

Introducing the SQLiteExample Application

For the remainder of the chapter, the `ch20/SQLiteExample` application will be used to highlight all of the key SQLite capabilities you might want to use when building database-driven Android applications. We will use simple `LinearLayout` and `ListView` to help demonstrate the use, and display, of data from a SQLite database. Figure 20-1 shows the UI that houses a `ListView` for showing known Android device models from a SQLite database. We have buttons for adding new device models and showing information about known devices.

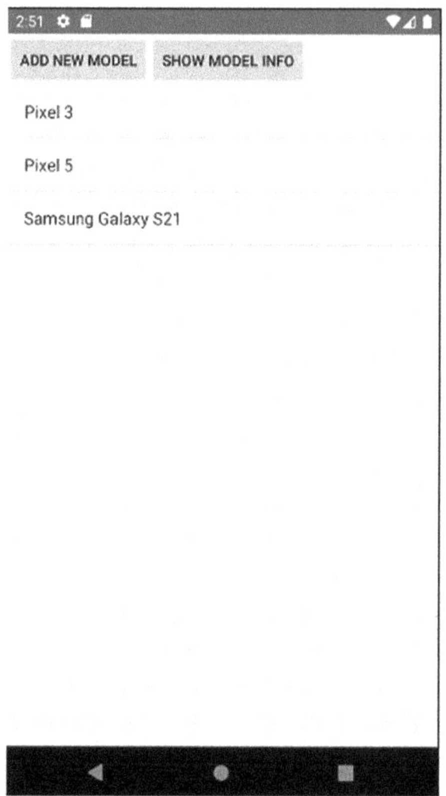

***Figure 20-1.** The SQLiteExample main activity and appearance*

This kind of simple layout and view should be familiar to you by now, so we won't dwell on that. Listing 20-1 shows the layout.

***Listing 20-1.** The SQLiteExample main activity layout*

```
<?xml version="1.0" encoding="utf-8"?>
<LinearLayout xmlns:android="http://schemas.android.com/apk/res/android"
    xmlns:app="http://schemas.android.com/apk/res-auto"
    xmlns:tools="http://schemas.android.com/tools"
    android:layout_width="match_parent"
    android:layout_height="match_parent"
```

```
    android:orientation="vertical"
    tools:context=".MainActivity">

    <LinearLayout
        android:id="@+id/buttonGroup"
        android:layout_width="wrap_content"
        android:layout_height="wrap_content"
        android:orientation="horizontal">

        <Button
            android:id="@+id/addNewModel"
            android:layout_width="wrap_content"
            android:layout_height="wrap_content"
            android:text="Add New Model"
            android:onClick="onClick"/>

        <Button
            android:id="@+id/getModelInfo"
            android:layout_width="wrap_content"
            android:layout_height="wrap_content"
            android:text="Show Model Info"
            android:onClick="onClick"/>
    </LinearLayout>

    <ListView
        android:id="@android:id/list"
        android:layout_width="wrap_content"
        android:layout_height="match_parent" />
</LinearLayout>
```

There are two points to note about this layout. First, I have defined two nested LinearLayouts. The outermost LinearLayout has the attribute orientation=vertical and contains the inner LinearLayout and the ListView with the stock Android id. The inner LinearLayout holds the two buttons, addNewModel and getModelInfo, with orientation=horizontal. This is a useful trick to have the UI widgets flow as we want them, but a more elegant solution could be devised with suitable weightings, gravity, and layout references.

Second, I'm using my common pattern of both buttons calling an onClick() method, which will have matching Java code determine which button was clicked and direct the logic from there.

Looking back at Figure 20-1, you can see some data about several devices is already listed. This means there is data in a database somewhere already being used to demonstrate the application. I performed this in the implementation of SQLiteOpenHelper used in the SQLiteExample application. The Java for this implementation is shown in Listing 20-2.

***Listing 20-2.** The MySQLiteHelper SQLiteOpenHelper implementation*

```
package org.beginningandroid.sqliteexample;

import android.content.Context;
import android.database.sqlite.SQLiteDatabase;
import android.database.sqlite.SQLiteOpenHelper;

public class MySQLiteHelper extends SQLiteOpenHelper {
    public static final String TABLE_NAME="devices";
    public static final int COLNO__ID = 0;
    public static final int COLNO_MODEL_NAME = 1;
    public static final int COLNO_RELEASE_YEAR = 2;
    public static final String COLNAME__ID = "_id";
    public static final String COLNAME_MODEL = "model_name";
    public static final String COLNAME_YEAR = "release_year";
    public static final String[] TABLE_COLUMNS =
            new String[]{"_id","model_name","release_year"};

    private static final String DBFILENAME="devices.db";
    private static final int DBVERSION = 1;
    private static final String INITIAL_SCHEMA=
            "create table devices (" +
                    "_id integer primary key autoincrement," +
                    "model_name varchar(100) not null," +
                    "release_year integer not null" +
                    ")";
    private static final String INITIAL_DATA_INSERT=
            "insert into devices (model_name, release_year) values " +
                    "('LG Nexus 4', 2012)," +
                    "('LG Nexus 5', 2013)," +
                    "('Samsung Galaxy S6', 2015)";

    public MySQLiteHelper(Context context) {
        super(context, DBFILENAME, null, DBVERSION);
    }

    @Override
    public void onCreate(SQLiteDatabase db) {
        db.execSQL(INITIAL_SCHEMA);
        db.execSQL(INITIAL_DATA_INSERT);
    }

    @Override
    public void onUpgrade(SQLiteDatabase db, int oldVersion, int newVersion) {
        // perform upgrade logic here
        // This can get quite complex
        if (oldVersion==1) {
```

```
            // do upgrade logic to new version
        }
        // and so on
    }
}
```

The Java listing for MySQLiteHelper shows the helper requirements that were outlined earlier in the chapter. The constructor takes the filename and version information and uses it to check for the existence of the SQLite database file, creating it if needed. I've chosen the filename "devices.db" as a somewhat meaningful name for the SQLite database file.

Looking at onCreate(), you can see it makes two successive calls to the execSQL() method, your first exposure to the common methods used to interact with SQLite databases. There are many variants of the parameters and return information available with execSQL(), but the most straightforward takes a String SQL statement as a parameter, which is the SQL command executed by the SQLite library. A successful execution of the SQL statement normally won't provide a return value – the "no news is good news" principle in action.

Each of the SQL statements used with the execSQL() calls is constructed in constant declarations at the top of the class. This approach to constant-based statements is not new, but it's worth noting a few of the additional constants in use here:

> Each of the three COLNO_* constants represents the column number (or ordinal position) of the columns in the table as I have defined it. So the _id column (discussed in the following) is at position 0, the model_name column is at position 1, and so on. These positions are important for some of the SQLite helper methods that implicitly use the default column order of a table for returning data.
>
> TABLE_COLUMNS is a String array of the column names in the table. A number of the methods we are about to explore make use of this collection of names.

Returning to the _id column of the table, this makes use of the autoincrement feature of SQLite to have it generate a unique integer value for each row, as the primary key for your table. The name _id is a convention used and expected by a number of the built-in Android tools, helper classes, and methods. I would recommend picking up this design tradition for all of your SQLite tables, at least until you feel you understand the consequences of doing things differently.

The next SQL statement invoked via an execSQL() call is the INITIAL_DATA_INSERT statement. The statement performs a multi-row insert to bootstrap an initial set of data into the one table in our schema. This kind of data seeding is entirely optional, and you certainly will have situations where you do want to do this and others where you won't need it. The syntax used for the insert statement itself is only supported in later versions of SQLite and therefore later versions of Android. For more details on SQLite versions and features vs. Android versions, check out the extra material on the book website at www.beginningandroid.org.

The final method in the helper class is a skeleton for onUpgrade(). In the example application, we are dealing with the first version of the application (DBVERSION equals 1 and is used in the constructor call). I left the outline of logic that you could use to work with the provided `oldVersion` and `newVersion` values to decide what schema changes, data changes, or other alteration actions might be needed as part of an upgrade to your application. When it comes to database schema upgrades, you will see many examples online of people simply dropping and recreating a database as the `onUpgrade()` implementation. It's a pragmatic hack, but it works to a degree, so long as you don't care about your users' data! Beware of this approach if you expect your users to store any data of value and want it retained even as the database schema is upgraded!

Creating a Database-Driven Activity

With an understanding of the purpose and structure of the `SQLiteOpenHelper` class, you are ready to use it in building a useful database-driven application. In the `Ch20/SQLiteExample` application, you see the logic as shown in Listing 20-3. This listing is quite long, though I've saved space by omitting another helper class I wrote named `DialogWrapper`. Read on for the Java code and then a walk-through of the logic.

***Listing 20-3.** The main SQLiteExample activity*

```
package org.beginningandroid.sqliteexample;

import android.app.AlertDialog;
import android.app.ListActivity;
import android.content.ContentValues;
import android.content.DialogInterface;
import android.os.Bundle;
import android.database.Cursor;
import android.database.sqlite.SQLiteDatabase;
import android.view.LayoutInflater;
import android.view.View;
import android.widget.ArrayAdapter;
import android.widget.Toast;

import java.util.ArrayList;
import java.util.Calendar;
import java.util.List;

public class MainActivity extends ListActivity {
    private SQLiteDatabase myDB;
    private MySQLiteHelper myDBHelper;

    @Override
    protected void onCreate(Bundle savedInstanceState) {
        super.onCreate(savedInstanceState);
        setContentView(R.layout.activity_main);

        myDBHelper = new MySQLiteHelper(this);
        myDB = myDBHelper.getWritableDatabase();
```

```
    displayModels();
}

public void onClick(View view) {
    switch(view.getId()) {
        case R.id.addNewModel:
            addModel();
            break;
        case R.id.getModelInfo:
            getModelInfo(view);
            break;
    }
}

public List<String> getModels() {
    List<String> models = new ArrayList<>();

    Cursor cursor = myDB.query(MySQLiteHelper.TABLE_NAME,
            MySQLiteHelper.TABLE_COLUMNS, null, null, null, null, null);

    cursor.moveToFirst();
    while (!cursor.isAfterLast()) {
        String model = cursor.getString(MySQLiteHelper.COLNO_MODEL_NAME);
        models.add(model);
        cursor.moveToNext();
    }

    cursor.close();
    return models;

}

public void displayModels() {
    List<String> modelEntries = getModels();

    ArrayAdapter<String> adapter = new ArrayAdapter<>(this,
            android.R.layout.simple_list_item_1, modelEntries);
    setListAdapter(adapter);
}
public void getModelInfo(View view) {

    Cursor cursor = myDB.rawQuery(
            "select _id, model_name, release_year " +
                    "from devices", null);

    cursor.moveToFirst();
    while (!cursor.isAfterLast()) {
        String model = cursor.getString(MySQLiteHelper.COLNO_MODEL_NAME);
        Integer year = cursor.getInt(MySQLiteHelper.COLNO_RELEASE_YEAR);
        Toast.makeText(this, "The " + model +
```

```
                        " was released in " + year.toString(),
                Toast.LENGTH_LONG).show();
            cursor.moveToNext();
        }
        cursor.close();
    }

    private void addModel() {
        LayoutInflater myInflater=LayoutInflater.from(this);
        View addView=myInflater.inflate(R.layout.add_model_edittext, null);
        final DialogWrapper myWrapper=new DialogWrapper(addView);

        new AlertDialog.Builder(this)
                .setTitle(R.string.add_model_title)
                .setView(addView)
                .setPositiveButton(R.string.ok,
                        new DialogInterface.OnClickListener() {
                            public void onClick(DialogInterface dialog,
                                                int whichButton) {
                                insertModelRow(myWrapper);
                            }
                        })
                .setNegativeButton(R.string.cancel,
                        new DialogInterface.OnClickListener() {
                            public void onClick(DialogInterface dialog,
                                                int whichButton) {
                                // Nothing to do here
                            }
                        })
                .show();
    }

    private void insertModelRow(DialogWrapper wrapper) {
        ContentValues myValues=new ContentValues(2);

        myValues.put(MySQLiteHelper.COLNAME_MODEL, wrapper.getModel());
        myValues.put(MySQLiteHelper.COLNAME_YEAR,
                Calendar.getInstance().get(Calendar.YEAR));

        myDB.insert(MySQLiteHelper.TABLE_NAME,
                MySQLiteHelper.COLNAME_MODEL, myValues);
        //uncomment if you want inserts to be displayed immediately
        //displayModels();
    }

    @Override
    public void onDestroy() {
        super.onDestroy();
```

```
        myDB.close();
    }
}
```

There are some key implementation steps in the preceding code to remember for all your SQLite-based Android development. A key step for any SQLite-based Android application is to create an object from your helper class and ensure it is kept for the life of the activities that need it. That usually isn't too hard, and my way of creating this from within the launcher activity is a common one.

Now that you have your helper object available, any time you need to work with the database, your interactions with it will start with invoking its `getReadableDatabase()` or `getWritableDatabase()` method to return a database object for your underlying SQLite database. As the method names suggest, a database object that is readable is used for only reading the database with `SELECT` queries, whereas the writable version allows DML statements like `INSERT`, `UPDATE`, `DELETE`, and DDL statements for object creation and alteration as used in our `onCreate()` helper class method.

When you are finished with a given task using the database object, simply call its `.close()` method, and the helper class will tidy up. This is normally done as part of your activity being finalized in `onDestroy()` or similar.

The `SQLiteExample` application creates the helper object and uses `getWritableDatabase()` to access the database in writable mode, proceeding to populate the `modelEntries` list using the `getModels()` method. With the results of this work, it then feeds our `ArrayAdapter` what it needs to inflate the `ListView` with the data returned from the database. The `getModels()` method is a short but powerful method, because it introduces and uses two major capabilities regarding SQLite databases and Android. The first concept is the query helper approach, which gathers data from your SQLite database, and the second concept is the cursor object for managing the results returned. Working proficiently with SQLite (and other) databases involves mastering both of these techniques, so let's look at them in more depth.

Choosing Query Approaches for SQLite and Android

While using a SQLite database in your application, you are presented with a choice of two main ways to retrieve the data it stores. Each approach utilizes the `SELECT` statement, but differs in how much hand-holding and assumed structure offered to you as a developer.

Using the Query Building Process

Approach number 1, as seen in the `getModels()` method of the `SQLiteExample` application, is to use the `query()` method. By using `query()`, you gain access to a very structured path to build up your desired or needed columns, source tables, predicate logic, and so on for the query, until you have the final form that will be issued on your SQLite database.

To use query(), you don't write the SQL SELECT statement directly yourself. Instead, you step through a predefined set of construction phases, with the query() method building your SQL statement for you under the hood:

1. Provide the name of the table to be used in the query.
2. Provide the column names to select (or "project" if you are into official relational database nomenclature).
3. Provide predicates for the where clause, including any optional positional parameters.
4. If positional parameters are used, provide the values for the parameters.
5. Provide any GROUP BY, HAVING, or ORDER BY clauses.

If you don't need one of the parts of the query, then you just provide null in the relevant parameter position for the query() call. You can see this in our call to query in the SQLiteExample code:

```
myDB.query(MySQLiteHelper.TABLE_NAME, MySQLiteHelper.TABLE_COLUMNS,
    null, null, null, null, null)
```

What this means is that we didn't use any predicates to add logic to the SQL statement's WHERE clause, had no parameters for the statement, and didn't use any GROUP BY, HAVING, or ORDER BY options.

That probably seems very straightforward, and in practice it is. The one significant limitation of this approach is lurking right there at step number 1. You provide the name of the table for your query – but only one table. And that's the drawback! With the query() method, you can only query a single table, which means no joins, and more subtly, you also cannot use any mechanism like subselects, correlated queries, or any other technique that would reference any other tables.

Using the Raw Power of SQL

If you yearn to break out of the query() method's limitations, then rawQuery() provides you pretty much the full power of SQL. As its name suggests, rawQuery() takes a "raw" string representing a SQL statement as a parameter and takes an optional array of positional parameters if you choose to use them in your SQL statement. Where you don't need parameterization for your query, you pass null as the second parameter.

You can see rawQuery() in action in the getModelInfo() implementation in the SQLiteExample logic:

```
myDB.rawQuery("select _id, model_name, release_year " +
                        "from devices", null)
```

With rawQuery(), you can go to town with whatever SQL gymnastics you can muster, including anything SQLite supports from the SQL standards such as nested subselects, joins, and more. This wide-ranging power comes with its own considerations.

Managing a small set of static queries with rawQuery() is fine, but the strings representing your queries become complex, or if you build larger and larger statements through dynamic creation of the SQL text, then there are some universal concerns you should worry about. First and foremost is the class of security issues known as SQL injections. SQL injection vulnerabilities are not an Android issue, nor are they a SQLite issue per se. These issues can affect any database-using application. The key to avoid SQL injection is the notion of string "sanitization," where you ensure the SQL created is not only valid but also not beyond the scope of what you intended.

Caution With the power of raw SQL come all of the complications and issues that can crop up when you are in total control of, and totally responsible for, query syntax, correctness, and more. If you are a beginner with SQL, I'd recommend testing the waters with the Query Builder approach and then doing side-by-side work with rawQuery() and Query Builder so you see where the pitfalls and sharp edges lay!

Managing Results from Queries with Cursors

Whichever query execution model you choose for working with your databases, results are presented to you (or your application) as an object known as a Cursor. A Cursor is essentially the same concept you will find in almost all database libraries, so the following description will be familiar if you have ever used other databases and their programming interfaces. If you are new to databases and/or cursors, you can think of them as a complete set of data resulting from a query and a pointer (or cursor position) to the current row of interest within the result set. Think of your favorite text editor or word processor and how the cursor sits at a certain point in the whole body of text in a document, and you get a rough idea. In database libraries, you can think of the cursor as both the whole result set and the current position in that result set.

This dataset-plus-pointer-to-position metaphor is key to understanding the power of a Cursor object as a developer. A Cursor empowers you to do the following and more:

- Move the cursor position and iterate over the result set with methods like moveToFirst() and moveToNext(),testing position with isAfterLast().
- Extract individual column values from the current row with getString(), getInt(), and other equivalent methods for other data types.
- Interrogate the result set to learn the names of columns, ordinal column positions, and so on with getColumnNames() and getColumnIndex().
- Get statistics about the result set with getCount(). Be warned, though, that attempting to count the results forces the entire result set for the Cursor to be read sequentially, which can consume considerable memory and take time for large results.
- Free all of the Cursor resources using the close() method.

A common way to process your results in a `Cursor` is to use a loop logic construct to iterate through its rows, performing whatever application logic you need on each row. The `SQLiteExample` application does this in a few places, such as this snippet from `getModels()`:

```
Cursor cursor = myDB.query(MySQLiteHelper.TABLE_NAME,
    MySQLiteHelper.TABLE_COLUMNS, null, null, null, null, null);

cursor.moveToFirst();
while (!cursor.isAfterLast()) {
    String model = cursor.getString(MySQLiteHelper.COLNO_MODEL_NAME);
    models.add(model);
    cursor.moveToNext();
}
cursor.close();
```

This shows the use of the `query()` method for a SQLite database object, to which we pass the name of the table and the `String` array with the column names that interest us. We receive in return a `Cursor` with a result set that looks like Listing 20-4.

***Listing 20-4.** Sample cursor result set for the SQLiteExample activity*

```
_id  model_name          release_year
---  ------------------  ------------
1    Pixel 3             2018
2    Pixel 5             2020
3    Samsung Galaxy S21  2021
```

To process the resulting `Cursor`, we invoke the `.moveToFirst()` method before entering the loop, which places the current row for the cursor at the `_id=1` row. As we step through the loop, we test that we have not moved to the end of the result set for the cursor with `isAfterLast()`, thus avoiding any errors from reading beyond our cursor's range. We call `getString()` by passing the `COLNO_MODEL_NAME` constant, representing the column position for the `model_name` column. This string is added to our `ArrayList`, and then we call `moveToNext()` to continue processing the next row.

> **Caution** It is very attractive to always rely on this approach to iterative row processing when dealing with databases – SQLite or otherwise. However, hidden in this pattern is the most common performance pitfall in all database-related programming. While loops and for loops are easy to code, but do not scale in ways that match a database engine's ability to perform set logic with native SQL. No matter how new or experienced you are with programming, it is worth remembering that SQL is pretty much always the best choice for computing and crunching data at scale. It's fine to use Java- or Kotlin-based iterative loops in your code for things outside of data processing logic, such as where data is bound to UI widgets or non-SQL-like processing is performed. But be vigilant, to ensure good performance for your users!

Moving beyond simple iteration and manual processing, you can use a Cursor object to seed a SimpleCursorAdapter for use in binding with a ListView or other selection UI widgets. In using any of the CursorAdapter options or subclasses, you will need to follow the table structure pattern introduced earlier in the chapter. You must create your table with a primary key column named _id and set it with the autoincrement property. The _id column and its value(s) will be expected by all of the adapter's methods, such as onListItemClick().

There are more advanced approaches to working with results when you hit the limits of cursors, such as the SQLiteDatabase.CursorFactory object and the queryWithFactory() and rawQueryWithFactory() methods that work with it. These are beyond the scope of this book, but you can learn more at developer.android.com.

Modifying Data with Your Android Application

Reading data from a database is certainly very useful, but is really only half of the story when it comes to database-driven applications. In almost all cases, you will want your users to add, update, and delete information from your SQLite database, and that means wanting to use the power of SQL's INSERT, UPDATE, and DELETE SQL DML statements against your database.

Android's support of SQLite extends to offering you two ways in which to execute DML statements that modify data. First up is the use of the execSQL() method, to which you pass a fully formed SQL statement. Looking back at the SQLiteExample application, it uses this approach via the helper class when the database is first created. As discussed earlier, execSQL() is suitable for any kind of statement that doesn't expect to return a result or cursor. As INSERT, UPDATE, and DELETE statements don't return results, they fit the bill. In the most up-to-date versions of Android, and therefore SQLite (versions 3.24 and higher), this includes the "UPSERT" variant of INSERT that implements ON CONFLICT support for updating existing rows via an INSERT statement.

If execSQL() leaves you feeling like you are flying by the seat of your pants, then the alternative is to use the SQLiteDatabase object's .insert(), .update(), and .delete() methods, taking the step-by-step approach to DML in much the same way that the .query() method helped you to build your desired SELECT statements. Each of these methods uses a ContentValues object, which offers you a SQLite-tailored map of values and columns.

Inserting Data

Reviewing the insertModelRow() method from SQLiteExample, you will see the .insert() method in operation:

```
private void insertModelRow(DialogWrapper wrapper) {
    ContentValues myValues=new ContentValues(2);

    myValues.put(MySQLiteHelper.COLNAME_MODEL, wrapper.getModel());
    myValues.put(MySQLiteHelper.COLNAME_YEAR,
        Calendar.getInstance().get(Calendar.YEAR));
```

```
myDB.insert(MySQLiteHelper.TABLE_NAME,
    MySQLiteHelper.COLNAME_MODEL, myValues);
//uncomment if you want inserts to be displayed immediately
//displayModels();
}
```

The call to `.insert()` in that listing is clear, thanks to the use of the helper class constants. Looking at the constants themselves, the first parameter takes the name of the table into which we are inserting, and the second parameter provides a column from the table that can accept nulls, which is an Android requirement rather than a design choice of mine. Its purpose is to sidestep SQLite's sometimes odd insert behavior, if the last parameter – the `ContentValues` object – is empty and is known as the "null insert hack."

Before using the `ContentValues` object, you typically populate it with the relevant data you want used. In the `SQLiteExample` application, we populate it with `String` data from the `DialogWrapper` object via that object's `.getModel()` method. Open up the Java source for the `DialogWrapper`, and you will see the `.getModel()` method returns the text the user enters in the pop-up dialog triggered by clicking the "Add New Model" button, as shown in Figure 20-2.

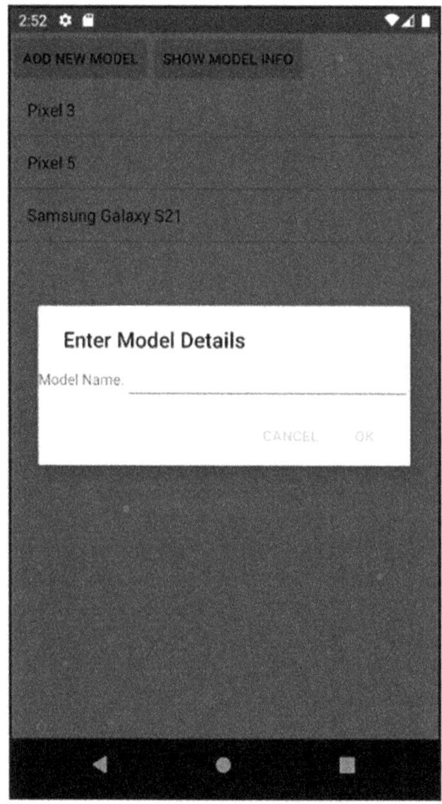

***Figure 20-2.** Prompting for new data to insert in the SQLiteExample application*

Whatever text gets entered becomes the value for the .put() call on the ContentValues object, along with the String value of the COLNAME_MODEL constant, which takes the role of the key. To come up a with a year value, we use a common Java technique to determine the current year. If you're interested in expanding the SQLiteExample application, you can adjust this to be part of the pop-up dialog and associated logic.

Updating Data

Updating data with the .update() method is broadly similar to the .insert() method. The one additional consideration over and above providing a String representing the name of the table to update and a ContentValues object that represents the new values the column or columns to be updated should have is that you can also provide an optional where clause. This where clause allows you to add any predicate logic you wish to refine which rows to target for update. It can include the question mark, ?, as a placeholder for values that substitute later prior to executing the statement, along with a final parameter, which is a list of values to use as replacements for any ? parameter placeholders. This is a very common technique for parameter substitution and is one of the (but not the only) techniques used to protect against SQL injection. You can protect whatever parameter values get used in the .update() with whatever logic you determine is needed – rather than just trusting a user's direct input.

The .update() approach is easy to use, but its simplicity comes at a cost. The values used for updates must be actual static values. You cannot pass a formula or calculation through the .update() method for SQLite to evaluate. In circumstances where you need this power, take the execSQL() approach instead.

Deleting Data

The last stop on our journey of helper methods for managing your SQLite data is the .delete() statement. It is also very similar to the .insert() and .update() statements you've already seen, being closest to .update(). The key difference for .delete() is that you need not provide any new data values, as you are deleting data, not adjusting it!

Invoke .delete() by providing it the name of the table that hosts the data you want removed, and also optionally include a where clause and any parameter values needed with the predicates to target the subset of rows you would like affected (assuming you are not trying to delete everything from the table). For example:

```
myDB.delete(MySQLiteHelper.TABLE_NAME, "_id=?", args);
```

You would provide a populated args value, which in our case would be the _id value for one of the rows holding phone model data, for example, "2" for _id 2. The statement SQLite sees and executes would look like this:

```
delete from devices where _id=2
```

The same caveat applies to .delete() as you saw with .update(). No calculations or dynamic formula can be passed in the parameters for SQLite to evaluate. To move to that level of complexity, you should again choose execSQL() instead.

Using the Room Persistence Library

Working with raw SQL statements, or even seeking help via the Query Builder method, still demands that you develop knowledge around SQL as a language and relational database concepts. In general, this is a very good idea. Some developers shy away from SQL, thinking it is too hard to use or too "odd" when compared to languages like Java and Kotlin.

There is a third approach to working with databases in general, known as an Object-Relational Mapping, or ORM, library. These have many pros and cons, but in essence give you a more Java-like (or Kotlin-like) way of working with databases. In the Android world, Google has made the Room Persistence Library available as part of androidx (Jetpack). Learning ORMs, including Room, can help both make your code less prone to errors with raw SQL and simpler to understand. Room by itself is a very large topic, and you can read more about it at `https://developer.android.com/jetpack/androidx/releases/room`.

As a new developer, building a basic understanding of SQL is critical to using any of the approaches Android offers – whether that's Query Builder, raw SQL, or Room – so starting with SQL is the right choice.

Packaging and Managing SQLite Databases for Android

When it comes to adding SQLite to your applications, there are some considerations beyond coding that will help you make good choices in designing, building, and supporting database-centric applications. Investing a little time and thought on some key issues like I/O, file placement, and seeding databases can payoff.

Managing Android Storage for Database Performance

Chapter 19 covered the details of managing and using files with your Android applications. There's no need to repeat that content again in this chapter, but a topic we didn't cover was the hardware technology used for storing those files. Almost all Android devices ship with on-board storage based on flash memory, built typically with NAND hardware. The quality and reliability of that memory differs markedly across different brands and manufacturers.

When building Android applications using SQLite databases, you will implicitly trigger reads from, and writes to, this hardware storage as your applications insert, update, and delete data on behalf of your users. One quirk of flash memory is its lack of predictability around fast writes. Ninety-nine times out of a hundred, you might get great, fast write performance, only to discover randomly that the next write you issue drops in speed because the flash storage has triggered some internal cleanup or management. The most common cause of this is "wear-level management," in which the flash storage management layer is trying to preserve the longevity of parts of its storage.

It can be hard to spot the performance problems this might cause, especially when testing your app in an AVD that almost certainly has its memory emulated by your notebook or desktop computer's very fast and very reliable RAM. You can mitigate a range of write performance uncertainties by using the `AsnycTask()` approach described in Chapter 18 to have database changes happen on an asynchronous thread, away from the main UI thread.

Another quirk of database management is thinking about what happens when the device fails – either from low power, unexpected crash, or the user simply choosing the power off button at a crucial moment of database activity. You are well supported by SQLite's abilities to recover from crashes and failures, using ACID database principles to preserve (make durable, in ACID parlance) changes to data. Being aware this happens is important, as part of the ACID guarantees of any database worthy of the name include the determination that transactions might need to be rolled back in order to preserve integrity.

ACID DATABASE PRINCIPLES

In all relational databases, including SQLite, there are four key principles that are the standard way to ensure data is protected, intact, and available when expected. These are known as the ACID principles, where those letters stand for Atomicity, Consistency, Isolation, and Durability.

Atomicity is the principle that all of the work in one transaction against the database either succeeds or is rolled back. No half-complete work should be allowed.

Consistency is the principle that data in the database is always in a consistent state and transactions can only adjust the data from one consistent state to another consistent state.

Isolation is the principle that the workings of a transaction will be invisible to other users of the database, until the entire atomic, consistent set of changes to the data caused by the transaction are made visible.

Durability is the principle that changes once made to the data will endure, even in the event of abnormal system events, catastrophes, and so on.

You should think about adding sanity-checking logic to your application to track and take action in those circumstances where you can be forewarned of issues. Low-power state is the most common situation you can detect, by registering a receiver in your application to watch for broadcasts like `ACTION_BATTERY_CHANGED`. By examining the intent payload, you can determine if power is running low and potentially defer write-heavy tasks.

Packaging SQLite Databases with Your Applications

My `SQLiteExample` application comes complete with a helper class that conveniently populates three rows of data to the device's table to seed the database. Great for this example, but it might leave you thinking, what if I need a few hundred, or even a few thousand, rows of data to make my database useful from the start? Performing this kind of mass-insert activity when first creating the database will present the user with a potentially very slow first execution of the program as all of that I/O is performed. Not only might this disappoint the user but such a long-running piece of work increases the exposure of your application to the chance of various errors at runtime.

If you want to provide a SQLite database populated with nontrivial amounts of data as part of your application, you package it with your other assets in the .apk. The appropriate place for the SQLite file is in a particular subfolder under your `assets/` folder, so that its location can be passed to the overloaded `openDatabase()` method, which accepts a full file location as its first parameter.

SQLite database files must be placed under the assets/ folder into the file system folder `/data/data/your.package.name/databases/`. Append the `String` representing your filename (e.g., `devices.db` from our example application), and you have the value to pass as a parameter to `openDatabase()`. In practice, for the `SQLiteExample` application, this full path and filename is

```
/data/data/org.beginningandroid.sqliteexample/devices.db
```

Choosing SQLite Management Tools to Prepare Databases for Packaging

Hand-crafting databases of any type is a tedious affair, so you will almost certainly want some tools to help design your database and populate it if you want to package a database file with your Android application.

Working with Built-In Tools

SQLite comes packaged with useful management tools, such as the `sqlite3` shell program that is shipped with almost all operating systems bar Windows (and even under Windows, it is trivial to download from `sqlite.org`). The AVD tools also provide access to the `sqlite3` utility, and you can invoke it from the `adb` shell utility once you are connected to your emulated device. For example,

```
$ sqlite3 /data/data/org.beginningandroid.sqliteexample/devices.db
```

Check out the documentation at `sqlite.org` for more details about using the `sqlite3` utility. The `adb` tool also provides some other useful general file management commands that you can harness for your SQLite database files, such as `adb push` to move a file to a device and `adb pull` to copy a file from a device.

Working with Third-Party Database Tools

When simple command-line tools don't stack up for your demanding needs, there are plenty of other, more sophisticated GUI tools available for you to help manage your SQLite databases. Some of the most popular include

- DBeaver: A tool growing in popularity for its support of many databases, not just SQLite. Cross-platform and offers a free community edition. Learn more at `https://dbeaver.io`.
- DB Browser for SQLite: Another cross-platform tool, specializing in SQLite management. Learn more at `https://sqlitebrowser.org`.

Historically, another tool called SQLite Manager was incredibly popular and very useful as it was packaged as a Firefox browser plugin. Unfortunately, with Firefox's significant architectural change in how its plugins worked, SQLite Manager ceased being supported. I mention it here so you don't go down the rabbit hole trying to find it – it's still mentioned widely in historic online posts and websites relating to SQLite.

Summary

You now have a firm working knowledge of the key steps to incorporate SQLite databases into your applications and build features and logic driven by and supporting the data contained therein.

We have also reached the end of the book – or at least the end of the printed and packaged version. There are additional topics and extra examples for many of the topics mentioned in the book, available from the website at `www.beginningandroid.org`.

I wish you every success as you continue on your path to becoming an Android application developer!

Index

A

G. Allen, *Android for Absolute Beginners*, https://doi.org/10.1007/978-1-4842-6646-5

G

H

I

J

K

L

M

N

O

P

Q

R

S

T

U

V

W

X, Y, Z

CPSIA information can be obtained
at www.ICGtesting.com
Printed in the USA
LVHW061057221021
701184LV00013B/727

9 781484 266458